D0948288

The union makes us strong

American labor history is typically interpreted by scholars as a history of defeat, accommodation, or incorporation. The radical unionism practiced by Congress of Industrial Organizations (CIO) locals in the middle-to-late 1930s is viewed as a momentary blip on the American labor movement's otherwise straight-line trajectory from craft to business unionism. Hidden by this conventional wisdom are a handful of American unions that did not follow the putative CIO trajectory. Long after more CIO unions started practicing business unionism, some unions organized themselves to challenge systematically and continuously management's rule on the shopfloor.

Based on three years of ethnographic research, this book takes a close look at one of the CIO unions that did not move from craft to business unionism: the International Longshoremen's and Warehousemen's Union's (ILWU) major longshore local (Local 10, San Francisco). American unionism looks quite different than conventional scholarly wisdom suggests when actual union practices are observed. One finds that in the ILWU, resistance to management's authority is collectively legitimated behavior, and explicitly acknowledged as good trade unionism. This case study suggests that American labor's trajectory is neither inevitable nor determined; that militant, democratic forms of unionism are possible in the United States; and that collective bargaining need not eliminate contests for control over the workplace. Under certain conditions, the contract is a bargain that reflects and reproduces fundamental disagreement; it is a document that states how production and conflict will proceed.

The union
makes us strong

Radical unionism on the San Francisco waterfront

DAVID WELLMAN

Community Studies Board
University of California, Santa Cruz

Institute for the Study of Social Change
University of California, Berkeley

CAMBRIDGE
UNIVERSITY PRESS

Published by the Press Syndicate of the University of Cambridge
The Pitt Building, Trumpington Street, Cambridge CB2 1RP
40 West 20th Street, New York, NY 10011-4211, USA
10 Stamford Road, Oakleigh, Melbourne 3166, Australia

First published 1995

Printed in the United States of America

Library of Congress Cataloging-in-Publication Data
Wellman, David
The union makes us strong : radical unionism on the San Francisco
waterfront / David Wellman.
p.   cm.
Includes bibliographical references and index.
ISBN 0-521-45005-5
1. International Longshoremen's and Warehousemen's Union. Local
10 (San Francisco, Calif.). 2. Trade-unions – Stevedores – California –
San Francisco. 3. Industrial relations – California – San Francisco.
4. Social conflict – California – San Francisco. I. Title.
HD8039.L82U74   1995
331.88′11387164′0979461 – dc20   94-10286
                                                                          CIP

A catalog record for this book is available from the British Library.

ISBN 0-521-45005-5 hardback

For my father,
Saul Wellman:
mentor, comrade, and friend

Solidarity forever!
Solidarity forever!
Solidarity forever!
For the union makes us strong.

Ralph Chaplin, 1915

CONTENTS

ix

Contents

PREFACE

THIS is not another sad tale about the demise of radical labor in America. It is not the story of how America's premiere militant union was defeated by bureaucrats, corporate liberals, collective bargains, or postindustrial technology. Quite the contrary. It tells a story of workers who currently and regularly fight with their employers over control of the workplace even though their union contract has officially settled the issue.

This is also not the story of an exceptional or "deviant" union, which, because of charismatic leadership and communist influence, was able to do what no other American union has done. The people in this book do not think of themselves as radical or politically "conscious." Left-wing organizers are not the leading players in this story. The major characters are typical American workers.

Finally, this book is not about extraordinary moments in history, those unanticipated explosions that reveal transcripts of resistance that would otherwise remain hidden. Rather, the story is located in routine settings, accepted union practices, and class conflict in institutional settings.

The story this book tells obviously does not follow what has become a traditional labor history narrative. Instead of beginning with might have been and asking why it did not, this book starts with what was and asks, what actually happened? Rather than looking for the operating rules of class relations in the contract, it locates them in the tensions generated between informally negotiated work practices and formally agreed-upon contractual provisions. Instead of assuming that contractual agreements eliminate class conflict, the contract is understood as a document that governs how production *and* conflict will proceed. And rather than asking how unions that practice militant, class-struggle unionism differ from the rest of American labor, it explores the features they have in common.

When one focuses on actual activities and routine practices instead of formal agreements and ideological principles, a new narrative emerges for class relations. This is an account in which the war between classes figures prominently and history does not end when contracts are signed.

When I began this project, I did not expect to find class-struggle unionism practiced anywhere in the house of labor. Like many of my contemporaries, I believed organized labor had been tamed. I thought labor history was, as Eric Hobsbawm had written, "by tradition a highly political subject" (1974:371), and the politics of this subject were straightforward. I expected to show how trade unionism diminished class consciousness and promoted capitalist rule. At the time, I thought the subject was strictly political. I do not recall being conscious of the personal dimension. In retrospect, however, the personal side of the subject is unavoidable. Both of my parents were CIO organizers in the 1930s and Communist Party functionaries throughout the 1940s and 50s. With hindsight, I now realize I was unintentionally challenging their politics.

Three years of field research with the San Francisco longshoremen's union, however, shattered my stereotypes of American labor. The experience forced me to substantially revise what I thought of unions.

The three years I spent with San Francisco longshoremen did much more than make me rethink my initial perspective. The experience has also given me a new appreciation for my parents' contribution to the American labor movement. It has given new meaning to the dialectic between the personal and the political. As an adult, I have always been critical of my parents' politics, especially when they supported authoritarian socialism in the former Soviet Union. That critical posture, however, did not distinguish between my parents' support for the Soviet Union and their contribution to American political culture. As I complete this project, I am discovering that the distinction is a necessary one. The unions they helped to organize look nothing like the Soviet Union they supported.

I believe there is a larger lesson in this realization. It is easy to discount and diminish the legacy of the old left in America. The good fights they fought can be discredited by their support of the Soviet Union and its subsequent failures. However, when one looks carefully at the surviving unions they helped build, the old left is not so easily dismissed. Although they failed to achieve their socialist goals, the militant democratic unions they helped establish, unions that would enable working-class Americans to participate in the decision making affecting their everyday lives, are a lasting achievement and profound contribution to American political culture. That may or may not be ironic. But it is an important and enduring legacy. That is why I have dedicated this book to one of America's most cantankerous and persistent old leftists: my father, Saul Wellman.

One of the important lessons I've learned from San Francisco's longshoremen is that work is a social accomplishment. However, whereas the longshore industry recognizes the social character of work, the academy does not. Individualism is the organizing principle of academic work; scholarship is constructed as a singular effort. In contrast, the organizing principle of longshore work is cooperation and the basic unit of organization is either a partnership or gang. Although this book was not created by gang labor or a partnership, it was produced by a series of collaborations. It never would have seen the light of day without the active involvement of a great many people who are not listed on the title page. My "gang" may not be the cohesive, face-to-face unit one finds on the waterfront. And it is not officially recognized. But it's real nonetheless and everybody in it made a unique and necessary contribution to the final product.

This book has been a long time coming and many people have participated in producing it. I therefore have a pretty big gang. I dare not count the number of iterations the book has been through, but there are three people who know the exact number because they have patiently and carefully gone through each iteration, page by page, line by line. Their participation in this project was absolutely essential to its successful completion. They helped me sharpen formulations and discovered promise where I found aggravation. Their faith in my abilities encouraged me to keep on when I wanted to quit. Jan Dizard, Howard Kimeldorf, and Jeff Lustig have redefined the outer limits of friendship. My indebtedness to them is hard to capture in words.

Numerous people have read various versions and pieces of the manuscript. Danny Beagle has been an all-purpose friend and colleague, patiently reading drafts, making suggestions, hearing me out, and giving emotional support. Jeremy Brecher took time from a hectic schedule to read an early iteration thoroughly and thoughtfully. His critical comments considerably enhanced subsequent drafts. David Brundage was always there when I needed him, offering intelligent, corrective, and supportive insights. Selflessly sharing his extensive knowledge of labor history, he treated me as a colleague when I felt like an intellectual intruder. Michael K. Brown and Elliott Currie gave new meaning to friendship and collegiality. Michael didn't tell me what I wanted to hear about the manuscript, but he told me what I needed to know. And he made fine suggestions for how to do it. Elliott picked me up when my confidence was at an all-time low; his enthusiasm for the book became infectious. Aaron Cicourel has been a loyal critic and a model who is impossible to emulate. I am deeply grateful for the hours he devoted to discussing research strategies during the earliest stages of this project. Troy Duster read early drafts. His comments set the standard for intelligent reflection and careful attention to details. His sense of perspective and theoretical sophistication were valuable resources for subsequent iterations. His friendship has been an important source of strength, insight, and affection. Gene Dennis-Vrana – longshoreman, writer, and ILWU Librarian – gave the next-to-the-last draft a careful and serious reading. The book is a wiser and more balanced account because of his efforts. I am grateful for his warmth and support throughout this entire project. Herman Gray has been a wonderful source of intellectual stimulation and theoretical enrichment. Our conversations about theory and methods provoked the methodological appendix. Early on, Jean Lave saw conceptual potential in what I thought was confusion. She taught me to appreciate the mental work of manual labor. Ron Lembo's friendship and intelligent reading of the manuscript were crucial to its completion. The insight, intensity, and theoretical elegance he devoted to the effort added a new dimension to the book. Eliot Liebow supported this project in two ways. He was director of the NIMH Metro Center, which funded the effort; and he offered excellent advice throughout the research process. Anselm Strauss's critical and encouraging reading of an early version of the manuscript was a lesson in craftsmanship and collegiality. Rachael Winfree joined Cambridge University Press in the final stages of this project. She devoted considerable attention to a thorough reading of the penultimate draft. The perspective and careful editing she provided gave the manuscript the energy and coherence it needed to finally become a book. Helen Wheeler copyedited the typescript with appreciation, craft, and precision. She improved the text considerably. Because I did not always follow the advice these people so generously provided, none of them should be held responsible for any errors, omissions, or misinterpretations the reader might find.

I actually do have a gang. It works at the University of California's Institute for the Study of Social Change. As director, Troy Duster is the natural and official leader of the gang. Janice Tanigawa, the administrative assistant, is also responsible for the wonderful atmosphere that encourages and facilitates intellectual work. I've shared pieces of this book with everybody in the gang. I couldn't have worked so long and hard at it without their receptivity, advice, and encouragement. I am grateful to the gang at ISSC: Dianne Beeson, Hardy Frye, David Matza, David Minkus, Howard Pinderhughes, Cynthia Sharp, Wendell Thomas, Alan Watahara, Deborah Woo, and Bob Yamashita.

This book originally began as a collaborative project with David Matza. Together we wrote a NIMH grant proposal, the success of which eventually funded the effort. Our plan was to do field research in two different sectors of working-class life and then jointly analyze and write up the materials we had collected. We devoted considerable energy to the joint effort, producing a published article, a draft of an extensive outline, and detailed elements of an emerging analysis. Ultimately, however, the collaboration was unsuccessful and we decided to write independently of one another. Nevertheless, David Matza has made a profound contribution to this study. His intellectual footprints can be found throughout it. They extend beyond the instances in which I formally cite the materials derived from our collaborative effort. The book has been enhanced by our collaboration.

Without Herb Mills's sponsorship, friendship, and mentorship throughout every stage of this project, there would be no book today. Herb introduced me to the longshore community and helped make sense of the visit as well.

I've been honored to share the evolution of this project with a number of dear friends and colleagues who patiently listened as I struggled to formulate it and generously offered helpful insights and encouraging words. I am especially grateful to Joan Acker, Rochelle Averback, Katherine Black, Joe Canale, Steven Deutsch, and David Milton.

My gratitude to the San Francisco longshoremen extends beyond their hospitality. Their contribution to this book exceeds the permission they granted an outsider to experience and write about their community. They educated me in the profoundest senses of the term. Through their example, I learned how ordinary people routinely make history and resist class domination. They taught me to appreciate community and find it in lived experience. I learned from them that there are homegrown alternatives to competitive individualism and racial hierarchy; that popular struggle has a distinguished record which, to paraphrase E. P. Thompson, need not be surrendered to the "enormous condescension of posterity."

Although my gratitude extends to the entire longshore community, a number of people were particularly instrumental in educating me: George Benet, Andrew Dulaney, Gene Dennis-Vrana, Rudy Garcia, Nick Granich, George Kaye, George Kekai, Leonard Malliot, Herb Mills, Bill Watkins, Cleophus Williams, Tony Winstead, and Larry Wing.

I am also grateful to the employers' association (the Pacific Maritime Association) for granting me permission to be on the docks and sit in their meetings. James Edwards and Alonzo Fields were especially supportive. Edwards was gracious with his time and his perceptive insights into the industry helped me understand it.

The emotional costs of doing a project like this one are extensive. The time and intensity devoted to it have taken their toll. I would not be able to sustain these personal costs without my very large and devoted extended kinship network: the Wellmans: Saul, Vickie, Ed, Estelle, Roni, Jeri, and Scott; Ian MacGregor, the Sheins: Sivi-Rae, Meagan, and Christopher; Meyer and Vera Baylin, Danny Beagle, Michael and Vivian Brown, Richard Clarke, Jan and Robin Dizard, Woody Donovan and Kathy Hughes-Donovan, Troy Duster, Nora Elliott, George and Willa Fields, George and Alma Hill, Ron Lembo, Jeff Lustig, Al and Juanita Rowland, Lisa Rubens, Orian and Rosemary Worden, and Deborah Woo.

I am especially grateful to Greta Fields Clarke, M.D., for being herself. Her intelligence, integrity, and support are natural cures for the hidden injuries of class. Her sense of confidence is an infectious therapy, her wisdom was sometimes communicable, and her sense of perspective was a useful antidote for overexposure to computer terminals and other academic occupational hazards.

David Wellman
Richmond, California
Labor Day, 1993

NOTES ON UNPUBLISHED SOURCES

T HIS book is based on three years of field research. That process is detailed in the methodological appendix. During this three-year period I generated and collected a substantial number of research documents. These materials are cited and quoted throughout the text. This note is intended to help the reader distinguish among the various documents.

As I indicate in the methodological appendix, I conducted approximately thirty in-depth interviews with longshoremen, union officials, and management representatives. When material is used from these interviews, it is identified by quotation marks. I do not provide the names of people interviewed, or the date of the interview, because I promised people anonymity. Sometimes quoted comments are attributed to "field notes." That means I did not conduct a formal interview, but recorded the remarks in my field notes and, for reasons discussed in the appendix, I am satisfied that using quotation marks for talk observed in the field is appropriate.

Because I recognize the constructed nature of sociological interpretation, and because I want the reader to have access to the materials within which my interpretations are grounded, I have chosen to include relevant passages from field notes in the text. I hope this approach will facilitate a dialogic relationship between reader and writer. Given sociology's continued preoccupation with what C. Wright Mills rightfully called "abstract empiricism," this is my way of emphasizing that field research, and the recorded observations it produces, is as legitimate as any other research practice, and therefore should be treated with the same degree of respect – or disrespect – as are the quantified representations of human group life that so frequently appear in social science writing.

In addition to writing field notes, I also collected leaflets, election campaign materials, documents passed across negotiation tables, and letters written by union and management officials. When these documents are quoted, they are cited as such. As I became trusted by the union and employers' association (a process that is discussed in the appendix), I was given a copy of written agendas before each Labor Relations Committee (LRC) meeting. I designated these documents "Research Documents," abbreviating them "RD," and for purposes of analysis, I numbered them. When material is used from these sources it is therefore cited as "RD # so-and-so."

The agendas contained complaints or grievances charged by one side against the other. In this industry, employer complaints are called "ECs" and union complaints "UCs." Each set of complaints is also numbered. Thus, when I quote from these written charges, countercharges, and responses, I cite them as either "UC" or "EC," using the LRC-designated numbers.

As noted in the appendix, I wrote in the margins and on the backs of these agendas or "Research Documents." They therefore became "field notes." But for some unexplainable reason, I did not categorize them as field notes. Instead, I filed them as RDs. Thus, in those instances where I quote from these field notes, I cite the RD as the source rather than identifying them as field notes.

Part I

LABOR RADICALISM REVISITED

1

UNSETTLING OLD SCORES: LABOR RADICALISM ENCOUNTERS CONVENTIONAL WISDOM

CONVENTIONAL WISDOMS

A new brand of unionism exploded on the American scene in the 1930s. Between 1934 and 1937, general strikes were waged in San Francisco and Minneapolis. Automobile and rubber workers staged sit-down strikes in Michigan and Ohio. Miners took over mines and steelworkers shut down steel mills in Pennsylvania and West Virginia. Throughout the country, workers previously ignored by or excluded from unions were busy being organized into the Congress of Industrial Organizations (CIO).

Working-class insurgency in this period was new in part because it was political in the broadest sense. More than ideologically radical, the CIO was radically "political." Unlike the American Federation of Labor (AFL) unions, at least initially, CIO affiliates were more internally democratic and, to the extent they practiced industrial unionism, antielitist as well. CIO unions were also, relatively speaking, more inclusive on matters of race and gender.[1] Their direct action tactics, moreover, made political participation an organizing strategy. These expressions of working-class insurgency were perhaps most profoundly political because they made workplace governance an issue. Workers insisted on the right to participate in decisions about work; and they forced factory owners to observe that right officially. They compelled owners to bargain in good faith; and they refused to work until employers formally recognized their organizations.

---

1 The CIO's practice regarding racial equality was uneven, reluctant, and often flawed. It should not be exaggerated. See Herbert Hill (1987). Relative to the AFL and past practices, however, the CIO represented a different kind of unionism.

CIO successes empowered ordinary workers and seriously restricted management's unilateral authority on the shopfloor.

By most accounts, this battle for industrial citizenship did not last very long. Like a meteor, it flashed across America's working-class horizon for barely a historical moment, leaving almost no traces. By World War II, or immediately after, CIO unions signed contracts settling the governance issue in management's favor. Workers were prevented from participating directly in production decisions. Laws were passed that outlawed secondary boycotts, and solidarity strikes became illegal. Bureaucratic organization was imposed on rebellious, radically democratic industrial workers. The CIO, some say, struck a devil's bargain with employers: In return for a labor relations system that guaranteed union recognition, the industrial union movement would forswear independent political action. Fights over who would govern the workplace, and how, were declared out of bounds. Militant CIO unionism rapidly became just another version of what some called "business unionism." In the words of one labor critic, unionists "chose to struggle only on the safe terrain of wages and benefits. . . . (T)he question of workplace regime was settled" (Moody, 1988:71).

Given this turn of events, scholars typically interpret American labor history as a history of defeat, accommodation, or incorporation. The unionism practiced by CIO locals in the 1930s is seen as a momentary blip on the American labor movement's otherwise straight-line trajectory from craft to business unionism. The standard account of the history of labor in America is one of "false promises," co-optation, and surrender. Militancy, shopfloor struggles over governance, and union democracy are located in the past, all prominent features of an exciting social experiment that either failed or was never given a chance.

The CIO's putative failure to expand the battle for industrial citizenship into a war for shopfloor control is taken by some to prove that AFL leader Samuel Gompers was right: Anything other than "pure and simple unionism" is doomed to failure. The demise of militancy, they conclude, confirms labor theorist Selig Perlman's insight that "the only acceptable 'consciousness' for American labor as a whole is a 'job consciousness'" (Perlman, 1928:169). Thus, left to its own devices, the natural state of the American labor movement would be conservative.

Over the years, Gompers's and Perlman's insights have become the conventional wisdom concerning American unionism and working-class politics. To Sombart's question, "why is there no socialism in America?" conventional wisdom responds: Ideas like class consciousness and class conflict have never taken root in American political soil because they are not native concepts. Rather, they are foreign seeds planted by people unfamiliar with the sociopolitical climate of North American class relations. In the United States, militant trade unionism is tamed into business unionism, incorporated and accommodated by corporate liberal capitalists. America transforms deeply democratic, radically participatory unions into bureaucratic versions of their former militant selves; it replaces class conflict with class cooperation by providing American workers with a package that combines contractual agreements and high wages. In the words of labor historian David Brody (1972:241), "the character of American trade unionism . . . made it an exploiter of radicalism rather than vice versa."

An unlikely consensus has emerged from this reading of labor history. People who would ordinarily disagree share a similar assessment of American trade unionism. From Vladimir Lenin to Selig Perlman, Robert Michels to Herbert Marcuse, or C. Wright Mills, Andre Gorz to Samuel Gompers, there is a consensus: In America, workers' organized efforts to gain or retain direction over their lives on the shopfloor are doomed to failure. Although they might dispute the reasons why, there is little disagreement on the outcome. Each would agree that despite various twists and turns, American labor history follows a relatively straight line: It begins with embryonic forms of "political" unionism and ends in "business" unionism. For political actors on the socialist left, this reading confirms their view that unions are not capable of establishing industrial citizenship; it is further proof of American "exceptionalism" and workers' "false consciousness." For activists on the libertarian right, the fate of unionism is another argument against it, an additional reason for individual and market solutions to workplace problems.

EXCEPTIONS THAT PROVE THE RULE

Hidden by this consensus is a handful of unions that did not follow the presumed CIO trajectory. The most notorious unions in this exclusive

5

club are the United Electrical, Radio and Machine Workers of America
(UE), the Hospital Workers' Union – Local 1199, the Independent Textile
Union (ITU), the Transportation Workers Union (TWU), the Interna-
tional Longshoremen's and Warehousemen's Union (ILWU), Mine, Mill,
and Smelter Workers' Union (MMSWU), and the National Maritime
Union (NMU). These unions are most often recognized for their
charismatic leaders and unabashedly left-wing politics. James Matles
(UE), Leon Davis (Local 1199), Joseph Schmetz (ITU), Mike Quill
(TWU), Maurice Travis (MMSWU), Blackie Myers (NMU), and Harry
Bridges (ILWU) were colorful figures, powerful leaders, and dynamic
articulators of a militant labor perspective. Six of them were accused of
being communists, and the seventh, Schmetz, was thought to be a socialist. Indeed, in 1949, the UE and ILWU were expelled from the CIO for
being under "communist influence."

Although they were notorious for the political eccentricities of their
leadership, these unions share a less sensational, but perhaps more fundamental feature: Long after most CIO unions purportedly began to practice
business unionism, they continued to pursue a version of early CIO
unionism. Some of them still do. Despite contractual agreements to cooperate, and even collaborate with management on matters of production,
these unions organized themselves to challenge management's rule on the
shopfloor and make the job site contested terrain. In the face of legislation
banning solidarity they found ways to unite workers across occupations.

Most Americans assume these unions were exceptions to the rule, and
that they probably still are. Scholars have analyzed them as "deviant" case
studies. Their influence has been minimized, and their significance restricted to the political margins. Many scholars have been more interested
in the color of the party card carried by the leaders of these unions than the
state of class relations on the shopfloors they organized, or the characteristics these unions share with other former CIO affiliates.[2] Because these
unions are assumed to be exceptions to the rule, a series of explanations

2 Fortunately, this is changing. A new generation of labor historians has recently focused on
  some of these unions. See for example, Fink and Greenberg (1989); Freeman (1988);
  Gerstle (1989); Kimeldorf (1988); Nelson (1988); Schatz (1983). For review essays commenting on the development of this new approach see Brinkley (1990); Isserman (1989);
  Lichtenstein (1989).

has emerged to account for their exceptionalism. Over the years, these constructions have become conventional wisdom. And like most conventional wisdom, these explanations are rarely questioned. Hardly ever does anyone ask, how unique did these unions actually turn out to be? Or, what do they *have in common* with the rest of American labor?

Recently, however, historiographic research has raised questions about just how distinctive these unions were and are. Rick Fantasia's case studies of the collective action exercised by ordinary unionists (1988), for example, indicate that "cultures of solidarity" and militancy are not restricted to these surviving radical unions. Lizabeth Cohen's history of the CIO in Chicago (1990) and Steven Fraser's biography of Sidney Hillman (1991) strongly suggest that the differences between "political" and "business" unionism have been overstated. The unions they examine fit both categories – sometimes simultaneously. Gary Gerstle's study of radical unionists in Woonsocket, Rhode Island (1989), moreover, shows that the spirit of radical unionism was sometimes clothed in conservative garb and spoken in the language of Americanism.[3]

This is a book about one of those unions: the International Longshoremen's and Warehousemen's Union (ILWU). Focusing on a major ILWU longshore local (Local 10, San Francisco), the book is based on three years of extensive field research: hanging out at the union hall and the bars surrounding it, sitting in on grievance committee meetings and contract negotiations, riding with business agents, and being aboard ships and docks when cargo was loaded and unloaded.[4] This careful look at the routine practices of San Francisco longshoremen in their everyday working lives suggests that in the ILWU, resistance to management's authority is collectively legitimated behavior, and explicitly acknowledged as *good* trade unionism. More than fifty years after the 1934 general strike that gave birth to this union, the San Francisco longshoremen still fight with management over workplace terrain. On the job, they use their working knowledge and working principles to challenge and contest management's contractual prerogatives; and, in the grievance machinery, they pursue disagreements over questions of workplace regime. Thus, the San Fran-

---

3 For a different view, one that argues communist unions left a distinctive legacy, see Stepan-Norris and Zeitlin (1989, 1991a).
4 A more thorough discussion of the research methodology can be found in the Appendix.

cisco longshoremen's union continues to wage what David Montgomery calls the "historic forms of working-class struggle" (1980:166). Longshoremen and their employers still fight over whose rules for how to work will be followed, which side's language will govern the workplace, and whose method for determining merit will prevail. The union continues to operate democratically, and has devised ingenious forms of contractual direct action on the job and in the grievance machinery. The exciting social experiment begun in the CIO five decades ago did not fail in this union; although modified, it is still practiced today.

EXPLAINING AN EXCEPTION

Most people, including many San Francisco longshoremen, would say that these findings confirm received wisdom: The union *is* unique. And they would explain the union's apparent uniqueness in four ways. Sociologists attribute the ILWU's evolution to two factors: domination by communists and other subversive elements, and the isolated character of longshoring.[5] According to this account, communists using the Bolshevik "organizational weapon" (Selznick) took over unions like the ILWU with a self-conscious strategy of disruption and manipulation. Operating secretly, often violating union democracy, they placed party cadre in key posts and thereby managed to infiltrate these unions.[6]

The second factor they would mention is that longshoring is isolated work (Lipset, 1963), which contributes to an "industrial propensity" for radicalism (Kerr and Siegel, 1964). In this account, certain industries breed radicalism because of their isolation. Radical politics, in this view, are supported by workers living in occupationally homogeneous communities that are isolated by geography and deviant work schedules, and therefore are not exposed to conservative middle-class influences. According to Lipset, lack of contact "with the world outside their own group" explains the radicalism associated with miners, seamen, loggers, fishermen, and dockworkers (1963: chap. 7).

5 This section relies heavily on Kimeldorf (1988: Chap. 1).
6 For other examples of this theory, see Barbash (1948); Epstein and Goldfinger (1950); Galenson (1974); Glazer (1961); Kampelman (1957); Pelling (1960); Prickett (1974); Selznick (1960).

San Francisco longshoremen have their own two-part theory for why their union is unique. The nature of longshore work, argue observant participants on the San Francisco docks, with its wide range of challenging and changing operational circumstances, makes it different than most industrial labor. The work requires a special combination of ingenuity, skill, and cooperative innovation, making continual supervision impossible. Thus, unlike factory work, longshore efficiency is intrinsically dependent on decentralized initiative (Mills, 1976; Mills and Wellman, 1987; Theriault, 1978; Weir, 1974). ILWU longshoremen also think their contract differentiates them. They point to contractual language which, in their view, makes the ILWU exceptional because it enables them to specify the conditions under which they will work and establishes grounds for refusing to work. They argue that these two circumstances, when combined, distinguish ILWU longshoremen from other American unionists: They can use the contractual agreement to implement their conception of what is safe, sensible, and proper work.

EXCEPTIONALISM REEXAMINED

Contrary to received wisdom, a close look at these accounts suggests they are seriously flawed; they do not explain why or how the ILWU is a unique American union. If the ILWU is unique, it is not because of communist manipulation or isolation. The union's practices are not explained by an omnipotent "red machine" that hijacked the union and secretly directed it. Quite the contrary. According to one student of the ILWU,

> Communist-supported insurgents rose to power by winning over the rank and file to their trade union program. Once in office, one of their first acts was to replace the old ILA constitution, which centralized power at the top of the union, with a more open and democratic set of procedures designed to guard against the kinds of organizational abuse that Communists were normally accused of practicing. (Kimeldorf, 1988:10–11)

The number of communists actually operating in the ILWU, moreover, appears to have been consistently exaggerated by both Cold War liberals and Communist Party (CP) sympathizers. One recent assessment concludes that, "in 1945, the high-water mark of American communism, only 237 West Coast longshoremen – a tiny minority it seems – were officially enrolled in the party. Subscriptions to the *Daily Worker* never exceeded five hundred" (Kimeldorf, 1988:163). Thus, professional revolutionaries "were a minority of the labor force" (Kimeldorf, 1988:163).

To complicate matters, despite its popular image, the ILWU was never, in any serious sense of the term, a "socialist" union. Although its founding president, Harry Bridges, and his supporters expressed socialist beliefs, the ILWU did not. The union never put forth a socialist vision for the future. Its constitution made no reference to "ultimate goals" or "collective ownership." In fact, being remarkably candid, Bridges is reported to have said: "You can't go getting mad at the employer because under our system he's in business to make profits. So you have to try to work out a solution within the system, and ours is admittedly a pretty selfish solution" (McConnell, 1966:327). Most longshoremen, moreover, voted for the Democratic Party, and Bridges voted Republican. Thus, although the ILWU may have had a disproportionate number of communist members, there is little reason to believe communists ran the union contrary to its membership's wishes, or that the union practiced "communist" politics.

Occupational isolation is an equally unconvincing explanation for ILWU practices. In fact, available evidence suggests the opposite. As Kimeldorf documents, on the West Coast waterfront, "isolation was *inversely* related to radicalism" (1988:13, emphasis added). Dockworkers in San Francisco were one of the ILWU's most consistently radical units. They were *not*, however, isolated from the city's general population. San Francisco's docks were at the core of the city's industrial geography. In San Pedro, however, the other principal California port some 400 miles south of San Francisco, dockworkers were very isolated from Los Angeles's cosmopolitan population and were much less responsive to radical politics than their brothers to the north.

The political history of longshore unionism in the Port of New York offers another example of the relationship between isolation and radicalism among waterfront workers. If anything, the self-contained world of New York longshoremen, insulated from the outside by ethnic community and casual employment, contributed to their conservatism and reactionary politics.[7] Isolation, then, is not a very convincing explanation for the ILWU's union practices.

The longshoremen's theory of why their union is exceptional holds up no better. A close look at the nature of longshore work and the contract signed by the ILWU suggests that this union has much more in common with American labor than the longshoremen's theory indicates. Work on Pacific Coast docks is, in crucial respects, similar to most work done by American labor; and the ILWU's longshore contract is, in important ways, a standard American union contract.

Because longshore work ranges from manual labor and skilled craftsmanship to operating technologically advanced machinery, the three major work categories associated with industrial labor are found on the waterfront. Dockworkers are simultaneously craftsmen, operatives, and laborers. The combination of activities required for longshore work, moreover, is required of virtually *all* industrial workers. When one focuses on the cognitive processes and physical activities necessary for longshoring, one finds that waterfront work has considerable common ground with numerous sorts of industrial labor.

All the energies needed to do the variety of work represented in David Montgomery's "house of labor" are necessary ingredients for moving cargo on the waterfront. Like craft labor, longshoring requires "skill and knowledge"; and, like craft labor, initiative is "indispensable to the operation of the enterprise" (Montgomery, 1987:45). Like the common laborer or the "human machine," longshoremen must know "teamwork, adaptability, and the use of such fundamentals of mechanics as inclined planes, pulleys, and levers" (Montgomery, 1987:61). To paraphrase Montgomery, like laborers on construction crews, longshoremen fetch and carry, load or clean up, whatever, wherever, and whenever (1987:63). Like the operative, longshoremen are specialists "bound to repetition of the same task in the same place" (1987:115). The personal qualities necessary for longshoring are comparable to those found among semiskilled workers and craftsmen: "experience, brain power, and adaptability" (1987:115). Like machinists, for dockworkers, "fitting parts together in assembly, or 'erection' of final

---

7 For a thorough comparison of the ILA and ILWU, see Kimeldorf (1988).

products, [is] as important a part of the trade as [is] the shaping of the parts" (1987:182).

Like the work done by skilled craftspeople, longshore work is, to use Shoshana Zuboff's phrase, "knowledgeable" work. It is based on "knowledge that accrues to the sentient body in the course of its activity; knowledge inscribed in the laboring body . . . knowledge filled with intimate detail of materials and ambience" (1988:40). Longshoring involves the knowledge of craft, the kind of knowledge Zuboff calls "know-how." It is based on knowledge derived from "action and displayed itself in action, knowledge that meant knowing how to do, to make, to *act-on*" (Zuboff, 1988:41, emphasis in original). Like other kinds of work organized by traditional craft practices, dockwork is also a "source of considerable pride, satisfaction, and independence" (1988:45).

In the last thirty years, longshoring has been transformed by the same technological revolution that has changed the face of most American work. A relatively simple, yet innately brilliant invention – the container – made that revolution possible. The container is a "box," twenty to forty feet long, that can hold twenty-four tons of cargo. Cargo is loaded directly into the container and handled just twice: when the box is "stuffed" and "unstuffed." Once the cargo has been stuffed, the container moves from truck, to railroad, then aboard ship and back again to truck. In the longshore industry, this is called an "intermodal system."

The container has modernized and automated San Francisco's waterfront. Longshoring is no longer a labor-intensive industry; it has become capital intensive. In the process, longshoring has become even more similar to most blue-collar jobs. Today many longshoremen are pinned down on container operations, making them clearly observable on the job. Their output can be easily monitored, which makes longshoremen less independent of management. Modernization, then, has reduced the distinctive features of conventional longshoring, making waterfront work more similar to other forms of industrial, blue-collar labor in America.

Longshoring on containerized waterfronts is more like mass production work than craft labor. The operation is no longer dependent on the special know-how of craftsworkers. The skills are more mechanical, repetitive, or "action-centered" (Zuboff, 1988:95). As with work in other automated industries, however, containerized longshoring has not eliminated the

12

need for skill. New skills are necessary. Like other workers in technologically advanced industrial settings, longshoremen are increasingly called upon to do cognitive labor, to exercise what Zuboff calls "intellective" skills. They continue to be knowledgeable workers who are called upon to think innovatively about and respond to unanticipated events in the workplace. Dockwork, then, shares numerous features with a multitude of industrial work.

Contrary to a widely shared belief on San Francisco's waterfront, the ILWU's contract with the Pacific Maritime Association (PMA) is also a remarkably traditional document. On paper, the union has relinquished workplace control; class conflict has apparently been replaced by cooperation. "Good faith" is guaranteed contractually by both sides as an explicit condition for coming together. The union also formally agrees to observe this commitment "without resort to gimmicks or subterfuge." According to the contract, the workplace is employers' turf; they choose what is to be done, how it is to be done, and at what pace. The union seems to have lost control over the workplace because the contract guarantees employer rights to "operate efficiently," "change methods of work," and "utilize labor-saving devices."

As to how the work will proceed, the agreement is clear-cut: It "will be performed as directed by the employer" (ILWU contract with PMA, p. 66, Section 10.6). And, with one simple declarative sentence, the union also renounces its traditional weapon for settling differences with the employers. As Section 11.1 states, "There shall be no strike, lockout or work stoppage for the life of this agreement."

Provisions pertaining to the management of disputes also work in the employers' favor. In the event that grievances or disputes arise on the job, states Section 11.31, longshoremen "shall continue to work as directed by the employer in accordance with the specific provisions of the Agreement." Thus, longshoremen are expected to do as they are told if they disagree with the employers. Even when disputes develop over matters not covered in the contract, the document concludes that "work shall be continued as directed by the employer."

The contract contains another provision that reads remarkably like the language found in agreements signed by "typical" American unions. Section 17.81 explicitly expects longshoremen to perform their work "cons-

13

cientiously" and with "sobriety." Members of the ILWU, continues the section, "shall not disregard the interests of the employer." The range of sanctions for people who do, moreover, is narrow and potentially harsh. Anyone found guilty of "deliberate bad conduct" can be either fined, suspended or, in certain instances, "cancelled from registration"; that is, be permanently removed from working on the waterfront.

Provisions of the ILWU contract that longshoremen think are exceptional, moreover, turn out not to be so. Like longshoremen, miners in the United Mine Workers union (UMW), for example, also have the right to refuse assignments that they believe place them in "imminent danger." They can do this "even if the employer can later prove that the belief was mistaken" (Witt, 1979:176). And like ILWU longshoremen, auto workers in the United Automobile Workers union (UAW) have the right to strike if health and safety issues "cannot be resolved in any other way" (Witt, 1979:176).

RECONSIDERING THEORETICAL CONVENTIONS

If the ILWU was not manipulated by communists and San Francisco longshoremen were not geographically isolated, if longshore work and ILWU contracts share key elements with other American unions, how does one explain the union's presumed uniqueness? Could it be that the ILWU is less exceptional than traditionally thought? Is something amiss in conventional wisdom about American unions? Or is it both? And if the union is not unique in the ways that have been traditionally suggested, even though longshoremen in San Francisco continue to practice the historic forms of working-class struggle, what is one to do with theories that presume unions like the ILWU are radical exceptions that prove the conservative rule of labor's demise?[8]

8 This is not to say the ILWU is a "typical" American union. Rather, the point is that received wisdom does not *explain* what is unique about the ILWU. Two points are relevant in this regard: (1) the ILWU, like other transportation-based unions, is distinct insofar as it occupies a highly strategic position in the expanded production process. Indeed, few unions outside of the transportation sector have the same capacity to disrupt production so effectively. This gives the ILWU tremendous power and endows its members with a sense of efficacy so often lacking among other workers. This disruptive potential is a real

Unions like the ILWU, unions that did not follow the supposed trajectory of the early CIO, provide scholars with a rare opportunity to study a kind of unionism assumed to have disappeared. Because these unions have been around for so long, they can no longer be dismissed as temporary aberrations soon to become just like every other American union. Thus, their very existence seriously undermines received wisdom about labor's fate in America. The fact that they have survived also makes it necessary for scholars to reexamine certain standard articles of faith, to take another look at traditional accounts of labor's demise. Their survival raises fundamental questions about theories that presume the fall of radical labor is inevitable, questions like:

What is meant by a "typical" union, and what are atypical, or "exceptional" unions?

What factors account for typical versus exceptional unions?

In what respects is the ILWU an exceptional union, in what respects is it typical, and why?

If the factors traditionally thought to explain the ILWU's exceptionalism don't, which ones do?

If the ILWU is less exceptional than previously thought, then might other unions be more like the ILWU?

Is the distinction between "political unionism" and "business unionism" a valid one? Is the trend toward bureaucracy and hierarchy inevitable, or is democratic participation an alternative? Do contract relations necessarily eliminate class conflict, or do they become a vehicle for it?

The central argument of this book is that the ILWU is much less exceptional than previously thought. In this context, "less exceptional" could mean two distinct things. It could mean that, except for their radicalism,

---

structural factor, which, although not unique to the ILWU, is hardly common to the rest of the working class. (2) Even though the ILWU is currently indistinguishable from other unions in terms of its work and contract, that was not always the case, as will be demonstrated in Part II. In fact, it was precisely its differences – in the nature of work, the capacity to resist, the hiring hall, and the contract – that distinguished it from much of the CIO prior to World War II. These features were the source of the political culture analyzed in Chapter 4. So even though the ILWU currently has much in common with other unions, it is still true that the ILWU's *history was different,* which may account for the political culture that can still be found on the waterfront. (Thanks to Howard Kimeldorf for this formulation.)

unions like the ILWU resemble other unions in terms of contracts, the nature of the work performed by their members, and the skills their members need to do the work. That is not what I mean by "less exceptional." I think there is another possibility: namely, that radical unions such as the ILWU resemble other unions in some very important respects, including their radicalism.

To recognize this possibility, it is necessary to reassess and reframe the theoretical construction that currently presumes labor radicalism is doomed in America, that unions like the ILWU are exceptions to that rule. Thus, one needs to ask: How is this formulation constructed? What are the conceptual components that determine what scholars will look for, and *not* look for? What is taken for granted; and what is researched? What kinds of evidence are produced by the methodological assumptions governing the sociology of American labor, and what kinds of evidence are systematically ignored?

What, in short, is this theoretical construction, and how might it be more usefully reconfigured?

2

SEALING THE FATE OF
RADICAL LABOR THEORETICALLY

T HE theory of labor's demise begins with an observation about which there is wide agreement. Labor historians who disagree on fundamental issues agree that something quite special happened in the early 1930s. From students of the traditional "Wisconsin school" like Irving Bernstein, and "iconoclastic" or "social democratic" historians like David Brody and Melvyn Dubofsky, to Stanley Aronowitz and Staughton Lynd, their "new left" critics, to the newest generation of "new" labor historians – Joshua Freeman, Bruce Nelson, and Ronald Schatz – there is essential agreement.[1] Even though they use different language, they see the period in remarkably similar ways. Bernstein calls the period "the turbulent years" (1970); Brody says the CIO had "some radical potential" (1980:141). Dubofsky uses concepts that Aronowitz and Lynd would endorse. For him, the 1930s were a time of "ferment," "militancy," "radicalism," "violence," "and perhaps even an altered working-class consciousness" (1986:212). In Freeman's view, this period represents "the most profound metamorphosis in the lives of working people since the Civil War and Reconstruction" (quoted in Brinkley, 1990:19). To Nelson these years were "a long overdue festive upheaval, a search for more humane

---

1 I am aware of the difficulties of pigeonholing historians into different interpretive schools. Such schemes can easily confuse as well as disclose. Nevertheless, I think it important to distinguish among groups of scholars in order to note what they have in common even when they disagree over other issues. Even though they are not "new left" historians, Brody and Dubofsky are typically seen as making a break with the "Wisconsin school." Unlike students of Perlman and Commons, they emphasize larger community issues and the broader political context. Although not completely satisfactory, the categories "iconoclast" or "social democratic" are used to distinguish them from "new left" historians and scholars in the Wisconsin school. I am indebted to David Brundage for this observation.

and just patterns of work relations, and the flowering of an insurgent consciousness" (1988:10). In Schatz's estimation, the early CIO stands "beside abolitionism, civil rights, and women's rights as one of the great movements for freedom and dignity in American history" (1983:117).

Although they agree that something special happened, however, labor historians disagree on what that was. They do not agree on just how turbulent the period was; Dubofsky's "new look" reads the 1930s as the "not so turbulent years" (1986). Nor do they agree on what the turbulence was about: Was it a "crisis of legitimacy" (Fraser, 1983:214, 1989), "citizenship rights" (Freeman, 1983:264), or "self-rule" (Brecher, 1974:265)? Was the issue "workplace rule of law" (Brody, 1980:96), "worker's control" (Montgomery, 1979a), or "a radical restructuring of the workplace" (Klare, 1978)? Disagreement extends to how people characterize the events. Was the era "militant," "radical," or "revolutionary"? Did the activities reflect "pure and simple unionism" (Brody, 1980), "syndicalism" (Nelson, 1988), or both (Kimeldorf, 1988)? Did they express "class consciousness" or "job consciousness"? Were industrial workers engaged in class conflict or radical interest group politics?

There is not even agreement on the depth of the turbulence. Was working-class unrest widespread (Brecher, 1974), or limited to less than 10 percent of the labor force (Dubofsky, 1986:214)? Finally, scholars do not agree on what direction the labor movement might have or should have taken. Was socialism on the agenda, or were the politics social-democratic? Did a "revolutionary situation" occur during the depression decade, as Dubofsky asks (1986:223), or, as Brody suggests, did the militancy itself inhibit the movement's radical potential (1980:152)?

Despite these disagreements, a consensus exists on the question this period raises for labor history. "Why did that militancy fade away so quickly?" asks Staughton Lynd (1971:52). "What was inherent in the labor militancy of the 1930s," asks David Brody (1972:242), "that gave it so short a life?" And, citing a number of radical projects that failed in the 1930s, Melvin Dubofsky asks, "why?" (1986:212). Why was the "militancy," "radicalism," "syndicalism," "class consciousness," or "revolutionary spirit" so short-lived? Why didn't something other than what happened, happen? Or, why did something *not* happen?

18

Much of recent labor historiography begins with these questions. Summarizing labor historiography in the 1970s, Bernard Sternsher writes that "the general burden of these inquiries was the *limitations* of rank-and-file militancy – its relatively short duration . . . and its involvement of only a minority of workers . . ." (1983:301, emphasis added). The scholarly focus is on deradicalization (Klare, 1978), the "radical possibilities" that faded (Brody, 1980:141), the labor movement's inability to develop a working-class culture capable of overcoming ethnocultural divisions (Gordon, Edwards, and Reich, 1982), the "demise" or "decline" of the labor movement (Goldfield, 1987; Moody, 1988), the problem of an "absent political class consciousness" (Davis, 1986:6). Verba and Schlozman explicitly frame their analysis in these terms: "What Didn't Happen in the Thirties" is the subtitle to their article on "Unemployment, Class Consciousness, and Radical Politics" (1977).[2]

Historians and sociologists offer two kinds of answers to the question of why what-might-have-been did not happen? One is that radicalism was defeated, and the other is that militancy was driven underground.

TRADING POLITICS FOR ECONOMICS: DEFEATING LABOR RADICALISM

The very success of industrial unionism, explains the first account, was the CIO's undoing. This labor movement forced factory owners to officially recognize organizations created by industrial workers; it empowered ordinary workers and reduced management's authority. Contained in this contractual victory, however, was political defeat: The right to contest workplace terrain – to act politically on the job – did not survive the success of industrial unionism. Three reasons are suggested for this development.

The first is that a bargain was struck. In exchange for giving up "political" demands, like control over the work process, labor was allowed to negotiate for a piece of the pie. According to this view, labor radicalism was

---

2 Kimeldorf's analysis of the ILWU as a "deviant case" does not follow this pattern. Instead of asking why the left failed, he asks why radicals succeeded in the industrial labor movement. See Chapter 1.

19

undermined by contracts these unions signed in which they agreed to shift their operations from political to economic terrain. In return for more money and union recognition, labor legally relinquished its demands for control of the workplace; instead of leveraging discontent, these agreements forced unions to manage it. Thus, the collective bargain radically altered class relations. Class collaboration replaced class conflict because the contractual agreement conceded workplace control to management. Workers could no longer legally challenge their employers' control over the workplace since these activities were preempted by collectively bargained agreements.

Stanley Aronowitz's analysis of labor (1973) is typical of this view.[3] Citing "long-term contracts" and "the structure of collective bargaining" as reasons, he argues that "rebellion remains a difficult task for several crucial reasons" (1973:216). Because of the obligations assumed by unions when they sign labor agreements, the modern labor contract, he asserts, provides employers with a stable, disciplined, and docile labor force (1973: 217). Class struggle has been preempted. Class collaboration has replaced class conflict in Aronowitz's view because "struggle at the point of production has become regulated" (p. 218). The contract "guarantees labor peace"; it enables employers to "avoid disruption."[4]

The second reason is that the workplace was transformed by bureaucratic structures. Different writers stress various phases in the process.[5] Richard Edwards (1979), however, offers the most comprehensive version of this explanation. Citing bureaucratic rules as evidence that workers have lost control of the workplace, Edwards argues the workplace was trans-

---

3 Other proponents include Atleson (1983); Green (1980); Jacobs (1969); Klare (1978); Lynd (1972, 1976); Milton (1982); Radosh (1966); Weinstein (1968).
4 Brody apparently agrees, arguing that "the contractual logic itself actually evolved into a pervasive method for containing shopfloor activism" (1980:201).
5 See Brody (1964, 1969) for a brief overview of the institutionalization process. Lipset, Trow, and Coleman (1956) specify the conditions leading to bureaucracy. Bernstein (1950) emphasizes the role of collective bargaining. For C. W. Mills (1948), oligarchy was an important factor in the development of bureaucratization. Millis and Brown (1950) focus on the regulating context of the Taft-Hartley Labor Relations Law. Lichtenstein (1982) stresses the co-optation of labor by the World War II administration and the bureaucratic habits associated with government work. Moody (1988) analyzes the imposition of bureaucracy on the CIO immediately after World War II.

formed in the last century; capitalist power is now institutionalized in bureaucratic control.

A transformation of hierarchical relations at the modern workplace has occurred, he contends, because "supervisory command" has been replaced by "rule of law" – the firm's law. Control is now bureaucratic: The sanctions imposed on recalcitrant workers are specified by organizational rules, not personal relations. Supervisors in bureaucratic organizations no longer formulate regulations, but rather apply them. Capitalist power today, according to Edwards, stems from an ability to "determine the terrain," to set the terms by which disputes will be settled. Bureaucratic rules invest power in the hands of capital, producing a new, "good" worker. Because of this development, struggles to control the workplace are no longer waged and labor's radical potential has been undermined.

The third reason focuses on changes in the work process. Class relations, it is argued, are profoundly altered when labor-intensive industries shift to capital intensity because capital-intensive industry means machine production. In this context, employers do not have to depend on workers' knowledge of the production process and workers thus become machine hands. As a result, they can no longer demand mutuality, much less respect. By appropriating technical knowledge, employers routinize work and control the job. According to this scenario, the technological revolution was counterrevolutionary; it has tamed a once unruly pool of labor.

Harry Braverman (1974) is probably the most prominent proponent of this view.[6] Working humanity, he argues, is transformed by technologically advanced industries into an "instrument of capital" for two reasons. One is that workers adjust to this form of work by becoming "habituated." The other is that modern technology eliminates skill, craftsmanship, and pride in work. How a worker performs a task in mass production work is not nearly so important as how many times the task is performed. Thus, automated work is not only simplified, but it is "degraded" as well. The conceptual, or thinking, side of work has been divorced from its execution. Capital-intensive labor, in this view, has been "de-skilled." Because de-skilled labor does not require much thought, management is freed

---

6 Other examples of this account include Edwards (1979); Noble (1977, 1984); Mills (1979b); Zimbalist (1979).

from its dependence on workers' knowledge of the labor process. Therefore, this transformed work process has ended labor's brief romance with radicalism and put employers back in control of the workplace.

WILDCAT STRIKES, INSUBORDINATION, AND PHANTOM UNIONISM: RADICALISM DRIVEN UNDERGROUND

A second explanation for what did not happen is that labor's radical potential was driven underground. When radical activities are officially banned from the workplace, workers devise other ways to rebel against management authority. Impressed by the human capacity to resist domination, yet conscious of constraint, this account discovers radicalism in slowdowns, work-to-rule actions, sabotage, insubordination, and wildcat strikes.

Labor radicalism was driven underground, according to this account, during World War II, when unions pledged not to strike until the war was over. "Unable to effectively use official union channels," writes Nelson Lichtenstein (1977:233–4), workers turned to "unauthorized methods" of direct action. The war's end, however, did not restore workers' rights to participate directly in the process of workplace governance. Passage of the Taft-Hartley Act meant that direct action on the shopfloor became illegal. "Boxed in by the legal framework," observes Garson (1973:115), workers had no choice but to resort to illegal walkouts. Labor's collaborationist posture during World War II, and the Taft-Hartley Act that followed, became management's rock and the union movement's hard place. Caught between, American workers had no choice but to take their struggles underground, to fight on subterranean soil.[7]

---

7 In this view, a large proportion of illegal work stoppages are precipitated by shopfloor disputes over governance; they are not spontaneous. World War II wildcats, it is argued, were caused by speed-ups, firings, and quotas, not wage disputes. Citing four primary and five secondary factors leading to wildcats in the auto industry, for example, one writer finds none relating to wages (Jennings, 1975:101–3). And analyzing 118 work stoppages in a two-month period, Homans and Scott could find only four that centered around wages or union organization (1947:280). The rest of the strikes, in their estimation, protested discipline, company policies, and firings. They were also "organized" since "a wildcat strike," write Homans and Scott, "presupposes communication and a degree of informal group organization" (1947:283). (For like-minded interpretations, see Green, 1975:39; Lichtenstein, 1977, 1989; Rawick, 1983; Weir, 1975.)

Postwar walkouts are offered as further proof that shopfloor problems had to be solved outside the union. The wildcat strike, in this view, is a protest, not only against management practices, "but also against the limits imposed by unionism" (Aronowitz, 1973:226). Illegal shopfloor actions and rank-and-file rebellions are interpreted as surface manifestations of a continuing contest for control over unions and the workplace.[8]

Critical of established unions, this view looks to other forms of organization for signs of insurgency. It finds oppositional cultures in primary work groups, which are informally constituted and antagonistic to bureaucratic union officials. These primary work groups, in the words of one commentator, function "as cells of organization in a guerilla war" waged as often against union bureaucracies as capitalist companies (Green, 1975:39).[9] They are seen as sources of independent power, as the "microorganizational units" that create "phantom unions," which are behind all wildcat strikes, slowdowns, and withdrawals of efficiency (Weir, 1973:56).[10]

This account is generated primarily by postulating two types of workers.[11] The first type is generalized from an incident known as the Lordstown phenomenon.[12] Influenced by the same winds of dissent and cultural revolution that fanned the flames of student rebellion in the 1960s, auto workers in Lordstown, Ohio, responded to speed-up and new forms of industrial organization with expressions of militancy and solidarity that most people assumed had died in the 1930s. The Lordstown

---

8 See, for example, Garson (1973); Gorz (1970); Moody (1988); Weir (1970, 1983). In certain instances, Montgomery subscribes to this view. "Today's steelworkers," he wrote in 1980, engaged in "personalized forms of rebellion on the job"; they carry on "communication by sabotage." He also noted that government rulings and management drives "have progressively tightened the legal noose around those historic forms of working-class struggle which do not fit within the certified contractual framework" (1980:166).

9 Brody also recognizes the importance of "work-group" activity, which he sees as an "expression of the irrepressible social organization of the shop floor" (1980:205).

10 For a critical view of phantom unionism and shopfloor guerilla war, see Burawoy (1985).

11 The following four paragraphs rely heavily on Matza and Wellman (1977). Some analysts of primary work groups as independent bases of working-class insurgency have arrived at this conclusion without theorizing these two types of workers. See, for example, Brecher (1974); Glaberman (1980, 1984); Rawick (1983), and Weir (1970).

12 See, for example, Aronowitz (1973: chaps. 1 & 8); Garson (1973); Gibbons (1972); Gooding (1970); Kremen (1972); Levison (1974: chap. 6); Norman (1972).

phenomenon was not, however, a repeat performance of "Lefty," the character who figured prominently in CIO organizing drives. Lordstown workers were more alienated from the work process, more cynical about traditional ideological politics, and more comfortable with direct action of less organized sorts. "Lefty" was the radical worker who helped organize the CIO. The Lordstown worker was Lefty's counterpart who had to cope not only with the boss, but with the unions Lefty created thirty years earlier.

The second type of worker is abstracted from a perspective that sees the worker not as worker, but as low-rider.[13] In contrast to the Lordstown phenomenon, the described rebellion of the low-rider takes place off the job in a relentless search for thrills, excitement, and proof of manly status. Although the low-rider obviously works, this perspective focuses on absenteeism, tardiness, poor performance, and trouble making. What the low-rider does aside from being tardy, absent, and troublesome is not addressed.

The low-rider uses the pseudo-freedom of empty time and avoids the coercion of the labor market, producing a space for action that is patrolled by the police. This dialectic with authority prods the low-rider to conceive new ways of "having fun" while evading the agents of order. The low-rider lives in a world where innovation is constant, rebellion is routine, and insubordination permeates, and even defines everyday life.[14] Essentially a "bad-ass," the low-rider is a rebel who resists workplace authority by rejecting, flaunting, or ignoring it. The politics of this rebellion are total, individualistic, and personal.[15]

Working-class radicalism, in the underground account, cannot be contained. Like a mighty river, it runs along the banks finding weak spots and penetrates them. Sometimes it seeps in, unnoticed until the river's banks have been eroded. Other times it washes over humanly constructed impediments and takes whatever space it needs for itself. Unauthorized, illegal direct action is an expression of what would be or might be, were

---

13 See, for example, Matza (1961a, 1961b, 1964, 1969); Matza and Sykes (1961); S. M. Miller and I. Harrison (1964); W. Miller (1958); Wellman (1968); Willis (1978, 1990).
14 Schwendinger and Schwendinger (1976); Werthman and Piliavin (1967); Willis (1978).
15 Marlon Brando's character in *The Wild One* is the prototypical bad-ass. When asked, "What are you rebelling against?" he answers, "Whadda ya got?"

workers not restrained and unions not collaborating or colluding with management. Lefty lives, in this view, not as politico, but as outlaw. Men and women organize illegal work stoppages rather than strikes; on the job they are subversives, and off the job they rebel in personal and stylized ways. Thus, working-class militancy persists *despite* contractual limitations and prohibitions. Labor radicalism was not defeated in the 1930s. It is alive and well, waged opaquely and illegally, on and off the job.

INFERENCE, PRESUMPTION, AND THE POLITICS OF PERSPECTIVE:BUILDING CONCLUSIONS INTO ASSUMPTIONS

Despite the differences between them, these two accounts have a common framework. They represent two answers to the same question. Thus, they are really two sides to one coin: two responses stimulated by the same fundamental question. That question is the one Sombart raised more than fifty years ago: "Why is there no socialism in the United States?"

If socialism had been on the American political agenda, and if the early CIO had been a socialist movement, this question might be a useful starting point. But socialism was never a serious item on the national American agenda, and although socialists and communists participated in CIO unions, the CIO was not a socialist movement. Thus, rather than starting with what actually happened, and then tracking its evolution, these two accounts begin with what might have been (some sort of incipient socialist consciousness), and analyze why it did not occur. As a result, "the history of American class consciousness," writes Sean Wilentz, "is not so much studied and written about as it is written off from the start" (1984:3).[16]

---

16 Brody and Dubofsky apparently agree with this formulation. "The interesting questions," writes Brody, and Dubofsky concurs, "are not in the realm of what might have been, but in a closer examination of what did happen" (1975:122). However, although neither of them subscribes to the "what-if" or "what-might-have-been" school of history, they do work in the "what-did-not-happen" tradition. Like their new-left critics, then, their work is framed by the question, "why not?" Thus, even though they reach different conclusions, their analytic emphasis turns around the same question, and their benchmark for assessing the CIO is similarly based on the negative criteria of what did *not* happen.

The way in which this history gets written off is crucial to the construction of theories explaining radical labor's demise. Three components are critical to the construction: (1) radical politics are equated with socialism; (2) a distinction is made between "political" versus "business" unions, and "typical" unionism in America is constructed as business unionism whereas political unionism is "exceptional"; (3) the operating rules of class relations are located in formal agreements, national political agendas, and institutional arrangements. Given these assumptions and the way they are combined, there is only one way to read American labor history; the conclusion is contained in the formulation: Radicalism is destined to fail.[17]

The first element in this construction can be seen in the way scholars treat the something special that happened in the early 1930s. Regardless of theoretical persuasion, labor historians use the same classic yardstick when they assess the 1930s. Whether it is new-left historians looking for "workers' control," "working-class self-activity," "syndicalism," "self-mobilization," and "revolutionary potential," or Wisconsinites and iconoclasts trying to find incipient traces of a "labor party," "advanced positions" on social issues, "socialism," and "communism," CIO unions are judged by their ideological politics. The benchmarks are classic socialist political abstractions.[18] Thus, the components of the CIO's "radical potential" listed by David Brody are: "an influential cadre of left-wing leaders; political activism, not excluding the formation of a labor party; and an aggressively advanced position on social issues . . ." (1980:141). And the political contours of the 1930s that Melvyn Dubofsky wants to explain are: Why "American socialism expired . . ., communism advanced only marginally, Roosevelt seduced the farmer-laborites and populists, [and] the CIO came to resemble the AFL . . ." (1986:213). In both instances, the focus is on ideological political consciousness. The issue is how close did

17 Again, Howard Kimeldorf (1988) is the exception. Although he accepts these assumptions, he concludes that radicalism did not fail in every instance. He does, however, equate radicalism with socialism, and analyzes successful socialists as "deviant." Thus, like the others, he considers radical unionism "exceptional."
18 Lizabeth Cohen's recent book (1990) is an important exception to this observation. Rather than hold CIO unions to the standard of class-conscious politics classically conceived, she argues industrial unionism in Chicago pushed for "moral capitalism," not socialism.

the CIO come to a socialist consciousness, or, what was its socialist potential?[19] The question of whether socialism should be the benchmark for radicalism is not addressed. The assumption is that it should.

The second element in this construction – the distinction between political or "social" unionism and business or "pure and simple" unionism – is not a new one. It is the same distinction American socialist and labor leader Eugene V. Debs made in 1921 between what he called "old unionism" and revolutionary industrial unionism (Debs, 1921). It is the distinction made by other labor radicals like Daniel DeLeon between "trade-consciousness" and "class consciousness."[20] In these formulations, political unions are class conscious whereas business unions are trade conscious. Class consciousness, in turn, is associated with radical or socialist ideology and the willingness to act "politically." Thus, social unionism, in Alice Kessler-Harris's words, is "collective activity in the community, the workplace, and above all in the political arena" (1987:32). Trade consciousness, on the other hand, is manifested in pragmatic, anti-ideological activities. In Kim Moody's terms, business unionism is "a unionism that sees members primarily as consumers and limits itself to negotiating the price of labor" (1988:xiv).

The distinction between political and business unionism is used to distinguish between unions like the ILWU, which, until quite recently, have been thought of as political, and the rest of American labor, which is considered business unionism. In this construction, political unionism is the exception proving the rule that, in America, labor's natural evolution is toward business unionism. Thus, the newest labor history accounts of unions like the ILWU assume they were different than most and then explain why. Instead of comparing the two traditions, the analysis is generally framed around questions such as, what makes radical unions so different from other trade unions? Or, what explains their exceptional history as political unions?

19 Sean Wilentz states the case well. Historians in this tradition, he writes, "assume that a powerful working-class socialist movement – a political species the American historians usually presume existed in nineteenth- and twentieth-century Britain, France, and Germany – is the sine qua non of true socialist consciousness" (1984:2–3).
20 See DeLeon (1921), as well as Goldfield (1987:49), and Lens (1959).

The ILWU's direction, for example, is attributed to a syndicalist mood, an occupational subculture, as well as the influence of the Communist Party (Nelson, 1988:4–10; Kimeldorf, 1988). The trajectory taken by the ITU and UE is explained by the distinctive characteristics of their founding leaders who were part of an elite stratum in their respective industry's workforce, a group that had emigrated from northwestern Europe or were the offspring of people who had, and were unionists with ties to either the Socialist or Communist parties (Gerstle, 1989; Schatz, 1983). Exceptionalism in the TWU is attributed to its "unusual combination of a heavily Irish membership and a leadership close to the Communist Party" (Freeman,1983:256). The Local 1199's distinctiveness is considered a legacy of its left-wing past in combination with being at the intersection of major social movements and structural transformations in postwar American life (Fink and Greenberg, 1989:ix–xi).

The first two elements in this construction write off class consciousness conceptually. Assuming that class-conscious politics are socialist makes radical unionism exceptional or deviant by definition. The third element in this construction writes off class consciousness methodologically. Because radicalism is equated with socialism, and because there have been no major socialist movements in America, it is assumed that radical unionism has declined since the 1930s. Thus, there is no reason to track the lived trajectory of founding CIO unions. Nor is it necessary to observe their actual routine practices in everyday life, up to and including the present. Instead, the rules of class relations are discovered largely in institutional, theoretical, or formal contexts and documents. This, of course, precludes the possibility of finding class consciousness on the shopfloor.

Aronowitz's assessment (1973) of class relations, for example, is based largely on his analysis of contractual obligations. His argument is mostly derived from close scrutiny of legal provisions in collectively bargained agreements. Like that of Aronowitz, Edwards's interpretation is based almost completely on his reading of rules, goals, and requirements of bureaucratic institutions. Similarly, Braverman's theory is based in great part on texts written by industrial psychologists, sociologists, and engineers. He cites the writings of people theorizing about "scientific-technical revolution" as evidence that the workplace has been transformed and management now controls the job. He also devotes considerable attention to engineering theory of machines and theories of scientific engineering. Thus, Braverman analyzes theory as though it were structural reality.[21]

Because they rarely look beyond the official, formal, or theoretical aspects of work, most people writing in this tradition do not fully explore actual shopfloor activities. They do not analyze disagreements routinely expressed on the job. As a result, labor's demise is constructed through conceptual assumptions or inferred from formal agreements and theoretical texts.

Aronowitz's assessment of class relations assumes that contractual obligations are fulfilled. He provides no direct evidence, however, that this actually happens. He never demonstrates that the contract successfully regulates struggles at the point of production. Nor does he establish a case for industrial peace. These judgments are either assumed or inferred from his reading of the contract. Thus, Aronowitz's epitaph for class conflict tends to be deductive; the state of class relations is determined by inference, not observation of actual disputes.

Like that of Aronowitz, Edwards's reading (1979) of class relations is also based on inference from rules, not accounts of struggles for power. Edwards focuses only on the elements of official organizational structure: formal rules, goals, and requirements. On the basis of these structural elements, he theorizes the "good" bureaucratic worker: someone who exhibits a "rules orientation," "habits of predictability and dependability," and "internalization of the enterprise's goals and values" (pp. 149–50).

The logic of this discovery is revealing. Qualities of a "good" worker are not established by observing shopfloor activities. Rather, they are inferred from job descriptions and management rating categories at the Polaroid Corporation. Thus, Edwards cites the company's personnel policy, which strictly prohibits "excessive absenteeism." He also mentions pay steps III, IV, and V, which require, among other things, "effective use of time,"

---

21 Apparently the methodological stance is intentional. In a candid footnote, Braverman (1974:180) admits he is describing a "theoretical ideal." The description, moreover, is from management's viewpoint. It is not an attempt to describe the "actual" course of events. "We are omitting for the moment," he writes, "the fact that workers are rebellious, and that the average pace of production is decided in a practice which largely assumes the form of a struggle, whether organized or not." But Braverman never returns to the subject of rebellion.

"thoroughness and accuracy," "orderliness," and "dependability." "Exceptional workers" at Polaroid are defined as "recognized leader-types" whose "quality stands out."

Not surprisingly, Edwards finds these traits rewarded by management. Workers' scores on these traits "predict" their ratings by supervision and "explain" differences in wages. On the basis of these findings, Edwards concludes that a new, predictable worker has been produced by bureaucratic control, and that corporations have consequently gained greater power.

Edwards's evidence, however, is only barely related to his theory. Orientation, habituation, and internalization are subjective categories. They are states of mind. But Edwards presents no data on workers' subjective understandings. He does not explore workers' orientations. Nor does he probe beneath the surface of their behavior to find internalized values. His only evidence is management's image of a "good" worker. And this he derives from rating categories in job descriptions. On the basis of these data, he infers the subjective state of workers in bureaucratic organizations.

But the inference is spurious. The subjectivity of workers cannot be ascertained through the rating categories of managers. That is the wrong place to look. If one wants to assess workers' orientations, values, and habits, then it is necessary to have access to their subjective world. But that assessment cannot be established by inference from the categories found on management's clipboards.

There is a more profound problem with this use of inferential analysis. The theory purportedly explains changes in control of the workplace. Nowhere in this analysis, however, does he provide direct evidence bearing on the issue of control. Instead, Edwards focuses on rules. And from this analysis of rules, he infers that bureaucratic control has been established.

Like the other two accounts, Braverman's assessment (1974) of class relations is either derived from assumptions or by deductive inference. His theory of habituation is a case in point. Braverman's contention that workers have been "habituated" is based on his reading of the motivation behind early industrial sociology and psychology. Pioneering industrial psychologists and sociologists, he argues, dedicated themselves to discovering the conditions under which workers would cooperate with

30

industrial engineers. Citing numerous books and articles, he makes a plausible case that these researchers tried to discover the conditions under which management–labor cooperation could be achieved. If they had successfully uncovered these conditions and implemented cooperation, Braverman might have data for his theory of habituation. But he provides no such evidence. Rather, he assumes that the research was translated into effective practice on the shopfloors of industrial America.[22] He infers habituation from his analysis of intentions.

When Braverman does cite direct evidence, he uses it to illustrate the theory, not test it. "A single illustration," he says, citing the Ford assembly line, "will have to suffice as an indication" of habituation (1974:149). Braverman's description of assembly line work at Ford, however, is not the source for his habituation theory. That theory is derived from his interpretation of industrial sociology and his "theoretical ideal" analysis of work. Having generated the theory from these sources, Braverman then applies it to the Ford assembly line, and ignores the extraordinary rates of labor turnover at Ford that might conceivably be interpreted as instances of resistance to habituation. Thus, although the argument appears to be grounded in observable events, it is actually generated by inference; the example is simply illustrative.[23]

These three explanations for the decline of labor radicalism are based on logical deduction and conceptual leveraging. They assume that contests for control are settled once rules are in place and that bureaucratic regulations translate into actual control. Instead of examining disputes over rules to see who, in fact, prevails, each one analyzes rules, contracts, and other forms of overt, formal, or official activity. They assume that contractual bans on overt struggles for workplace control have settled the governance issue; that official prohibitions on challenges to managerial authority prevent contests from being waged; and that, because ideological politics are not practiced, unions are no longer radical.

By themselves, however, rules do not constitute power. Rules are disputed, broken, negotiated, manipulated, finessed, and sometimes ignored. They have to be used, and used effectively, if one side is to control

22 For a similar critique, see Clawson (1980).
23 Aronowitz also argues by illustration (1973:223). For a more detailed discussion of the pitfalls hidden in argument by illustration, or "exampling," see Glaser and Strauss (1967).

another. Often, rules are used in ways not intended by their authors. And even when rules are obeyed it is risky to assume they have been "internalized." Predictable work habits do not necessarily mean that management is in control, or that workers are habituated. The defeat of labor radicalism, the idea that unions have given up their fight with management, then, cannot be established by fiat. It can be determined only by looking beyond contractual language, formal organizational structure, and technical-scientific texts. Direct evidence must also be provided. The issue has to be decided empirically, not inferentially.

In contrast to the theory of labor's defeat, the notion that labor radicalism has been driven underground is not constructed through inference. Rather, conclusions are based on observations of actual human activities. The account does not assume that resistance to management's authority has ended. Instead, rebellion is discovered in new locations and recognized in multiple guises. In this view, working-class history is made by human actors and subjectivity is featured prominently. The emphasis is on human activity, on the ingenious ways workers have devised to subvert authority, resist domination, and endeavor to maintain their self-respect against seemingly overwhelming odds.

The search for subjectivity and activity in the belly of domination and constraint does, however, produce a limited sense of the possible. Although there is hope for a more coherent and organized working class movement, that hope is located in the future, not the present. For the time being, struggles over governance are possible only when they are waged independently of unions, in opposition to them, off the job, or through symbolic, personalized forms of rebellion. Workers can object, withhold, withdraw, disrupt, sabotage, reject, ignore, be insubordinate and troublesome. But they have no institutional or organizational power. Militancy is restricted to negative, covert, illegal struggles where workers, independently of their unions, merely place barriers on management's power. At no time is management presented with "autonomous forms of workers' power" (Gorz, 1980:49). Conscientious withdrawal of efficiency and restriction of production are seen as negative answers to management ideology and union betrayal (Matza and Wellman, 1980:25). Practiced privately, however, furtive resistance can be double-edged – more problematic for the refractory than for management. After all, management "knows" workers are sloppy, forgetful, dumb, and untrustworthy. Thus, to behave in ways that even hint at confirming these negative stereotypes is to become complicitous in self-depreciation. Insofar as most people actually wish to be thought of as "good workers," resistance of the furtive sort can be a psychically risky business.[24] From this point of view, then, even though working-class radicalism survives legal and political prohibitions, it cannot currently wage contests for "real" power.

This account, however, is also flawed. Like the theories of defeat, it assumes that legal restrictions actually do prohibit unions from engaging in contests for control; thus it explores the matter no further. It also assumes that politics means ideological politics, or class-oriented social agendas. And because it finds none preached or practiced at work, the search for militancy is either abandoned, or moved elsewhere, to other kinds of behavior. What actually does go on between management and labor, however, is never analyzed.[25] Instead, it is assumed that class differences can be expressed only in covert behavior or deviousness; that contests over control cannot be waged through unions; and that struggles for workplace terrain have therefore been moved elsewhere, either transformed into conscientious withdrawal (Veblen, 1964), or replaced by games restricting production (Burawoy, 1979). Unions are assumed to be unresponsive bureaucracies, organizations that maintain the current order of class relations (Moody, 1988). The grievance machinery is dismissed as being either ineffective, or as a sophisticated device for deflecting working-class discontent. But all of this is assumed; the actual relationship between unions and management is not analyzed. Unions are held to an ideal-typical standard associated with revolutionary organizations. When confronted with the contradictory realities of unionism, unionism in toto is dismissed.

Thus, both constructions are based on political assumptions about what labor *should* do, not what workers and their unions actually do. The two constructions write off labor radicalism conceptually and methodologically. They both assume that radicalism means socialism; that radical unions share very little with other labor organizations; and that the

---

24 I am indebted to Jan Dizard for this insight.
25 See, for example, Atleson (1983); Goldfield (1987); Klare (1978); Millis and Brown (1950); Milton (1982); Moody (1988).

operating rules of class relations are found in formal, institutional, and ideological documents. Each one assumes that it is impossible to wage struggles for control on the shopfloor, or in unions and, without exploring beyond contractual language or directly observing actual union activities, that is exactly what they find. Thus, both conclude what they assume: namely, that the struggle between labor and capital either no longer exists, or has been relocated.

3

A FRAMEWORK FOR AMERICAN
UNIONISM

A more complete and complicated framework is needed to assess American unionism, one that distinguishes between formal and informal rules; between stated principles and routine practices; between political principles and the politics of everyday life; between ideological politics and actual contractual relations. An expanded conception of politics is needed, one that includes struggles over power, not just ideology; that includes battles waged on multiple fronts, on informal as well as formal terrain, and argues in colloquial as well as ideological languages, "politics" in the same sense that Big Bill Haywood meant syndicalism was socialist: "with its working clothes on."[1] Another method for assessing the state of class relations is necessary, one that does not locate the operating rules of class relations in the contract, but rather in the work process and grievance machinery; one that looks for the actual rules governing class encounters in tensions between practices negotiated informally at work and contractual provisions formally agreed upon at the bargaining table. Needed too, is a new framework for assessing the early CIO's accomplishments. If socialism wasn't on the national agenda, what was the "something special" that happened in the 1930s?

A NEW YARDSTICK FOR AMERICAN LABOR RADICALISM

Since neither socialism nor working-class consciousness as defined by a priori socialist expectations was on the 1930s agenda, the question asked of American labor movements should not be why no socialism. Rather, it should be, what *did* the CIO actually accomplish? What did it seek to do,

1 William "Big Bill" Haywood's definition of syndicalism. See Haywood (1905).

and how close did it come to achieving its goals? The analytic emphasis changes radically when these questions are asked. As Michael Kazin puts it: "Instead of the elusive 'what if,' . . . an emphasis on workers who sought constantly to increase their collective power without having socialism as a goal can liberate us from regarding them as somehow lacking in perspicacity or will" (1982:16). This focus enables one to see expressions of worker solidarity and class consciousness that have been, as Rick Fantasia points out, "ignored in social analysis because they do not meet the standard or classical model of what class consciousness *ought* to look like" (1988:23, emphasis in original). Sean Wilentz states the issue nicely: "The question posed by Sombart two generations ago should be turned on its head; rather than ask why there is no socialism in America, or no class consciousness in America, historians should find out more about the class perceptions that did exist" (1983:76).

When this advice is followed, a different assessment of the CIO emerges; another set of benchmarks, a new yardstick for evaluating its radicalism can be constructed. Socialist class consciousness rooted in the European experience is just one measure of radicalism. The CIO, however, was radical in another, more indigenously American way. The promise of the CIO, its radical potential, was that it put on the political agenda the issue of working-class participation in American institutions. In the workplace, the early CIO stood for union and shopfloor democracy; in national politics it promoted industrial democracy and an Economic Bill of Rights.[2] Although socialism was never a major item on America's agenda, participation certainly was: Rank-and-file CIO members insisted on self-governance in their everyday lives. Even though they did not explicitly demand "workers' control," they hotly contested management's right to rule, demanded a say in shopfloor decisions, and made their voices heard on social issues as well. As Lizabeth Cohen observes, industrial workers in the 1930s "had demanded, and were beginning to receive, a say

---

2 This may not differentiate between the CIO and the AFL. When one focuses on industrial relations, the two kinds of unionism appear to have engaged in similar practices. Gompers's style of unionism (Fraser, 1991) and the Commons-Perlman approach to industrial relations were posited on the worker's property right in the job and constitutional-legal limits on the employer's power and authority to regulate the labor process unilaterally. Thus, AFL unions could also be militant on shopfloor issues.

in the two institutions that wielded the most power over their lives: the state and the corporation" (1990:293). Thus, it is the CIO's participatory politics, not its missing socialist principles or numbers of left-wing cadre, that should be the benchmark by which it is assessed. When this is the measure of labor radicalism, the CIO's radical moment extends beyond the "turbulent years," the ILWU appears much less "deviant," and the distinction between "business" and "political" unionism becomes a false dichotomy.

CITIZENSHIP, THE CIO, AND A DUAL AGENDA

Citizenship in national politics

The early CIO made participation an issue on two agendas: in national politics, and in the workplace. At the national level, the CIO conducted one kind of struggle for citizenship. Unionists insisted their voices be heard on social issues, not only matters of work. Thus labor's organized muscle on the job was flexed off the job as well. Workers registered to vote, became a "constituency," backed candidates, and voted as a bloc. Liberal, social-democratic legislation was proposed and actively supported by many CIO unions. They pursued a social as well as an economic agenda; alliances were forged with groups previously excluded from organized labor, and some CIO leaders saw unionism as a movement to promote the general welfare of all Americans.

Dubofsky (1986:212) describes this period in commonly accepted terms:

> Masses of hitherto politically apathetic workers . . . went to the polls in greater numbers. And Roosevelt broke the last links that bound millions of workers . . . to the Republican party. Lewis exulted at the results of the 1936 election in which for the first time since the depressions of the 1890s, Democrats swept into power in the steel and coal towns of Pennsylvania and Ohio, winning office on tickets financed by CIO money and headed by CIO members. A new consciousness appeared to be stirring among the nation's industrial workers. A social scientist sampling attitudes and beliefs among Akron rubber workers . . . discovered that the vast majority of CIO members valued human rights above property rights and showed little respect or deference for the prerogatives and privileges of corporate property. Akron's workers . . . apparently

37

distinguished between purely personal use-property and property as capital. . . . Such an altered consciousness fed the dreams of Popular Fronters and third-party activists.

When World War II broke out, the labor movement embraced a welfare-state program. The agenda, according to Brody (1980:216–17),

> took form in President Roosevelt's Economic Bill of Rights, which elevated basic security to the status of human rights and expanded the scope of those rights beyond income to include health, education, and housing. Pushing past FDR's generalities, the progressives advocated national planning on the one hand, and, on the other, an economic policy designed to assure full employment.

The CIO's political activities were expanded during the war to include a nonpartisan Political Action Committee (PAC). Made up of fourteen regional offices, and, in some areas, an extensive precinct level organization, PAC "signified the new importance attached to political involvement by the industrial-union wing of the labor movement" (Brody, 1980:217).

When it is said that the early CIO had radical potential, these are the activities to which labor historians and sociologists typically refer. And when the CIO is accused of failing to achieve its radical potential, this is the potential to which they refer.[3] The focus is on the CIO's explicit national political agenda, its support for economic bills of rights, welfare-state legislation, full employment policies, and national planning procedures. Political enfranchisement and realignment are seen as hopeful signs, a new majority in the making. Blacks and women were being organized into CIO unions.[4] Immigrant workers who became Americans were joining unions, registering to vote, and voting Democratic. Native workers were leaving the Republican Party. There was even the possibility for a third party, maybe a labor party, since the CIO was seeking an independent

---

3 As Lipset states the case: "In the U.S. . . . the absence of an aristocratic or feudal past, combined with a history of political democracy prior to industrialization, served to reduce the salience of class-conscious politics and proposals for major structural change" (1985:243).

4 This is not to suggest that the CIO was completely inclusionary. As Herbert Hill argues convincingly (1987), the CIO also practiced a high degree of racial discrimination. The point is that, in some important instances, industrial union organizing distinguished itself from craft union practices by including black workers and women where previously they had been excluded.

political identity and its leaders were suspicious of entangling alliances with the two existing parties. Remarkable changes in working-class consciousness also inspired radical hopes. In institutional and ideological terms, then, a case can be made that working-class America was lurching leftward, if not moving in an incipiently socialist direction. That it moved no further to the left is taken as an indication of the CIO's failure.[5] This is the demise of labor to which so much scholarly energy is devoted.

Politicizing everyday life at work

The CIO, however, had another political agenda, one that was not written into party platforms, not pursued through electoralism, and not debated in explicitly ideological terms. CIO unions were also political in the practical, commonsense meaning of citizenship; they were about issues of control and participation in the everyday lives of ordinary workers. Thus, the CIO made citizenship an issue at work as well as in national politics.[6] CIO unions fought with management over who would govern the shopfloor, and industrial workers waged lively battles among themselves for control of their unions. Industrial unionists waged this struggle for control of their everyday lives on three fronts.

The shopfloor was the most obvious and notorious terrain. Because union recognition marked the end of unilateral managerial prerogatives, by its very existence the CIO challenged management's authority to control the labor force and workplace. But the CIO's attack on managerial unilateralism was not simply symbolic. Industrial unions also contested management's right to rule by waging the "historic form" of working-class struggle, the struggle for shopfloor control. CIO union demands went beyond wages and hours. In a 1941 survey of American collective-bargaining methods, economist Sumner Slichter discovered that three-quarters of the agreements (290 out of 400) signed between 1933 and 1939

5 Alan Dawley articulates this position succinctly when he claims that "the ballot box was the coffin of class consciousness" (1976:70). Michael Goldfield is even more explicit: "The weakness of trade unions in the United States," he writes, "and their long-term decline are again confirmed by examining their influence in national politics" (1987:26).
6 Marshall's notion of citizenship captures what I mean by the concept: "a status bestowed on those who are full members of a community. All who possess the status are equal with respect to rights and duties with which the status is endowed" (Marshall, 1965:92).

contained restrictions on employers' freedom to make layoffs (cited in Schatz, 1983:107). Confirming this finding in one major industry, Schatz writes that except for a brief period in 1936–7, United Electrical (UE) union organizers "based their appeal to workers primarily on non-monetary issues" (1983:150). They concentrated instead on demands for equal distribution of work in slack periods, seniority as the chief criterion for layoffs and rehiring, resolution of shopfloor disputes, and union recognition. Summarizing the accomplishments of early CIO organizing, Robert Zieger comes to a similar conclusion. "The CIO era's struggle to achieve external control," he writes, "was a shining victory" (1985:510). He argues that if the definition of workers' control is broadened to include "such practices as union participation in job evaluation, careful regulation of seniority lines, closely calibrated pay scales according to job content, protection from arbitrary discipline, and so forth, external control – 'workers' control' . . . was indeed at the heart of the CIO" (Zieger, 1985:506).

Citizenship was a shopfloor issue because CIO unions demanded a say in who would work, and how. The West Coast "Big Strike" of 1934, writes Bruce Nelson, represented "a desire to transform the world by fundamentally reshaping the patterns of authority and organization in the realm of work" (1988:6). In the Midwest, observes Lichtenstein, "auto workers waged a protracted conflict with the bosses over control of the work routine and distribution of power in the factory" (1983:284; see also Lichtenstein, 1984). And in upstate New York, "the struggle to . . . change the power relationships among people in the factories," Schatz writes of the UE, "really began only after the union won recognition" (1983:105).

In some instances the union movement actually implemented its plan for industrial self-governance. The settlement that came out of the dramatic events of 1934 on the Pacific Coast included contractual provisions "under which the longshoremen could mount a successful struggle for job control" (Mills and Wellman, 1987:171). And they did. According to one waterfront observer, "authority to direct work upon the docks passed from the hands of the foremen into the hands of dock and gang stewards. . . . They establish the manner in which, and the speed at which, work is to be performed on the waterfronts of the Pacific Coast" (cited in Nelson, 1988:161). One UAW local (299) introduced a group incentive plan "run by the workers themselves" (Friedlander, 1975:91). And unionized textile workers in Woonsocket, Rhode Island, instituted a system of work distribution they felt was "fair" and "just." Their share-the-work scheme "recognized the fundamental equality of all workers and did not discriminate on the basis of ethnicity, sex, or age" (Gerstle, 1989:145).

Textile workers clearly understood the implications of this scheme. "The union took over and did the job of foreman," said one (cited in Gerstle, 1989:141). The experience of electrical workers was similar. "With the coming of the union," wrote a UE business agent, "the foreman finds the whole world turned upside down. His small-time dictatorship has been overthrown and he must be adjusted to a democratic system of shop government" (cited in Schatz, 1983:117). A local union leader put the matter more graphically: "Finally . . . [the workers were] throwing off the shackles and saying to the boss, 'Go to hell! You've had me long enough. I'm going to be a man on my own now!'" (cited in Schatz, 1983: 117). Transit workers in New York City were no exception to this development. According to Freeman, the union gave workers who had once been passive a sense of liberation and empowerment, an escape from what many transit employees equated with slavery. "On account of this organization coming into existence," said one turnstile mechanic, "we are able to go to our bosses and talk to them like men, instead of . . . like slaves" (cited in Brinkley, 1990:19).

CIO unionists also fought for control of their everyday lives in a second location: They inserted themselves directly (sometimes literally) into the relationship between management and labor. Because they were impatient with, and skeptical of, established organizational forms that prevented people from actively participating in the process of making social change, CIO unionists engaged in direct action. They organized sit-down strikes and factory takeovers.

It is estimated that in the first six months of 1937, more than four hundred thousand workers participated in 477 sit-down strikes (Dubofsky, 1986:209). Twenty-five sit-downs erupted in January 1937, 47 in February, and 170 in March. According to *Time* magazine, "Sitting down has replaced baseball as a national pastime" (quoted in Dubofsky, 1986:209). The most distinctive feature of sit-downs was that they were self-initiated, highly participatory forms of collective action. "The initia-

41

tive, conduct, and control of the sit-down," comments Jeremy Brecher (1974:226), "came directly from the men involved." "Most workers distrust . . . union officials and strike leaders and committees," wrote Louis Adamic, who observed sit-downs firsthand,

> even when they themselves have elected them. The beauty of the sit-down or the stay-ins is that there are no leaders or officials to distrust. There can be no sell-out. Such standard procedure as strike sanction is hopelessly obsolete when workers drop their tools, stop their machines, and sit down beside them. (cited in Brecher, 1974:226)

The sit-downs were social events that countered the isolation of factory work. "Sitting workers talk," Adamic noted:

> They get acquainted. And they like that. In a regular strike it is impossible to bring together under one roof more than one or two thousand people, and these only for a meeting, where they do not talk with one another but listen to speakers. A sit-down holds under the same roof up to ten or twelve thousand idle men, free to talk among themselves, man to man.

Sit-downs were also an example of what 1960s new-leftists would call "participatory democracy." Workers occupying factories had to organize themselves for life inside the building. A firsthand observer at Fisher Body No. 1 in Flint, Michigan reports that the basic decision-making body was a daily meeting of all strikers in the plant. "The entire life of the sit-down," writes Henry Kraus (1985:93), "came into review here and most of its ideas and decisions originated on the spot." "The chief administrative body," notes Brecher, "was a committee of seventeen that reported to the strikers; available records indicate that virtually all its decisions were cleared with the general meeting of strikers" (1974:241).

Organizing themselves for daily life meant strikers had to create their own institutions for control and discipline. Thus, sit-downs became concrete expressions of self-rule and sovereignty.

> Workers established courts to punish infractions of rules. The most serious 'crimes' were failures to perform assigned duties by not showing up, sleeping on the job, or deserting the post. . . . Punishments were designed to fit the crime; for example, men who failed to take a daily shower were 'sentenced' to scrub the bathhouse. The ultimate punishment, applied only after repeated infractions, was expulsion from the

plant. The courts were generally conducted with a good deal of humor and treated as as source of entertainment. (Brecher, 1974:243)

The third front in the battle for control was the unions themselves. The struggle over workplace regime was extended from the shopfloor to CIO union halls throughout the country; during the initial organizing period, local unions were typically subject to rank-and-file control through various forms of direct and indirect democracy. Following passage of the Wagner Act, for the first time working people had the legal right to express themselves through majority rule in organizations of their own making. In Brody's estimation, the CIO responded to this challenge "brilliantly" (1980:96). "Typically," he writes,

> an intricate network of unpaid posts was established in CIO plants, so that "more men are given responsibility, and our organization becomes more powerful and more closely knit." The aim was to avoid "bureaucratic" rule by putting the leadership, as one organizer said, not in a few hands, but in "the whole body, in one acting as one." (1980:97)

Some CIO unions were accused by impatient members of practicing "just too damn much democracy" (Matles and Higgins, 1974:12). On the West Coast, Maritime Federation officials had to "submit every action of the slightest importance to a majority vote of the membership" (Nelson, 1988:257). *San Francisco Chronicle* labor reporter Arthur Eggleston was impressed with the degree to which waterfront unions had transformed the autocratic structure and practice of traditional AFL unions. "Referendum election of officers," he writes, "referendum votes on agreements, referendum votes on practically everything of importance and extremely easy methods of recalling officers constitute a grave threat to the less risky method of machine and convention control" (cited in Nelson, 1988:257). The UAW, according to Bert Cochran, was equally democratic. "[T]he union practiced a democracy," he notes, "and was able to elicit a rank-and-file participation in its affairs that was only partially or episodically achieved by others" (1977:108).

The principle of representation was taken seriously by industrial union organizers. The ITU, for example, encouraged high levels of membership participation and therefore decision-making powers were distributed to a large number of elected officials.

Each local met once a month to discuss its own business. Once a year the members of each local elected three general officers and two stewards from each department to administer local affairs between monthly meetings. The general-officer positions . . . were dominated by male, skilled workers, but the representation of each department in local governance insured that the interests of lesser skilled female and male workers would be represented as well. (Gerstle, 1989:146)

"Democratic practice," observes Gary Gerstle, "arises only in part from the character of representation of an institution's governing bodies; it depends as well on the quality of participation" (1989:147). The quality of participation in industrial unions was, by most standards, quite high. Gerstle describes textile workers' union meetings in these terms:

Meetings were well attended and exciting. All kinds of union members, even those limited by a faulty knowledge of English or fear of public debate, spoke their minds on issues that mattered to them. The most eloquent statement of the importance of democracy in the union consisted not of words, however, but of one unionist's mementos. . . . At a certain point late in the interview . . . he excused himself for a few moments and returned with a highly polished gavel and a dog-eared paperback copy of *Robert's Rules of Order*. He had used these tools to run the meetings of his Falls Yarn local in the 1930s. These, the only materials he had saved from his lengthy union career, spoke volumes about the centrality of democratic rules and procedures to his union experience. They conveyed, far more effectively than words, what democratic participation must have meant to individuals long subjected to autocratic foremen at work and long excluded from the democratic promise of American political life. (Gerstle, 1989:148)

The politics of participation practiced by the early CIO and the struggles it waged for control over the everyday lives of industrial workers should be the benchmark against which its subsequent trajectory is evaluated. Socialist principles, left-wing cadre, and potential labor parties are not the only criteria for assessing radical potential. And in an American context, these constructions of radicalism probably obscure more than they clarify. The early CIO was radical not by the standards of European socialist theory but rather because of its participatory politics and because it politicized everyday life at work. Evaluated this way, the early CIO – indeed, the entire industrial union movement – accomplished remarkable

44

results. It established capital-labor relations, in Gary Gerstle's words, "as a political, even moral, issue of cardinal importance" (1989:187). Like Irish nationalism, writes Joshua Freeman, industrial unionism was "an expression . . . of the demand for the full rights of bourgeois citizenship, including . . . participation in economic and political decision-making" (1983:264). When one considers not only the CIO's national political agenda for industrial citizenship but also its programs for citizenship in the everyday meaning of the term, it becomes apparent that labor radicalism did not end in the 1930s.[7] Some of the CIO's oldest unions still practice participatory politics in much the same ways as they did in the old days. And in this respect, the ILWU may not be an exception that proves the rule.

TOWARD AN ALTERNATIVE FRAMEWORK

"American workers," observes David Montgomery, "share an opaque but potent heritage of on-the-job struggles to control the terms under which they labor for a living" (1979a:154). That heritage is "opaque" in large part because working-class life in America is typically evaluated according to a particular political version of what it ought to be or might have been. "What has gone on at work," he writes in another context, "cannot be learned simply by reading the prescriptive literature for managers, any more than the on-the-job practices of a twentieth-century union can be learned by reading its constitution and by-laws" (1980:492).

Montgomery offers a necessary corrective to that approach. "American experience," he notes, "forces us to begin with the world of practice, and then to probe some of the ideological implications of that practice" (1979b:7). When one focuses on practice, the understanding of unions that emerges contradicts conventional wisdom. As Montgomery has found,

> American workers have waged a running battle over the ways in which
> their daily work and the human relations at work were organized over

---

7 This understanding of citizenship is somewhat different from the meaning advanced by T. H. Marshall (1965:122), for whom industrial citizenship means trade union representation. I mean something more: participation in workplace decision making.

the last century, and in the process they have raised issues which go far beyond the confines of "wage and job consciousness" or "bread and butter" unionism, into which historians have long tried to compress the experiences and aspirations of American workers. (1979b:7)

The focus on practice raises a new set of questions. Instead of asking what might have been, students of labor history are encouraged to ask what was. Instead of equating radicalism with European socialism, the early CIO's politics of participation become the benchmark. Instead of assuming that labor's battle with capital was either defeated by contractual agreement, bureaucratization, technological change, or driven underground, scholars can explore what actually happens on American shopfloors. Instead of distinguishing between "business" versus "political" unionism, the focus is on what unions have in common and what they actually do. It is possible to move from the history of attempts to win union recognition and written contracts to the story of contract implementation. Questions that once were considered answered can be transformed into questions again.

Assuming that something special did indeed happen to labor in the 1930s, this book asks, what actually happened to one such special union after fifty years of contractual agreements and revolutionary technological change? But instead of building answers into a theoretical framework the issue is addressed empirically. Theories purporting to explain labor's demise have been transformed into a series of questions that organize this book: (1) Instead of assuming the festive upheaval ended in the late 1930s and union leadership became institutionalized, the question becomes: Under what conditions did bureaucracy emerge and subvert democracy, and how was bureaucracy restrained in certain unions? (2) Rather than assuming technological changes undermined traditional skills, thereby preventing workers from regulating the workplace as they did in the 1930s, the question becomes: What is skill and how is it used in modern contexts? (3) Instead of starting with the premise that the antagonistic relationship between management and labor became cooperative when the contract was implemented, this book asks: Was the conflict waged in other arenas and does it persist? (4) If, in some instances, conflict between the two sides did continue after the contract was signed, how is it waged?

When one listens to what the two sides in the labor process talk about when they are forced by the contract to meet – concentrating on how they use the language created in this context, and how they act on these issues – class relations do not resemble conventional wisdom. Unions like the ILWU practice neither political nor business unionism. Rather, they have established a method for carrying on class conflict within the confines of the contractual agreement. The collective bargain does not channel class conflict into activities that are relatively nonthreatening to capital.[8] Instead, conflict takes place in the discourse made necessary by the contract. Deep disagreement is expressed and profound conflict is pursued in this talk. When one focuses on the activity created by contractual obligations rather than on contractual language itself, the rules for class relations look different than conventional wisdom would predict. They are rules for conflict based on and expressed through collaboration.

If the San Francisco waterfront is any indication, the points of contention that erupt over the contract go to the heart of class relations. These disputes constitute a set of regular features. It is not just a desire for better economic benefits that defines the ILWU's stance in relation to employers. Instead, San Francisco longshoremen try to manage their own work, denying the legitimacy of capital's authority over the workplace. This conflict is reflected in opposing images of production, conflicting vocabularies, and differing world outlooks. It is expressed in disputes over which side's people will inhabit and supervise the workplace and whose interpretations of the contract will prevail. The sociologies of knowledge used by each side have very little in common. The conflict runs deep, approximating a struggle between rival systems for organizing production.

Class relations on the Pacific Coast waterfront suggest that class conflict has not been eliminated by contractual agreements. Rather, the conflict has been relocated and is now waged within the confines of the contract. In the process, the contract has become a weapon in ongoing disagreement. The essential class disagreement between the two sides continues. Class conflict in contractual contexts is conducted through the creative use of language. Space is provided within the contractual relationship for

8 The following paragraphs are based on Matza and Wellman (1981).

47

struggle over and within the agreement. Thus, the contract is a bargain that reflects and reproduces fundamental disagreement. It is a document that states how production *and* conflict will proceed. The contract, in other words, can be seen to contain conflict in both senses: It limits some potential disagreements and it provides the context within which other disagreements can continue to occur.

Part II

LOCAL COMMUNITY AND "TUMULTUOUS" DEMOCRACY: THE SOCIOCULTURAL FOUNDATIONS OF UNIONISM ON THE SAN FRANCISCO WATERFRONT

W HAT happened to that something special that captured the imagination of industrial workers in the 1930s? Why was the festive upheaval, the celebration of self-governance in everyday life so short-lived? What happened to the democratic cultures of solidarity and resistance?

Organized pluralism and democratic political culture were undermined, some historians answer (Lichtenstein, 1984; Moody, 1988), in the late 1940s and early 1950s when the CIO formalized its relationship with capital. The new relationship between management and labor reduced rank-and-file participation in union affairs. Bureaucracy replaced democracy as an organizational principle in the CIO.

Two reasons are given for this development. One is that nationally negotiated contracts led directly to the rise of bureaucratic power. The contractual relationship required labor to commit itself to procedural rule, predictability, and order. Therefore, as the relationship matured, union power was transferred from the shopfloor to international headquarters. Since national contracts required national organizations to negotiate and enforce them, local unions had less power to control their internal affairs. The national contracts also centralized negotiable items, and issues that were once delegated to locals, like production standards, became the responsibility of national officers, leaving less for locals to bargain. As a result, power was increasingly centralized.

But bureaucracy did not result solely or inevitably from the CIO's

49

contractual relationship with capital. It was also a political accomplishment.[1] Recalcitrant shopfloor militants and oppositional politics had to be defeated; organized political pluralism had to be either destroyed or strictly limited. It was destroyed, a number of historians argue, in large part by an anticommunist crusade that began in the 1940s. In the process of purging communists, CIO officials defined rank-and-file disagreement with union officers as disloyalty.[2] Opposition was equated with being an outsider and considered disloyal behavior. Ironically, then, in the fight against totalitarianism, organized political pluralism was destroyed in many CIO unions.[3]

The CIO's postwar bargain with capital also contained a political strategy.[4] As World War II ended, it became clear that the CIO would not be politically independent.[5] Instead, it would operate as a pressure group within the Democratic Party. The vehicle created to do this, the Political Action Committee (CIO-PAC), would mobilize labor's vote for the Democrats.[6] This strategy, CIO critics claim, made unions entirely dependent on the good will of the Democratic Party and other political forces beyond their control. It forced organized labor to defend itself through pattern bargaining (Moody, 1988:38). As a result of this strategy, the CIO's national social-political agenda was sacrificed. Industrial labor compromised on its concern for the welfare of all Americans. By the end of the postwar period, then, organized labor was focusing primarily on economic matters; issues of social justice and equality were left for others to pursue. As a consequence, notes Kim Moody, by the end of the 1940s the CIO no longer practiced "social" unionism. Industrial unionism had been transformed into bureaucratic, service-oriented "business" unionism.

If this account explains what happened to the special participatory qual-

---

1 Kim Moody (1988:28–35) develops this point at length. See also Daniel Cornfield (1989, 1991).
2 Union antipathy to dissent did not begin with the Cold War. It has a long history in the labor movement, including left-led unions. See the essays by J.S. Hardman in *American Labor Dynamics in the Light of Post-war Development* (1928).
3 This argument is elaborated in Moody (1988:35).
4 See Aronowitz (1973); Goldfield (1987); Milton (1982); Moody (1988).
5 For analyses of this development see Brody (1980); Lichtenstein (1982); Milton (1982); Moody (1988); Preis (1964).
6 See Lichtenstein (1982) and Moody (1988:35–6) for discussions of this political strategy.

ity of most CIO unions, it certainly does not apply to the ILWU's subsequent history.[7] If the CIO did indeed strike a deal with employers that ended the participatory festive upheaval, the ILWU was not a party to the bargain. It was not allowed to be. And although it would be accused of many political sins, rarely did anyone charge the ILWU with being a bureaucratic, service-oriented business union.

Because a number of high-ranking officials were associated with the Communist Party, the ILWU was treated as a pariah union during the anticommunist crusade launched after the Second World War. Founding President Harry Bridges was the object of numerous prosecutions for alleged communist associations. While denying membership in the Communist Party, he refused to condemn the organization and frequently praised its stands on labor issues. A number of other ILWU officials were known as radicals before joining the union and refused to testify before congressional committees investigating communist activities in the labor movement. As the Cold War matured, a resolution was adopted at the CIO's 1949 convention that prohibited union officers and board members from belonging to the Communist Party, or any "Fascist or totalitarian organization." Following perfunctory trials, the ILWU and ten other unions with leftist leaders were expelled during the next two years.

The ILWU's expulsion from the CIO was just one in a series of events that kept it outside organized labor's house, or more accurately, in its dog house. The union's very existence was problematic. The ILWU hiring hall was specifically targeted as being illegal by sections of the Taft-Hartley Act. The U.S. government persistently tried to jail and deport the union's leadership. Between 1934 and 1945, Bridges was the object of three deportation proceedings. In 1949, two high-ranking officials in San Francisco (Bob Robertson and Henry Schmidt) went on trial with Bridges, having been accused of conspiracy and fraud for stating on citizenship applications that Bridges was not a communist. In 1951, a leading ILWU official in Hawaii (Jack Hall) was jailed along with six other people for allegedly violating the anticommunist Smith Act. Left-wing, rank-and-file longshoremen along the Pacific Coast were prevented from working cargo that

---

7 I am not convinced the account *does* explain what happened. But that does not matter here. Regardless of how one assesses the accuracy of this account regarding other CIO unions, it does not explain the ILWU's trajectory.

required a security clearance. The Waterfront Employers Association also added to the ILWU's problems. Sensing the union's vulnerability, and anticipating government support, they forced two very costly and troublesome strikes on the union in 1948 and 1950.

Thus, at that very moment when CIO unions were developing a businesslike relationship with employers and political officials, the ILWU was under serious and sustained attack. At the time when most CIO unions were allegedly trading shopfloor power for economic incentive, the ILWU was fighting for organizational survival. The bargain CIO unions ostensibly made with capital was not an option for the ILWU.[8]

One of the serendipitous consequences of the sustained and intense political attack on the ILWU was that it did not become bureaucratized. The union's democratic political culture was never destroyed. Attempts to suppress the ILWU played a crucial, although paradoxical role in this process. Instead of crippling the union, the anticommunist crusade actually intensified its democratic tendencies. If the union was to survive legislative, political, and economic assault – if it was to weather outlaw status – it had to practice the spirit not just the letter of democracy. Beleaguered legally and politically, the ILWU could not afford to give its enemies additional reasons to attack and undermine its leadership. But democratic organization was not simply a defensive tactic; democratic practices also strengthened the union. Rank-and-file participation created a sense of belonging and gave ordinary longshoremen a valuable stake in the union. Internal pluralism transformed social and political diversity into unity and solidarity.[9]

8 Although it is accurate to say that the ILWU was not allowed to cut a deal with capital after World War II, a "new look" emerged after the 1948 strikes that eventually achieved a rapprochement of sorts. The union no longer sanctioned "quickie strikes" or regular work stoppages. The employers' association was also reorganized, and deemphasized its principled opposition to the ILWU's existence. Apparently both sides realized they could not deliver a knock-out punch and therefore agreed to live together, not necessarily as friends, but as distrusting partners. I am grateful to Howard Kimeldorf for this insight.
9 Even the ILWU's severest critics recognize the democratic character of the union in these formative stages. See, for example, Swados (1961); Weir (1964, 1974:276–8). This development may have occurred in other CIO unions. Stepan-Norris and Zeitlin (1991a,b) argue that the chances of constitutional democracy in CIO unions were increased if they were led by communists and allied radicals.

The combined government-employer attack on the ILWU created a new kind of human relations among West Coast longshoremen. The shared experience of militant activities and defiance of government produced a community of workers.[10] Consolidating the "festival of the oppressed" (Nelson, 1988:157) that was celebrated on West Coast docks during the General Strike of 1934, longshoremen created a "culture of solidarity" (Fantasia, 1988), or a "culture of unity" (Cohen, 1990) that was sustained by government and employer hostility. A new identity emerged: Swedes, Russians, and Italians became "longshoremen," "ILWU." Union membership was added to ethnicity and skill as another basis for distinguishing between people.[11] The longshoremen viewed themselves as subjects of history who could define their own relations. They created a new language of social action and invented a politics that empowered them all. They called each other "brother"; they talked about "one big union" of maritime workers; and they adopted the slogan, "an injury to one is an injury to all."[12]

This sense of community, or culture of solidarity, was translated into a distinctive organizational form. The union they created was radically democratic. It was a loose confederation of tightly knit locals, each one autonomous from yet closely linked to the international offices in San Francisco. The organization was antiautocratic. Local officials could hold office only for two consecutive terms and then they had to return to the docks. The organization was also antihierarchical; full-time officers were paid no more than working longshoremen. The locals soon became famous for participatory politics. Anyone who wanted to speak, could, and did, usually for a long time and always using colorful waterfront language.

---

10 The following discussion is based on Mills (1976, 1978a, 1979b) and oral histories conducted with J. Bulcke, Henry Schmidt, Bjourne Halling. See also Bruce Nelson (1988).

11 Although unionist was added to the identity of ethnic dockworkers, ethnic identification did not diminish. What longshoremen called "ethnic gangs," for example, persisted well into the 1960s. Racial identity, moreover, was *not* included as part of the sense of inclusive ILWU brotherhood on the San Francisco waterfront until at least the 1950s. And outside of San Francisco (and Hawaii), the historical record is complex, as Nancy Quam-Wickham suggests (1992). In a number of West Coast ports (especially in the Northwest), the "wages of whiteness" predominated.

12 This discussion of community has benefited from Aronowitz's preface to DiFazio (1985).

Meetings lasted for hours as people freely spoke their minds, many of them for the first time in their adult lives. Issues were debated with passion, often without regard for Robert's Rules of Order. Ballots were not the only way to count votes; people also expressed themselves with their feet and fists. It was a rough and tumble, Western-style union democracy.

As the union grew, the working knowledge for longshoring expanded.[13] Cultural, political, and linguistic skills became necessary.[14] Longshoremen needed to know how to be "a good union man," how to fight with management, how to get along with union brothers, how much work to do, and how to follow waterfront codes for proper behavior. These skills became critical features of their working knowledge, and were passed on to successive generations of West Coast longshoremen.[15] Contained in the working knowledge of longshoremen, then, were the principles of militant unionism.

The ILWU continued to practice that special kind of unionism that emerged during the 1930s in large part because the effort to isolate it was so successful. It was not only denied access to the CIO's postwar bargain with capital. Since it had been expelled from the CIO, the ILWU was also not part of the political strategy either. Working through Political Action Committees was therefore not an option, and the ILWU was not permitted to practice pressure group politics in the Democratic Party. Thus it was forced to be politically independent. As a result, it never became dependent on political forces beyond its control, and it did not rely on legislative strategies to protect itself. An unanticipated consequence of exclusion was that the ILWU could not defend itself through pattern bargaining. It could defend itself only by vigorously and militantly defending its membership at the point of production, on the waterfront. The ILWU could not concede the issue of citizenship at work because the union's very existence depended on its being political in this sense of the term.

---

13 The concept of "working knowledge" is developed and elaborated by Kusterer (1978).
14 I am not suggesting that these skills are unique to San Francisco longshoremen. Rather, the idea is that these skills became important components in the ILWU's organizational culture.
15 For a full discussion of how these principles were reproduced between longshore cohorts, see Kimeldorf (1988).

Employer and government strategies to destroy the ILWU backfired. Instead of crippling the union, these efforts actually helped create a powerful political community that, as the following three chapters suggest, could be – and still is – used to resist management's authority on the docks, and, when necessary, can be aimed at union officials too.

4

POLITICAL COMMUNITY ON THE
SAN FRANCISCO WATERFRONT

None of us is smart as all of us[1]

I N the classical sociological literature, community is said to exist when certain feelings or values are present. For Tönnies, these values are kinship, love, loyalty, and honor. When Weber wrote about communal relationships, he mentioned a sense of belonging, and being implicated in other people's existence. Durkheim found community in groups formed by intimacy, emotional cohesion, depth, and continuity.[2]

Local 10 members use different words to describe these feelings. They consider themselves a social world, and in some important ways, they act like a traditional community. "We're part of a neighborhood," said one of them. "We have an image. We're part of a way of life; we're part of a subculture. We're also a job. And we're an emotional, economic, and political entity. That's what we are, all of those things."

In an earlier historical context, a different set of concepts was used to talk about the feelings associated with community. The French Revolution constructed the experience of community around three dimensions: liberty, fraternity, and equality. Within a community, these dimensions have an organic relationship; without community, they are driven apart. Taken together, liberty, fraternity, and equality stand for union, or solidarity; thus, they are critical features of political community. The French Revolution's conception of community provides an excellent framework for analyzing the political community one finds among San Francisco longshoremen.[3]

1 Poster above the desk of Local 10's president.
2 This summary is based on Nisbet (1953:42–106).
3 From today's vantage point, one is reluctant to lionize or romanticize fraternal relations because they seem so gender laden and exclusionary. Given the historical and social setting

The values and traditions that make community a lived experience on the Bay Area's waterfront are effectively organized along the three dimensions of community enunciated by French revolutionaries.

The experience of community, and its institutional expressions, are resources Local 10 members draw upon in their struggles for control of the workplace. The principles of community have produced a political culture; public politics and a culture of participation have become organizational mainstays in the life of Local 10. Longshoremen in the Bay Area can therefore contest management's rule because they participate in nearly every aspect of the union. The bases for resistance to domination from within, and across class lines, are rooted in the union hall, which is the fabric of this union.

THE UNION HALL

For fifteen years prior to the 1934 general strike, productivity on the San Francisco docks was driven by a relentless competition for employment.

described in this book – a world that was and essentially still is exclusively male – the concept of fraternity is descriptive of both the roles and ideals of San Francisco longshoremen and of their gender composition. Although one can be critical of the union's past exclusionary practices, that judgment does not diminish the usefulness of fraternity as a dimension for analysis, or its importance as a critical element in a male community. The all-male character of the longshore workforce, moreover, is a complicated question, and one that cannot be simply attributed to male chauvinism. The physical requirements of traditional longshoring were, in some respects, gender neutral. Small men were excluded from work on the waterfront; and until recently, California labor laws prohibited women from lifting more than twenty-three pounds.

It should also be noted, in all fairness to the ILWU, that in those industries where women worked – canneries and warehouses – they exercised roles of leadership and authority in the union. The union's official position on women and work has traditionally been progressive. Speaking before the Sixth Annual Convention of the California CIO Council in 1943, for example, Harry Bridges said: "The idea that a woman can't do as good a job as a man in industry is ridiculous. In some cases of physical labor that may be true, but even then it is only partly true. In many jobs that men have always done it is already found that women can do them equally well" (Bridges, 1943).

The union's official position notwithstanding, the longshore division was and basically remains an all-male community. For years, the union's admission policy, which required sponsorship from a member, effectively kept women out of the regular workforce. Women were not allowed in longshore locals until 1975 when Billie Padilla was admitted to Local 13 in San Pedro. The first female dockworker in San Francisco (Mattie Lawson) was registered in 1979. It took a Federal Court decree in 1982 before women were regularly included as registrants on the West Coast waterfront.

Longshoremen hanging out in the hiring hall of Local 10 after the morning dispatch. San Francisco, 1979. Copyright © by Pat Goudvis 1979.

Competition was organized in several ways. Hiring was done at an early morning "shape-up," or "shape" held in front of piers berthing the vessels to be worked. Since anyone desiring work could join the shape, and because unemployment was normally very high, the hire was riddled with bribes, kickbacks, favoritism, and discrimination. Competition was not limited to hiring, however. It extended to the work, where casual gangs competed with their steady counterparts for regular employment. Competition for contracts between stevedore companies also pitted the steady gangs of one company against those of every other. To complete the competitive picture, the various ports around the San Francisco Bay competed with one another. The shape-up, then, dominated longshoring in the region. By the early 1930s it had created a dangerous and brutal speed-up. Those who resisted were either fired or blackballed, and replaced with a casual hired from among the unemployed who lingered around the pierheads along the Embarcadero.

The 1934 strike settlement provided longshoremen with a contractual opportunity to dismantle the shape-up. The arbitration board's ruling provided for a coastwide contract. That provision eliminated port-by-port competition. Within each port, the board ruled, employment would be restricted to a "registered" and "preferred" workforce. Employers could therefore no longer choose anyone they pleased to work. Instead, employment preference was restricted to people who were jointly recognized and registered as longshoremen by the union and the waterfront employers association.

Competition between registered longshoremen was eliminated by the board's 1934 ruling that a hiring hall be established. Even though the hall was to be administered jointly by employers and the union, the work was assigned by dispatchers elected annually. Assignments were handed out by job categories on a "rotary" basis. That meant each man in a job category had a right to a job before another longshoreman in that category could be dispatched a second time. Through this dispatching system the hall equalized longshoremen's opportunity to work. Thus it became the institution through which a community was fashioned among dockworkers in each port on the Pacific Coast. As a result, longshoremen on the West Coast came to say of their union, "the ILWU *is* the hiring hall."

Originally located in the Alaska Fisherman's Union building on lower

Clay street, close to the Embarcadero and the waterfront, the "hall" was actually space leased by the local. Described as both "run-of-the-mill, over-crowded" (Mills, 1980:18), and providing a "real sense of belonging and control of premises" (Weir, 1974:139–40), the hall had an undisputable reputation for being an important space where a sense of community was experienced among longshoremen. It was a place where the men hung out and socialized before the dispatch, and played cards when they did not get a job. There was a lively sense of politics on the premises. The offices of elected officials were immediately adjacent to the dispatching area and accessible to rank-and-file longshoremen. Meetings were open to all members and it was difficult to know where unofficial business left off and official business began.

The hall was moved to its present site in 1959. Located in two spacious buildings specially designed for and built by the union, which together occupy an entire city block of prime real estate, the hall is very close to Fisherman's Wharf. A large statue of a serenely smiling St. Francis stands watch over the longshore complex. Until recently, the neighborhood surrounding the hall was occupied by working fishermen. Marine supply shops, dry docks, repair centers, and dockside cafes dotted the area (see Mills, 1980). In the words of one longshoreman, "I guess you could say that it really was a 'fishermen's wharf.' And because we respected and enjoyed their community, we were always made welcome by our neighbors."

Contemporary historians like Foucault emphasize that meanings are built into the way buildings get put together. The architecture of the new Local 10 hall was a matter of considerable planning. The idea behind the hall was to make it a community center built around the crucial symbol of job control: the hiring hall. In this way a community of labor with the possibility of freedom was architecturally designed around the central necessity of workers: the job.

The building's architecture encourages activity and facilitates community. The centerpiece of the complex is a large octagonal building that houses the hiring hall. From the outside, the hall looks like a modern, concrete circus tent. The octagon is highlighted by eight concrete beams that move from the ground midway up the building at slight angles and then sharply angle toward the center where they become one. The build-

61

ing is constructed in wood, concrete, and glass, which gives the architectural design the appearance of a temple. The hall is easily accessible through four entrances of multiple glass doors.

The interior of the hall is cavernous. The main floor is surrounded by chalkboards. Job categories, workers' names, and the number of hours worked are written on them. The floor is dotted with bulletin boards announcing activities, union actions and decisions, and longshoremen's registration numbers in order of job availability. A second floor with rows of seats from which the activities below can be viewed slopes gently upward toward skylights.

During the dispatch, the main floor opens directly onto a narrow corridor leading to a glass-enclosed office where the dispatchers work. The dispatchers' office is two tiered, with a panoramic view of the entire hall. On the top tier, the dispatchers receive orders from stevedoring companies for complements of longshoremen; the orders are arranged according to job categories. These jobs are then dispatched from desks behind glass on the ground level. When the hall is used for meetings, a partition that closes off the dispatchers' office from the rest of the building is lowered. A vee-shaped office building and parking lot surround the hall. The offices of elected officials, secretarial staff, record keepers, welfare officers, and the Pensioners Club are found in the office building; meeting rooms are on the second floor.

The neighborhood surrounding the hall has changed dramatically since 1959. It is no longer a fisherman's wharf except in the tourist sense. The hall is currently ringed by hotels, condominiums, parking lots, artisans peddling their crafts on the street, and expensive restaurants. The longshoremen consequently stand out from the tourists in the area. The hall, however, continues as a sort of capital of the longshore community; it is the headquarters of this small part of the Bay Area's working class. Its location in a busy and interesting part of San Francisco adds to the attractiveness of a place where people gather and come to work before going to the job.

During the day, the hall is a vibrant place. It comes alive between 6:00 and 6:30 in the morning as the men arrive for the day's dispatch. The hall buzzes with noise and activity. There is a feeling of great energy just before the dispatch. Small clusters of men engage in animated conversation; there is jiving and movement. Along the sides of the room some longshoremen sit by themselves while others read.

The hall empties out after the dispatch nearly as quickly as it fills up before. The men spill out into surrounding restaurants, the parking lot, or off to the job. Longshoremen who didn't get a job hang around, talking with friends; some of them wait for a job that has been allocated late. Since the hall is open for a couple hours in the morning and afternoon, it is a place where people meet when they don't work. They play dominoes, cards, or just talk.

The office building and parking lot become centers of activity when the hiring hall closes. At the office building the longshoremen pay fines, check on personal records, pick up newspapers, and socialize with officers and secretarial staff. In addition to being the place where union officials work, the building provides space for committee meetings. The pensioners have an office there, and in addition to monthly meetings they gather regularly just to hang out. Some of the rooms are rented out for entertainment, benefits, and political speakers. There is always something going on: a meeting, an argument, a conversation.

When the weather is good, the benches around the hall serve as a front porch on the parking lot. People visit, share a drink, watch women. Sometimes the men work on their cars, repairing or polishing them. Spontaneous bazaars emerge every so often and items of unknown origin are sold. The winter rains do not completely wash out the sense of community among longshoremen. Instead, it gets moved into cars or campers, bars and cafes, and the hall too, when it is open.

THE LONGSHORE COMMUNITY

Liberty, fraternity, and equality are not simply abstract principles in Local 10; they are also observable union practices and they serve as powerful counterweights to hierarchy in either managerial or union guises. Because San Francisco longshoremen practice the principles of political community routinely, in their everyday work lives, they can be insubordinate and disobedient – they are able to struggle with employers for control of their work despite contractual prohibitions. The principles of community are observable in two areas of Local 10: One is institutional, where the formal and organizational expressions of community are practiced. The other is cultural, where the informal and routine expressions of community are found in longshore talk and practices.

FRATERNITY

The most concrete expression of community is fraternity. Like community, fraternity is affection rooted in shared values and goals. Fraternity, however, is not usually found in American life.[4] The language of fraternity is not typical in American talk.[5] In religious services men are sometimes called "brother"; certain Christian sects publicly call men "brother." Some trade unions still use the language of fraternity. But, in general, fraternity is recognized precisely because it is so rare. Fraternal language is seldom heard in America, and when it is used, the words are spoken self-consciously, almost like a foreign tongue. Examples of fraternal behavior are even rarer. Very few standards exist for appropriate fraternal behavior among adult men. Perhaps the most common expression of fraternity in American life occurs as a sign-off, "fraternally yours," at the end of a letter.

In striking contrast with most of American life, a sense of fraternity is clearly experienced by San Francisco longshoremen. It is heard routinely in the language they use, it is seen in the personal ties that bond them, and it is found in the interaction between them.

THE LANGUAGE OF FRATERNITY AMONG LONGSHOREMEN

The language of fraternity is a regular feature of longshore life. Official union documents routinely preface longshoremen's surnames with the word "brother." The poetry, essays, and novels written by and about long-

---

4 For an extended discussion of the loss of fraternity in modern society see McWilliams (1973). See also Mary Ann Clawson, *Constructing Brotherhood* (1989).

5 There are notable exceptions typically found in communities that have been historically excluded from the American mainstream. Black men in working-class communities, for example, regularly address one another with fraternal terms like "brother" or "blood." Working-class youth in Latino neighborhoods use the expression "carnal" when referring to each other. Translated literally, "carnal" means "of the flesh." In Latino communities, however, a person called "carnal" is a "brother." In fact, "mano," the term frequently substituted for "carnal," is an abbreviation for "hermano," which in English translates as "brother."

shoremen are also heavily sprinkled with the word "brother."[6] One cannot be among San Francisco longshoremen very long without being struck by how central "brother" is to their vocabulary, the ease with which it is used, and how natural it sounds. Longshore conversations are typically punctuated with the title. The term, moreover, is not reserved for ceremonial occasions. It is used routinely in conversations around the hall, on the job, and even during leisure-time activities. The widely used expression has a variety of uses in longshore talk:

• It is used as *title:* "It's like brother so-and-so was saying." Or, "When's the last time you saw brother what's-his-face?"

• When longshoremen do not know an individual's name, the expression is used to suggest the person to whom they are referring. Thus, it is used as *identification:* "The brother driving winches at the forward hatch told me." Or, "You know, the brother with the old Mercedes."

• The important distinction between management and labor is also captured and maintained by the word "brother." Management is verbally excluded from the fraternity of longshoremen by the title "Mr." Thus, saying "brother" is a way to express *class differentiation:* "And then the brother looked at Mr. so-and-so funny and said something to him." Or, "Mr. so-and-so came on deck and the brothers crowded around him."

• When a critical principle shared by longshoremen is violated, "brother" is invoked as *a standard of behavior:* "Act like a brother, goddammit!" or "Well, he sure don't act like a brother."

• The racial composition of the union also makes it necessary for longshoremen to specify the basis of the fraternity they are talking about. Nearly two-thirds of Local 10's membership is either black or brown and in the black community "brother" refers to black men.[7] Thus, in Local 10, when a longshoreman's color is an issue, "brother" is used as an expression

6 See, for example, Carson (1979).
7 Arriving at a precise figure for longshoremen of color in Local 10 is difficult. For years it was illegal for unions to collect data pertaining to race. However, in 1979 the union took the employers' association before the EEOC, claiming the PMA discriminated against minority longshoremen in promotions to walking boss. At that time the PMA asserted that 55 percent of Bay Area longshoremen were black and 12 percent were Hispanic or Asian. The union challenged the figures, arguing that the longshore population the PMA was counting included people working in the Stockton and Sacramento ports. At any rate, the Local says of itself that two-thirds of its membership consists of racial minorities.

of *union solidarity:* "The black brother on the winches was . . ." Or, "The white brother said . . ."

- Stylistic changes and slang abbreviations originating in surrounding racial and ethnic communities find their way into the usage of the term "brother" among longshoremen. The phrase is therefore used as a form of *jive:* "What's happening, bro'?" Or, "Right on, bro'."

- Finally, the term is used as an expression of *affection:* "I love him like a brother," as well as for *emphasis* or *punctuation:* "And that's no bullshit, brother."

Speaking in explicitly fraternal terms is only one way that longshoremen express fraternity. They speak an even deeper language of brotherhood that surfaces when longshoremen repossess explosive words from the American vocabulary of antagonism and derogation. Nicknames, for example, can be a source of ridicule or embarrassment; they are not suffered quietly. In the context of fraternity, however, these names are connotatively converted into expressions of endearment and affection that reaffirm the spirit of community rather than destroy it. Through nicknames, longshoremen say things about one another that in any other context would be "fighting words." Given the fraternal context, however, these labels are tolerated and sometimes promoted, even though the bearer is reminded of personal pain.

Some examples: A gang boss with second- or third-degree burns about portions of his face is called "Crispy." "Bimbo" is a rotund, balding, squat holdman with large protruding ears. "Hungry Mike" was known for working every day in the year except two or three; his hunger for money was so intense, it is said he wore secondhand work pants. "Moaning Jack" is always negative, and everything is wrong in his life. "Drugstore Hank" used heroin and drank a fifth of whiskey every day in his life as a longshoreman. "Tuna's" proper name is Charlie. He is also known as "Sorry Charlie" because, like the tuna in the Starkist television commercial, he has been metaphorically and literally known to miss the hook. When he makes a proposal that is voted down at a union meeting, the room fills with a chorus of "SOORRRYYY CCHHHAAARRRLLLIIIEEE." A gang boss who is known for missing work regularly, or "flopping," is called "Floppsy." The origin of "Dirty Neck's" nickname is obvious. "Cue Ball's" head is cleanly shaven.

Surface meanings not withstanding, the nicknames are terms of endearment. The men who bear them are spoken of fondly, and they are objects of affectionate folktales. Moreover, the names are not imposed without taking the recipients' feelings into consideration. Nicknames are not used if the recipient objects.[8]

THE BONDING OF BROTHERHOOD

Talk about sports, gambling, and sex is an important medium through which fraternal bonding occurs among longshoremen.[9] This talk is to work what litany is to Catholic mass and the chorus is to Greek plays. The talk is communion, an act of sharing. It represents a common possession to which each individual can contribute and in which he can participate. It is a kind of glue that binds men together and provides them with rites denoting membership in an exclusive fraternity.

The expressions they use, the stories they swap, the graffiti they write, and some of the nicknames they create give voice to their intense interest in sports and gambling. "Number Five Jack," for example, has a reputation for betting the number 5 horse in every race. He doesn't even bother to buy the racing form. His habit is a topic for conversation. When one of his partners found out that Jack was born under the sign of Cancer he was told: "Your lucky number is 2, Jack; you're betting the wrong fucking number." Two longshoremen worked one ship for five days and spent a great deal of their time trying to calculate Jack's losses. "As close as we could figure, since 1939, he'd lost $162,000 on the horses." "Hack" Wilson used to play a pretty good game of baseball and was named after another "Hack Wilson": the National League record holder for home runs (56) in one season, who played for the Chicago Cubs.

A good deal of energy is expended on matters of this sort. In fact, sports events compete with union activities. When fall meetings are scheduled for Monday evenings (during nationally televised football games), they are poorly attended, and sessions that overlap with the professional basketball

---

8 For additional accounts of longshore nicknames and a somewhat different, although not contradictory, interpretation of them, see Pilcher (1972:105) and Weir (1974:269–70).
9 I am indebted to David Minkus for formulating and phrasing the following paragraph.

championships in the spring are sometimes canceled for lack of a quorum.

The rituals of sex talk are also a particularly binding form of communion. Sex talk assumes the listener is trustworthy and loyal since the subject matter is so sensitive. Thus the talk about sexual exploits and experiences creates a brotherhood. Sex talk is a medium for both hierarchy and leveling. On the one hand, it establishes a pecking order based on sexual prowess and preference. Men who might otherwise be ordinary are elevated by a reputation for being "good with the women." The talk also levels as well as elevates. Knowledge and power are passed around and shared in an intimate circle of democracy. The uninitiated are introduced to sexual secrets; the braggart is taken to task. A longshoreman known to be a good elected official is taken down a few pegs by libelous graffiti.

A recognizable kind of waterfront storytelling also exists and it routinely ends with punch lines that establish the trustworthiness and reliability of longshoremen, reaffirming the bonds of their brotherhood. These stories begin with an agreement between workers, an agreement that might be easily betrayed. But that never happens. The following story is typical.

> George told of the night he was working "four-on-four-off" in a gang. One of the guys didn't show up at the agreed upon time when he was supposed to do his "four-on." Where was he? the guys wondered. About a half hour before the job ended the guy showed up. He had towels wrapped around his neck and arm. What was the problem? He'd caught his wife in bed with another man and as he was beating up on the man, his wife took an axe to him and cut the hell out of him. The guy hadn't yet gone to the hospital. He told the gang what had happened and then said: "I came here first because I wanted you guys to know that I hadn't walked out on you." (Field notes)

These stories are didactic; they give voice to the values held dear by this political community. Speaking of storytelling on the San Francisco waterfront, one longshoreman observes, "stories are essentially intended to convey a lesson or at least an observation about our working and union life" (Mills, 1978b:26). Like talk about sex and sports, stories about heroism among longshoremen are a kind of communion. The bonds of brotherhood are affirmed in them and the community's principles for membership are passed on. The folklore of fraternity creates common ground among longshoremen, enabling them to avoid those issues that divide them. Thus, the folklore activity counteracts human fissures that can potentially fracture community.

Expressions of fraternity among San Francisco longshoremen are not restricted to talk. The men also act toward each other in fraternal ways. Fraternity is rooted in the organization of longshore work: The men work with "partners." The hazards and difficulties of longshoring routinely require acts of courage and this also binds the men together into a brotherhood. Longshoring is dangerous work. When longshoremen are killed on the job, work stops for at least the duration of that shift. All the men "stand by" until told to do otherwise by a local union official. As one described it, this is a way for "honoring a fallen brother."

When a Local 10 member dies there is a ceremony at the hall during which public expressions of affection, grief, and respect are shared. At monthly membership meetings and gatherings of pensioners, the names and registration numbers of longshoremen who have died during the last thirty days are read while the survivors stand in respect.

> "Did you hear that?" said an old-timer poking the person standing next to him in the ribs. "He said 'Big Dago' died." "Big Dago died"; "Big Dago died," whispered a number of people in shock and disbelief. The room got very quiet. I could see some eyes glistening. And then somebody gasped: "Not big Dago!" "Big Dago is dead!" (Field notes)

Public intimacy and tolerance are not typically associated with American men. The literature on working-class life suggests that intolerance predominates, and the feminist critique maintains that machismo precludes routine expressions of affection among men in America.[10] San Francisco longshoremen stand in sharp contrast to this received wisdom. They regularly exchange affectionate greetings and openly display feelings of intimacy. These expressions range from playful punches, to hale-fellow-well-met slaps on the back, to genuine bear-hug embraces, to men sitting next to each other with arms draped sensitively over one another's shoulder.

---

10 For examples of these two points of view, see Lipset (1963: chap. 4) and Rubin (1976).

The longshoremen's reputation for being a bunch of brawling, intolerant tough guys says more about the power of folklore than the actual situation of Local 10 members. Their toughness is not a matter of dispute. Neither, however, is their tolerance for and patience with one another. For example, meetings are frequently interrupted by longshoremen, some of whom are drunk. People talk without being recognized, and they speak their mind even when they are not addressing the issue at hand. If disrupters persist after numerous warnings, they are assessed a fine. When that does not work, the men handle the matter informally. So patient are longshoremen that there are times when disruption, belligerence, and even racial heckling are tolerated from an inebriated brother. The meeting gets stalled, the business postponed, and precious time is wastefully consumed by remarks that are personally and collectively abusive. Still, the men rarely respond in kind. Within the bonds of fraternity there is tolerance and gentleness.

EQUALITY

An injury to one is an injury to all.[11]

Community is rooted in equality as well as fraternity. Typically, however, equality is a hope, a goal toward which groups aspire, not a reality. Usually, it is an I.O.U. on orthodox theories of citizenship, a theoretical yardstick against which real differences are measured. Thus, talk about equality tends to focus on inequality. People worry about the gap between stated rules and normal expressions of equality in routine settings.

Despite the work that union dockworkers share, the longshore community is made up of diverse human categories. Longshoremen differ by job classification, seniority in the industry, ability, race, ethnicity, age, and political orientation. In many areas of American society, these differences are bases for advantage. In Local 10, however, they are not. Expressions of equality are located not only in the official organization, but in the substance of everyday union life as well. Equality is found institutionally in the rotational dispatch that provides longshoremen with an equal chance to work. The dispatch undercuts a traditional source of inequality: com-

11 ILWU motto (previously used by the Knights of Labor).

petition for the opportunity to work. Institutional expressions of equality are also embodied in the architecture and organization of the hiring hall. Longshoremen can literally see if the institutional forms of equality are being abused. Finally, equality is practiced in the everyday lives of long-shoremen. Reciprocity takes the form of social bartering and it is a promi-nent feature of longshore relationships. Trades and exchanges are made with trust as collateral; equality is the interest that is drawn on the principal.

The institutional architecture of equality

Equality between San Francisco longshoremen is rooted in basic work arrangements. The wage schedule minimizes possibilities for serious pay differentials between longshoremen. Only six rungs extend above the "basic" wage on the income ladder. Moreover, ninety-five cents an hour is all that separates the highest paid longshoremen from the lowest paid. This narrow hourly wage gap means that one traditional source of inequal-ity is effectively checked.

The wage schedule does not, however, regulate the number of hours worked by longshoremen. Because waterfront workers are paid by the hour it is possible that people with better access to work opportunities could make more money than the rest. Access to work could, if not otherwise regulated, be weighted in traditional directions of advantage in America: on the basis of age, race, or ethnicity. But longshoremen have developed a method for dispatching people to work that insures the job "pie" is cut up equally.

Local 10 members who work out of the hall are organized by skill categories called "boards": hold board, dock board, lift board, winch board, special equipment board, and so forth. Each board is subdivided by shift. Thus, for example, there is a day and night dock board. The union's commitment to distribute advantage evenly is reflected in its dispatch system. Longshoremen are dispatched by boards. The dispatch system insures that work opportunities are evenly distributed. No one can be dispatched off a board to more than one job before everyone else in that category has had an opportunity to work. As a result, work is distributed equally within boards.

71

The process for distributing work, however, is complicated by the unpredictability of the maritime industry. "Them ships are like bananas," say longshoremen. "They come in bunches. It's either feast or famine." And when work is available, it is not always distributed evenly between boards. Some ships provide work for only certain skill boards, creating a situation in which there is more work than available longshoremen on a given board. In this instance, jobs are dispatched to men on the next highest skill board. This keeps work chances even; boards are prevented from hoarding work.

Cutting up the job pie equitably is difficult and complicated. When it is successful, the dispatch underwrites a very basic form of equality: It guarantees equal access to the work. Longshoremen do not have to compete with each other or curry favor to get a job. Work opportunities depend on the amount of work available, not the personal characteristics of longshoremen.[12]

The dispatch, however, cannot guarantee that all longshoremen work the same number of hours. In part this occurs because Local 10 members have the contractual right to refuse a job. The imbalance in hours worked is also attributable to the uneven distribution of work between the various boards. The most serious obstacle to equalizing work opportunities, however, is the category of "9.43 men," a category that emerged when the historic Mechanization and Modernization (M&M) agreements were signed in 1966, modifying dispatch rules and job categories.[13] Longshoremen who work "9.43" work "steady," and are guaranteed a monthly minimum of 173 hours. Thus, they work more hours than the longshoremen who take their chances with the dispatch. The discrepancy caused by this contractual provision is an important source of controversy. Opponents of the category argue it undermines the dispatch system, and undercuts equality of work opportunity. The imbalance created by Section 9.43 also threatens to divide Local 10 members by income, not just hours worked. Despite the narrow gap between skill levels, income inequality is a possibility because some longshoremen are guaranteed steady employment.

The union has wrestled with this controversy since the category was

12 For a more extended discussion of the ILWU dispatching system, see Larrowe (1955).
13 The term "9.43" refers to the section of the contract that allows employers to hire longshoremen on a steady basis.

created. The "9.43 men" category was a central issue during contract negotiations in 1971, 1975, and 1978. In 1975, a cap was placed on the hours 9.43 men could work. The limit was 176 hours a month. In 1978, a formula for equalizing work opportunities was reached. The ILWU and Pacific Maritime Association (PMA) agreed to rotate 9.43 men and hall men in and out of the hiring hall. This agreement established a limit on the work opportunity gap.

The bottom line was established when the union agreed to allow modern technology on the waterfront. In return for work lost to modernization, the union negotiated a Pay Guarantee Plan (PGP). PGP was designed to cushion the unemployment produced by the containerized technology. It was intended to maintain the income of longshoremen who are available for work five days a week, at a weekly equivalent of thirty-six hours at the basic wage rate. The pay guarantee establishes an income below which longshoremen will not fall so long as they present themselves to the dispatch as available for work. Although PGP does not equalize the income gap between 9.43 and hall men, it provides a minimum lower limit to the discrepancy.

The principle of equal access to work is upheld on the docks as well as in the dispatch. Jobs sometimes last longer than one day. Longshoremen call these jobs "callbacks," because people are called back to work the next day or days. Determining who will get callbacks is an important decision. Longshoremen fear that, left to their own devices, "walking bosses" (foremen) will assign callbacks to their friends or people most compatible with the company. That would, of course, create imbalances in the distribution of work. To counteract this, the union has a uniform policy for callbacks. When longshoremen are dispatched to a job, dispatchers write the order of dispatch on the job-slip. And if there is a callback, the men are returned according to dispatch seniority: The first dispatched are the first called back. This system checks favoritism and maintains equality of job opportunity because, over time, everyone has the same chance to be the first one dispatched.

Like the best laid plans of mice and men, however, policies aiming toward equality are often violated unless they are institutionally protected and routinely enforced. Equality is rapidly and effectively subverted when activities are conducted in private, because people outside the inner circle

73

do not know what is happening. This situation goes unrecognized until equality has been visibly replaced by inequality. At this point it is difficult to reverse the process. Carrying out business publicly and openly is therefore crucial for protecting egalitarian principles.

The architecture and organization of the hiring hall enable longshoremen literally to "see" imbalances in work opportunity if any exist. Who works off of which skill board is public knowledge. Longshoremen's registration numbers are publicly posted by skill board. When openings occur on skill boards, announcements are made and attached to bulletin boards throughout the hall. And once the promotion committee is convened (a committee of elected longshoremen and appointed employer representatives), it deliberates at the hall, in full view of all interested parties. Each person's standing in the daily dispatch is public knowledge. Under the "low-man-out" system (the person with the fewest hours worked is the first one dispatched), the number of hours a person works is listed next to his name. The information is posted on sign-in sheets found throughout the hall. With the rotary system (no one is dispatched until everyone has been rotated through a dispatch cycle), longshoremen's names and numbers are listed in relation to their location in the dispatch cycle.

The dispatch itself is a very public event. Who receives a job and who does not is immediately obvious. The kinds of work available on a given day are also observable. Dispatchers work behind large glass windows, and the job-slips are spread out on a counter in front of them. When longshoremen walk up to the window, work opportunities are immediately visible.

But seeing is not always believing. Thus, records are kept by the union and the employers, and people are able to confirm or disconfirm what they think they have seen. Located a couple of yards away from the hiring hall, the records office is open to union members. Longshoremen are free to look at the records and see how many hours people have worked in a quarter. Each person knows how many hours he has worked by writing them in his "record book." If he thinks someone is getting better treatment, he can validate the suspicion with a trip to the records office. Thus, the hall provides numerous ways for longshoremen to see who is getting jobs. The principle of equality of work is embedded in the hall's organization.

74

Trading and sharing: Keeping things even

The principle of equality is not limited to institutional contexts in the longshore community. It is also expressed routinely in relationships. One form of equality is reciprocity, and reciprocal relations are typical among longshoremen. They trade off advantage and injury. Financial relations among longshoremen, for example, are typically based on reciprocity and trust, not just self-interest. Money is routinely borrowed and lent without so much as an informal I.O.U. There seems to be no need for written assurance of repayment; the operating assumption is that it will happen. Apparently it does, because longshoremen who ask for repayment before it is volunteered are regarded as "up tight." The request is taken as evidence that the asker has not fully accepted the trust that unites longshoremen.

"He still isn't all that comfortable among the longshoremen," said an old-timer of a college drop-out who began working on the waterfront in 1969. "He'll ask about the couple of bucks he lent someone a couple months ago."

The trust involved in financial relations is revealed in exchanges like the following. In the researcher's presence, one longshoreman gave another a five-dollar bill.

"What's that for?" asked the recipient.

"Well, the last time you were drunk, you owed me two dollars," answered the donor. "I told you that it was seven dollars and you were so drunk that you didn't know any better and you gave me seven. So I've owed you five dollars for the last three years."

With a big smile on his face, the recipient accepted the money. "It will be three years in February since I've had a drink," he explained proudly to the outside observer (field notes).

Just how seriously longshoremen take the assumed state of reciprocity between them is shown here by the fact that scores are settled even when one party did not know they needed to be. The principle is also revealed in a saying one frequently hears when someone says that repayment might take awhile.

"That's all right," is the response. "Somehow it all gets evened out over time."

Reciprocity occurs routinely among longshoremen. It begins in the morning before work and often continues on into the evening. The workday starts with ride sharing. Expenses as well as cars are shared according to an unwritten rule. Reciprocity is also practiced in partnerships. Partners share the unpleasant task of being at the dispatch hall early in the morning to pick up a job. This allows the other some extra time in bed.[14] At work, longshoremen "cover" for each other so that people can leave the job. They also routinely trade off bad jobs.

"I'll take the steel discharge job; you can have the auto ship because I know your back is bad," a longshoreman was overheard telling his friend at the hiring hall early one morning. "I know you'd do it for me" (field notes). At lunch and dinner, food is traded and shared among the men.

In addition to food, money, and work, longshoremen also share insults. Ethnic humor and put-downs are routinely and openly exchanged. Hand trucks are called "Mexican diesels," and brooms with short handles are known as "Jap brooms."

"Don't you have to make a bed check pretty soon?" an Asian longshoreman said to his black partner over a drink at a bar late one night. The insinuation was barely disguised: His partner should be on a work-release furlough from jail.

"When did they let you motherfuckers out of the camps?" responded the black longshoreman.

"You niggers never got out of the camps," quipped the Asian longshoremen, not to be outdone (field notes).

Throughout the exchange smiles never left their faces.

Longshoremen also trade "fighting words" (words that in most circumstances result in violence). And like ethnic slurs, they are typically the source of laughter.[15]

Routine expressions of equality continue after work. Unpleasant tasks are traded and enjoyable activities are shared. For example, union mem-

14 See Theriault (1978:7–14) for a description of this process.
15 Pilcher makes a similar observation for Portland longshoremen: "The mutual vituperation of the working longshoremen expresses exactly the opposite of its overt meaning. When one longshoreman calls another a 'dirty cocksucker, a shiteating asshole' or addresses him by any other obscene terms, he is expressing affection and reaffirming a deeply felt personal regard" (1972:103).

bership meetings are held monthly. Attendance is mandatory and people who fail to show are fined. Union books are stamped at the end of meetings as proof of attendance. For some longshoremen, however, the meetings are an unpleasant task. After a long and hard day at work, their union commitment is reduced by their impatience with the details of democracy. Men who feel this way attend meetings on alternate months. They trade off attendance with friends who take their books and get them stamped. Although democracy suffers in the process, an unpleasant chore is shared.

When meetings end, nearby bars fill with longshoremen. Round after round of alcohol is consumed, with longshoremen taking turns buying rounds. If the evening ends before each person has bought one, they make up the difference next time. Just like reciprocity in financial relations, longshoremen assume implicitly that he who has not yet bought a round will stand for the following one – the next time if need be.

A deep sense of equality runs through the longshore community. Thus, what would be insults in other contexts are traded among longshoremen without apparent injury. There is, moreover, opportunity for real exchange. Insults are traded rather than simply hurled. The verbal exchanges therefore reinforce relationships based on equality instead of undermining them. They serve as a kind of social cement; the vocabulary of hostility and inequality is inverted into an expression of equality and a source of amusement. As trust replaces competition, money ceases to produce anxiety or tension between friends.

LIBERTY

Equality is an important component of community. By reducing differences, it encourages trust and promotes reciprocity. But the leveling process can also stifle creativity. If people are not free to express their individuality and personal potential, community in the fullest sense of the term does not exist.

In the United States, freedom is usually defined negatively. It is thought of as being free from arbitrary control or exemption from compulsion – a right that protects individuals from restriction. Freedom, however, has another meaning, one that goes beyond the state of being *not* subject to control. Being free also means the freedom *to* act in a manner of one's

77

choosing.[16] Both meanings are expressed in the longshore community. Freedom and independence are important elements in this social world.

First of all, longshoremen think of themselves as self-selected workers; not everyone is cut out to do the work. It is dangerous, physically demanding, complicated, strenuous, and intermittent. Anyone who fears water, ships, working high above or down below sea level will not want to do longshoring. In this regard, longshoremen are like long-haul truckers, lumberjacks, merchant seamen, and iron workers. The work attracts certain kinds of people. No one can be forced to do these jobs; people make that decision for themselves.

Longshoremen are selected in another way. Not everyone who wants to is able to work on the docks. More people want to do waterfront work than there are openings available. Thus, the number of registered longshoremen is carefully regulated, and jointly agreed to by the union and the employers. The combination of choosing the work and being selected by the industry allows longshoremen to think of themselves as a special workforce. "What you do for work represents a large portion of what you are," commented one of them.

> I think that work is important and that if you're a longshoreman, that has a stamp on your personality. You're a little tough-minded, opinionated, sentimental and pretty easy with money. And probably a little arrogant. There's a little arrogance that goes with the longshoremen because of the Big Strike. (Field notes)

Independence is also rooted in the way longshoremen are paid. Asked what they do for a living, Local 10 members invariably reply, "I am a longshoreman." They don't say they work for a particular stevedoring company. That is because the stevedoring firms do not actually pay the longshoremen. Rather, they pay the employers' association (PMA) and the PMA issues checks to longshoremen. So officially speaking, longshoremen work for the Pacific Maritime Association, not the various stevedoring firms that contract for their labor. Being paid by an employers' association guarantees longshoremen an important freedom. It insures against arbitrary control by management. They can refuse to work for a

16 For a detailed discussion of this distinction, see Marcuse (1966).

particular steamship line or stevedoring company without jeopardizing their registration.

Longshoremen also work with a great deal of freedom. They can reject jobs without penalty. If they do not like the job that comes up at the dispatch, they can wait for another, or refuse to work that day. This is called taking a "flop." When someone "flops," technically speaking they are not available for work that day. Thus, they risk the pay guarantee by flopping. But if a longshoreman is willing to risk that, he does so without losing his place on the waterfront.

Within certain limits, longshoremen can also choose the amount of work they will do. They have to be available for work when their number comes up, and work must be equally distributed throughout the Local. So long as they don't take more than their fair share of the work and are available to work (be present at the dispatch), the men decide how little or how much they will work. Reflecting on the industry, one longshoreman commented: "There's a freedom, without being so casual that you don't get paid, and it's a casualization that doesn't let you get lost in the freedom."

Longshoremen also choose the kind of work they will do. So long as they are willing to flop, they cannot be required to accept a job at the dispatch; nor can they be compelled to work even after arriving on the docks. When work is plentiful and their number is low in the dispatch (meaning they must be dispatched before anyone else is), longshoremen can also choose among a number of jobs in their category.

To some extent, longshoremen can also decide where they will work. Waterfront work in the Bay Area covers over a hundred miles of coastline. The work starts thirty miles south of San Francisco in Redwood City, proceeds up the peninsula to the city's docks, across the bay to Oakland and then ten miles north to Richmond and thirty miles northeast to Benicia. When there is plenty of work and they qualify for multiple jobs, longshoremen therefore have a number of sites from which to choose their work.

Liberty to speak one's mind is a striking feature of conventional long-shore work. Restrictions on talk are minimal and social support for the freedom of expression is strong. The hall is also a place where longshore-men can openly express themselves without fear of reprisal. The men speak freely about the employers and the union at the hall. An elaborate grapevine has sprouted among longshoremen and it effectively spreads all kinds of news. The men are encouraged by free time, and each other, to swap stories and tell what they think happened during the day. Because longshoremen circulate through the hall daily, and work at new locations with different people each day, information is disseminated rapidly. An example: Local 10's Executive Board meets Thursday evenings. One Thursday night, the Board voted to change the Local's policy for selecting baggage handlers on passenger ships, a prized job. The meeting lasted until nearly midnight.

At 6:00 a.m. the following day, the daytime Business Agent came in the hall to relieve his nighttime counterpart.

"Did you hear what the Executive Board did last night?" the night Business Agent asked.

"No," said the day B.A.

"They voted to eliminate the baggage men's list altogether," said the union officer who was going off duty. "Baggage men will be chosen from among dock men and all dock men will be eligible to be baggage men."

At 6:15 a.m., the researcher went into the hall and stopped at the dispatcher's office. People were already talking about the Executive Board's decision. One of the dispatchers said there would be problems at the dispatch; the men who had previously been on the baggage list would be incensed.

At 6:30 a.m. the dispatch began. The hall was already abuzz with news that the baggage list had been discontinued (field notes).

Liberty takes other forms in the longshore community. For example, longshoremen literally take "liberties" with each other, with conventionality, and with the union. Examples include the nicknames they develop, the racial insults they trade, and the language of personal put-down they use.

Nicknames express liberty in an additional sense, as shown by the nicknames themselves. In addition to "Crispy," "Dirty Neck," and "Tuna," there is "Baseball Eddie" (he pretended to throw a baseball and catch it every once in a while); "Bicycle" Larry (he always rides a ten-speed bike); "Mountain-climbing Larry" (he teaches mountain climbing for the Sierra Club); "Strong-arm Louie" (a "powerful guy," known as a toilet paper stealer – two or three rolls a day – and someone who would empty napkins off restaurant tables); "Honey-dripper" ("can 'sweet talk' the ladies like no one else"); and "Honey Bear" ("big, tough, not afraid to throw a punch; when he drinks a lot he gets a little mean, but a very, very good-hearted guy"). As these nicknames suggest, a wide variety of "characters" and activities are tolerated on the waterfront. Within limits, then, the long-shoremen are free to be who they want to be. The community encourages this and takes pride in it as well.

The freedom they experience is a source of pride and amazement among San Francisco longshoremen. "I am so free it's unbelievable," said one of them. "I go down sometime and volunteer to work because I get lonesome. That sound unbelievable? I get a little lonesome sometimes for the guys and just go down and see if I can get a pretty good job so I can work and bullshit with them."

Liberty, fraternity, and equality are built into everyday life in the world of San Francisco longshoremen. In addition to being principles for com-munity, these practices are also resources for being disobedient, warrants for challenging management's control of the waterfront, and weapons for resisting centralizing, bureaucratic tendencies in the union. The organiza-tion of opposition to domination by management or the union is created by the sense of community San Francisco longshoremen experience. The community bonds create a powerful sense of unity and solidarity, rooted in trust and loyalty. Within this community, longshoremen learn they can trust one another. That is proven every day in routine ways. They are also educated in loyalty through the stories, folklore, jokes, and nicknames they exchange daily. This experience of community teaches tolerance for difference and dissidence. And tolerance, of course, is an especially neces-sary quality for fashioning unity and solidarity out of heterogeneity. The longshore community reminds dockworkers that their "us" implies a "them," and that loyalty and trust are important for the organization of opposition to domination.

81

5

THE STRUCTURE OF
PARTICIPATIONIST POLITICS

ANYONE who walks into the San Francisco longshoremen's hall on the third Tuesday of the month around 7:00 p.m. will witness a monthly spectacle. If that person is a stranger, the activities look chaotic, they seem neither focused nor organized. The hall is filled with longshoremen. Some mill about, talking and joking. Others are seated in rows of chairs, listening to speakers on a raised platform near the front of the room. The noise level is high; hearing even amplified voices is frequently difficult. Periodically someone goes to a microphone near the front of the hall and addresses the group. Speaking with passion, he argues vigorously, sometimes verbally attacking the people seated on the raised platform.

The men seated on the floor participate in the proceedings with continuous verbal commentary. "Act like a president, goddammit!" shouts someone to a man standing on the platform in front of a microphone, during a heated and confused exchange. "Take the nails out!" yells someone else when a speaker claims he is being treated unfairly.

Dialogue is routine: "Put a fine on his ass!" hollers somebody, referring to a disrupter. "Do you want me to fine him?" asks the man at the microphone on the platform. Judgment is rendered swiftly. "Yes!" roar the assembled, sounding more like the chorus in a Greek play than the jury in American courts (field notes).

If the stranger knows political theory, a cursory glance suggests that, on the surface, the proceedings are democratic. A good number of people are present; the men are directly participating, and in ways of their own choosing. Issues are discussed publicly, and the majority rules. Thus, the student of political theory will immediately see in this room a very rough-hewn, and deeply participatory, expression of what theorists call "democracy."

Longshoremen call it a "membership meeting."

Fifty years after it was founded, the San Francisco longshoremen's union continues to operate along participationist, egalitarian lines. Local 10 members control their union by practicing what CIO activist and journalist Len DeCaux once called "tumultuous democracy." The "rank-and-fileism" practiced by early CIO affiliates is still observable in the San Francisco local. The tumultuous democracy practiced by ILWU locals is the second source of opposition to employer control of the waterfront and an obstacle to centralization in the union. Because politics are public, and a culture of participation emerged early in the ILWU's history and was carefully nurtured thereafter, democracy has flourished, bureaucracy has been checked, and longshoremen can insist on participating in decisions that affect their everyday working lives.[1]

1 In 1963, 82 "B" men in Local 10 were deregistered for allegedly violating dispatch rules. They contested the decision and eventually sought redress in court. Supporters of the B men allege that their firing was political, part of a campaign by International President Bridges to stifle opposition to the M&M plan. As a result, they argue, the ILWU became a "bureaucratic" and "undemocratic" union (Jacobs, 1964; Pierpont, 1967; Weir, 1964, 1969). How, then, one might wonder, can the concept of democracy be used in relation to the ILWU?

Even with the wisdom of hindsight, it is difficult to know Bridges's motivation in this incident. He consistently denied the frame-up allegation; and in 1976 a Federal District Court Judge in San Francisco ruled that "there is not proof in the record that Stanley Weir was considered to be a thorn in the side of Harry Bridges. . . . There was no evidence that a 'frame-up' contributed to the de-registration" (quoted in *The Dispatcher,* September 10, 1976).

Although one may never know Bridges's actual motives in this incident, there seems to be some merit to the charge that the B men were treated unfairly. They were apparently convicted of rules established after their deregistration, which were then applied retroactively. Recent court decisions have ruled in their favor in this regard. Does this therefore mean that the concept of democracy is no longer applicable to the ILWU?

The allegation of "bureaucracy" is not persuasive. Union critics (Jacobs, 1964; Weir, 1964) use the word polemically. They present no evidence indicating how the organization has become bureaucratized.

The question of union democracy, however, is more complicated. Apparently Local 10 lived up to its democratic principles throughout this affair. According to union critics, Local 10's membership consistently voted to reinstate the B men, and local leaders vigorously represented the deregistered longshoremen (Weir, 1964). Bridges thwarted local efforts and achieved his purposes, according to this account, through "intimidation" of

THE ORGANIZATION OF PARTICIPATION

Hearing and healing differences

If the outsider looks beyond the surface, he or she will see more profound examples of participation in these meetings. A virtual stream of people moves back and forth between their seats and the microphone. Considerable movement and activity centers around the microphone. Almost every issue raised by one speaker elicits comment from another. The style of involvement, moreover, invites participation by people unschooled or unimpressed with formal parliamentary procedures. Rules are frequently bent and procedures stretched. No one objects. Although Robert's Rules of Order are routinely invoked, parliamentary formalities are typically replaced with substantive commentary. "Point of Order, Brother Chairman!" someone calls out, knowing that declaration brings immediate recognition. Having taken the "deck" (the floor), the longshoreman then speaks to a substantive point. But very rarely is the violation flagged; apparently no one objects to the innovative use of parliamentary procedure.

Particularly controversial disputes engage virtually everyone. The results of one announcement are typical.[2] The Local's Appeals Committee

rank and filers and "manipulation" of local leaders.

It is both beyond the scope of this book and difficult to assess whether Bridges "intimidated" and "manipulated" or "persuaded" and "convinced" his colleagues. The numerous attacks on him by the government and employers certainly produced considerable membership loyalty to Bridges. He could also be quite persuasive. He was renowned for his ability to use organizational principles brilliantly and effectively orchestrate membership support for his policies. It is not so clear, however, that these qualities compromised the essentially democratic culture and structure of the union at either the local or the international level. Bridges was always challenged and questioned by his membership; public criticism of him was and is a routine feature of ILWU culture. Thus, Bridges was more likely to co-opt his critics than to purge them.

On balance, then, as the next two chapters demonstrate, the concept of democracy applies to Local 10's politics. Whether or not it is applicable to the ILWU's international organization is another question. The relationship between international officials and local unions in the ILWU is as complicated as it is contested. It defies easy characterizations and deserves careful, critical analysis. But my less-than-exhaustive exploration of that relationship suggests that when a thorough investigation is concluded, the ILWU will be evaluated, overall, as one of the most democratic trade unions in North America.

2 The following paragraphs are based on field notes.

84

overruled a Grievance Committee decision to discipline two prominent union members for fighting. Within moments of the announcement, men were lined up ten deep at the microphone; the hall was buzzing; the atmosphere was electric.

The first speaker was a Grievance Committee member who was livid. "We've done our job. We won't hear the case again."

That statement outraged someone else. How could anyone on the Grievance Committee make up his mind not to hear a case without finding out why the decision was repealed?

Two members of the Grievance Committee announced they were resigning.

The longshoreman who had lost the fight was the next speaker. He made an impassioned plea for "justice."

"Why pick on one person?" countered another Local 10 member. He reminded people that the victim of this incident had been the aggressor in another situation. In that case the Grievance Committee had not been overruled. "Besides which," he added, "longshoremen ain't symphony concert goers."

"I'm the cat so-and-so [the victim in this incident, who was the aggressor in another fight] Sunday punched," announced still another speaker, adding parenthetically, "even though I kicked his ass and he was never formally charged."

The chaos continued before the chair interjected himself: "There are details that people are forgetting," he said angrily. "Somebody mistakenly put the matter in the grievance machinery."

"Why?!" came a loud chorus from the floor.

Ignoring the question, the chair continued: "I got the matter out of the Labor Relations Committee and put it back in the hands of the union where it belongs. I've helped other brothers too. I don't see why this case should be treated any differently."

Pushing, shoving, and yelling erupted around the microphone. A substantial number of men started to walk toward the door in disgust. "Let's go home!" they yelled.

Instructing the sergeants-at-arms to clear the mike, the chair gaveled the meeting to order. When peace was restored, he explained that if the membership wanted to change the Appeals Committee's decision they first had to set up an investigating committee to determine if the Appeals Committee had violated its constitutional mandate. After more arguing, someone moved that an investigating committee be appointed. The motion was roundly defeated by a voice vote.

Participation in membership meetings is not always so obvious. Some of the opportunities are more subtle. When committee meeting minutes are read, for example, an intriguing turn of events occurs. Longshoremen go to the microphone and "take exception" to something that was read. Taking exception to minutes means longshoremen disagree with a committee's decision. The simple statement, "I take exception to these minutes," puts the committee under public scrutiny; its deliberations become the entire membership's business. Exceptions are considered, debated, and voted on when the evening's agenda is concluded. If the membership disapproves of a committee's decision, it is overturned by majority vote. Thus, in this union, sovereignty is located in its rank and file at general membership meetings.

Another chance to participate also appears during committee reports. According to ILWU tradition, when more than one person is reporting, members speak in alphabetical order. Thus, the speaker's list is not determined by status, influence, or physical power. The topics to be reported, moreover, are evenly distributed among committee members; each member is assigned one issue to speak on. As a result, the membership does not depend upon one person's recollection. The chances for complete and candid accounts are increased by another Local 10 tradition: Speakers typically exceed their allotted time and topic. Debates are therefore fully aired, differences are expanded upon, and competing interpretations get discussed.

Public politics

The possibilities for participation in Local 10 extend considerably beyond membership meetings. Private committee meetings are not permitted in this union. "Executive" sessions or "closed" committee meetings are unheard of. All meetings are open, including the weekly strategy sessions of elected officials. Held in the office of either the president or secretary-treasurer, these sensitive "officers' meetings" are regularly and actively attended by rank and filers who "happen" to be around.

Public meetings are also standard practice for every standing committee. Committees meet at regularly scheduled times and places. Meetings are publicized and longshoremen know when committees deliberate. Everyone knows the Grievance Committee meets weekly on Monday mornings; the Executive Board meets twice a month, in the evenings of the second and fourth Thursdays; the Labor Relations Committee convenes on Wednesday mornings. The meetings are as public as they are publicized. When a controversy is expected to erupt at the Executive Board, or the Grievance Committee is to hear a complicated case, longshoremen know that in advance and can attend the meeting if they wish. Many do. Thus, meeting rooms are usually half filled with longshoremen interested in committee deliberations. And the meetings are not attended passively. Longshoremen are permitted and, in some instances, encouraged to participate actively.

These opportunities for union participation are facilitated by two aspects of West Coast longshoring. Because of the daily dispatch, the men are around the union hall routinely. And because they interact with each other regularly, longshoremen know when issues will surface. Their flexible work schedules allow them to be at the hall when they wish. Longshoremen are therefore unusually free to attend meetings when they please. Thus, union participation is encouraged because longshoremen have the contractual right to determine when they will work. In combination, these two elements of longshoring make possibilities for union involvement into operating realities.

The elaborate grapevine that has sprouted among San Francisco longshoremen also enhances union participation. Longshoremen share intimate details, sometimes bordering on gossip, of their personal lives, which are passed along at work and around the hall. This informal network keeps longshoremen informed about the union, the work, and the officers. The grapevine enables longshoremen to participate in union activities even when they are not present physically.

The grapevine, the daily dispatch, and flexible work schedules empower longshoremen to "check up on" or "keep an eye on" elected officials. Through the grapevine, or in conversation during the dispatch, they learn what officers have done or will do about an issue. And, if they are not working, or decide to "flop," they can actually look over an officer's shoulder. When the contract is being negotiated, for example, local officers are routinely joined at the bargaining table by rank and filers. If Local 10 members know a special issue will be argued, they take off work and attend the talks. Although not permitted to negotiate, the rank and filers are consulted at caucuses and their input has an immediate effect.

Local 10 practices a kind of "raw" democracy. Many of the opportunities for participation in this union are not formal or institutionalized. This does not, however, mean that officers can act unilaterally, or disregard the membership. The public politics practiced by Local 10 effectively insures that officers take into account varying interests; it prevents them from acting on their own or "taking over" the union. Politics in public enables rank-and-file longshoremen to be actively involved in the union. And actively participating in the union is another way to control elected officials. In this version of tumultuous democracy, officers are immediately and routinely accountable to their membership.

THE OBLIGATIONS AND PROSCRIPTIONS OF PARTICIPATION

Participation in Local 10 is also promoted institutionally, extending to virtually every aspect of union life. Certain activities are constitutionally obligatory. Attending membership meetings, for example, is not optional. The meetings are "stop-work meetings" so that every active longshoreman can attend them. This means that one evening every month the waterfront closes down. Work stops, and longshoremen are expected to be at the union hall. Fines are levied against members who are absent. Voting in the Local's yearly election is also mandatory.

Whereas certain instances of participation are obligatory, others are formally proscribed. Local elected officers can succeed themselves only once. They must return to work after serving two consecutive terms. This back-to-the-bench rule prevents anyone from assuming office for life. It also increases the opportunities for being an elected official. The rule formally restrains "pork-choppism": Since holding office is not assured, office holders must pursue more than self-interest. Because their position is not guaranteed, officers must be responsive to the membership. If they expect to be reelected, they have to run for office.

There are other restrictions on office holding. Anyone who wants to become wealthy does not run for office. Local 10's by-laws require that officers be paid basic longshore wage rates and no more. Elected officials therefore cannot earn more than longshoremen working in skilled categories. In fact, officers typically earn *less* than rank and filers because officials are not paid overtime or skilled wage rates. This reflects a general pattern in the ILWU. ILWU officials are among the lowest paid union officers in the Bay Area. In 1978, for example, the International president of the ILWU ranked 35th among the 50 highest paid labor officials in the area.[3] Although opportunism is obviously not completely eliminated by the officers' pay rate, it does make office holding unattractive to those who want to become personally wealthy. Longshoremen in the ILWU do not run for office to get rich.

The pay formula limits more than opportunism. It also prevents a financial division between officers and rank and filers. The wage structure maintains income parity and financial equality among all union members. Equality in this sense contributes to the high quality participation in ILWU politics that can occur only between people on equal footing.

Equality among Local 10 members is reinforced by equal access to the union's means of reproduction. The Local publishes a weekly bulletin that is produced by elected members of the "Publicity Committee." Anyone can write for this publication. *The Bulletin* is not an officer's mouthpiece, however. Rather, it is written by Publicity Committee members. When the officers want their views known, they publish an "Officers' Bulletin." Longshoremen keep in touch with union affairs through the *Bulletin*. It also provides members with a public outlet for their views and critical commentary on officers.

THE CULTURAL-INSTITUTIONAL CONTEXT OF DEMOCRATIC UNIONISM

One hallmark of democracy is participation. By itself, however, participation does not translate into democracy. Sometimes participation is restricted to deciding issues already determined beforehand by a small set of self-designated leaders. In these instances, participation is reduced to ap-

3 *San Francisco Examiner,* October 1, 1978, Section A, page 21.

proval or disapproval. The knowledge assumed in the choices is neither shared nor public. Thus, participation is illusory. It is restricted to endorsing decisions made by others.

The appearance of democracy can also be manipulated by self-defined leaders working behind the scenes. Oligarchy emerges when backstage actors are able to restrict leadership to a trusted few and thereby block members from access to real power. Membership participation in this context is minimal and superficial. But it does serve a purpose. Even the most limited forms of participation can be used to legitimate essentially undemocratic procedures. Thus, an entrenched leadership, working secretly, can undercut participation while keeping up democratic appearances.[4] To blossom, democracy must therefore be rooted in open and public politics. Cultural and institutional limits on oligarchy are also necessary. Both of these exist in Local 10.

Limiting ambitions

Local 10's constitution puts institutional checks on oligarchy. The obstacles to oligarchy in this union, however, run much deeper than formal restraints. Organizationally speaking, Local 10 does not leave much room for oligarchy. There are only five full-time, paid officers: president, secretary-treasurer, and three business agents. This sets limits on political opportunities. Office seekers can move up only a few rungs on the political ladder before returning to the docks. And since the union's International staff is quite small, even the most ambitious politicians must limit their aspirations. Only six titled International officers are elected, and no more than ten people fill appointed positions. In other words, this union does not provide many paid leadership opportunities. The ILWU's structure therefore discourages political ambition. It just isn't big enough; the possibilities for patronage are too few.

Ambition is limited in other ways. The job of a union official is not an enviable one: The hours are long, time off is rare, and the pay is low. They are not paid overtime and their time "off" is routinely interrupted. The

4 For discussions of the uses and abuses of participation see Kornhauser (1959); Lipset (1956, 1963); Michels (1962); Selznick (1957).

pressures are enormous and the rewards are minimal. Compared to waterfront work, the perks are insignificant.

The culture of insubordination

Union officers rarely receive accolades; gratitude and deference are not perks on this job. ILWU officials are frequently objects of ridicule, hostility, and abuse. The following exchange between a Local 10 member and an International officer at a membership meeting is typical.[5]

"I'm not trying to bait you, Brother," a longshoreman said somewhat sarcastically from the floor mike. "I just have a few simple questions for you."

The questions were neither simple nor few. "What local does the organizing staff come from?" he asked.

"You know the answer to that," responded the official.

"Just answer the question," shot back the longshoreman.

"You know the answer: It's Local X."

"Why?"

The International officer tried to provide a context for the issue: He inherited his staff; he didn't want to fire anyone; the current staff could handle the job.

The longshoreman was not convinced. "Why are no members from Local 10 on the organizing staff or regional directors?" he said/asked, barely disguising the insinuation that Local 10 was being treated unfairly. The men hooted and howled in appreciation. They clearly shared his sentiments. The longshoreman acted like a cheerleader, encouraging membership dissatisfaction, and the members responded appropriately.

The International officer finally lost his composure and yelled: "Goddammit, you know the answers to these questions. You're just trying to embarrass me!"

"No, Bro'," replied the longshoreman in a pseudo-fraternal tone of voice, "I'm not trying to embarrass you; I'm just trying to get answers to questions." The hall shook with laughter.

Sometimes the attacks on officers are personally abusive. At another

5 The subsequent paragraphs are based on field notes.

membership meeting, a black longshoreman called into question the racial identity of a black officer. He called the official a "white person with black paint on his face." Elected officials are typically targets of frustration. "I move that the titled officers be given thirty days off for not enforcing the dispatch rules," shouted a longshoreman half-seriously during a debate over the rules.

ILWU union officers are always under public scrutiny, and they are routinely accountable for their activities and whereabouts. When they appear to be treated better than rank and filers, local members demand an explanation. At one membership meeting, for example, the Local president reported that longshoremen were getting "time off" at the Labor Relations Committee for "no-shows" and coming to work late.

Speaking from the floor, a union member asked sarcastically why the officers were not "cited" when they showed up for work late. "I've been in the office any number of times and you officers are nowhere to be found. Where were you? Why don't you get written up the way we do?" The hall exploded with approving whistles and catcalls.

Officers who execute their duties unsatisfactorily are publicly admonished. At one Executive Board meeting, a member told the committee that the titled officers were "not together." He was particularly critical of one officer, noting he had called no staff meetings recently. And when staff meetings were called, he argued, the time was not publicly announced. He had taken a day off to attend one, only to find out that the meeting had been canceled. He observed that a number of issues were raised this evening that the officer was unaware of because he was out of touch with other officers. The officers, he felt, were not in communication.

"Fellows," he pleaded/demanded, "we got to get together. When you decide to have a staff meeting, goddammit, you make sure that everyone on the staff is there. Work out a strategy; work it out beforehand. But goddammit, find out what the other guy is doing."

It is also common for officials to be publicly lectured on how to do their job. An exchange at another Executive Board meeting is typical.[6] The president was asked for a report on the status of dispatch rules. He re-

---

6 The following paragraphs are based on field notes.

sponded by handing over a copy of the written rules. This visibly angered a number of Executive Board members.

"That's not what you were instructed to do," said one of them.

The president responded petulantly: "The rules for rotary dispatch have been written, these are the rules, that's what you asked for. Here they are."

"That's not what we asked for," countered an Executive Board member. "The rules have obviously been modified and what we want is a modified set of the rules. This is no way for a leader to act."

Another committee member agreed: "This is the second time you've kicked back an issue to the Executive Board without working on it."

"Don't give me a lecture on how to run the union," responded the local official.

"You are not exercising leadership," asserted one of his critics, having the last word.

A union official's job is difficult in any circumstance. But whatever troubles are inherent in the job, they are compounded considerably by the insubordination and individualism of Local 10 members. They constantly challenge, scrutinize, and outright defy elected officials. This obviously makes office holding a very difficult and trying experience. As a result, Local 10 members think seriously before running for office. And in many instances, they must be actively encouraged. Officers typically look forward to a year on the docks after two in office. They speak gratefully of the back-to-the-bench rule.

Oligarchy is unlikely in this context. Because of the culture and organization of San Francisco longshoremen, political ambitions are seriously limited. Democratic unionism is therefore enhanced by the longshore culture of insubordination. This culturally sanctioned, fiercely independent spirit retards antidemocratic tendencies.

The politics of candor

Democracy in Local 10 is reinforced by the union's deeply respected, long-standing tradition for conducting business not only publicly, but candidly as well. An outsider is profoundly impressed by the candor and openness that characterizes the operation of this organization. Sensitive and potentially embarrassing matters are not kept private, or restricted to inside dopesters and inner circles. Instead, they are discussed frankly and publicly. For example, one young longshoreman raised a troubling issue at a steward's training program. "If the local arbitrator is agreed to by the union," he asked naively, "how come we got one who always sides with the employer?" The answer he received was a detailed history of the appointment: He was publicly told the inside story.[7]

Local 10's officers publicly talk about deals and compromises that in most organizations would be covered up or played down. At an informal, off-the-record meeting, for example, one official asked his PMA counterpart to delay arbitrating pay guarantee abuses.[8] If the issue went to an arbitrator, he said, neither side could win because it would be out of their hands. Then, taking the manager in his confidence, the unionist shared a secret: Local 10's Executive Board was working on a solution that required membership approval. He thought the proposal would be approved but needed time. The employers would be smart to wait until the membership met before arbitrating. The employer's representative agreed.

The union official was in an awkward position, at best. He was sharing union strategy with the employers, and that could be used against him by his enemies. Thus, he had good reason to keep the encounter secret. And if the exchange became public, he could have denied saying anything, or played down its significance as an off-the-record comment. Despite considerable personal risk, and without taking refuge in secrecy, the official publicly revealed the agreement on his own initiative. In an absolutely fascinating display of candor, he shared the entire exchange with Local 10 members. Speaking to a membership meeting during "Officers' Reports," he told the details of his conversation and agreement with the employers. He left out nothing, even the specifics that were unfavorable to him personally.[9]

In addition to conducting business openly, union officials also treat the

---

7 The union and employers "trade" appointments along the Pacific Coast. One of the union's appointees had personal problems and was replaced. Since the employers allowed the union to replace the problematic appointee, the union could not object to the employer's choice for San Francisco.

8 The following paragraphs are based on field notes.

9 His description was accurate. I checked it against my notes for the earlier meeting. He kept nothing from the membership. His report contained the essence of everything said on both sides.

membership respectfully. Rank and filers are treated as equals by Local 10's officers. One membership meeting, for example, scheduled for noon, was late getting started. The officers were out of sight. Before impatience had a chance to build, however, a business agent appeared on stage, turned on the microphone, and told Local 10 members that the officers and convention delegates were meeting with the International officers. The membership meeting would therefore be delayed fifteen minutes. The announcement did more than convey courtesy; it also turned a private meeting into a public one. Thus, it became knowledge the membership could use to evaluate the delegate's reports and hold officers accountable.

Conducting union business openly is an institutionalized practice in Local 10. Negotiations are public. Even private "caucuses" are open to members. Arbitrations are no different: Anyone can observe them. This is sometimes uncomfortable for employer representatives because some union officials use the occasion to impress rank and filers by dramatically dressing down their adversaries. The weekly Labor Relations Committee meetings are also open, as are their caucuses.

Very few opportunities exist in Local 10 for conducting official union business in private, behind closed doors. It is nearly impossible for officers to secretly make informal binding agreements. Neither the institutional apparatus nor the political climate allows such arrangements. And even if formal restraints on secrecy were violated, tradition would oppose deals agreed to outside of public scrutiny. Neither precedent nor sentiment would sanction private agreements. To further complicate matters, flexible work schedules and intricate grapevines also make it difficult for officers to conduct official business privately. Some rank and filer is always about. And the waterfront is alerted momentarily with the slightest indication of something going on behind closed doors. In combination, these elements of longshore life make open and public politics a normal occurrence in routine settings throughout Local 10.

PATCHWORK ON POLITICAL QUILTING: THE SOCIAL FABRIC OF DEMOCRATIC UNIONISM

Democracy is as fragile as it is delicate. And, sometimes it can be used against itself. Organizational flexibility and openness, for example, encourage membership participation. The same organizational format, however, is also a formula for vulnerability. Because they are open, democratic organizations can be penetrated, and democracy legally subverted. Candid and public politics are another mainstay of democracy. But public discourse is not always carefully considered; it does not always produce good judgment. Public politics sometimes becomes demagoguery.

Aware of these possibilities, classical political sociologists qualified their enthusiasm for democracy. They worried that, unless modified, the democratic process would render ordinary people vulnerable to manipulation from above and experts unnecessarily exposed to pressure from below.[10] Secondary centers of power were necessary, they argued, to guard against the misuses and abuses of democracy. By mediating between the state and the individual, these institutions would keep some power in the hands of private citizens and decelerate the growth of powerful political apparatuses.

The intermediary centers of power to which modern political sociologists devote their attention are "voluntary associations." According to pluralist theory, democracy's chances for success are enhanced by pressure groups and political parties. Individuals can exert a measure of control over them; would-be tyrants are stopped by multiple and competing centers; and stable democracy flourishes in the process.

When sociologists assess the potential for democracy in an organization, they typically look for formal voluntary associations. If they find official pressure groups or self-conscious political parties, they assume that a variant of democracy is being practiced.[11] Were this criteria applied to Local 10, no mediating centers of power would be found. Official political parties do not exist, and neither do formally constituted pressure groups.[12] It would be incorrect, however, to conclude that organized competition and mediation do not count in Local 10's politics.

10 See, for example, Michels (1962) and Tocqueville (1945).
11 A good example of this is the volume by Lipset and his collaborators (1956).
12 Although they no longer exist, competing political parties, known as the red slate and blue slate, did function during the 1950s. Impressed by this multiparty arrangement, Lipset et al. suggested that Local 10, together with the International Typographers Union, might be the only two exceptions to Michels's "iron law of oligarchy" (1962:149).

Local 10 is a multisided organization. Longshoremen are organized into official and unofficial categories by which they are known and with which they identify. These categories reflect divisions within the local that are the bases for social bonding. Because the people in each category typically share interests, union leaders treat them as constituencies. Thus, even though Local 10 claims no formal pressure groups, longshoremen are organized along numerous informal categories. Elected officials treat these groups respectfully and their unofficial spokesmen have an important voice in the unions' official affairs.

Like patches on a quilt, these categories are individually recognizable and overlapping. They are patterned in ways that resemble a political quilt. The quilting keeps political democracy alive in Local 10.

Cohorts and generations

San Francisco longshoremen typically identify themselves as "'59," "'63," "'67," or "'69" men. The year refers to the date they were registered as Pacific Coast longshoremen. The identity is an important one because it goes beyond the number of years worked on the waterfront. It is also a way of talking about age: Longshoremen registered recently tend to be younger. Thus, registration dates are associated with lifestyles. Marijuana tends to be the tonic of choice for longshoremen registered in the late 1960s. People who began working on the waterfront before that appear to prefer alcohol. Styles of dress also seem to be related to registration dates.

The correlation between age and registration date, however, is not a perfect one. The union has a policy of providing work for political activists exiled from other occupations. This permits people to begin longshore careers at mid-life. Thus, age does not always predict registration date. As a result, people are referring to more than their age when they talk about their registration year. Each date stands for a set of shared experiences that create a common waterfront identity. When longshoremen speak of their registration date, they are identifying with a generation or cohort of dockworkers. The identification is often explicit: "We came up together," longshoremen say of someone in their cohort. Generational identities are one source of pride and organization in Local 10.

Longshore cohorts are produced by shared waterfront experiences. Each generation informally apprentices together. They are exposed to the tricks of their trade as a unit; the "ropes" are learned in common. Unofficial initiation into the longshore community, or "hazing," is experienced collectively. Through these processes of becoming longshoremen, reputations are made and selfhood is proven. Shared experiences also become sources of comparison and grounds for distinguishing between generations. People in cohorts "remember when" together; they share the same "good old days." Generational identities are created out of these experiences.

Cohorts are bases for bonding. Longshoremen are organized inside the union by cohort. Because generational circumstances facilitate friendships, when longshoremen "hang out" together, they do so typically with people in their cohort. Sometimes friendships extend beyond work, to weekends and families. Waterfront generations also share preferences for recreation. Like tonic, recreational choices tend to be generational and these shared experiences are further grounds for association.

Waterfront generations are also an important ingredient in union politics. People are distributed throughout the union's political hierarchy largely on the basis of their registration date. As new generations come on the waterfront, their predecessors are pushed up the political ladder. As a result, each cohort tends to control a level of political office holding in the union. Thus, political power, loyalties, and alliances are deeply embedded in generational identities.

Local 10 houses five waterfront generations. Until 1959, every San Francisco longshoreman was registered either before World War II, or immediately after it. This is the generation that made the union's political history so colorful. Some of these people participated in the general strike, and most helped organize the union in the 1930s and survive the 1950s. They are the "old-timers." Their reputation is powerful and they are treated with profound respect. They are a cohort to be taken seriously. The old-timers still participate in union business; most of them remain active long after retirement. Local 10's Pensioners Club meets monthly; a union-wide pensioners' convention is an annual event; a pensioner sits on the union's Negotiation Committee; and pensioners vote on contracts. These avenues of expression enable the pensioners' voices to be heard and their will to be exercised.

The first longshoremen registered after World War II arrived on the waterfront in 1959. Called " '59 men," this generation has become the "old-timers" as the veterans die. Over thirty years on the docks has enabled these longshoremen to establish a group identity and take control of strategic positions in the Local. Nearly all its full-time elected officials are " '59 men."[13] This cohort is also heavily represented on the Local's Executive Board, Negotiating Committee, and International Convention Delegations.

The third San Francisco longshore generation was registered in 1963. Following the pattern of " '59 men," they are moving up the local's political ladder. At least one of them is annually elected as a full-time officer; a fair number of them sit on the Executive Board, and a good proportion of the Grievance Committee and Promotion Committee's members are '63 men. The fourth and fifth waterfront generations, registered in 1967 and 1969, already figure in union politics. They are stewards and sit on the Appeals and Publicity Committees.

A complicated political-generational patchwork has emerged in Local 10 over the past thirty years. The cohorts play a strategic role in this arrangement. Each generation is simultaneously constituency, resource, and veto group. Issues that impact on longshoremen are not experienced uniformly; saliency varies by cohort. The more seniority one has on the waterfront, for example, the more likely asbestos poisoning will be an issue for them. Longshoremen nearing retirement age also become preoccupied with the details of pensions in contract packages. On the other hand, longshoremen looking toward another twenty or thirty years on the waterfront are especially concerned with the shipping industry's future. Because they are experienced differentially, social issues become the political property of particular generations.

The social issues associated with each cohort, however, are only one patch on the political quilt. Over time, generational spokesmen emerge. Although they are not official representatives, certain individuals are

13 During the period of this study, all but one full-time officer was registered in 1959.

known to "speak for" a cohort, or an issue. They are viewed as "spokesmen" because most hold elected office in the union. Longshoremen are notoriously loquacious, but the mantel of "spokesman" is reserved for people with observable constituencies. Spokesmen are consulted when problems erupt; rank and filers bring them individual troubles they want handled at higher levels.

Generational spokesmen are crucial patches on the local's political quilt. No one cohort is a majority. If someone is to be elected or a decision made, more than one cohort must therefore be persuaded. Generational leaders are important in this process. Receiving their endorsement increases one's chances for winning votes.

Cohorts are also veto groups as well as swing votes. Because of their location in the Local's political apparatus, one generation can subvert another's "program" by ignoring it or not implementing it. For example, a proposal that negatively affects "'59 men" is not likely to succeed. Most full-time officers identify with this cohort and they will not implement it. Cohorts are explicitly invoked when spokesmen worry that proposals will affect their generation negatively. "As a '69 man', I can't support a motion that would effectively eliminate the possibility of container freight," said a young longshoreman to a membership meeting deliberating who would be eligible for containerized work (field notes).

This patchwork of political generations is critical to Local 10's version of democracy. Generational identities and organization operate as checks and balances. The generations are also buffers between officers and rank and filers. Officers typically take into account generations, not individuals, when formulating policies. Finally, cohorts give longshoremen power because they have more strength as generations than as individuals.

Race and ethnicity

Before World War II, Local 10 was racially homogeneous and ethnically diverse. Large numbers of Scandinavian, Slavic, Italian, Portuguese, and Irish people lived in the Bay Area and many of them were longshoremen. Ethnicity was crucial to people's chances for working on the waterfront. It either helped or hindered. Longshoremen were recruited informally by people already working on the docks and they picked fellow countrymen.

100

Inside the Local, ethnicity was also important. Work was organized along ethnic lines: Gangs were known as much for their ethnicity as for their productivity. Some longshoremen still talk about the Portuguese, Maltese, and Slav gangs that worked on the waterfront.

Black people did not come on the docks in appreciable numbers until the Second World War. And when new generations were registered in the early 1960s, the union recruited heavily in Black and Hispanic communities. This self-conscious effort to attract non-Europeans was successful. Longshoremen of color became a numerical majority in Local 10 by the end of the 1960s.

Ethnicity, however, is still an important category in the union. Local 10's membership does not divide into clear-cut categories like black, brown, and white. Longshoremen identify with and organize into ethnically defined groups. Euro-Americans continue to cluster in ethnic formations. Hispanic longshoremen distinguish between "Latinos" and "Chicanos."[14] Thus, race and ethnicity persist as principles for group formation and consciousness on the San Francisco waterfront.

As a category that organizes consciousness, race is modified by social ecology. Neighborhoods are still an important component in longshoremen's identity. Black longshoremen typically live in Oakland and Richmond, and they frequently identify with these cities. Thus, residence is crucial to their self-identity. Hispanic longshoremen tend to live in San Francisco's Mission District or East Oakland. They identify with these areas and cluster in groups organized around residence. Euro-American longshoremen who identify ethnically also tend to live in specific enclaves.

Powerful and concrete bonds are contained in racial and ethnic identities. Chances are good that longshoremen who share an age and ethnicity also share a history: They either grew up together or near each other, went to some of the same schools, or knew one another in the military or criminal justice system. Shared history produces intimate bonds among San Francisco longshoremen. Ancestral identities enable groups of longshoremen to share common histories, languages, secrets, and symbols. And unlike cohort bonding, the glue created by ethnicity is more powerful

14 "Latinos" are people from Central and South America; "Chicanos" are people of Mexican ancestry born in the United States.

than age. Thus, longshoremen who share neighborhoods or ancestries have loyalties that go deeper than age or registration cohort.

The ties produced by heritage and ecology are reinforced on the waterfront. They are principles for organization at work and association around the hall. Ancestry is still one of the grounds for inclusion in gangs, even though no gang is currently organized exclusively by that criterion. Partnerships, however, continue to be based on ascribed characteristics. Evidently the trust established by shared neighborhood and ethnic history extends to work. Apparently reputations made off the job are shared on the job and partnerships are based on them.

Race and ethnicity figure prominently in Local 10's politics. Latin and South American foreign policy is predictably salient for Hispanic longshoremen. Black dockworkers, on the other hand, are especially interested in trade with South Africa. Longshoremen are also divided by race on internal union policies. Blacks and Hispanics are especially sensitive to traditions that advantage Euro-American longshoremen. Gearmen and walking bosses, for example, were disproportionately recruited from the ranks of Euro-American longshoremen because seniority was the principle for inclusion. No one was surprised, therefore, that when the local moved to substitute new criteria, union officials were supported mainly by longshoremen of color.

The ethnic and racial patches on Local 10's political quilt contribute to the democracy it practices. Although formal caucuses are not recognized, longshoremen routinely caucus informally. Much of this caucusing, moreover, occurs in racially and ethnically homogeneous circles. Thus, even though the union is politically opposed to organizing longshoremen by racial categories, Local 10's membership in fact routinely organizes itself along ascriptive lines. It is therefore quite natural that racial and ethnic constituencies have emerged with unofficial representatives acting as spokesmen. Thus, the Local's Executive Board is typically made up of members of each ascriptive group. As a result, most ancestral groups are represented in some fashion in the union's political deliberations.

Local 10's racial patches enhance its political democracy in yet another way. No one racial group can impose its will on the Local. Afro-American longshoremen may be a numerical majority. They do not, however, vote as a category to the man. As a result, even though 55 percent of the Local's membership is Afro-American, Euro-American and Hispanic longshoremen are routinely elected officers and committeemen. Because longshoremen do not blindly vote their racial category, successful politics and candidates must be acceptable to more than one racial group. In this context, "minority" groups have veto power and this, in effect, makes for an effective, informal system of checks and balances.

Racial and ethnic segmentation serves the democratic process in additional ways. Ethnic spokesmen act as go-betweens. Rank and filers turn to them when redress does not come from above. And full-time officers listen to ethnic representatives when they need an immediate reading of a group's pulse. The Local's ascriptive leaderships therefore mediate between levels of union hierarchy. Ethnic segmentation also bonds longshoremen who are divided along other lines. Whereas ascriptive ties divide dockworkers by one standard, they decrease other divisions. Racially salient issues, for example, diminish differences between "'59" men and "'69" men.

Job categories

Another source of identity and organization on the San Francisco waterfront are the "boards" on which longshoremen work, their job categories. As noted earlier, twelve job categories – or boards – are contractually recognized. These boards organize longshoremen into twelve separate units. The units are differentiated by pay rate, job opportunities, time spent in the hall, and relationship to supervision. In this respect, the boards create divisions between Local 10 members. But the boards are also crucial sources of unity for longshoremen. People who share job categories, share work experiences. The boards, therefore, are another patch on the union's political quilt.

Longshoremen working a particular board routinely touch shoulders. They wait in the same line during the dispatch and they work next to each other on the job. They share working conditions; they are paid the same hourly wage; and they are exposed to similar insecurities. Thus, boards are a source of association for longshoremen.

Working in a gang is another opportunity for unity. The same group of people work together each time a gang is dispatched. Over time, therefore,

103

intimate bonds develop among gang members. People share rides, coffee breaks, lunch, and beers. Gang members are typically "family" for each other.

Gangs and boards bring longshoremen together. They provide the grounds for solidarity. Under certain circumstances, however, they are also sources of differentiation. Because Bay Area ports are heavily containerized, gang work has been reduced considerably. As a result, gang men depend on the Pay Guarantee to supplement their income. And because they work infrequently, they are also isolated from other longshoremen. People working off the "dock board" share a similar fate: They also get very little work. Special Equipment Operators, on the other hand, benefit from containerization.

Because the rewards of containerization have not been distributed uniformly, issues created by the new technology divide longshoremen by boards. Dock men and gang members, for example, speak favorably of the Pay Guarantee. They are not happy that it is necessary, but they appreciate the cushion against technologically produced unemployment. Longshoremen working off boards rewarded by new technologies, on the other hand, speak scornfully of the Guarantee, calling it "welfare." Because containerization has been experienced differentially, longshoremen are divided on the topic by job category. Boards typically have conflicting, and sometimes opposing, interests on the issue. Their differences are sufficiently important that interest groups have emerged out of job categories.

The transformation of job categories into interest groups adds another patch to the Local's democratic quilt. The common interests held by people in job categories unify longshoremen otherwise divided by race, ethnicity, and cohort. Skill boards overlap sociological categories. They are a kind of glue that bonds longshoremen together. Since no job category is large enough to dictate union policy, another system of checks and balances has been established de facto. It is impossible for one board to determine union policies and elections. Put differently, these "interest groups" protect the Local from being captured by a clique or cabal.

The quilting on Local 10's political fabric was not self-consciously created. These social patches were not devised by someone intending to create participatory union democracy. Unintentional or not, the arrangement has

104

provided for a lively form of democracy. An unofficial system of checks and balances has emerged. Leaders must actively circulate in the Local. The union's informal organization insulates rank and filers from leaders and protects officials from the general membership. Divisions within the union are healed by overarching loyalties that cut across cleavages. These overlapping identities bind the entire Local together. In combination, these patches are a quilt that shapes and maintains a union that is political in the participatory or democratic sense of the term.

6

BEING POLITICAL IN LOCAL 10

TWICE a year the longshoremen's hall is transformed into a polling place. Candidates line up outside the main entrance and hand out campaign literature. As longshoremen walk into the hall, they pass through a gauntlet of people who have elective office on their minds. The atmosphere is festive; the building buzzes with excitement. When candidates pass out election material, they say, "do the right thing when you get in the voting booth, brother."

"I've gotcha," is the usual response.

When longshoremen speak of politics, they mean more than political participation. They are also referring to people who hold union office. "Political" is the name they use for longshoremen who pursue elected office. Thus, alongside politics in the participatory sense, Local 10 members practice a more traditional, opportunistic sort of politics. A group of longshoremen with "track records," who run for office on "programs," represent and serve union constituencies. These people are known as "politicos." Their routine activities are called "being political."

The longshoremen's consciousness of the cynical side of politics is another weapon in the battle to maintain control over their union, as well as to resist management's authority. When used properly, cynicism can be a restraint on antidemocratic tendencies and managerial talk about sharing a common enterprise. Because Local 10 members are able to see through participatory images, they are less likely to be fooled by self-serving politicians and managers using the ideology of participation either to undercut the process of democracy or the contest for workplace control.

BEING POLITICAL

Calculating options

One obvious way to be political in Local 10 is to run for office. And when they do, political people act strategically; they carefully calculate their options. Political careers typically begin on committees, not in titled offices. "You've got to learn about political things from the bottom up if you want to move in this local," said a seasoned political veteran (field notes). Getting started in politics also means running for office even when the chances for success are slim. Like politics in any context, the objective is to create name recognition. Political newcomers also take labor relations classes or grievance management seminars to increase their political attractiveness. Longshoremen typically begin political careers as stewards. Acting strategically, moreover, is not limited to newcomers; long-time activists calculate their options, too. Some sit out elections when incumbents are likely to win. And kindred spirits periodically agree not to run against each other.

Longshoremen strategize in other areas of their lives as well. Work, for example, is organized around political aspirations. Rarely resting on their laurels, politicos self-consciously rotate work schedules to increase contact with rank and filers. When they are back on the docks after two years in office, some politicos work six months in a gang, and six months out of the hall, six months on the night side and six months on the day shift. Rotating in and out of the hall, and between shifts, increases visibility. And visibility helps them get reelected after a year or two out of office.

Longshoremen with coastwide political aspirations also use flexible work arrangements to their advantage. ILWU members can work temporarily in any port on the West Coast. This enables politicos to work the entire coast promoting a political program. "I expect to hustle work up and down the coast after I get out of office next spring," explained a titled officer who was testing the coastal political climate. "I think I'll work out of San Francisco, Sacramento, Eureka. I intend to know the work situation in northern California thoroughly. I might even work in Los Angeles."

Making the record

Anyone in Local 10 who is politically ambitious establishes a record to stand on. Records are lists of accomplishments, issues raised, and programs proposed. They are also reasons to vote for someone. When longshoremen talk about someone "making the record," however, they do not refer only to a candidate's accomplishments. They also refer to posturing. Creating the appearance of militancy is sometimes viewed as "making the record," especially when that stance is used later on to solicit political support. Politicos make the record for their militancy in two locations: across bargaining tables and at union meetings.

Labor Relations Committee (LRC) meetings provide excellent opportunities to construct records of militancy. Even though the LRC has broad jurisdiction, its authority is limited. LRCs cannot force disputants to resolve disagreements. If the two sides are unwilling to agree, the unresolved dispute goes to an "Area LRC." And when agreement is not reached at the regional level, the dispute is sent to a "Coast LRC" and/or an arbitrator. The LRC is also restricted by its narrow mandate: It can adjudicate disagreements only over contractual violations.

Because of these restrictions, LRCs *hear* more disputes than they settle. Thus, they serve as natural settings for politicos to establish militant *bona fides*. LRCs encourage politicos to act militantly for a number of reasons. First of all, longshoremen feel strongly about the issues being disputed. Second, they want the disagreements settled rapidly, and locally. They don't want to wait for a Coast arbitrator to rule. And finally, Local 10's members don't limit their complaints to contractual violations. Longshoremen routinely grieve practices that are contractually permissible, *and* disagreeable. Thus, the stage is set for militant-sounding talk.

Disputes over practices that are contractually permissible make particularly good opportunities for militancy. The running dispute over "manning" is a case in point. The contract is permissive regarding the number of people required to work a job. "The employer shall not be required to hire unnecessary men," states Section 15.2 of the agreement. Employers use this language to justify hiring a minimum number of longshoremen. But union members obviously disagree; they want more men hired.[1] This

1 For a detailed discussion of these differences, see Mills (1979b:33–47).

dispute erupts regularly at LRC meetings. Sometimes Local 10 officials visit other ports and detect different manning practices. When they discover ten-man gangs in other ports, they protest the practice at LRCs because gangs in San Francisco work with only eight longshoremen.

"Goddamn it," said one official returning from southern California, "we're undermanned around here. The union wants the minutes to show that we want the same number of men in gangs as they have in Los Angeles."

The PMA did not object to recording the union's preferences. The local manager did, however, note that the practice "in no way is a violation of the contract." Sometimes union officials escalate matters. They make a motion to discontinue the practice. In these instances, the PMA "disagrees," and insists the issue be arbitrated.[2] Even though these arguments are colorful and heated, the dispute typically goes no further than the local LRC minutes. Nevertheless, these exchanges are repeated regularly, sometimes weekly.[3] Although the exact wording varies, a pattern emerges: Union officials demand equity in manning; and employers insist the practice is contractually permissible. The two sides appear to be reading from a script. But the ending is as patterned as it is inconclusive. The dispute never gets resolved.

Looking from the outside in, this pattern is inexplicable. The observer sees only inconclusiveness. Handled locally, at an LRC, disputes over manning accomplish very little because gangs working "shorthanded," and discrepancies between manning scales are not contractual violations. And if the contract has not been violated, the dispute cannot be decided by an LRC. To complicate matters, if the problem is with the contract, the LRC cannot solve it because the contract can be redrafted only by a coastwide negotiating committee. Thus, disputes over manning are not very effective methods for changing the contract, or the number of longshoremen working. What, then, is happening?

Longshoremen who are knowledgeable about union politics offer an insight. Officials raising the issue, they explain, are acting opportunistically. Manning scales are a long-standing source of bitterness between

2 Quotes based on field notes.
3 During one eight-week period, it was raised at every LRC meeting.

longshoremen and employers.[4] By raising the issue at an LRC, and getting it into the minutes, union officials can claim they are representing the membership effectively. Actual outcomes are irrelevant to this claim. What matters is that the practice be protested, the protest recorded, and the minutes become public record. Thus, the official is "making the record." Or, as a longshoreman less conversant in contractual nuance put it: "The brother's just politicking" (field notes). In other words, manning disputes are used by political people to establish a record they can run on.

The interpretation is credible. Although political longshoremen are always "making the record," they raise manning disputes with particular frequency and intensity every fall. It hardly seems coincidental that this takes place immediately before election time.

Politicos also make the record at LRCs by raising issues that are completely unrelated to the contract:

"We want to sit in on Local 75's LRC, the guard's local," announced a union official during "general business." "These goddamn guards are doing work that's not theirs: They're taking dispatch tickets on the night side. That's not their work; it's supervision's and we want supervision doing that, not the guards. We want to deal with this at their LRC meeting."

"The longshore LRC cannot make a decision on this matter," responded a PMA officer. "If you want to be present at Local 75's LRC, that will have to be worked out between Local 10, Local 75, and the PMA. But we can't decide it at this LRC."

"OK," said the unionist, "but I want the minutes to show that we don't like them taking these tickets at night" (field notes).

Longshoremen may not like guards taking dispatch slips. There might even be contractual prohibitions on the practice. But in this instance, the objection was not contractually grounded. No contractual provision was cited as a basis for the objection. The demand to participate in the guard's LRC was also unrelated to the contract. Clearly the official was making the record. He raised a noncontractual disagreement in a meeting authorized only to manage contractual violations. When the PMA representative

---

4 For more extended discussions of the manning controversy see Hartman (1969) and Fairley (1979).

110

pointed out the LRC had no jurisdiction in this matter, the union official did not pursue the disagreement. He was more concerned that the dispute be recorded than it be settled. And during the next election, he cited the exchange as an example of how he had represented longshoremen in LRCs.

Section 9.43 is frequently the source for record making at local LRCs. One of the especially objectionable aspects of this provision is that it places no limits on the number of "steady men." When people argue for limits on 9.43 men, they are therefore toiling in the vineyards of resentment and dissatisfaction. They are obviously cultivating a potentially high-yield crop of unhappy voters. But "making the record" depends on how they raise the issue. One union official, for example, was straightforward. He demanded a "cap be placed on the number of people who could go 9.43." When he offered his reasons why, it became quite clear he was making the record. He argued that because the PMA wanted San Francisco to become a "Low Work Opportunity Port," no more 9.43 men should be dispatched.[5] With a cap in place, he contended, work in the port would be equitably distributed.

The PMA ignored the substance of his argument. They made no mention of equity or redistributing work. Instead, they raised contractual issues: The union had not accepted the employers' motion to declare San Francisco a "Low Work Opportunity Port," said one PMA representative. Since both sides had to agree on the designation, technically speaking, San Francisco was not a "Low Work Opportunity Port." Second, he argued, the Low Work Opportunity Port provision said nothing about limiting 9.43 men. So even if the union and the employers agreed that San Francisco was a Low Work Opportunity Port, there were still no contractual grounds for capping the number of 9.43 men. The demand was therefore inap-

---

5 "Low Work Opportunity Port" is contractual language created to insure there be no reduction in the longshore workforce. A Low Work Opportunity Port is said to exist when two conditions obtain: The average hours worked by "B" longshoremen (nonregistered) are reduced to less than twelve hours per week for a continuous six-week period and when the average hours worked by "A" longshoremen (registered) are reduced to less than eighteen hours a week during a six-week period. When an area is declared a "Low Work Opportunity Port," longshoremen in that port can transfer to areas requiring additional labor (supplement III, 1978 contract, pp. 172–8).

111

propriate. The union official had not established contractual grounds for limiting steady men.

The unionist did not contest the contractual interpretation. "We want the minutes to show," he said, without even acknowledging the employer's reasoning, "that the union wants a cap on 9.43 because you guys say this is a Low Work Opportunity Port."

"The brother is doing a little politicking by getting noncontractual items onto the LRC records," commented a fellow officer later on. "He makes a real habit of this. I think he imagines that he can then claim he is really struggling for the men" (field notes).

When someone is said to be making the record, or "politicking," his sincerity and motives are questioned. Behavior is neutralized, its significance minimized, when longshoremen are suspected of making the record. The assumption is the person does not know how to use the contract and therefore blusters, or knowingly inserts noncontractual issues into the discourse to establish militant credentials. In either instance, making the record has a negative connotation; the phrase is used to discount or belittle someone's words or deeds.

The discount rate for making the record may be high. But that does not mean it is unacceptable behavior. When people make the record, they are often enthusiastically encouraged. The union official arguing for a cap on 9.43 men is a case in point. Even though he was unable to persuade the PMA, longshoremen appreciated his effort. The attack on Section 9.43 was well received by Local 10 members attending the LRC. Even when longshoremen are obviously making the record at membership meetings, they are frequently encouraged energetically. The necessary ingredient for encouragement is that voice be given to a strongly felt sentiment. The issue need not be a contractual violation; and the speaker may not even offer a solution. But if a resonant chord is struck, approval is immediately registered, even when everyone knows the speaker is just making the record.

Speaking militantly on mobilizable issues is another obvious way to make the record. Making the record in this context, however, is done differently than during negotiations with employers. This record does not require issues to be packaged in contractual language; nor does it necessitate contractual sophistication. Obvious posturing is not a liability. This

112

kind of reputation is not created by being accurate or effective. The speech is the record.

A record is made in speeches when one of two options are established: Either the speech prepares grounds for future claims to insight, or it invokes hindsight to show the speaker's visionary qualities. One of the characteristics of this record, then, is self-aggrandizing language. Standard talk for staking claims on the future includes: "You mark my words," or, "if you'd listened to me when . . . ," or, "like I said last time. . . ." These assertions then become the "record."

This record is created independently of how it is received. Sometimes politicos promote sectarian issues. They make foreign policy resolutions, or, they renounce the two-party system, demanding a worker's party. Some politicos are insensitive to the membership. They frame topics in a fashion guaranteed to arouse the ire of the assembled, or they continue to debate issues long after all interest has evaporated.

"Isn't it true?" said one longshoreman, a prominent member of an old-left sectarian splinter group, referring to a new contract, "that the caucus did nothing about working conditions? Isn't it true that they were only concerned with wages and hours?"

Without waiting for an answer, he explained in excessive detail why the contract should be rejected. When he began talking about the next topic, it was introduced with the same preface: "Isn't it true that . . . ?" This was necessary because the chair had ruled against making statements; only questions were permitted. As the litany proceeded people started booing. He continued on doggedly; then laughter filled the hall. When he finally got the message (or ran out of topics), he walked away from the microphone.

At first glance, the incident is difficult to explain. Why would political people so totally disregard their audience? Why act in such a self-consciously alienating manner? This is very strange behavior for people who call themselves "political." A clue emerged when an equally insensitive sectarian spoke later in the meeting. "Let's set the record straight!" he announced at the conclusion of his speech (field notes).

Both speakers were making the record. The fact that their message was received with hostility does not change this. Being received negatively does not prevent one from making a record. Speakers taking unpopular

113

stands can still claim to be correct in the future, or look back with the power of hindsight vision. Thus, it does not matter if the message is accepted or rejected. In either instance, the speaker has made the record. Rank and filers are aware of this. Asked why some politicos alienated the union's membership, one Local 10 member said, "they always want to be right. They don't care what people think; they're politicking, making the record." His analysis was confirmed a couple months later.

"I told you before, and nobody listened," said one of the politicos mentioned earlier. "The caucus is only concerned with wages and hours" (field notes).

Having made the record, now he was using it.

Programs and platforms

Political longshoremen must stand for something. Thus, each one has a program. When politicos are asked what they stand for, they mention a platform or program. Sometimes a platform is one's record, but not always.

Programs of the word. Two kinds of programs surface in Local 10. One is written down and printed. It is handed to voters during election campaigns. This program is packaged in a number of forms and sizes. The simplest, most common example is a small card (2″ × 4″) with the candidate's picture, name, and the office or offices he seeks. Strictly speaking, the cards contain no program. They simply state, "vote for" or "elect."

Another version of the written program is a brief statement or principle printed alongside the candidate's picture, name, and the office being sought. Examples of this kind of program include: "for rank and file control"; "the man who can get the job done right and fair"; "the best man to run to get the job done"; "will do the job right."

Sometimes candidates expand on these principles and offer a more elaborate program:

"I believe that all jobs on the waterfront should have a manning scale. I will work for this throughout the years."

"Your vote for ———— is more than just a vote. It is a statement for change. We must work harder for fairness in our union and fairness on the job. ———— has that special talent. Union experience, respect for his fellow man . . . to help make a better day."

The final form of written platform is found on leaflets where a complete and comprehensive statement of the candidate's intentions is presented. This statement is explicitly called a program. One such program announced the following demands:

1. Bridges and Goldblatt Should Not Run Again.
2. We Should Continue As An Independent Union.
3. The Contract . . . Now What The Hell Do We Do??? I want to end the PGP. No 9.43. Would you tie the coast up for a six hour day and retirement at 58?
4. The Business Agent . . . What He Should Do.

Programs of the deed. Longshoremen also run on unwritten programs that are not stated explicitly. These programs are not found on leaflets. Rather, they are seen in the deeds and heard in the spoken words of politicos. Time and sophistication are necessary before these programs can be recognized as such. Careful observers of their union notice that officeholders regularly raise and pursue particular troubles. This pattern is recognized as a program by the union's observant participants, which is what they call it.

Unwritten programs are not observable to the naked eye, however. To see them, the outsider needs patience and coaching from union insiders. Over time, endless, inconclusive arguments are seen in a new light; they take on new meanings. What appears at first glance as repetitious wrangling, a failure of the grievance machinery, turns out to be one union official's "health and safety program." It took a month of observations and an insider's insight before this program became visible.

"Crescent," said the union official during general business at an LRC in late March.[6] "Some of your lifts are smoking. We're going to be looking into that, there's been some backsliding. Some of your equipment isn't working right and when we find it we're going to pull it."

"You should refer these sorts of things to the Joint Safety Committee," responded the PMA spokesman.

6 Field notes.

"There's no problem with that," the unionist said quietly. "But if you want to avoid work stoppages you should clean up your act. If you don't, work'll stop."

At 8 a.m. the next morning, the union officer drove along San Francisco's Embarcadero.[7] As he drove through a shed, he spotted unsafe lifts. The exhaust pipes were not high enough. After putting a note on one, he told the walking boss the machines would have to be fixed before they could be driven.

Patrolling the Embarcadero one week later, he stopped at another dock.[8] As he walked through it, he noticed a load of insecticides. He carefully read the label, discovering that the chemicals contained atropine. "I've been looking for this kind of cargo," he told the observer. "It contains the most dangerous kind of poison longshoremen handle. If you come in contact with this poison," he explained, "it'll turn you into a vegetable within five minutes." He said he would tell the LRC that when this chemical is shipped, paramedics would have to be present. Later that month, at an LRC, the union official made a motion that paramedics be present when chemicals containing atropine were shipped.[9] The PMA would not agree; a work stoppage would be necessary before the motion was considered.

"Typically indecisive," noted the observer to a rank and filer attending the meeting.

"Oh no," explained the longshoreman, "that's 'so-and-so's' *program*. He's always bringing that up" (field notes).

With this new perspective in place, the observer began to see programs in exchanges that were previously viewed as inconclusive arguing. Squabbles over bathrooms could be seen as "health and safety programs."

During general business at an LRC in early June, another union officer raised what he called "the shithouse issue."[10] He could find no toilets within 200 feet of the docks on Pier 96. "That violates the health and safety regulations," he said.

---

7 Field notes.
8 Field notes.
9 Field notes.
10 Field notes.

"We're operating in compliance with the regulations," a PMA representative noted simply.

The union official drew a picture to show they were not.

"Show me where the regulations state 200 feet," demanded the PMA officer.

The unionist took out his book, and with great glee pointed to the regulation. He told the employers if they didn't live up to the regulations, he'd have the men leave the job to relieve themselves. He might even shut down the job because of health and safety violations.

The issue was raised again at the next week's meeting.[11] Nothing had been done since the last meeting, said the union official. He told the employer representatives in an angry tone of voice, "we'll bring down that job on health and safety if you don't clean it up."

The PMA had obviously done their homework; they had read the regulations carefully. "The toilet situation on Pier 96 does not constitute an immediate endangerment to health," a regional PMA officer stated matter-of-factly, "because there are means available to get the men a toilet nearby."

"I'll bring the place down," reiterated the unionist.

Four months later, the same union official asked the PMA what it was doing about the "situation with the shithouses at Encinal?"[12]

"We're in compliance," said a spokesman, smiling.

"If you don't get some portable shitters out there soon," the angry union officer threatened, "I'm gonna bring down a ship on health and safety."

Ten minutes later, the same unionist announced that the toilets at 9th and Grove Street in Oakland were not being maintained properly. "If you don't clean them up," he said in a very businesslike tone of voice, "we'll have to tell the men to use the toilets downtown. It might take them a half hour and they'll be on the payroll. But if that's how you want to handle the issue, that's what we'll do."

Unwritten programs have a number of recognizable traits. They focus on issues that never get completely resolved. One aspect of the problem may be adjudicated, but the basic dispute continues. They are also associ-

11 Field notes.
12 Field notes.

ated with particular union officials. Each officer typically pursues a program of his own. These programs, moreover, are usually not local union policy. No resolutions have been passed that mandate the officers to pursue them. These activities therefore represent independent programs waged on behalf of the membership. Another feature of programs is that they are called such by rank and filers, even when politicos use another name. The final characteristic of these programs is that they are used by politicos when running for office. "This is what I've been doing," or "I'm working on these problems," say people who point to their programs when they solicit votes, or justify another term in office.

THE POLITICOS

Elections, running for office, making records, and programs are considered one kind of politics in Local 10. Being political, in San Francisco's longshore local, however, has more than one meaning. Longshoremen also use the word "political" to communicate a deeper, more profound understanding of certain behavior. Being political has an *abstract* meaning in their vocabulary. Some people are routinely political. Called "politicos," these longshoremen do not need elections to be political. Everything they do is interpreted as political.

For example, longshoremen regularly travel between ports on the Pacific Coast. Transferring between gangs and the hall is routine. But everyone who transfers is not "running for office." Militant talk, arguments over the contract, and hindsight vision are typical among longshoremen. But not every speaker who does this is suspected of making the record. Many Local 10 members have a standard set of grievances and they regularly voice them. Every list of complaints, however, is not a "program" or a "platform." Most of Local 10's members are not "political" in these senses of the term. For the majority of them, political involvement is restricted to attending membership meetings, voting in union elections, or simply paying dues. Their political participation in the union is minimal and obligatory.

Being political in Local 10 is limited to a relatively small group of longshoremen, people who participate regularly and extensively in union activities. These people, affectionately called "politicos" by other long-shoremen, seek election to union office; they routinely speak at meetings; they are quoted by the media; they sign union petitions and leaflets. Almost everything they do is interpreted as being political. Although it is difficult to define politico precisely, an obvious criterion is whether or not the person holds an elected position in the local. Despite some difficulties with this definition, it has advantages. One is that there is no disputing who is elected to union office. Another is that this definition probably undercounts the number of politicos because it does not include people who actively participate in the union even when they do not run for office. Thus, it does not exaggerate the number of politicos. In this chapter politicos are defined as people who are either elected to office in primary elections, or participate in runoffs. The positions they seek are: president, vice-president, secretary-treasurer, business agents, dispatchers, Board of Trustees, sergeant-at-arms, Publicity Committee, Promotions Committee, and Executive Board.

Regardless of how the politicos describe their behavior, no matter what they do, rank and filers usually call it: "running for office," "making the record," or "establishing a program." Local 10's members have good reasons for talking about politicos in these terms. If the results of elections during the period when this study was conducted are any indication, it most certainly looks as if they are being political. Of all the people eligible to run for office only 5 percent ran. Only 2.4 percent of the voting membership were elected in the primaries, or advanced to a run-off election. Nearly two-thirds (59 percent) of the elected officials, moreover, held more than one office. Better than three-quarters (77 percent) of the offices were held by people elected to more than one position. If one person holds two offices, and sometimes three or four, one has obvious reason to interpret office holding as being political. The uneven distribution of office holding among politicos, then, confirms the belief that they are being political, even when, on the surface, their behavior is indistinguishable from everyone else's.

The offices sought by people seeking multiple positions also give credibility to this interpretation. Two-thirds (68 percent) of the Local 10 members who pursued multiple candidacies sought positions that would take them off the docks for a year or two.[13] Thus, rank and filers have good reason to accuse office seekers of being political. What clearly looks like personal gain is one result of office holding.

Elected officers appear political in still another way. Virtually everyone who stands for election runs for the Executive Board. The Executive Board seats thirty-five people. Most committees have five openings; titled offices offer only one or two. The chances for getting elected to *some* office, then, increase considerably when multiple offices are sought and when one of them is on the Executive Board. Rank and filers know this. Thus, they have reason to believe longshoremen are being political when they run for Executive Board. The goal seems to be election insurance, not principled behavior.

The kinds of work union activists do, and don't do on the waterfront, the boards they work and don't work, also give credence to talk about their behavior being political. They work in job categories that make it possible to be political. They work almost exclusively in conventional longshoring. When the field research was done for this book, none of the elected officials were Special Equipment Operators. They worked either in conventional categories, for the union, or did not work because of occupational disabilities. Not one politico was a 9.43 man.

Conventional jobs provide longshoremen with wonderful opportunities to be political. Because conventional holdwork and winch driving allow for an incredible amount of freedom, longshoremen working in these categories can be politically active at work. Because the work moves them around ships and docks, they can see troubles on the job and be seen, too. Politics and conventional longshore work also require common skills. Like politics, longshoring is a talk-intensive activity; communication skills are important. Since politicos are usually gifted talkers, conventional longshoring is a natural place to launch and cultivate political careers.

It is hardly surprising that politicos work in conventional job categories. Because a large percentage of Bay Area longshoring is containerized, conventional work is sporadic and infrequent. As a consequence, longshoremen doing conventional work frequently use the Pay Guarantee Plan to supplement their finances. Being on PGP is a mixed blessing. Because one

---

13 President, secretary-treasurer, business agent, dispatcher, and dispatch sergeant-at-arms.

is paid for not working, people on PGP have considerable free time on their hands. The politicos on PGP have therefore transformed technologically produced underemployment into an opportunity for union involvement. In 1980, almost half the politicos (46 percent), either did not work on the docks (they were on disability or working for the union); or they worked in job categories receiving nearly 90 percent of the PGP payments ("dock," or "dock preference," or "gang").[14]

These jobs enable longshoremen to be political. If they work, people in these categories know in advance when they will work. Thus, they can plan meetings. And, if necessary, they can attend late sessions when there is no job the next day. These jobs also give longshoremen plenty of time for union activities. Gang men work only two or three days a week and people on the "dock" and "dock preference" boards work even less because they are disabled or injured. Many politicos work the night side, a notoriously slow-moving shift that is even less supervised than the day shift. These jobs, then, offer a natural workplace for longshoremen who want to be political.

The self-selection of politicos into slow moving, conventional categories is another reason why rank and filers often discount the accomplishments of elected officials as just being political. Apparently when longshoremen who work off fast-moving boards address meetings it is assumed that they are not being political because their work does not encourage office holding. If they wanted an office, the reasoning seems to be, they would work in another job category. Thus, longshoremen's job categories make talk sound "political" when delivered by one person, and just a "speech" when spoken by someone else.

If liberty is secured by vigilance, democracy in Local 10 is healthy. The longshoremen's ability to see the cynical, self-serving side of being political is an important resource for democracy, and democratic possibilities. This consciousness enables them to discount, minimize, or contextualize the significance of the politicos' accomplishments. Put differently, this consciousness prevents longshoremen from being "snowed" by politicians. It allows them to see through high-sounding rhetoric and selfless

14 Based on PMA document passed across LRC table.

rationales covering up self-interested motivations. Thus, this awareness provides Local 10 members with a kind of x-ray vision into the political process. They realize that elected union officials, like presidents of the United States, to paraphrase Bob Dylan, "must sometimes have to stand naked." As a result, longshoremen don't put politicians on pedestals. They see them, rather, as mere mortals, whose behavior must always be monitored with a modicum of cynicism, whose speeches need to be taken with a certain amount of metaphorical salt, and who, therefore, can and *should* be regularly and periodically replaced. Given these insights into the political process, longshoremen are not easily dominated, taken advantage of, or fooled. No one is permitted to stand too far above or away from the rank and file.

This does not mean the union practices pure and unblemished democracy. Like most humans, longshoremen have been known to take liberties with the democratic process. Elected officials have embezzled union funds. Dissidents have been physically assaulted. And Local 10 members have used union office to advance their private pecuniary interests.[15] The patchwork on this political quilt has, however, provided the Local's rank and file with institutional opportunities for making informed choices and with safeguards when the process is jeopardized. Thus, democratic deviations are short-lived and, overall, exceptional because annual elections do not give memories time to get short. Elected officials get taken to task for what they do and don't do. And the back-to-the-bench rule helps in those instances when memory fails the democratic process. Were one to chart the Local's political trajectory, the line would therefore not be unidirectional. However, despite some serious fluctuations, it would move consistently in the direction of maintaining and repairing an essentially democratic political posture.

POLITICAL COMMUNITY AND SHOPFLOOR CONTROL

The idealism, morality, and vision that distinguished West Coast longshoremen in the 1930s is kept alive, in good part, by the community ILWU

15 None of these democratic digressions occurred while I was doing field research. Nevertheless, according to numerous union sources, there was a period in the late 1960s and early 1970s when the Local's democratic process was abused.

members experience daily. Longshoremen learn through practice, every-day, that community can be an operating reality as well as an ideal. Since they need not compete with each other for work, longshoremen can – and their fraternal feelings encourage this – treat each other as objects in themselves instead of instrumentally, as means-to-an-end. Their experience with the ILWU teaches longshoremen that the principles of community are not just remnants of ideals passed. They are living realities, too. Treating each other as equals encourages longshoremen to take responsibility for their fellow union members. They learn through experience that what happens to a brother affects the entire fraternity, that an injury to one really *is* an injury to all. Thus, longshoremen are encouraged to be moral, as well as economic actors. Their community uses a language and set of principles that provide them with the grounds for doing things because it is "right" to do them, not only because it is necessary.

San Francisco longshoremen maintain the view that they can define relations between them, act on history, and be "a little arrogant," because their experience as workers serves as a benchmark against which operating realities can be measured *and* resisted. Freedom, equality, and brotherhood are experienced concretely by longshoremen. They routinely talk about these principles. Longshoremen therefore know when community is at risk, and transgressions of it are neither accepted as normal nor treated like business as usual. Violations of what they experience as freedom, equality, and brotherhood become objects for attention, comment, and action. Their experience of community then, is a source of opposition to bureaucracy in the union and domination at work. Thus, these principles of community have created a political culture in the union that underwrites the enforcement of democratic practices and undermines employer domination of the workplace.

Union democracy as practiced by Local 10 members is also a weapon in the contest for control of the waterfront. Because longshoremen actively participate in union affairs, shopfloor disputes are immediately shared, collective responses can be formulated and mutually enforced before moderating influences are imposed. The culture of insubordination fuels this process, encouraging militancy and union officials who share this inclination. Direct participation in union affairs is transferred to the docks, and the public politics practiced in the union hall prevents elected officials

123

from making deals with employers that do not have rank-and-file approval. The grapevine, the flexible work schedule, and the daily dispatch empower longshoremen to keep tabs on elected officials and discipline employers. The back-to-the-bench rule discourages protracted solutions to problems that can be solved immediately on the docks.

Local 10's participatory politics educate San Francisco longshoremen in the details of practical democracy. And the lessons learned in the union hall are practiced on the docks. The points of contention between employers and Local 10 members, then, are not mediated or masked by the union experience. If anything, union participation gives voice to the legitimacy of grievance and enhances the sense of outrage experienced by union members when they are not taken seriously or treated as equals by their employers. In combination, the sense of community experienced by Local 10's membership and the radical democracy practiced by the union have produced a vibrant political culture among San Francisco's dockworkers. Because the principles enunciated by this community are also resources for insubordination as well as self-actualization, that political culture, as the next three chapters suggest, enables longshoremen to use knowledge and codes created on the job, along with collectively bargained contracts, as weapons in their continuing battle for shopfloor citizenship.

Tugboat bringing crane alongside ship to lift a load too heavy for the shipboard cranes. Pier 27, San Francisco, 1979. Copyright © by Pat Goudvis 1979.

Part III

UNIONISM, WORK, AND
TECHNOLOGICAL CHANGE

Without our brain and muscle not a single wheel could turn . . .
From "Solidarity Forever," by Ralph Chaplin

L OCAL 10's political culture was seriously tested by McCarthyism
in the 1950s. It was also put to a second test in the early 1960s. This
time, however, the challenge came from a contractual agreement signed by
the union, not from the government or the employers' association. The
agreement came to be known as the "Mechanization and Modernization
Agreement" (M&M),[1] the first of which was signed in 1961. This agreement allowed employers to introduce radically new technologies on the
waterfront.[2] Once in place, these new technologies seriously transformed
the operational circumstances of West Coast longshoring. The industry
became capital intensive and work came to resemble factory tasks. Compared to conventional dockwork, the job became routinized and machine-
paced. Traditional craft skills became unnecessary, the sequencing of ship
work was preplanned by computer, and control of the labor process was
centralized. The second M&M, signed in 1966, also had a profound impact on the waterfront. That agreement modified dispatch rules and job
categories. Section 9.43, for example, was added at this time. The new
M&M Agreements reduced the union's ability to use the contract as a
weapon, and initially allowed employers to determine manning scales.

All the conditions were present for class relations on the waterfront to
be radically altered. Shifting to capital intensity would, if critics of automation proved correct, free employers from their dependence on workers'
knowledge and initiative, settling the issue of workplace regime in man-

---

1 For detailed accounts of the M&M, see Fairley (1979); Hartman (1969); Larrowe (1977);
Mills (1979b).
2 This paragraph paraphrases Mills and Wellman (1987:192–4).

agement's favor once and for all. The new technology would accomplish what the government and employers' association had been unable to do.

But that did not happen for two reasons. First, as the following three chapters will show, the technological revolution did not live up to its advance billing. Because the union decided not to oppose technological innovation, the nature of dockwork *did* get radically changed. But that did not settle the matter of workplace governance. Although some traditional skills became less important, new ones were needed. The work continued to demand initiative, and employers still relied on longshoremen's knowledge to move cargo. The new technology did not transform class relations in ways that were expected.[3]

The principles of political community learned by longshoremen also played a part in deciding the fate of technological change. Longshoremen were encouraged by these principles to insert themselves actively, mentally, in the work process, to take responsibility for their actions, to object when their skill went unacknowledged and unrecognized. They insisted on being taken into account, being consulted about how work would proceed. And when they were disregarded or ignored, they objected, sometimes stopping work, sometimes slowing down, and sometimes refusing to be dispatched. Both the political community and institutionalized union practices longshoremen had established during the ILWU's first thirty years enabled them to maintain their autonomy, to enforce self-regulating codes, and to fight with management for control over technologically advanced terrain. Thus, although containerization radically transformed the longshore work process, it did not destroy the longshore political community.

Dockworkers continued to insist on being treated as citizens of the waterfront. The longshore culture of struggle and solidarity was too well entrenched to be defeated by technological innovation. The evolution of class discourse could not be contained. To paraphrase William Sewell, the "conceptual or discursive transformations" that radicalized the French and English working classes in the 1830s had transformed West Coast longshoremen in the 1930s. And, like the situation in Europe a century earlier, "the genie of class discourse, once created, proved very difficult to get back

3 For alternative and critical interpretations of this process see Mills (1976); Swados (1961); Theriault (1978); Weir (1974). The reasons for the discrepancy between my interpretation and theirs is discussed later in this section.

into the bottle" (Sewell, 1990:71). Indeed, the controversy surrounding the M&M Agreements sharpened rank-and-file longshoremen's ability to debate intelligently and self-consciously the issue of job control.

The new technology did not fundamentally alter class relations or create the brave new workplace predicted by critics of modernization. But it did produce an ugly debate between longshoremen. The political fabric of Local 10 is increasingly dominated by two social strands. Like loose threads running through the center of a coarsely woven fabric, they threaten to unravel the political quilt which, until now, has unified a radically heterogeneous group of workers. By transforming traditional skills, the new technology has created a volatile argument over the nature of skilled labor on the modern waterfront. The disagreement reproduces the controversy over de-skilling that has been debated by scholars.[4]

The dispute is waged with loaded and self-interested language. Modern longshoring requires "sophisticated" equipment, argues one side, which equates skill with containerization. In this view, the more complicated the machinery, the more skill is required. The oppositional case is equally straightforward. "Your grandmother could drive the biggest container crane in the world," reports one longshoreman (Mills, 1977:23). Another says: "I found out that operating any piece of equipment is nothing but self-confidence. It's got nothing to do with skill. The machine almost guides itself, so it's all self-confidence."

One side highlights the necessary skills required by the containerized technology; the other downplays them with ridicule. Of course, the stands people take are influenced by their social location in the work process. Not surprisingly, people who emphasize the skills necessary to do modern work tend to be longshoremen who are working "steady" on container docks, and union officials defending the M&M Agreements. Longshoremen working out of the hiring hall, or in gangs (the people who work with conventional technology), on the other hand, tend to discount the amount of skill needed to drive cranes.

---

4 Proponents of the de-skilling thesis include Braverman (1974); Clawson (1980); Edwards (1979); Gordon, Edwards, and Reich (1982); Mills (1976); Noble (1977, 1984); Weir (1974); Zimbalist (1979). For a critical look at the de-skilling hypothesis and an alternative interpretation for the modern work process see Adler (1986a, 1986b); Blauner (1964); Doeringer and Piore (1971); Finlay (1988); Hirschhorn (1984); Sabel (1982); Salzman (n.d.); Spenner (1983); Thurow (1975).

Each side talks about skill using self-interested language. Justifying steady employment because of skill enables 9.43 longshoremen to ignore the allegation that their steady employment is a reward for loyalty to their employers.[5] The argument made by hall men, on the other hand, is equally self-interested: If steady men are not skilled, then longshoremen doing conventional work cannot be defined as being less skilled than 9.43 men.

The depth of this controversy, however, is not understandable by simply identifying the disputant's social location. Although the side people take is related to their place on the waterfront, that does not explain the intensity of the argument. Unless something else is at stake, why should longshoremen be so invested in an issue that is clearly not an either-or matter? Buried beneath and hidden by the talk about skill are some deeper issues.

Until recently, longshoremen had a common conception of skilled labor. All longshore work, regardless of contractual category, was recognized to require ingenuity, initiative, and judgment. The new technology, however, has fractured that shared understanding. The social definition of skill has become problematic, and taken-for-granted assumptions about competence are now contested. Thus, the very language and logic by which the industry defines and redefines itself, sets priorities, and establishes financial reward is at stake in this controversy. Because the new technology has reduced opportunities to work, the argument over self-definition, priorities, and worth is waged along mutually exclusive, either-or lines. Advantage is gained by highlighting differences, not by emphasizing shared features of the work. As a result, people have a stake in invidious comparisons.

---

5 These people were called "steady men," or "nine point four three men" (9.43 men) until 1978, because, like gearmen, they worked "steady" for a stevedoring company. The term "9.43" referred to that section of the 1966 contract that allowed employers "to employ steady, skilled mechanical or powered equipment operators." Instead of being dispatched from the hiring hall, "9.43 men" went directly to the job; they were guaranteed at least one month's work. In 1978 the contract was amended to equalize opportunities for crane work. A formula was created that allowed crane operators hired out of the hall to share the work with 9.43 men. For every 9.43 man an employer put on the payroll, one crane driver had to be hired from the hall. The new contract also kept crane drivers in contact with the hall. It specified that Special Equipment Operators (SEO men) cycle in and out of the hiring hall, working two months as steady men and one month off the dispatch.

The intensity of debate is fueled by another matter. Before the modern technology was introduced, the term "old-timer" designated more than seniority. It took years to master conventional longshoring and the title recognized that accomplishment. The old-timer was a respected long-shoreman; young dockworkers aspired to be one, and community "elders" took pride in the prestige that accompanied this title.

Old-timer, however, no longer refers exclusively to skilled longshore-men. Although still a term of endearment, it is now invoked independently of seniority and ability. Longshoremen are currently certified as "skilled" once they complete a four-week training session conducted by the PMA. The modern technology has therefore created a new meaning of skill. It is a contractual understanding and the employers, not longshore-men, determine who has achieved it. This definition of skill is neither produced nor shared by longshoremen; it is imposed from outside and it has wreaked havoc with their tradition of respect for experience and their sense of self-worth. People no longer need to spend years on the water-front to earn the title and, more important, have it conferred by the community.

The new technology alters the relationship between age and skill in yet another way. Because the work involves physical strength and quick re-flexes, the SEO category puts a premium on youth. Special equipment operators therefore tend to be relatively young. As a consequence, the people who, contractually speaking, are the most skilled are also the youn-gest and newest members of the union. The traditional relationship be-tween experience, ability, and reward, then, is inverted; the conventional longshore currency for self-worth is devalued.

The future of longshore community is also an implicit issue in the argument over skill. When longshoremen become 9.43 men their rela-tionship to the community is seriously altered. Although their earning potential is increased, their dependence on the union is decreased, which makes acceptability to supervision crucial if one is to be employed under Section 9.43. Thus, steady employment seriously threatens the fraternity, equality, and freedom that has traditionally underwritten a sense of com-munity among San Francisco longshoremen.

The debate over skill has therefore become verbal terrain upon which the struggle for community is waged. The language of skill allows longshoremen working 9.43 to express union loyalty even though they are employed steady. By invoking skill, they can claim their employment is based on their merit, not their loyalty to an employer. By the same token, however, hall men who minimize the skills of modern longshoring are making the loyalty issue a high priority item on the community's agenda. Because, in their view, containerized work requires minimal skills, they can insist that the only reason why 9.43 men are steady employees is because they are loyal to stevedoring companies.

What gets lost in this argument over skill, what gets hidden by the heat, is that skill, like most human concepts, is defined socially. The social definitions of it, moreover, are negotiated, located, and debated. Because skill, like death, is clear-cut and simple only when defined nominally, skilled labor cannot be conceived abstractly, in binomial, ordinal terms. And when it is, equally powerful – and contradictory – cases can be made that skill has been eliminated – or enhanced – by the containerized technology. Given one's conception of skill, both positions are correct because the same job is assessed by competing and conflicting criteria. As a result, like scholarly debates over the consequences of modern technology, the two waterfront sides talk past each other – and with the same consequences: The de-skilling controversy becomes an intellectual cul de sac in both locations.

Because they share the same set of binary distinctions, longshoremen and scholars of modern technology talk in remarkably similar ways with predictably similar outcomes. Both assume that skill is either the product of craft technology, or correlated with machine complexity: Longshoremen argue over whether the modern technology "de-skills" or "upgrades" work; sociologists distinguish between "mental" and "manual" labor. Both dichotomize between types of work: Longshoremen contrast "simplified" versus "complicated" work, or "supervised" versus "autonomous" jobs; sociologists debate "habituated" versus "self-actualizing" work, or "routinized" versus "self-regulating" jobs. The trouble with these binary distinctions, to put the matter simply, is that routine work practices do not neatly fall into one or the other category. They combine elements of both.

To move out of this sociological blind alley, these ideologically loaded concepts need to be defused, and the terms of debate seriously revised. Rather than assume skill is a binary quality, one needs to observe actual workplace practices and explore the complex, cognitive processing required by all jobs. Instead of dichotomizing between kinds of work, it makes more sense to analyze nuances of initiative necessary for any job to be accomplished. Thus, the approach advanced in this book takes neither side in the argument over skill as it is currently formulated. Rather, it offers another way to think about skill and the relationship between skill, technology, and class relations.[6] By reformulating the terms of debate, this approach assumes that all work involves continually engaged *cognitive processing,* and that this mental energy is translated into *initiative,* without which work does not happen (or it happens slowly, or poorly, or both). Worker initiative, in turn, makes employers *dependent* upon the workforce. And employer dependence, in its turn, gives workers *potential* power vis-à-vis their employers.

This conception produces an understanding of the relationship between skill and unionism that is different from the two sides debated on the waterfront and in the academy. The connection between work process and shopfloor control is seen in a new light. Assuming that work of any kind requires knowledge and initiative, the question this conception asks is not does modern technology eliminate skill? Rather, it asks, how is initiative organized? And, under what conditions is labor's potential power actualized in its relationship with capital?

6 I am indebted to Jan Dizard for this formulation.

Holdman (longshoreman) working at Pier 32, San Francisco, 1979. Copyright © by Pat Goudvis 1979.

Longshoreman working in the hold as a lift driver discharging cotton from a ship at Pier 27, San Francisco. Copyright © by Pat Goudvis 1980.

7

WORK, KNOWLEDGE, AND CONTROL: CONVENTIONAL LONGSHORING

L ONGSHORE work is shaped largely by the maritime industry's technology. That technology has three components: the cargoes being transported; the vessels used to transport cargo; and the gear necessary for moving cargo to and from its place of shipboard stow. Coordinating and integrating these components creates a range of challenging and changing operational circumstances for dockworkers. Longshoremen routinely work cargoes of differing size, weight, and packaging. Differences in ship design and deck configuration also complicate the work considerably. Each ship varies with respect to its design, capacity, and the state of its shipboard gear. To compound the diversity in circumstance encountered by longshoremen, loading sequences are dictated by the ship's subsequent ports of call. Adding to the complexity of longshore work is the wide variety of technology used on the docks.

Given this complicated configuration of technology, longshore work requires not only physical strength and stamina, but also initiative and ingenuity, diverse skills, and experience, an ability to innovate cooperatively. Indeed, because the pace and difficulty of longshoring is not just a function of technology, and because the work does not lend itself to continual supervision, efficiency on the docks depends upon the decentralization of initiative.

Focusing on five types of longshoring in two technological contexts, one can see how potential power is generated, and sometimes realized, on San Francisco's docks. The cognitive work necessary for doing conventional longshoring, and the initiative required of the work, is analyzed in this chapter. The cognition and initiative required of containerized work is discussed in Chapter 8. These chapters show how waterfront employers are dependent on longshoremen in both contexts. Although containeriza-

137

tion has changed the terms, it has not reduced the need for employee initiative.

In the conventional context, the jobs analyzed are "holdman," "winch driver," and "gearman"; the containerized categories are "holdman" and "Special Equipment Operator" (SEO). Each job category is analyzed along two dimensions: (1) the intelligence, or cognitive work necessary to do the job; and (2) the degree of autonomy, or initiative associated with each kind of work. These five job categories are a sample of waterfront jobs; they present a picture of the range of work done in this industry, from the oldest to the most modern forms of dockwork.

HOLDWORK

As long as sea-going vessels have carried cargo, there has been holdwork. And until less than thirty years ago, "holdmen" in San Francisco and Phoenicians in the holds of ancient ships basically did the same work. In conventional longshoring, holdwork is labor done in the hold of a ship. The work varies from "hand handling" cargo – literally moving cargo by hand – to driving lift trucks; from putting "dunnage" – pieces of wood – between cargoes to building ramps or "skids" along which cargoes can be moved; from hooking on cargoes to lashing cargoes to decks; from humping 500–600 pound bales of cotton to lumping hides of dead animals.

The hold of a ship is its basement. Cargo is stowed there many feet below the vessel's deck. The hold is also the basement from which longshore careers begin in San Francisco: Every person in Local 10 must work at least five years in the hold before being promoted to deck- or dockwork.

Contractually speaking, holdwork is the most unskilled labor on the waterfront. Since everyone's introduction to longshoring takes place in the hold, the work serves as a kind of apprenticeship. To the casual observer, the job seems to depend strictly on brawn. "There is a stereotype of a longshoreman walking past most people's eyes," said an observant participant: "His back is a little hunched, he's got powerful arms, he wears work-type clothes, a white cap, and he carries big hooks."

Things look different through the eyes of holdmen, however: The job is routinely challenging, it requires multiple skills, it calls for critical judg-

138

ments, and even has pleasurable moments. The modest pleasures occur mostly when holdwork is done on conventional operations. The work is out of the weather. "If it's hot," said one holdman, "you're cool down below. But if it's cold outside, you're warm down below. So the job goes with the weather." The work is rarely routine: "There's a different ship, a different look, a different dock, a different man and a different cargo everyday," observed another longshoreman. "Every time I go to work, I'm doing a basically different job."

Depending on the type of cargo and its location, accomplishing a "tight stow" on loading jobs involves special abilities and judgment. The work is not routine, and it taps mental as well as physical abilities. Knowing how and where to stow the nearly infinite variety of cargoes is challenging. Certain cargoes fit nicely in the bow, others in the wings of the hatch. Building and stowing cargoes can be like working a complicated jigsaw puzzle with do-it-yourself pieces. The task is an important one and the stakes are high. If cargo is not stowed properly, it will shift at sea causing the ship to list, endangering the lives of crew members. Thus, handling cargo in the ship's hold involves a great deal of ingenuity.

The ingenuity required enables longshoremen to leave signatures of their personhood on the work and to have pride in it as well. One expression of the personal signature is known in San Francisco as putting a "Yankee Face" on the cargo. A Yankee Face is the last tier of cargo stowed in a "slam-bang" fashion. The cargo is handled sloppily until the last tier. This tier is stowed perfectly because it is observable from the ship's deck. Thus anyone looking down on it will think the holdmen have done an excellent job stowing cargo. Sometimes odd-sized cargo is finished off with a Yankee Face. In Los Angeles a Yankee Face is called a " 'Frisco Face," which is evidently the southern California definition of phony.

When the work is done well, the men take pride in it. "I can do the job better than anybody else," said one; "that's why I'm a longshoreman. I'm not a rinkey-dink cherry picker." The hostility expressed toward people who do not do their job well shows the pride holdmen take in their work. Someone who builds sloppy loads unintentionally is sarcastically and derisively likened to a person who does not know how to work with his hands. A longshoreman who does a poor job and does not know it, is, as

139

one longshoreman remarked, likely to be told, "You work like a fucking shoe salesman! What the hell are you: a shoe salesman or a longshoreman? How come you're working so stupid?"

The cognitive dimension of holdwork

Holdwork is governed by rules, or principles that longshoremen must know and be able to improvise around. The basic activity of holdmen is to lift cargo and move it. Mental energy enters the work at the point where the skill level implicit in everyday lifting is surpassed. Anyone can lift but everyone cannot lift. As an occupation, lifting begins with what everyone knows about it and then proceeds mentally to refine, elaborate, and perfect the state of the art. One direction of improvement over merely human power is the strength of horsepower and fuelpower. The machine, however, is not a thoughtful lifter. The asset of human power is improvisation and ingenuity, and holdmen improvise around a number of principles.

Knowing how to lift. Principles of lifting are one set of circumstances around which longshoremen work creatively. The variation in cargoes requires that holdmen be able to adjust their techniques of lifting to the cargo at hand. There is no uniform way for handling bales of cotton, sacks of coffee, or variously sized boxes and lashings. Unique cargoes call for multiple principles of lifting.

The act of lifting is itself an object for thought. Being able to lift continuously for eight hours or more is possible only when holdmen grasp principles of lifting and use them creatively. Some holdwork cannot be accomplished with human power unless the people working know how to do it. A 250-pound drum will break the back of anyone uninitiated in the rules of human lifting. Most people would have difficulty even budging the object. There is a knack to moving heavy barrels and people discover it if they are going to do waterfront work. Longshoremen learn how to bend down, get underneath the drums, and flip them so they can be lifted without injury or immediate exhaustion.

Bales of cotton sometimes weigh more that 500 pounds. The men handle these bales with large "cotton hooks." Knowledgeable longshoremen working partners move cotton in a manner that is deceptively effort-less. The bales are rolled and bounced, apparently with a minimum of effort. Waterfront neophytes quickly learn, however, that brute strength does not move cotton. The longshoreman who relies strictly on force finds that he, not the cotton, is the object that moves.

"The first time I worked cotton," an old-timer recalled, "these two southerners rolled a bale down to me and hollered: 'Hey you! Get it.' I grabbed it, and it almost threw me down. I didn't know how to handle that stuff."

Lifting bales of cotton is reflexive work; it requires concentration. To pick up cotton, longshoremen squat down, shift the bale onto a lift truck with a little bounce, and then pull back on the hand truck. Once the bale is in this position, the men can turn it in any direction. Longshoremen call this kind of lifting "standing cotton on its lip." If the bale is not tilted correctly against the bulkhead of a ship, it falls and the men are unable to move it.

Working partners. Most longshoremen "work partners," where two people work together as a pair. "Working partners" decreases the amount of work one person must do. The arrangement also allows longshoremen to avoid the daily dispatch since partners can "pick up jobs" for each other. Because partnerships often last years, they become marriages of sorts, with all the attendant joys and difficulties. Thus, choosing partners is carefully done; it is an important part of the work.

Finding partners is not easy. A "good partner" has many attributes. He is protective, both physically and psychologically. Working with a "good partner" means four eyes are looking for loose material that might cause a fall; an extra pair of eyes is searching for a "bite [knot] in a line" that could catch a leg. Good partners also know how to work safely and properly; they carry their weight and sometimes even more. A partner can make the difference between a good day and a bad one. "I like to work with that guy," one San Francisco longshoreman is fond of saying, "he makes hard jobs easy, and easy jobs a rhumba." The work may be hard, and even quite dirty, but the rewards of partnership make it worthwhile. In the words of another Local 10 member, "the emotional relationship between partners is more important than tonnage, weight, and statistics." Finding and sustaining waterfront partnerships is complicated; knowing how to do it is an important part of longshoring.

Working partners requires another kind of mental energy. Partnership can be achieved only when longshoremen know the principles that underwrite the relationship. Lifting cotton, for example, requires more than reflexivity and concentration. Cooperative ingenuity is also needed. Lifting bales of cotton is difficult, and sometimes harmful, for partners. Partnership happens when two longshoremen learn to lift as one. But knowing how to lift as one is not so simple as it sounds. Sometimes one longshoreman is weaker than his partner; other times one of them has not properly placed his hook. Unaware of this, the other partner comes up with all his strength. When the lift is not synchronized, serious back injury is a strong possibility. Working partners requires knowledge of a partner's strengths and weaknesses, the ways in which he moves, as well as his working idiosyncrasies.

Working partners is also psychological work. Partners' moods are critical in determining how to work. Because partners work in close physical proximity, being able to act as a team is crucial. If one is in an ugly mood, the other has to know when to be sympathetic, when to cajole, and when to get angry. Thus, knowing how to facilitate interpersonal relations is another working principle of partnership.

Stowing cargo. Longshoremen are routinely called upon to improvise around stowage principles. Ships are not square. The hold of conventional freighters is not constructed at right angles; the walls are not perpendicular to the deck. The hold is concave, curving gently from the ship's main deck to its hull. At either end of a ship, the hold sweeps forward or aft, narrowing in width as the vessel's sides becomes its bow and stern. Holdmen have to stow cargo in this odd-sized and shifting terrain. Considerable mental work goes into evenly stowing uniformly sized boxes in conventional holds. The sloped walls in the hold of a ship conflict with the geometry of boxes. Despite this, longshoremen are expected to stack boxes evenly, both vertically and horizontally. The cargo "face" is expected to be uniform, as if the hold were square.

Longshoremen have a concept for this process. They call it "taking out the sheer." Since every conventional ship is unique, and no two cargoes the same, taking out the sheer is conceptual work. Successfully accomplishing the task on one ship, moreover, does not guarantee it can be done the same way on another. Thus, this cognitive energy is rarely transferable.

"Tying" or "locking" cases or sacks requires knowledge of another stowage principle. Every other layer of cargo is begun with the first case or sack turned so that the narrow end faces the center of the hold. In maritime language it is turned "athwartships," and pulled out to be flush with the cargo face. The cargo is staggered like bricks in a wall, and a built-in lock, or tie, is created to prevent slippage at sea (Weir, 1974:246). Being able to take out the sheer and tie cases requires ingenuity and resourcefulness; the work is intensely mental, calling for three-dimensional vision and foresight.

Maintaining the body. The most important work tool used by longshoremen is their body. The physical strength generated by holdmen is crucial for moving cargo. An injured body is therefore damaged equipment. But the possibilities for injury are considerable because lifting is as hard on the human body as it is dangerous. Thus, longshoremen are robbed of their youth prematurely; age creeps into their faces at a point in the life cycle when many cohorts in other jobs still look youthful. Waterfront language gives voice to this process. Longshoremen frequently comment about another, "he's all beat up from hard work." Sometimes they say, "he's got the word 'work' tattooed right across his forehead." Recognizing the dynamic between body and work, longshoremen improvise around rules for lifting. The object is to work the work, to use the work to condition the body.

"The kink in my back is gone," writes author-longshoreman Eric Hoffer, commenting on the dialectic between work and body, "yesterday's work did it" (Hoffer, 1969:14). Hoffer could get rid of the kink because holdwork requires a variety of lifts. Various parts of the body are used with different kinds of lifting. When cargo is lifted above one's head, the back muscles are strained. Lifting objects directly off the floor, on the other hand, taxes the thighs and stomach. Carrying a lifted item requires arm muscles. Longshoremen have a working knowledge, an implicit understanding of the principles of physiology, anatomy, and physics. When possible, they improvise on these principles to maintain the body as an

143

effective instrument for labor. They vary lifts during a shift to prevent one part of the body from being consistently exposed to injury or fatigue. Longshoring, then, is cognitive work – it is not simply physical labor. The mind as well as the body is used; loading and unloading ships requires ingenuity and innovation. In a word, the work involves intelligence, or, in Anthony Giddens's terms, "reflexive monitoring" (Giddens, 1979:53–9; 1984:5–14).

THE SOCIAL ORGANIZATION OF INITIATIVE IN HOLDWORK

To improvise around the principles of holdwork, longshoremen must communicate. Longshoring facilitates communication with numerous opportunities for talking. In conventional longshoring, the job itself is an occasion for talk. The work must be explained, it cannot simply be ordered. The holds of conventional ships are densely social scenes when longshoremen are working. There is much talking on this job: talk about how to do the work, the origin and destination of the cargo, the ship and its gear. The talk is a form of communion, like the ritual song in the traditional workplace. Jiving adds rhythm to the patter of talk, thus moving it halfway toward the ritual use of songs. An outsider is struck by the sociability of longshore work:

> As I walk down the ship's deck I come to a hatch opening and I lean over to see what the guys in the hold are doing. The hold sounds alive with chatter. "Thatta boy!" exclaims a holdman to his partner. "Knew you could do it," he encourages sarcastically. "Way to go, way to go, way to go," harmonizes someone else. "That's right baby!" calls out a holdman to a hatch tender on deck. "A little more over here, over here . . . yeah, that's it. You got it poppa!" he shouts, signaling that the hoist is proceeding without problems. (Field notes)

An old-timer, writing fiction, describes the scene similarly:

> It is just past eight o'clock, and the men turn-to with a boisterous spirit, singing, whistling, hammering at themselves with good natured profanity.
>
> The yard boom, the one nearest the dock, is being pulled by hand out over the dock.
>
> Charley's eyes are constantly aloft. He shouts and swears with exaggerated intimidating intent.

144

Charley: Slack the fuckin' mid-ship guy! You – the cherry with the ponytail! Shake hands with the goddamn preventer chain, will ya?

A young hippie, hair tied back, gawks over his shoulder at Charley, cowed by his presence. He pulls awkwardly on a heavy, grease-covered chain.

Charley: That's a good girl. Careful ya don't get yer fuckin' hands dirty! All right, get the boom out, for Christ's sake!

There are men at work everywhere you look. Forklifts weave in and out of the shed bringing various kinds of gear alongside the ship. Again, the sounds of the dock match those on deck – profane, happy, musical. (Hamilton, 1979:67)

In addition to requiring cognition and communication, longshoring calls for ingenuity. Longshoremen are not tied to machines nor paced by assembly lines. Longshore work is not started, integrated, or paced by physically located machines. Efficient longshoring therefore requires that dockworkers know how to exercise judgment and use initiative. Because conventional longshoring relies on these kinds of know-how, management is quite literally dependent upon dockworkers if waterfront cargo is to be effectively and expeditiously loaded and unloaded. Supervising stevedores too closely is therefore counterproductive; longshoremen must be left to their own cognitive devices, and encouraged to work independently. Management knows this. They realize that conventional holdwork requires skill and technical knowledge; and they assume longshoremen know what they are doing. Thus, generally speaking, they treat holdmen respectfully; they recognize the personhood of their employees. When they do not, supervisors jeopardize the working relationship, and production as well. As a result, most conventional holdwork is not directly supervised by gang bosses or walking bosses.[1]

---

1 Contractually speaking, "gang bosses" are "supervision." They can fire gang members. But using this sanction successfully is complicated and gang bosses rarely act as supervision in this sense of the word. The position is an elected one, and abuse of it can result in a petition for removal. Gang bosses also belong to the same union local as gang members. They therefore share an organizational affiliation and loyalty with the people they are supervising. Finally, a longshoreman who is "fired" can be dispatched to the job from which he was fired. Given these complications, the line dividing gang bosses from gang members is not sharply drawn. In fact, gang members routinely view gang bosses as "time keepers." There are differences between the categories to be sure: Gang bosses receive a small pay differential (twenty-five cents an hour); they transmit instructions from the walking boss to the

145

Hold gangs work with relative autonomy. So long as holdmen keep the cargo moving, supervisors need not be in the hold. Gang bosses know the quality of work their gangs can do; they assume holdmen know how to work and will ask if they have questions. Thus, when the work is getting done, the gang boss remains on deck. He assumes that if the cargo disappears into the hold, the men below are capably doing their job. The principle governing this process is revealed in a waterfront saying: "Keep the (cargo) hook moving," as San Francisco longshoremen say. When this principle is followed, waterfront supervision is inconspicuous.

Supervisors determine neither how the work is to be done, nor its pace. Instead, work practices are influenced by the cargo, the gang's experience and ingenuity, and the pride and cooperation with which the men work. Indeed, overzealous bosses who scrutinize work too closely routinely find that production drops. Thus, the relationship between gang bosses and holdmen is typically respectful; the terms are established through reciprocity. Deciding how to work is a cooperative project, and plans evolve through give-and-take. According to one longshoreman, the following kind of exchange is typical:

> Holdman: What do you got on the dock there?
> Gang boss: We got some drums and some rugs and a tank. What do you want?
> Holdman: Send me the drums first 'cause we got a place under the coaming here where we can put these drums and then you can send the rugs. We'll put some rugs on top of the drums.
> Gang boss: What if I send the tank first?
> Holdman: No, god, don't send the fucking tank down here because the tank won't fit in the wings.
> Gang boss: Are your sure?

gang; they inform the gang about work locations; they keep the time sheets, and sometimes they suggest how the work might proceed. Practically speaking, then, gang bosses are not supervisors.

Walking bosses, on the other hand, are more clearly supervisors. Walking bosses are foremen assigned to walk the length of ships and docks to supervise the work. Hence, the origin of the job title. They are not elected; rather, they are selected by stevedoring companies. They have their own local union within the ILWU. Their job is to convey the superintendent's plan for loading or unloading a ship, and they can fire people. They see that the work proceeds expeditiously. They are management's representative on the ships and docks.

Holdman: Well, throw me down the tape and I'll measure it. How tall is
   the tank:
Gang boss: The tank's 12 feet.
Holdman: We don't have room under the coaming to get it in so you'll
   have to put it in the square of the hatch.

Since holdmen are rarely pinned down by close supervision or machines, the work allows for an incredible amount of freedom. As a result,
the pace and quality of conventional holdwork are determined by the
relationships that develop between longshoremen, not by the scrutiny of
supervisors. When holdmen work conscientiously, they do so out of a
sense of self-respect, or because they want to be regarded highly by their
partners and other members of the gang. Reputations earned in the hold
have serious consequences; they extend at least to the hiring hall. Holdmen working out of the hall who are known as poor workers discover that
partners are difficult to find. The rewards for hard work, on the other
hand, come in smiles and greetings, along with offers to work partners at
some future date. In conventional holdwork, then, hierarchies are established by work performance as judged by the men themselves, not the
employer.

The rules for how to work are not found in official documents. Rather,
they are established on the job and enforced flexibly. So long as the hook is
not "hanging" (either waiting for a hoist or with a load), gang bosses ignore
a wide variety of proscribed work practices. If the men choose to spell each
other, and alternate the work between two teams, gang bosses will not
intervene so long as the work gets done. Even though it is contractually
banned, gang bosses will occasionally allow longshoremen to work, "four-
on-four-off." The men who are "off" do as they please for four hours. If
someone has a doctor's appointment, that person can leave the hatch and
remain on the payroll.

Since the operational circumstances of longshoring are complicated and
unpredictable, formal rules need to be relaxed for the work to be done
effectively. Officially agreed-upon rules for handling cargo have to be
modified when ships are late or stevedoring equipment is not up to code.
Sometimes, gangs do not "fill" (someone fails to show for work), or
longshoremen dispatched to a job do not have the appropriate skill credentials, or someone leaves the job early. These situations are routine, and

147

when they happen, management and labor work "around" the problem; they generate informal agreements for working. The operational circumstances of waterfront work therefore create the potential for power from below. Longshoremen are in a position of strength because management depends on their working knowledge to get the job done and relies on them to flexibly enforce contractual rules.

Longshoremen frequently act upon this unofficial but potential source of power. They make a variety of "deals" with management around work practices. These deals are possible because each side recognizes and respects the other's potential power. The deals represent exchanges between equals, both of whom have access to a different source of power and a recognized ability to use that power. Thus, the deals involve quid pro quos. For example, the men agree to work faster than normal, exceed speed limits on auto discharges, go without lunch or coffee breaks, work "shorthanded" (work with fewer hands than are contractually required), or do unsafe or onerous work, in exchange for being allowed to leave work early.[2] Sometimes management "permits" people to work without a skill card. This deal allows supervisors to keep the job going without waiting for a "skilled" longshoreman to be dispatched. It also permits longshoremen who make the bargain to work enough hours to be credentialed eventually.

Because both sides have access to power in these encounters, the agreements are routine and explicit. In contrast to deals struck between sides without equal power, these deals are quite open and visible.[3] Waterfront deals are underwritten by the potential power that is generated by holdwork. If longshoremen had no power in the work process – were management not dependent on the knowledge contained in their skill and initiative – there would be no need to make deals and recognize them

2 Longshoremen are contractually entitled to eight hours' pay when they present themselves on a job to which they have been dispatched so long as they are not fired during a shift. The men are paid for six hours at straight-time rates and two hours at overtime rates, regardless of how many hours they actually work. Known in the industry as "six and two," or the "eight-hour guarantee," these terms were awarded by arbitration after the 1934 strike. With the guarantee, longshoremen can be induced to work faster without suffering potential loss of pay.
3 For further discussion of "deals" and modifying work rules on the West Coast waterfront, see Fairley (1979); Finlay (1988); Larrowe (1955); Mills (1978a).

publicly. Supervisors could do as they pleased without the consent of longshoremen and the work would still get done. Thus, the deals are an openly effective and reciprocated use of potential power.

WINCH DRIVERS AND GEARMEN

After holdwork, winch driving is the next oldest job on the waterfront. Exactly when winches appeared on sailing vessels is difficult to establish. Winches were, however, observed on the docks in the late 1880s (Hobsbawm, 1967:244). Before winches, longshoremen drove "donkey engines": steam-driven machines. Probably the first fuel-driven power used by stevedores to make a hoist, the donkey engine was most likely introduced soon after the steam engine was invented in the early 1800s. The industry's first winch drivers were therefore known as "donkey engine drivers"; they appeared on the docks at the beginning of the nineteenth century.

Gearmen, in their own estimation, are the "heart" of the longshore industry. They make it possible for the work to be done. Longshoremen working in the "gear locker" maintain the equipment, or gear, used to load and unload ships. All the chains, bridles, hooks, and lifts used on the waterfront are kept in working order by gearmen; they make the gear available to longshoremen at the beginning of the day and they collect it at shift's end. They build, repair, handle, and haul all stevedoring equipment.

The mental labor of dockwork

Winch drivers work the ship's gear. They work vessels that typically contain between five and eight hatches. The ship's gear is mounted on the deck, located next to each hatch. "Gear" refers to a series of masts or booms mounted at one or both ends of each hatch. At the center line of the vessel, near each hatch opening, are two adjacent winches. Wire ropes or "falls" pass through blocks at the top of each boom. The falls permit booms to be independently lowered or hoisted by winches. Two falls are attached to the ship's cargo hook, or "blacksmith"; each fall runs from the hook to the winches passing through blocks at the head and heel of the positioned boom. One boom is placed or "spotted" directly above the

149

hatch and the other is located above the dock area where cargo is "slung" or "unslung." Once the hook has been shackled to the free end of both falls, it can be traveled between the dock and the hold. When cargo is being loaded aboard ship, the cable attached to the "inshore" winch – the winch closest to the pier – lifts the fall that is connected to the hook. Cable is taken up on this winch and played out on the "offshore" winch. The winch driver then lowers the cargo into the hold using the offshore winch.

Winch driving is intensely mental work. It carries significant responsibility. Each time the hook moves, holdmen working below labor in harm's way and the winch driver is directly responsible for their safety. Working safely is therefore one of the primary principles for properly driving winches. Knowing how to do that requires a considerable amount of knowledge. Winch drivers also work a different job each time they are dispatched. To complicate matters, winches vary from ship to ship in terms of design and state of repair. Ship design and hold configurations also vary widely among vessels sailing to the Bay Area. The variety of cargo handled on conventional operations adds to the complexity and depth of knowledge required to drive winches.

Like cognitive work in any industry, winch driving is as much an art as a skill. When winch drivers lower heavy cargo into the hold, they work the two winches against each other to keep the load from swinging. They must anticipate the movement of cargo and control the swing by playing out cable on one winch while taking up slack on the other. "When something swings," said a winch driver, "you shift it the other way and that stops its swing. I know guys that can have a hook really swinging and they go: boomp-boom! They stop it just like that: boom! It stops right there."

"You get to be talented on it," he concluded, "it's like a ballet almost."

Operating winches is complicated seriously, and requires extra mental energy when the operator drives "blind." Sometimes winch drivers cannot see where the hook is being worked. Their view is obscured either because of the configuration of the hold or the location of the winch controls. "Driving blind" means a winch driver relies on the "hatch tender's" signals. The hatch tender stands where he can see the operation and read signals from longshoremen in the hold or on the dock. Sometimes acting like a police officer directing traffic, other times like a symphony conductor, the hatch tender signals with his hands, his arms, subtle movements of his fingers, and often with his entire body. The hatch tender's performance is accompanied by a steady stream of verbal patter mostly to himself. The mental effort necessary to drive blind is extensive. In this instance, longshoremen are called upon to make calculations according to an elaborate although implicit set of physics principles, to interpret and communicate through a complicated and rich set of gestures, and literally to envision a process they cannot actually see.

The cognitive work winch drivers do, and the mental energy they expend, is recognized and rewarded by the longshore industry. They receive a wage differential, earning fifty cents an hour more than holdmen. The high regard fellow longshoremen have for winch drivers' cognitive skills is also reflected in the rich lore they share about the "great" winch drivers, and their talk about the "brains it takes" to do the job.

Gear work also requires cognitive energy. Gearmen must be proficient with other kinds of skills that engage the mind. These longshoremen are competent actors in at least three skilled activities. They must be a combination machinist-repairman-welder, who can drive large semitrucks over the highways, be knowledgeable about the principles of holdwork, and know how to drive winches as well. Just being able to perform these tasks, however, is not enough; gearmen must also be a master of each one. In addition to knowing the gear and how to keep it working, they are sometimes called upon to actually *create* it.

Gearmen and winch drivers do mental work different than other longshoremen. They do not use the same working principles as holdmen. Winch drivers need not be concerned with stowage principles, and gearmen do not "shake hands" with the cargo. Thus, although their work takes a toll on the body, the price they pay is not nearly so high as the one exacted from holdmen. As a result, winch drivers and gearmen do not think about their bodies in the same terms as holdmen. Even though safety is always an issue, winch drivers and gearmen are not directly exposed to the hazards of holdwork.

Driving winches and working in the gear locker is, however, governed by principles that require considerable mental energy. Winch drivers concentrate intensely on the operation while making a hoist; little else is on their minds. They are preoccupied with hand-eye coordination, safety considerations, and nonverbal, signaled communications. Viewed from

151

the hold, where exhaustion is produced by physical labor, the winch driver upstairs appears to have it easy. He sits, and between hoists his arms are folded.

When holdmen become winch drivers, however, they quickly develop a different perspective on the job. The task does not require extensive physical energy, but it is mentally exhausting. "You don't have to break your back" is the way one winch driver put it, "but you got to use this," he said pointing to his head. Keeping an eye on the men below, another on the cargo being hoisted, or on the hatch-tender's signals, and operating the winches without looking directly at the handles is cognitive work in the most basic sense of that term. And like mental labor in other contexts, it takes a toll on the driver. Some winch drivers find that when lunchtime arrives, because of the tension produced by intense concentration, they are unable to eat. And at the end of a day, they leave work "all shook up," said an old timer.

Repairing equipment and treating it well is also cognitive work. Gearmen must know how to work creatively and be able to improvise to keep the gear in working order. They have to know the principles of welding, machine repair, and equipment building. The work itself also requires mental energy. As gearmen put it, they work "with their wits." Gearmen who can devise a new piece of equipment or repair an old one with available materials are invaluable. Like all cognitive work, the demand for new ideas is built into the gearmen's job.

THE SOCIAL LOCATION OF HIERARCHY AND INITIATIVE IN DOCKWORK

On the winches

Like holdmen, winch drivers and gearmen work relatively autonomously. Management's dependence on their working knowledge is recognized, and, although their relationship with supervision is more complicated than holdmen's, their personhood is respected at work. Winch drivers either work with a gang or out of the hall, "off the plug." Once dispatched, they work for a gang boss or a walking boss. They work "for" someone, however, only in a limited sense of the word. They relinquish neither

152

mind nor responsibility to supervisors. Winch drivers need not be told how to work. They know how to drive winches and, because they have been longshoring for at least five years, they know to keep the hook moving.

Although winch drivers are quite knowledgeable about the work, they must still discuss it. Like holdwork, the job requires cooperation, which makes communication essential. Since winch drivers are often well respected, the talk is conversational when they communicate with holdmen and "supervision." They sound like people engaged in a common project. The topic is mutual problem solving, and the banter between hatch tender and winch driver described earlier is typical. Thus, as with holdmen, supervisors do not tell winch drivers how to do the job or how fast to work.

Winch drivers are essentially in charge of their work and management honors that fact. Successful supervisors interact with winch drivers carefully and respectfully. They do not remind winch drivers that the hook is not moving – there's no need to. And because contractually "correct" procedures for making hoists do not exist, it is counterproductive to insist that winch drivers hoist cargo in a particular way. Firing a winch driver for judgment calls is also difficult. The contract is ambiguous and so firings cause serious disputes. Even when winch drivers are "successfully" fired, the dispatch system recycles them to jobs supervised by bosses who originally terminated them. Thus, supervisors do better when they make proposals and discuss alternatives as opposed to firing winch drivers. And unless they are invited, supervisors tend to stay out of discussions when winch drivers and holdmen talk about how the work should proceed.

Winch driving is not, however, unsupervised work. Sitting above deck in the pivotal job connecting dock and hold, winch drivers work in full view of everyone. There is no one on the waterfront who cannot see the winch driver. And if the hook is hanging, or moving erratically, everyone can see it. Thus, unlike holdwork, winch driving is carefully observed. This visibility makes fellow longshoremen supervisors who are not indifferent to the quality of work. Since longshoremen are at risk when winch drivers work carelessly, or are under the influence of alcohol, it is holdmen who typically "suggest," in colorfully blunt waterfront language, that the driver be more careful or go back to the hall. Management is usually not even consulted. This kind of supervision from below, by holdmen, amounts to an implicit expression of workers' control over winch drivers.

Supervising is, however, done from above as well as below. Since winch drivers are not completely ignored by employer representatives, it is difficult for them to take "hikes" as frequently or for as long as holdmen. Nevertheless, they can and do work deals with gang bosses to cover for them. As a result, winch drivers sometimes attend personal business during a shift. However, because the winch drivers' competence is more visible than the holdmen's, winch drivers are more vulnerable to supervision even though options for handling incompetence are limited contractually. Thus, ironically, although winch drivers are, contractually speaking, "skilled" laborers, and holdmen are not, winch drivers do not have as much freedom on the job or control over it as holdmen do.

In the gear locker

Unlike winch drivers, gearmen work "steady" for stevedoring companies. Like 9.43 men, they go directly to the job; they are not dispatched from the hall. This arrangement works well for gearmen. First of all, bypassing the hall means they can leave home for work later. Gearmen also make ninety cents an hour more than winch drivers. But most important, working steady guarantees a week's work. Having a job therefore does not depend on ships being in port, and gearmen's pay is not influenced by shipping schedules, weather conditions, or chance.

The employers also benefit when gearmen work steady: Through regular association with the company, the men become familiar with the gear, its location, and company practices. Thus, supervisors do not have to show new men where the gear is located and how to use it. If gearmen work steady, work can begin promptly when the shift starts.

The employers gain more than convenience, punctuality, and efficiency from steady employment status. A deeper advantage is produced by this arrangement. Gearmen tend to be loyal workers. Since they are not dispatched by the union according to universal criteria, gearmen working steady can be hired for personal traits desired by companies. Employers can hire whomever they please as steady gearmen and they unilaterally

154

select longshoremen by name and registration number.[4] Given the advantages of steady employment and the unilateral basis for inclusion, unlike holdmen and winch drivers, gearmen are encouraged to be loyal to their employers. As one of them remarked in a moment of unguarded candor, "We're actually company men."

The arrangement sometimes works against gearmen. Steady employment depends on loyalty as well as skill, so union protection is limited. Because they work at the pleasure of a stevedoring firm, gearmen can be released and returned to the hall on grounds the union cannot contest. In contrast to holdmen and winch drivers, the relationship between gearmen and supervision is therefore a delicate one. Employers need gearmen's skills, reliability, and loyalty; and gearmen want steady employment. Thus, unlike holdmen and winch drivers, gearmen are guarded around supervision. Under normal circumstances they don't openly disagree with or disregard the employer's representatives. When proposing procedures for work, they invoke the company's "interests." They are susceptible to management's verbal darts. The price of steady employment, then, is the appearance of loyalty.

Loyalty, however, also has its toll. Gearmen work on their own; they are rarely supervised directly. Unlike holdmen and winch drivers, they do not work for gang bosses or walking bosses. They are immediately responsible to superintendents who tell them what the job is, and they are rarely seen thereafter. Thus, gearmen themselves determine priorities, strategize about tactics for repair, weigh alternatives, order parts, and generally decide how the work should proceed. In this respect, they are among the most autonomous workers on the waterfront.

The job of caring for and nurturing equipment is critically important. When gear is not properly maintained, stevedoring companies incur additional expenses: Longshoring takes longer, or the union stops work. Thus, unnecessarily antagonizing gearmen puts the entire operation at risk. It is therefore difficult to know where the gearmen's loyalty ends and their employer's dependence begins. Gearmen have an equally complicated relationship with fellow longshoremen. Their steady employment status

---

4 There is a strong sense of resentment among union members about this practice; people feel abused. The union has formally accused employers of using race as a criterion for hiring gearmen, but so far the charge has not been sustained by an arbitrator.

and apparent employer loyalty make them suspect to men working out of the hall. Nevertheless, their skills command respect, and longshoremen depend on quality maintenance work for their physical survival.

The complicated relationship between gearmen, supervision, and long-shoremen is created by the strategic location of gearmen in the work process. Gearmen work at the point of the production of safety. Equipment maintained in good working order is presumably safe to operate. Part of the gearman's job, then, is to intercede in the ongoing debate over abstract considerations of the "proper" working order of gear when disputes erupt between management and the union. In arguments over safety, the gearman's area of expertise is not that he knows better than anyone else whether a piece of equipment really needs repair. He does, however, know more directly, because he can see what is actually to be done. The judgment he renders is inherently controversial: His concern for the equipment's state of repair is sometimes construed by other workers as taking the employer's position; other times his concern for the men's safety is taken as evidence for being on the longshoremen's side. This aspect of the gearman's job is complicated seriously by the union's inability to defend him successfully.

In the cab of a container crane. Copyright © by Pat Goudvis 1980.

Crane operator going to work. Copyright © by Pat Goudvis 1979.

8

WORK, KNOWLEDGE, AND
CONTROL:
CONTAINERIZED LONGSHORING

WHEN a freighter loaded with Hawaii-bound containers left San
Francisco's Matson docks early one June morning in 1958, most
people had no idea what would happen to longshoring in the wake of that
sailing. Moving along the waterfront like a tornado through a town, the
container transforms everything it touches. Truck trailers have been replaced by vans that sit on interchangeable chassis. Railroad boxcars have
given way to flatcars that carry only containers. Ships the size of aircraft
carriers, which only transport containers, have taken over for tramp
steamers carrying general cargo.

Even the waterfront's landscape has been transformed. Continental
railheads used to end miles from the docks; an overland highway connected rail and sea. Now trucks, trains and ships begin and end their
journeys within sound, and, in some instances, sight of each other. The
ribbons of railroad end abruptly at the coast where they are connected to
rows of warehouses framed by a skyline of cranes. For a moment at least,
the various components of the transportation industry come together.

The contrast between containerized and conventional longshoring is
dramatic. Conventional longshoring is concentrated. It is restricted to
piers. The piers occupy five to seven acres of land. Like fingers on a hand,
they extend offshore and connect cities to ships. In comparison, modern
container facilities are scattered throughout a port area. They require fifty
to one hundred acres of land.

Other differences are equally obvious. The "hook" in conventional
longshoring is a ship's "blacksmith," or cargo hook. It is powered by the
vessel's winches. In a container yard, the "hook" is a towering, four-legged
crane on tracks that travel the length of a ship. Sometimes three or four
cranes work simultaneously. Whereas it used to be said that longshoremen

were one of the few categories of worker who climbed down a ladder (into the ship's hold) to work, longshore crane operators now climb nearly seventy feet *up* to work.

In the relatively short time since the Matson ship sailed, the total tonnage handled by Pacific Coast longshoremen increased nearly five times.[1] During this period, the total revenue tonnage coming through Bay Area ports nearly doubled.[2] Although the amount of tonnage increased dramatically, however, longshoremen worked less. In 1971, Bay Area longshoremen worked 3,840,727 hours. By 1980, the numbers had dropped to 2,050,388.[3] Productivity and labor costs were altered profoundly during this period. The number of tons per hour handled by longshoremen increased nearly six times.[4] At the same time, however, the number of hours worked per ton decreased almost ninefold.[5] These figures reflect the important impact that containerization has had on the longshore industry: It dramatically changed the nature of cargo coming through the Bay Area port. Nearly four-fifths (78.6 percent) of the total tonnage coming into Bay Area ports in 1980 was either automobiles or containers.[6]

The social consequences of containerization have also been profound for the longshore workforce. Achieving higher productivity while lowering labor costs through a reduction in the hours worked by longshoremen meant many fewer dockworkers would be needed in the future. The number of registered West Coast longshoremen therefore dropped accordingly, from 11,724 in 1971 to 8,389 in 1980. This drop in numbers hit the Bay Area especially hard. Local 10 lost almost half its membership in the 1970s.[7]

The new technology has quite obviously and radically changed waterfront work. It has not, however, produced the dire consequences predicted by critics of modernization. Were these predictions realized, three

1 From 23,892,210 tons in 1958 to 113,992,702 tons in 1980. PMA Annual Report (1980:17).
2 From 9,573,167 tons in 1971 to 15,460,292 tons in 1980. PMA (1980:18).
3 PMA (1980:22).
4 From .837 tons per hour in 1960 to 5.498 in 1980. PMA (1980:16).
5 From 1.195 hours per ton in 1960 to .182 hours worked per ton in 1980. PMA (1980:16).
6 Calculations based on figures in PMA (1980:19).
7 The membership dropped from 3,466 longshoremen in 1970 to 2,034 in 1980. PMA (1980:20).

new developments should be observable on the waterfront: (1) Containerized longshoring would have eliminated judgment, ingenuity, and initiative from the San Francisco docks; (2) modern waterfront work would no longer require cognitive labor; and (3) reciprocity would no longer extend across class lines because management would no longer depend on dockworkers to exercise skill and initiative, and supervisors would not need to recognize the personhood, or citizenship rights of longshoremen.

When one observes actual workplace practices, however, that is not what is found. The skills necessary for containerized longshoring obviously differ from conventional skills, but the modern technology has not eliminated skill. New skills are required, and thus, in some contexts, re-skilling is occurring. Mental activity is also necessary on the modern waterfront. Longshoremen working on container docks are thoughtful actors, using an implicit body of working knowledge to accomplish their tasks. And so, though the bases for cognitive work have changed, the possibilities for it still exist.

There is also continuity in class relations. Reciprocity between longshoremen and their supervisors continues. Management still recognizes the personhood of San Francisco's dockworkers; citizenship rights are respected on the waterfront. And when they are not, the denial is contested. Thus, in this respect, longshoremen remain independent and autonomous workers. Finally, cooperation and freedom are regular features of work on the container docks. In a number of crucial contexts, management still depends on the patience, ingenuity, and initiative of longshoremen driving modern equipment.

COGNITIVE WORK IN CONTAINERIZED LONGSHORING

Containerized work is not very romantic, dramatic, or mysterious. So far as longshoremen are concerned, "a van (container) is a bunch of pallet boards loaded three or four high, like they were loaded in the old days."

"They're just put into the van and put up against each other so they don't slide too much, and then the door is closed," said one longshoreman. "That's all a van is."

Compared to conventional longshoring, modern work is standardized. The slingload never changes. Neither do the moves cranes make. When

161

containers are loaded and unloaded, they go to predetermined places. Their dockside and shipboard destinations are planned in advance by computers. The work is monitored, audited, sequenced, and controlled.[8]

Holdwork

Some holdwork is easier using modern technology. Powerful equipment does the heavy lifting; and holdmen put dunnage between the cargo or arrange it for the lift driver. Sometimes holdmen drive modern cargoes on and off ships. Driving cars is a frequent hold job in San Francisco. Although the cars are "cargo," the job experience is not handling cargo; it is driving cars, like working in a garage. Holdmen get in a car, start it, drive it off the ship, park it on a field adjacent to the dock, and then get in a truck that takes them back aboard the ship.

Containerized holdwork can also be difficult and dangerous. Most of it is "lashing": attaching or releasing the various fasteners ("turnbuckles," "cones," or wire ropes) that secure containers to the deck of a ship. The work is hard and dirty. Lashings are coated in grease, and some weigh almost one hundred pounds. Wrestling lashings about a deck is therefore strenuous. Lashing can also be dangerous: Holdmen frequently lash containers stacked three or four high. Known as "working on top," some thirty-five feet above the ship's weather deck, the work is always hazardous. It is especially dangerous at night or during heavy rains and strong winds.

Six-foot turnbuckles weighing seventy-five pounds are always lethal, regardless of the weather. The gear can "get away" from a longshoreman and seriously hurt him. Modern lashings are less heavy and greasy than the chains they replaced, but the mechanisms for securing tension are more dangerous. To get tension on modern lashings, a longshoreman pulls up on a handle that tightens the gear. When he has the handle in a tight position – all the way up – he has to "unbutton" or release it without losing the tension. This is done very carefully. If he is not skillful when he lets it go, and does not stay above or behind the mechanism, it is, in one man's

8 For an extended discussion of differences between conventional and containerized long-shoring in San Francisco, see Herb Mills (1976, 1977).

words, "like looking in the face of a bear trap." Stories abound of hands and feet having been broken by gear that has "gotten away." Longshoremen have been killed lashing.

In addition to being dangerous, lashing is, as one longshoreman said, "hard-ass work." Sometimes the men work ships they call "ro-ro's," or "roll-on-roll-off" ships. Cargo is literally rolled on and off these vessels with tractors driven by longshoremen. Local 10 members lashing on ro-ro's work inside the bowels of a ship. Workspace is extremely tight because clearance between containers is only a foot and a half. The lashings are attached beneath the vans in the dark. "It's a fucking nightmare down there," said one holdman.

Certain aspects of holdwork in containerized longshoring live up to its critic's worst fears. Longshoremen working in a modern hold very rarely get to use the skills they have mastered for conventional operations. There is not much room for error on this job. The work must be done right or vans will shift at sea. There is no need for a discussion about how to do the work. Only one way is correct. Thus, opportunities for ingenuity, experiencing a sense of accomplishment, and leaving a personal touch on the work have been transformed. Modern holdwork, however, is not without its mental challenges, skills, and even bases for pride. "Stuffing" containers may be routine work, but it is not possible to do routinely. "You have to show a little class when you load one of them containers," said a holdman. "You've got to use all the space." That is usually easy, he allowed, since the boxes being "stuffed" are typically of the same size. Nevertheless, it takes ingenuity to load odd-sized boxes. "They don't want no space left in there," he observed. "Because empty spaces don't make no money."

The sources for pride in work have changed. The personhood of individual longshoremen is rarely imprinted on modern jobs. It is impossible to put a Yankee Face on containerized cargo. Nevertheless, it is possible to earn personal reputations for doing the work well. "Mule and George," for example, are partners and they reportedly seek out lashing jobs. They are reputed to have the work "down to a science." The word is that "they're the best there is on the Coast. They're tops." Legend has it that when they board a ship to do lashing, the walking boss leaves; there is nothing he can tell them about the work. Longshoremen who mention the team know little about "Mule and George" personally. And the fact that George's surname and Mule's real name are unknown probably reflects the extent to which containerization has depersonalized the work process. Nevertheless, although Mule and George may not be able to leave their personal stamp on the containers they lash, they have established their imprint upon longshoremen: "All I know about them," said one man, "is that they're the best on the coast."

Being able to survive hazardous working conditions has also become a source of pride and an evolving skill. Occasionally, longshoremen who typically aim for the safest work will take a dangerous job, just to see if they can still do it. They will volunteer to lash atop containers three high. "It's a matter of pride," said one. Holdmen gain satisfaction from the realization that, as another man put it, "there is no longshore work I can't do."

Like holdmen doing conventional longshoring, holdmen on modern operations do cognitive work even before they reach the job. They must still think about the kind of work they want to do. Modern technology has reduced their options, but choice must still be exercised. Some of the modern facilities are already in poor repair; the container ships, moreover, were not designed with longshoremen's comfort in mind. Riding on tractors with solid rubber tires for eight hours or more over chuck holes and protruding metal locks feels like it can destroy a man's body. The older men must take this into account when choosing work; younger longshoremen can afford to ignore it. Equipment also varies by ship as well as by facility: Matson ships secure cargo with "Peck and Hale" lashings. Other companies use chains and six-foot, twenty-five-pound turnbuckles. Although equally difficult and dirty, some equipment is considered more dangerous than others. Thus even with modern work, longshoremen are engaged in thinking about suitable jobs.

Cognitive activity does not end when holdmen arrive at the modernized workplace. Longshoremen are not passive victims of new technology – they actively struggle with it. The modern hook may make standard moves in directions that humans do not determine. But the hook is more like a metronome beating out a regular tempo than a murderer of cognitive activity. Just as the position of a sliding weight determines the rate at which the inverted pendulum of a metronome beats time, the pace of the modern hook is determined by the hands of longshoremen on levers in cranes and lashings on containers. At times longshoremen collectively decide to work faster, to increase the speed of the hook. Since they are guaranteed eight hours' pay when the shift begins, they have an incentive to work faster on jobs where there is less than eight hours' work. Thus, the pace on "short" days is considerably faster than when there is enough work to fill eight hours.[9]

Establishing the pace of work on container jobs requires cognitive labor. Supervisors know the number of vans that can be lashed, or the number of cars that can be discharged in a given hour. They also know how many container moves can be made in an hour. But management's expectations do not determine the work pace. Rather, as is the case with conventional holdwork, these expectations become one of the many objects longshoremen take into consideration when they figure out how fast they will work. The men also consider weather. Weather affects the speed with which vans are lashed and cranes moved. Wet, windy weather can be cause for working slower. Equally important, because of contractual provisions requiring safe working conditions, weather is invoked as the cause for a change of pace. Longshoremen use weather as the grounds for a slowdown. Safety is another issue that is both cause and grounds for altering the work pace.

Supervision is a critical consideration in the determination of work pace, although not for the reasons one might suppose. Walking bosses and superintendents who act as though longshoremen are mules, and not worthy of respect, typically have a negative impact on output. Longshoremen slow down when they are treated as machine tenders. They work to rule, or slow down invoking either safety or weather, instead of openly questioning authority. Driving cars off auto ships at the legal limit (five miles per hour), for example, has a dramatic impact on production quotas.

Thus, cognitive labor is still necessary even in the most routine longshore work. Pace is not entirely a function of machine, and thinking is still required to do the work. Like musicians playing to the beat of a metronome, longshoremen working modern technology improvise on and around the tempo of the hook. They speed up, slow down, and sometimes just keep up with the crane. They spell each other and cover for people taking unauthorized breaks. Talk continues and respect is demanded. Thinking has not been eliminated by the modern machines.

9 For a detailed discussion of pace setting in containerized longshoring, see Finlay (1988).

165

Special equipment operators

Special equipment operators, or "SEO men" as they are called, drive the powered equipment at container facilities. They operate straddle trucks or "strads," tractors, lift trucks, and cranes. Crane driving is to modern dockwork what winch driving is to conventional longshoring: Cranes move cargo back and forth between dock and ship. Driving cranes is therefore very much like driving winches. Both operators are located some distance above the ship's hold; the moves they make depend on the eyes and ears of their fellow longshoremen. Like winch drivers, crane operators do hand-and-eye work; the job requires skillful hand-eye coordination. The crane driver's eyes dart back and forth between the container and its destination. His hands and feet look like they move independently of his eyes. He makes moves like an accomplished musician. "Isn't it beautiful how we do it," said one crane driver, as if to confirm the outsider's observation. "It's just like playing a piano. You know, like playing a song" (field notes).

Unlike winch drivers, crane operators receive their instructions over a two-way radio:

"What's next, Joe?" asks a crane driver working seventy feet above the docks.

"Flat-rack in the second cell off-shore, Jimmy," crackles a voice over the speaker.

"Got you poppa" (field notes).

The driver "gantrys" (positions) the crane abreast a designated hatch. Manipulating levers, he then extends the gear across the ship's deck directly above a cell in the hatch. With a flick of the wrist, he lowers the "bridle" that will hook on to a container. Even though each cell has guides along which the lifting device travels, and the bridle's "flippers" also guide it, hooking on to a container is hardly routine work. No two moves are exactly alike. When containers are unevenly distributed throughout a ship, the vessel lists to one side. The tides affect the ship's position in relation to cranes, and choppy water causes even the heaviest ships to bob. Thus the ship is frequently a moving target. To complicate matters, the cells are quite narrow and the driver is typically unable to see them directly. When there is no hatch-tender around, he has to estimate the angle of the cell

166

using shadows and beams as benchmarks. His benchmarks move, however, as the day wears on and the sun travels through the sky. Hooking on to a container while sitting some seventy feet above it is very much like threading a moving needle. It requires coordination, concentration, and unlimited patience.

The cranes move rapidly over ships. They stop at a hatch and hook on to a container. Below deck, in the ship's hold, the vans are stacked up to eight deep. The crane yanks up one of the containers, quickly moves back off the ship, and then lowers the big box onto a chassis pulled by a tractor. It makes these moves at least twenty times each hour. The cranes operate at impressive speeds. Some 35–40-ton cranes are able to hoist and lower at a speed of 225 feet per minute. As one stevedoring company advertisement says of its newest crane: "it wastes no time."

Driving cranes is taxing work. Because the operator constantly looks down between his knees to position the containers, the work puts considerable strain on his back, neck, and shoulders. The work also requires concentration, and this produces strain. As in the work of air traffic controllers, the margin for error is minimal: One mistake can be fatal. If a crane operator does not pay enough attention to the job, and a van comes loose, the consequences are serious. In addition to damaging the van, the ship might require repairs and that could keep it from going to sea. The stress and strain of driving cranes makes relief necessary. As a rule, crane operators are relieved at least every two hours during an eight-hour shift.

Special equipment operators also drive straddle trucks. Sitting twenty to thirty feet above ground, with communication restricted to a two-way radio, strad drivers have a unique perspective on the container yard. Because of blind spots, turning radii, and the cab's location, they have a better view of the whole yard than the area immediately adjacent to their machines. Their hearing is obstructed by high levels of machine noise, the "ear muffs" they wear to reduce that noise, and the raucously loud beeping sound of the warning device attached to the equipment cab. Strad drivers pick up containers in the yard, take them to the dock, and drop them beneath the hook where they are hoisted aboard ship by crane. The process is reversed on discharge operations.

Some longshoremen complain that driving strads is boring work, espe-

167

cially on loading operations. In order to keep up with the crane, they have to work hard and drive fast. Although not monotonous, the work is, however, quite repetitive: Find a container, pick it up, drop it under the hook, again and again. There is very little time for unofficial breaks and, because the docks are like a freeway, these longshoremen seriously concentrate on driving. The work is difficult: Not only do the operators sit some twenty feet above ground, but they also sit at right angles to the direction in which they are traveling. Thus, they drive in an unnatural position, looking over their shoulder.

Strad drivers and crane operators are the heart of the containerized technology; they make the contemporary industry move. The amount of time ships spend on berth is related to the speed with which these longshoremen work. When a container vessel is on berth the docks are like a freeway. Since four cranes sometimes work one ship, each with four to six strad drivers assigned to it, the yards are congested. Container operations are as noisy, congested, hazardous, and difficult to negotiate as a highway during rush hour. Driving strads, like driving cranes, is therefore a taxing job.

Driving strads and cranes requires considerable skill and competence. Special equipment operators enjoy the competence and they relate it to a sense of technical command. In American culture, all driving jobs contain an element of adventure, especially the ones blessed with high levels of horsepower. Cranes and strads are powerful machines. Thus the operator is an empowered individual. Being in the air also contributes to a feeling of adventure and creates fears or fantasies about flying.

The skills required for SEO work approximate gaming or athletic abilities. It is therefore not surprising that SEO men use sport metaphors when they talk about work. Finding a container below deck is called "fishing." Getting ready for the day's work is referred to as "warming up like a pitcher." Shifts are called "games": "The day game starts at 8. Will you be ready?" The special equipment operator's job contains a sense of responsibility, controlled danger, and fun. The work may have its routine aspects, but it is also interesting.

Like other longshoremen, SEO men do cognitive work. They devote mental energy to the task, weather conditions, and other job-related matters. Compared to holdmen, they are preoccupied with the task at hand. Their steady employment status also tends to reinforce their preoccupation with the work. SEO men speak of leaving work "mentally tired"; some say their "head hurts" by the end of a shift. Holdmen typically find this difficult to understand. In contrast to conventional holdwork, which requires a thorough grasp of stowage principles, crane driving is utterly routine. The sling-load is standard. Crane drivers do not decide which containers are to be worked, their destination, or the sequence in which they will be worked. These decisions are made by other people using computers and their determinations are communicated by walking bosses or clerks over two-way radios.

Despite these limitations on cognitive activity, however, the work requires considerable mental energy. The mind must be engaged when SEO men drive blind, or load containers aboard ships that are listing. Their job is complicated enormously when they drive a crane that was designed to service a ship with different features than the one being worked. Crane driving is also discretionary work. For example, hatch covers on container ships weigh up to 56,000 pounds. When a crane driver is told to pick up a hatch cover and move it, he has to make a decision: Does he raise the hatch cover, and gantry with the cover hanging directly over the vessel? Or, does he lift the cover, position it over the dock, and then gantry to the next hatch? The first move takes less time. If, however, the cover comes loose and crashes onto the ship, the crane driver could be "grounded" (either sent back to the hall or taken off cranes). The second move is safer. If the hatch cover comes loose over the dock, only the cover gets damaged. But this move takes more time and crane drivers are judged by how fast they work.

Discretion is only one kind of mental work done by crane drivers. They must still "think ahead" on the job. Even though SEO men are not responsible for the sequence in which vans are handled, they have to anticipate what will be done next without being told by clerks or walking bosses. For example, crane drivers do not wait to be told that a hatch needs to be covered. They know when the hatch is completed, and they cover it without a word being spoken. They often know which hatch is to be worked next and go there directly before being told. To unsympathetic

169

holdmen, the crane driver's anticipatory work is considered "ass-kissing," or "kissing-up to supervision." But the crane driver's self-interested explanation is also plausible: "I don't like to work late," said one crane driver as he guided his crane rapidly to another hatch without being told. "Every time you wait a couple of minutes to be told what to do, you increase the possibility of working overtime. And I don't like to work overtime."

SEO work requires certain kinds of mental work that are not necessary in the hold. Unlike holdwork, SEO jobs can rarely be disattended; the task at hand can never be taken for granted. The skill involved is not the only issue. SEO men can be easily observed by supervisors. Thus, even if they are not preoccupied with the job they have to appear as if they are working. Their delicate relationship with supervision makes SEO men attend to management when they are not concentrating on the work. They have to impress these people if they are to be employed steady. Thus when SEO men are not preoccupied with the job, they often have management on their mind.

Even though operating special equipment requires one's undivided attention, the job allows longshoremen to think actively about things unrelated to the task at hand. The work is not always continuous. Computer error is common and longshoremen either misplace or can't find containers. When this happens, the strads cannot keep up with the cranes and crane operators have to wait or "stand by" for the next container. Even Matson, the Bay Area's most sophisticated longshore operation, has been unable to completely eliminate periods during which crane drivers stand by. The crane servicing ships at Matson's revolutionary facility in Richmond is fed by two other cranes: a "yard gantry crane" and a "mobile yard crane." The two yard cranes bring containers to a conveyor. Known as the "mousetrap," this conveyor holds up to five containers at one time.[10] Theoretically, the mousetrap keeps the ship-side crane working continuously. But the mousetrap stops when the yard cranes are feeding it. This, of course, gives the crane operator working the ship an unofficial breather. During these interruptions, he can read a newspaper, daydream, write in his time book, or look around and take in the scenery.

10 According to local lore, the name comes from the American folk saying, "If you want to succeed in business, build a better mousetrap." The container conveyor is Matson's "mousetrap."

THE SOCIAL LOCATION OF HIERARCHY AND INITIATIVE

The new technology reduces the freedom waterfront work has traditionally provided. Physical movement is limited; longshoremen are
pinned down on container jobs. The rhythm of the work responds more
to technology than to humans. The work can be audited and monitored
and is usually done in full view of supervision. It is therefore difficult to
wander between hoists, to spell one another, to cover for someone. The
new technology has also reduced management's dependence on labor's
ingenuity. Steady employment makes certain categories of longshoremen
vulnerable to employer priorities. Thus, open and heated arguments about
the work process are rare on the modern waterfront.

Holdwork

Even when holdmen work below deck, it is difficult for them to control
the pace of this work. Direct surveillance is not necessary to monitor the
job. Supervisors know how many containers need to be lashed, or cars
unloaded for a job to be completed. And walking bosses don't have to be
present to keep track. They know, at least to the hour, the time it takes to
lash vans or drive cars off a ship. And if the work is not moving fast
enough, there is no need for walking bosses to intervene directly; it is no
longer necessary for them to encourage or cajole slow-moving holdmen.
Because the work can now be monitored, supervisors are able to determine how many longshoremen are needed to complete a slow-moving
job. If necessary, they can call the hiring hall at mid-shift and order additional holdmen. As a result, the job does not depend upon cooperation to
the same extent as in conventional longshoring.

Modern technology has changed the relationship between holdmen and
supervision. Traditionally, the relationship revolved around reciprocity
and mutuality, and management depended on holdmen to figure out how
to do the work. Now computers decide. Thus, supervisors depend less on
holdmen's good will to get the job done. And walking bosses no longer
need deals to maintain a certain pace. Holdmen working modern technology consequently do not have the informal bargaining power that they
exercise in conventional longshoring.

171

This relationship, however, has not been completely transformed. Walking bosses acting unilaterally and arbitrarily find out that what is normally a half-day's work cannot be finished without additional long-shoremen working overtime. Deals continue to be made. Longshoremen lashing containers are permitted to leave early if they finish before shift's end. People discharging cars are encouraged to work fast in return for a shortened workday. Thus, management still depends on holdmen to get the work done; holdmen have not lost all of their bargaining power.[11]

The new relationship between management and labor, moreover, is by no means a completed project. It is emergent, an object for struggle in a contest over who will govern. There is not one kind of management–labor relationship on the modern waterfront. At a minimum, there are two: one produced by the needs of conventional longshoring, and the other by containerized work. These two relationships are sometimes within eye-sight of each other, separated by only a few wharfs. And within the period of one week, hall men cycle in and out of both kinds of relationship. Resistance to their loss of power is therefore fueled in this process; crucial aspects of the good old days remain in force and frame a current standard against which the possible future is assessed.

Operating special equipment

Special equipment operators occupy a particularly vulnerable place in the work process. In exchange for a regular, high-paying income, SEO men who are employed steady give up their right to choose when they will work and what they will do. They also relinquish the freedom to argue forcefully with management about how they will work. Longshoremen dispatched from the hall don't risk very much when they argue with walking bosses. The worst that can happen is they get sent back to the hall and lose a day's pay. But when SEO men get into a dispute with manage-ment they jeopardize the very terms of their employment. If an SEO man is returned to the hall the union can do almost nothing to save his steady job. Like gearmen, then, these longshoremen have a complicated and sometimes compromised relationship with supervision. They have to be

11 For an extended account of "deals" on the containerized waterfront, see Finlay (1988).

careful about what they do, guarded in their talk, and sensitive to production quotas.

Nevertheless, the relationship between steady men and management is not a one-way street with all the initiative coming from the employer's direction. Supervisors want to use their modern equipment to its fullest capacity. If this is to happen, SEO men must be treated respectfully and given opportunities to make decisions. Thus, cooperation and reciprocity are features of their relationship with employers.

Special equipment operators do not work in gangs that are recognized contractually. Employed as individuals, technically speaking, they work by themselves with supervision from walking bosses. In fact, however, SEO men work in groups that they speak of as "gangs." In this instance, the gang contains a walking boss, crane drivers, strad operators, and clerks working together regularly.[12] The relationship between crane drivers and walking bosses in these modern gangs resembles relationships between management and labor in conventional gangs. Crane drivers are not ordered around by walking bosses. When instructions are given, the tone of voice is conversational; directions are formulated as requests; the characteristic exchange is give-and-take. The following exchange, which was overheard in the cab of a container crane, is typical:

"Hector, what's the number on that box [container] in the fourth cell in-shore?"
"15854, my man."
A couple of moves later: "When you drop that box, Hector, would you pick up that hatchcover on 15 and put it on 9?"
"Right on, Jim."
"Thanks."

Management still relies on the initiative of workers in modern longshoring and their relationship is still reciprocal. Obviously, important changes have taken place in relations between these two sides. Walking bosses now work with computer printouts that tell them where containers are located and in what sequence they will be handled. This gives management an understanding of and control over the work process, which is

---

12 Clerks or "checkers" keep track of cargo. They record which cargo has been loaded or unloaded, where it is stowed aboard ship or placed on the dock. They have their own local unions in the ILWU.

unknown in conventional longshoring. Nevertheless, because container ships are so large, walking bosses cannot actually see the containers until they are hoisted by crane drivers. This gives the crane operator an advantage. From his seat, he can see the entire operation as well as specific containers. Thus, even though he does not know what his next move will be, he is the only one who can actually see where all the vans are located. In this respect, then, the walking boss continues to be dependent on crane drivers. It is therefore not surprising that good-natured ribbing and humorous bantering can be heard over the two-way radios in container cranes. An example:

> "Hey Gino," calls the walker over the phone, after Gino has deposited a van on the pier. "What are you trying to do, dust the docks?"
> "No man," replies Gino as he holds a microphone in one hand and a lever in the other without even slowing down, "Joe's already done it this morning." (Field notes)

Deals continue to be struck between men in these gangs. Sometimes, for example, crane drivers work what they call a "three-legged job."[13] This occurs when two crane drivers are periodically relieved by a third operator. These three longshoremen rotate between the two cranes. When relieved, the drivers are free to do as they please. Since the relief driver does not start until two hours into the shift, he can attend to personal business in the morning. The men decide among themselves who will drive first and who will drive relief. Management stays out of this decision. On some operations, crane drivers also work "partners": One man drives the crane and the other "tends hatch." Although the typical arrangement is to drive two hours and tend hatch two hours, partners sometimes vary the time they spend in the cab or on the ship. The decision is made independently of supervision.

Crane drivers are not machine tenders and they do not automatically follow orders. When they have reason, they argue with walking bosses. For example, while one crane driver was observed loading a hatch an order came over the two-way radio to gantry down the dock, pick up some

---

13 In conventional longshoring a "three-legged job" refers to a practice where three winch drivers work one hatch. Two sets of winches are driven in cooperation with each other while the third longshoreman tends hatch. The term is used in modern longshoring even though the operational circumstances are quite different.

holdmen, and lift them aboard ship to lash. "Wait a minute, man!" he responded. "I only have a couple more boxes before this hatch is finished. Let me do this hatch first and then I'll pick them up."

"OK," said the walker, "but let's try and move it."

Asked why he objected to the order, the crane driver explained that "going down the dock to pick them up takes time. I'm going in that direction when I finish this hatch. If I have to gantry down and then back before I finish, it'll take me forever to get done" (field notes).

Special equipment operators are often suspect in the eyes of longshoremen dispatched from the hall. The suspicion is generated by their steady employment status and their apparent loyalty to employers. There is, however, a deeper source for suspicion. Because of the very place they occupy in the work process, special equipment operators sometimes co-opt management's standpoint. The men operating cranes and strads have a larger picture of the work process than any other longshoremen. Working high above the dock, they can scan and observe the entire operation from above. They see the various tasks done by other longshoremen in relation to their overarching job of swinging cargo from place to place. From these heights, the empowered part of the process is taken for granted. And as a result, special equipment operators complain frequently about the slow work pace performed by holdmen. They apparently do not take seriously the different machinery empowering holdmen who basically work manually. Thus, the broader view of management is built into the special equipment operators' physical location in the work process, not simply because of factors like aspiration, ambition, or loyalty to the employers.

Anyone working in the SEO category finds himself in an unavoidably difficult job. The work is hard, sometimes dangerous, always isolated, and typically observable. The men's loyalty is questioned by fellow longshoremen and manipulated by employers. The union's ability to defend them is severely curtailed by the terms of their employment. And finally, the coincidence of management viewpoint with the work process picture coming from the heights of powerful machines routinely brings these men into conflict with people from their own union.

The longshoremen's relations with management are complicated by yet another feature of the containerized waterfront: There are fewer opportunities for talk on this job. Longshoremen are isolated on container

175

docks. Hand-drawn stowage plans that require discussion have been replaced by computer printouts; face-to-face exchanges have given way to
squawk boxes and walkie-talkies; the social density of a ship's hold has
been supplanted by the individual intensity required in the cab of a crane
or strad. These changes make it difficult to share grievances and plan job
actions; SEO men cannot talk face-to-face while they work.

But the modern technology does not stop communication. A complicated conversation of gestures goes on between longshoremen and between longshoremen and supervision. The air waves at container yards
also crackle with human voices. The talk is obviously restricted, but it has
not been eliminated. When lashing aboard container ships, holdmen are
denied the ease of talk they find in the hold of conventional vessels. They
do, nonetheless, create the social space necessary for talk. Working partners and getting ahead of management expectations for output permits
people to talk, even if it is momentary and irregular.

A considerable amount of communication in modern longshoring has
been relocated to social spaces that are not directly part of the work. Coffee
and lunch breaks take on added importance in this context. Relief periods
on the modern operation permit more than relaxation from hard work;
they are also moments for establishing human contact in the midst of
socially isolating work. Coffee breaks, however, typically do not allow
enough time for longshoremen to recharge their cognitive batteries. Modern facilities are so vast, and the men so separated from each other, that
fifteen minutes is insufficient for people to touch bases.

The lunch break has therefore become especially significant. An hour
off work gives men in container yards an opportunity to come together
and share the day's work experience. One of the by-products of geographically isolated modern facilities is that longshoremen are encouraged to
take lunch together. Container work is sufficiently distant from restaurants and cafes so that in order to take full advantage of the hour, longshoremen bring their lunch to work and eat it in lunchrooms provided by
the stevedoring companies. Ironically, then, although the modern operation isolates longshoremen at work, it brings them together during lunch
in ways that conventional longshoring does not. Conventional docks are
so close to local neighborhoods that during lunch the men spread out to a
myriad of restaurants, cafes, and bars.

176

The new locations for talk on the modern waterfront clearly alter the kinds of conversations that occur. People do not talk as much about work issues as they do when they work conventional jobs. The conversation that is permissible on conventional longshore jobs does not exist on the modern operation. And the possibilities for making jobs more fun through verbal activities are limited. Nevertheless, opportunities for talk have not been eliminated by the modern technology. Conversation has not ended; rather, it has been relocated. Thus, longshoremen are still able to share complaints about management and talk about how to settle them.

When one analyzes the cognitive work necessary to accomplish a given job, it becomes clear that a certain amount of knowledge and initiative is required of all work, whether or not it is officially recognized. The issue then becomes, how is this initiative actually organized? In the case of longshoring, from the least skilled conventional jobs to the most skilled containerized operations, the work is relatively autonomous. Dockworkers are encouraged to do things without being told. And, although there is considerable variation, supervisors realize that they are dependent on holdmen, winch drivers, gearmen, and special equipment operators to execute the work. The ways in which San Francisco longshoremen transform their employers' dependence into formal and informal recognition of their personhood is the subject of the next chapter.

9

"DOING THE RIGHT THING": WORKING PRINCIPLES AND CODES OF CONDUCT

In aristocratic societies the poor man is familiarized from his childhood with the notion of being commanded. . . . In democracies servants are not only equals amongst themselves, but it may be said that they are in a way the equals of their masters. . . . At any moment a servant may become a master, and he aspires to rise to that condition. . . . Why then has the former a right to command, and what compells the later to obey?

Alexis de Tocqueville
Democracy in America

THE cognitive work performed by longshoremen and the initiative expected of them are sources of potential power. These two features of waterfront work prepare longshoremen to take themselves seriously as self-conscious actors and to resist intrusions on their selfhood. By themselves, however, cognition and initiative do not translate into actual power. Something else must happen. San Francisco longshoremen are able to wrestle with their employers, and sometimes to capitalize on their potential workplace power, because codes of conduct, or working principles, have been generated by the union's political community and are enforced on the docks. In combination, these codes, along with the employers' dependence on longshoremen, have produced a situation where personhood is reciprocally acknowledged on the San Francisco docks, where longshoremen are recognized as citizens of the waterfront and accorded all the rights and obligations associated with such status. And when personhood is not acknowledged, or citizenship rights are not recognized, work stops.

Over the last fifty years, San Francisco longshoremen have devised principles for how to work, and how *not* to work. These principles of self-regulation accomplish two apparently contradictory outcomes: They en-

178

able Local 10 members to work autonomously *and* they allow supervisors to get production. In the longshore community these principles are called "watching the game" and "doing the right thing." In addition to guiding work, these self-regulating principles are also weapons in the contest for control of the waterfront. The principles are political resources. In some contexts, they affirm, and, in others, they oppose certain kinds of work practices. These codes are standards for resistance *and* accountability. When longshoremen ignore agreed-upon rules, or management violates accepted procedures, the principles are invoked. At that moment, controversy begins and work frequently stops. Because these codes establish acceptable work practices and productivity levels, they determine the parameters of management's authority. Thus, they are the "real" rules governing the workplace, the actual terms of class relations. Passed on from generation to generation, they have become the criteria against which orders are evaluated; they are the bedrock of autonomy and resistance to management's authority.

WATCHING THE GAME

Longshoring is dangerous work.[1] To physically survive, longshoremen must be mentally alive. They therefore put considerable energy into handling the hazards of work. To avoid being hurt, longshoremen must think about danger. When lashing containers, for example, they routinely encounter grease and water. They want to walk gingerly because, in the words of one man, "it's so fucking easy to step in the water and the grease and sail off that van, it's not even funny." But longshoremen cannot tiptoe on containers, because being fast is important. Thus, they have to know how to move quickly without slipping.

Longshoremen know that danger is not dependable. And so thinking about danger must be routine. When working beneath the hook, they calculate possible moves for escape. Because longshore work is so dangerous, dockworkers can never completely disregard even the most

---

1 The national average incidence rate for all private sector employment in the United States in 1977 was 9.3 occupational injuries and illnesses per 100 full-time workers. The number of lost workday injuries and illnesses per 100 full-time longshoremen on the Pacific Coast in 1978 was 13.4 (Pacific Maritime Association, *Annual Report,* 1980, p. 33).

routine tasks. Holds of ships are thick with hazard-related talk. The men may be casual about the task at hand, but, as one of them put it: "you can't be casual talking about danger." Thus, job talk routinely focuses on safety issues and principles of safety are communicated through a special short-hand language. "Never turn your back on a good deal," San Francisco longshoremen say frequently. Among holdmen, the meaning is clear: Do not hook up a load and then ignore it. Always keep an eye on cargo being hoisted so that, as one holdman put it, "you can run in case it starts back down on you."

The longshoremen also routinely tell one another to watch the game. As an admonition, the saying is typically accompanied by a wink of the eye. Pointing an index finger to the speaker's eye also works. There are varia-tions on the phrase. Sometimes it is used evaluatively; the implicit sugges-tion is that a practice should be altered, as in: "You're not watching the game." The various ways in which this saying is used point to numerous principles for working safely.

In the hold, while a hoist is being made, watch the game can literally mean "watch," or keep an eye on the cargo. A former holdman elaborates on the phrase and suggests a broader principle: "Anything that moves on the waterfront that's got power – put your eyes on it. Any time you hear the winches move, you've got to watch it. This is a dangerous job down here if you're not watching what you're doing. The most important thing is watching the game."

The saying can also communicate approval. For example, when hold-men stand in the wings of a hatch while a hoist is being made, out of the winches' "drift," they are said to be "watching the game." Generally speak-ing, when holdmen speak of "watching the game," they are referring to safety rules.

Longshoremen who endanger themselves or others are likely to be told: "watch the game." The words, however, need not be spoken to communi-cate the warning. Longshoremen know the meaning of a wink with an index finger pointed to the eye. To an outsider the gesture might say, "use your head." Longshoremen say: "watch the game." This silent language permits them to communicate despite noise, and without attracting super-vision's attention.

Winch driving and gear work are not as routinely hazardous as hold-

Coffee weighers and strappers at Pier 54, San Francisco. These longshoremen weigh and stack up coffee bags, one of the most back-breaking jobs on the waterfront. Copyright © by Pat Goudvis 1980.

work. Nevertheless, winch drivers and gearmen must know how to work safely. They know how to watch the game because they have worked at least five years in the hold. And even though they are not personally at risk, they are very much implicated in the well-being of people working below them. If a load spills on a hoist, or a faulty piece of equipment injures a holdman, it is either a winch driver or a gearman who is responsible. Thus, the principles for safety are as important above deck as below.

There is no one on the waterfront who does not know what it means to watch the game. And anyone who does not "watch it" will be replaced, either from above or below. Knowing how to watch the game extends beyond working safely. The "game" is everything. In addition to safety, it is politics, productivity, and community. Watching the game therefore means being aware; being alert to activities that are dangerous to the union; and being "alive" to options for survival. Translated into a different language, watching the game is being socially conscious. Longshoremen who watch the game are therefore said to be "doing the right thing."

THE RULES OF WORKING ETIQUETTE: "DOING THE RIGHT THING"

Because longshoring entails cognitive work and is mostly unsupervised, longshoremen have considerable latitude for determining the quality and pace of work. But there are also limits. A certain degree of productivity must be met, and at an agreed-upon level of quality. There are additional restraints: Longshoremen determine neither which cargo, nor how much of it will be worked. Marx's observation on the relationship between agency and history is therefore appropriate in this regard. Longshoremen make history, but not in circumstances of their own choosing. There is a tension, then, between freedom and restraint. Longshoremen are routinely called upon to make choices; they must figure out how to work. Local 10 members have to decide how fast to work, and, in certain instances, when and if to formally challenge management.

The dynamic between freedom and restraint makes a kind of working etiquette necessary for waterfront work to be accomplished. Longshoremen must know how to work with freedom, without abusing it. The collectively bargained contract establishes only the outer limits of permissibility. Thus, over the years, rules have emerged for how to maneuver the limits of freedom on the job. The principles of this working etiquette can be heard in numerous waterfront expressions.

"Do the right thing" is a frequently heard expression on the San Francisco waterfront. The phrase is used in numerous contexts and its meaning is variable. "Doing the right thing" on the job means, among other things, to "do the work right." When longshoremen talk about "doing the work right," they sometimes mean "work safely." Thus, in this context, "doing the right thing" means "watch the game."

"Doing the right thing" or "working right," however, involves considerably more than "watching the game." It also means "working union." "Working union" refers to figuring out solutions for problems on the job and coming up with ideas that do not sabotage the union or the men. "Working union," then, is one aspect of "doing the right thing."

Working union, however, is not as simple as it sounds. Knowing how to work union does not mean doing sloppy work, and it does not mean holding back on production. Longshoremen who work union take pride in their skills and competence. Someone working union is, in longshore language, keeping the hook moving, or "meeting the hook." Someone who does not keep the "hook moving" is not considered working union or doing the right thing. In fact, longshoremen who are not doing their share are likely to be told: "Face me or face the ladder." When they are doing the right thing by "meeting the hook," dockworkers are typically facing one another. When they work in the hold, partners literally face each other. Thus, when someone is not working to capacity, he is often facing in other directions. He is therefore told to "face the ladder." In other words, "climb the hatch ladder" out of the hold and leave the job.

This tradition goes back at least to the union's inception. "In spite of all my contempt and hatred for the goddamn ship owners," said a charter member and a CIO militant,

> once I took a job I felt an obligation to work. I didn't understand the guy that took a job and didn't want to do a goddamn thing. And I frequently told the guys, I said: "You aren't worth twenty-five cents an hour." I figure if you went to work, you know, you put in some work. You didn't kill yourself, but you work.

183

He recalled the period between 1934 and 1936 when the union successfully reduced sling-loads to 1,800 pounds.[2] Defying the employers and expressing their independence, some longshoremen would build sling-loads weighing considerably less than 1,800 pounds. Union activists objected:

> I used to tell them, "Look, you've got to do some work, you know. You can't go collect your money without showing some work."

But working union is not a synonym for speed-up. Doing the right thing does not mean doing the right thing for the employer. In the words of one man, "working union" is definitely "not kissing ass." There is a delicate balance between doing the right thing and "working too hard." Some people are rejected as partners because they work "too good," or are "too eager" to please employers. Thus, as a former holdman puts it: "The best combo on the waterfront is a worker that's pretty good or good, not excellent, good; who is also a good union man and who is also interesting because it helps everybody make their day."

Although doing the right thing means coming up with ideas for how to work, there are limits on the amount of ideas men can come up with. Working etiquette requires propriety. Longshoremen who come up with too many ideas, or figure too many angles, may be sanctioned with a version of the following expression: "You got a head that belongs in Washington, but your ass belongs right here on the waterfront."

Free time is common in conventional longshore work. It comes between hoists, when the job is finished early, when the cargo requires fewer men than are present, or when the men spell each other. When this occurs, longshoremen can leave the job so long as the work is "covered" and the hook is moving. The time is used to do chores, make medical appointments, pick up children. On many jobs, however, these liberties are not possible. The cargo requires that everyone on the job work it. And in this instance, longshoremen doing the right thing will not leave the job. If they have made an appointment, they will cancel it. Someone who intends to "take a hike," or leave the job in this circumstance, is told to "watch the game." Put more directly, he is told not to leave.

2 For an analysis of this period see Mills and Wellman (1987).

184

During extended periods when there is no work, on the other hand, watching the game means taking advantage of free time. Speaking of such a situation, one longshoreman said, "The guy I was working with told me, 'Why don't you go home and have a long lunch with your Dad. Leave at 11:00 and come back at 2:00 because at 2:00 we have to relieve the other hatches.' And I said, 'Well, maybe.' 'No,' the guy said, 'you don't always get these kinds of jobs so you might as well do it while you get a chance.' He was watching the game for me." When longshoremen know how to interpret these complex cultural cues with multiple meanings they are practicing a working etiquette. Because they are able to watch the game they can therefore do the right thing.

The work etiquette regulates other contexts in which the line between freedom and its abuses is a thin one. The isolated and hidden terrain of conventional longshoring makes pilferage easy.[3] Of itself, longshoremen do not frown on pilferage. And stevedoring companies overlook "acceptable levels" of it. Too much, however, and in the wrong place, becomes a problem. When this happens, another meaning of doing the right thing emerges: Do not take advantage of freedom. The outer limits of freedom have been reached when longshoremen take more than they can consume,

---

3 For obvious reasons, it is difficult to establish precise figures for pilferage on the San Francisco waterfront. Official government estimates put "documented cargo loss" figures at between $250,000 and $500,000 a year (Emch, 1978). This should be contrasted to the Port of New York which, according to the Department of Transportation, loses upward of $3 billion annually. Underwriters, Customs officials, and management representatives all agree that pilferage on the Bay Area waterfront consists mainly of "thefts of opportunity" as opposed to organized crime. People find an item they can use personally and take it. Containers have cut the possibilities for pilferage, but not entirely. Some containers have cartons destined for different areas and must be "broken down" on the docks. Known as "less than container loads," or "LCLs," these containers provide opportunities for pilferage.

Local 10 officials take exception to the government estimates. "It is biased, slanted, and doesn't mention that management is involved in the biggest heists," said a union representative angrily at a Labor Relations Committee meeting (field notes). "We take the fall for the biggest heists. Whenever cargo is missing, we get blamed. Last year 3,200 boxes of corned beef turned up missing. We goddamn well didn't take those boxes out under our coats."

There is no denying that pilferage happens. The waterfront is thick with humorous tales about clever "crimes of opportunity." Nevertheless, during the period in which this research was conducted, only three official complaints of pilferage were filed against longshoremen.

and flaunt it. In this instance they are admonished to watch the game or do the right thing. The warning results from practicality not morality. "Too much" pilferage brings the wrong kind of attention to longshoremen. Gang bosses, walkers, and security guards are forced to attend to the act if it is overdone. Thus, longshoremen who take advantage of opportunities for theft are violating another rule of the working etiquette; namely, as one of the men put it: "Don't bring any heat on yourself, the game you're in, or your partners."

There is considerable leeway between the inner and outer limits of freedom, between "thefts of opportunity" and "too much." The space between these extremes is not precisely covered by the working etiquette: How much is "too much"? Which place is the proper one? The etiquette provides only principles; how to interpret and enforce them, however, is decided by the men as they determine what will be tolerated.

Knowing how to practice the working etiquette is not easy. The practitioner must be able to manage a conflicting set of expectations and calculations. One way to do the right thing, for example, is to figure out the easiest, safest way for working a cargo. Longshoremen are encouraged to work with a minimum of effort. Since the work is typically unsupervised, this is not a problem. And when a labor-saving idea is proposed that allows a partner to leave, the proposal's author is said to be "watching the game." If, however, the labor-saving idea is not used judiciously, it might be noticed by management. And if the practice persists, management eventually orders less men for the job. This however reduces the opportunity for work and therefore directly violates community standards for "working union," which means, among other things, not sabotaging the union or other longshoremen. Thus, without foresight and calculation, doing the right thing can lead to not watching the game.

Doing the right thing, the men remind each other, does not mean doing the right thing for the employer. If they are watching the game, longshoremen who leave work early must think through the consequences of their behavior. Immediate time-off has to be balanced against future employment. "As a union man," one longshoreman said, "I'm not inclined to do it [take a hike] when it's so visible that it will eliminate men from the job. But it's a constant problem because we're encouraged to do it." In this circumstance, the working etiquette is as much a problem as a solution.

The tension between union and non-union ways for working reveals another feature of the working etiquette: Longshoremen must know how and when to involve the union in work disputes. Because there are no suggestion boxes on the waterfront, procedures for doing the work "right" are worked out between the men themselves. Some work practices are long-standing. They go back to the early days of conventional longshoring when the work was labor-intensive, requiring numerous longshoremen, and took a good amount of time. Today, however, time-consuming work practices involving more than a minimal complement of people are an anachronism. Nevertheless, so long as each person on the payroll is present and gives the appearance of working hard, supervisors typically do not challenge the practice. "It's pretty hard to write us up [file a complaint]," notes one longshoreman, "when we're struggling and sweating down there."

But problems do begin to emerge when longshoremen decide, for example, to modify a long-standing labor-intensive work practice by using a forklift. Adding the machine makes the work easier. Employers rarely object to this modification of an accepted work practice. But eventually they invoke the innovation as grounds for reducing the number of longshoremen on the job. And this is the point at which disputes arise: Longshoremen object to the reduced manning; but employers justify it by saying the machine reduces the necessary number of hands.

At this moment, longshoremen must make another choice: "You've got to decide," said one of them, "whether you're going to make a big case out of it or not." If the union is called, the matter is taken out of their hands. The dispute is settled contractually and precedent is established. On the other hand, however, if the men do not call the union, and continue to use the machinery, eventually their numbers will be reduced. If they decide to work without the machine and not raise the issue, all of them will work, but harder. What it means to do the right thing in this situation is hard to know. Sometimes there is a tension between doing the right thing and "working union."

Being able to identify the "right thing" is an important talent on the waterfront. When properly applied, the knowledge helps longshoremen choose between conflicting demands. Knowing what is the right thing, however, is not easy. The expression contains an extremely complicated and fluid principle, governed by multiple, layered, and sometimes competing meanings. Determining the right thing can be enormously difficult. One longshoreman's account of his deliberations makes the point. He recalls doing dockwork one rainy day not too long ago. A popular jitney driver had just driven his machine off a slippery pier into the bay. The man drowned. This event was fresh in the storyteller's mind as he tried to move railroad flatcars. His walking boss had told another jitney driver to get a tractor and move the cars with it. The jitney driver was nervous: "I haven't driven a tractor very much before," he told the walker. And then he asked the assembled longshoremen, "have any of you guys driven a tractor?" The storyteller was volunteered by his partner. But he didn't want to do it. Driving the tractor would mean he was working out of his job category. He thought another jitney driver should be hired from the hall. Despite these reservations, he agreed to do it; that way he would keep the job going.

Everyone was pleased with the decision except the driver; he had mixed emotions.

"Is that working union?" he asked sincerely.

"What would you call that? I don't know. What should I have done?"

Thinking through the matter, he concluded: "I did the right thing for the walking boss; the right thing for my partner and I, as far as we were concerned individually. And I did the right thing for the jitney driver. But I'm not too sure I did the right thing for the union."

Knowing how to do the right thing is as difficult as knowing what it is. Longshoring is a complex world where right and wrong are rarely obvious. Knowing how to apply the working etiquette once the right thing is known can therefore be complicated. Appropriate principles for action are always being assessed and once determinations are made, more thought goes into applying them. For example, during the Vietnam War longshoremen loaded napalm bombs. The men knew they were loading weapons that would ultimately be used on civilian populations, including children.

"What do you call 'doing the right thing' there?" asked a longshoreman who had loaded the deadly cargo.

"Our contract is to load and unload ships," he continued.

188

"We load dangerous cargo, we load obnoxious cargo. Sometimes we load cargo that we don't think is morally correct cargo. But we do it. Now, is that 'doing the right thing' or what? Most of us do it."

WORKING PRINCIPLES AND CONTAINERIZED LONGSHORING

The meaning of principles like "do the right thing" gets blurred by the modern technology. The delicate balance between working union and doing the right thing in conventional longshoring has a new meaning in the cab of a crane or strad. Technological limits on freedom simplify the rules of working etiquette. The new restrictions on freedom limit its abuse and leave little room to reflect on what might be the right thing to do. Technological restraints on discretion are also reinforced by the steady employment status of special equipment operators. Thus, certain aspects of containerized longshoring seriously undermine the working etiquette developed by West Coast longshoremen. The new technology makes it difficult for ILWU members to implement principles for working properly. The principle of "working union," for example, is sabotaged by steady employment, limitations on flexible work rules, and a reduced workforce.

Despite these restrictions, longshoremen continue to work union, even on container operations. One morning, for example, a hatch-tender dispatched from the hall was paying no attention to the job. Instead, he was talking to a cluster of men standing on the ship's deck. The crane driver had to strain to see the hatch so as not to damage containers. "Why don't you say something to him?" the SEO man was asked.

"He has to make a living, too," he replied. "If I say something over the radio, they'll hear it in the headquarters and he'll get fired" (field notes). The crane driver was working union; he was "doing the right thing."

Union principles for self-governance are difficult to implement under the new technology. As a result, they are not asserted frequently. Thus, it sometimes appears as though doing the right thing is a principle of the past. The longshore working etiquette seems to be a victim of containerization. This conclusion is plausible, however, only until the etiquette is violated, until someone does *not* do the right thing. When that happens, the principle is invoked, and if it continues to be ignored, conflict results. When, for example, a recognized rule of indulgence is unilaterally retracted, fairness becomes an issue and the dispute turns into open conflict. And, as one superintendent in charge of an automobile discharge found out, the disagreement can be waged fairly fiercely, even on modern terrain. The incident was cause for excited conversations around the hall during a dispatch early one summer morning.[4]

"Did you hear what happened at Benicia yesterday?" asked one long-shoreman. Benicia is a small town north and east of San Francisco. It sits on the Carquinez Straits, where the Sacramento River empties into the northern-most part of the San Francisco Bay. The docks in Benicia are used almost exclusively for discharging automobiles.

> "No," said his buddy, "I haven't."
>
> "We were dispatched to a 9:00 start," replied the storyteller, barely able to restrain himself. "But the goddamn ship didn't arrive until 10:30. We were ready for our usual coffee break at 11:00 but the fucking superintendent wouldn't let us take one. He said we'd already had one because we started an hour and a half late. So when the coffee wagon shows up, this motherfucker takes a cup of coffee and a donut for himself and tells the driver to leave. Can you believe that?! Man, were we ever pissed off. So we decided to slow down, to really cake-walk the cocksucker. We drove cars off that ship at five miles an hour.
>
> "That pissed him off. At first he cursed every car as it went by him. But then, as it was getting clear that we were serious, he tried to trick us. He would say there were only a couple more decks of cars and that if we would speed up, he'd let us off early. But we knew the ship was filled with cars.
>
> "When he realized we were going to take as much time as we possibly could, he started telling us that if we would hurry up, he'd pay us until 8:00. We wouldn't go for that either. So we worked until 8. And we left seven cars aboard ship so that the company would have to hire more men for the next day. Fuck that shit!"

By story's end, a number of participants in the action were clustered around the narrator. They all looked very proud of themselves, grinning from ear to ear, nodding in agreement with the conclusion. And like a Greek chorus, they validated the account chiming in with comments like, "Who the fuck does he think he is!?"

"We showed him!" said another.

4 The following paragraphs are based on field notes.

A coffee wagon was parked across the street from the hall. In front of it was another cluster of men recounting the same incident.

"It was a matter of dignity," explained a speaker. "The sonofabitch takes a fucking cup of coffee for himself and tells the driver to leave us standing there! That ain't doing the right thing."

The men recounted their tale to one of the Local's business agents who had stopped for a cup of coffee. He smiled when they finished, and told them he was impressed. "When seventy guys do something like that," he said, "they're better than the best business agent on the docks."

This job action suggests that competing principles for what is right and wrong, fair and unfair, continue to generate struggles over how work will be done on the modern waterfront. It is still possible to contest the other side's principles. In this instance, the men were so deeply offended by the superintendent's conception of fairness that they successfully organized a slowdown, one of the most difficult job actions to accomplish on the waterfront. In comparison, work stoppages are easier to do: The men agree among themselves that work will stop; they announce that decision to supervision; and then they wait for union and company representatives to adjudicate matters.

Slowdowns are much harder to do. They require internal coordination and enforcement. The men must rely on their own resources for persuasion since matters are settled directly without the employer association or union. Because work does not stop, the men have to decide upon the pace. They have to determine how slow is fast enough to get their point across without giving the supervisor grounds for calling in the arbitrator.

Work slowdowns are especially difficult to organize while discharging automobiles. The men really do not work with each other on these jobs. Cars are driven off the ship one-by-one, individually and separately. The work is done in isolation; people can't talk to each other while driving cars. Given these circumstances, it is quite a feat to successfully organize a work slowdown. In the words of a seasoned business agent who does not usually sprinkle his talk with superlatives, "What these guys did out there was really something." The magnitude of their accomplishment underscores the significance they attach to principles of fairness.

The men self-consciously transformed adversity into advantage. Even though they were isolated while driving cars off the ship, they returned to the vessel aboard trucks in groups of ten. "When they were bringing us back," said a longshoreman who was instrumental in the action, "we got to talking about, 'Fuck that guy, man. We can play that game too.'" Discussing matters among themselves on return trips, the initiators realized certain factors were in their favor. The ship was large, the cargo numerous, and the exit ramps few. A couple of people could therefore immediately and effectively slow down the entire operation. On subsequent return trips the ringleaders addressed the fears of men who were reluctant to join. According to one of the organizers, they explained that there was too much work for the superintendent to fire them.

> We told them, "look, you ain't gonna get fired because it costs 7 to 8 grand a day for that ship to sit in port." We told them that we were pretty sure the ship had a contract with the stevedoring company that said that if the stevedoring people caused a labor problem they had to pay the ship's crew's wages.

Those longshoremen who were not persuaded by this analysis were, however, convinced by the superintendent's behavior that a protest was necessary. After an initial display of hostility, the company representative became more reasonable and made the men an offer. In the words of one participant, "he told us 'no matter what time you guys get done, you're going to get paid for ten hours.'" But that strategy backfired. The longshoremen felt it was an insult to their integrity and intelligence. "It really pissed the guys off," said an instigator, "because he was like trying to buy them off, you see. So they slowed down even more."

By the end of the day the men had their revenge. They may have lost a coffee break. They did, however, get paid double-time for two hours of overtime; they forced the company to hire more men to finish the job the next day; and they were quite sure that in the future, the superintendent would do the right thing.

WHEN CODES OF CONDUCT BECOME STANDARDS FOR RESISTANCE

Principles like do the right thing and watch the game are codes of conduct. They distinguish between acceptable and unacceptable – fair and unfair – work practices. They also establish standards for accountability. When

192

these principles are recognized and *enforced* by longshoremen, they are principles for self-regulation. Because most supervisors are former longshoremen, they know the codes and recognize them as legitimate working principles. In fact, walking bosses typically invoke these principles when expediting the work. By recognizing the legitimacy of these principles, management is, in effect, acknowledging the personhood or the citizenship rights of longshoremen on the docks. And so long as the acknowledgement of personhood is reciprocated, class distinctions are suppressed. Local 10 members will actively cooperate with management to get the job done; they will act as though everyone had an equal stake in its completion.[5] On the other hand, however, when supervisors act unilaterally, disregarding the citizenship rights of longshoremen by refusing to acknowledge their personhood, work stops, and class antagonisms erupt. Business as usual ceases and class relations become hostile; the principles for self-regulation are transformed into standards for resistance.

When longshoremen are told to do the right thing or watch the game, the assumption is that they know "the game," as well as the "right thing," and can detect violations of community standards. Being told to watch the game or do the right thing, then, is a reminder that actions have consequences, that jobs are performed within a context. These injunctions call for thought; they remind longshoremen to consider their activities in relation to a system. When telling someone to stay on the job, for example, longshoremen point out that taking a hike might jeopardize other people or make the work unnecessarily difficult. People are free to do as they please, the explanation continues, so long as the job is "covered." Thus, when explained as a system, the order to stay on the job allows being covered for or spelled by another worker.

If, on the other hand, someone is told to stay on the job without explaining why, an order is being imposed, in both senses of the term. It is an order, not a suggestion, and neither flexibility nor improvisation are permitted. The injunction puts order and control around what appears from outside to be chaos. The purpose of imposing an order is to decide if the job is actually being covered by management standards. Tone of voice is not the difference between imposing an order and explaining a system.

5 I am indebted to Jan Dizard for this insight.

193

Each contains a different set of principles for being told what to do. One disregards the longshoremen's cognitive skills, their ability to think things through, and do the "right thing." The other encourages and uses these qualities and principles.

When the personhood of longshoremen is recognized, and orders are explained, work proceeds relatively smoothly, even if Local 10 members have contractual grounds to stop the job. As an experienced participant on the San Francisco waterfront observes:

> If the employer and/or the ship admitted there was a problem, the men might proceed as best they could and with extra caution. For example, upon the initial rigging of the gear it was once discovered that the off-shore topping lift winch was "creeping," except when physically locked against such movement. A young British mate of serious and exacting demeanor was approached on deck. "That offshore topping winch creeps." The response was a serious, but disarming: "Everything aboard this vessel creeps." The response was almost predictable: "Well, I'll be damned! Mr. Mate, that's one fine answer! OK. We'll keep an eye on it and do the best we can." (Mills, 1978a:24)

Longshoremen routinely agree to "work around" problematic situations when, for example, supervision explains that an unanticipated problem has surfaced and asks for help or indulgence. So long as the personhood of longshoremen is acknowledged, class distinctions are suppressed and Local 10 members actively cooperate to finish the job.

But this is not always possible. Although they work the same docks, longshoremen do not share a common social location with their supervisors. The two groups are paid to do different jobs. Local 10's members are paid to *handle* cargo; their supervisors, on the other hand, are paid to *expedite* the handling of cargo. To complicate matters, the two sides operate with different meanings of the "right thing." Thus, it stands to reason that, periodically, the different tasks and competing principles will come into conflict. Sometimes the supervisor's responsibility for moving cargo quickly runs counter to the longshoremen's notion of the "right thing." Sometimes it is impossible to explain an order. Either time does not permit it, or the explanation is insufficient. And given that the two sides work with different sociologies of knowledge – they inhabit radically different social worlds, act according to competing working principles, and

194

consequently experience conflicting phenomenologies – some things can never be explained. When this occurs, longshoremen's citizenship rights are ignored, their personhood is unrecognized, and, as a result, they refuse to follow management's orders.

Evidently this occurs relatively frequently. In a recent two-year period, for example, the stated reason for better than one-fourth of management's complaints about Local 10 members was a dispute over orders. The formal complaint charges these longshoremen with "refusal to work as directed."[6] The wording of this complaint, however, does not adequately communicate the depth of the dispute. The formal language ignores – and to some extent hides – the deeper sources of the trouble. As disputes escalate into open confrontation, and one observes the unfolding process, the actual stakes become visible. One incident illustrates what is at issue.

"How's it going?" inquired a business agent as longshoremen came down a ship's gangway on a lunch break. "Any problems?" Every so often he would spot a winch driver. "How are the winches?" he wanted to know. The typical response was "fine," or "no problems." One winch driver stopped, however. He was having a little trouble: One of the winches pulled to the right when it was in neutral. The business agent took note of the hatch and said he would be there after lunch.

When lunch ended, the business agent climbed up to the winch driver and asked about the problem. The man allowed that the machine wasn't operating properly but said it wasn't "too big a deal." It just wasn't operating right and he was having some trouble. The walking boss arrived during the exchange and said there was no problem: "That's the way these winches operate. It's like the Westinghouse gear, the same thing." The winch driver didn't argue; he nodded in a noncommittal manner.

In the meantime, the superintendent walked up, very agitated. "Get down off there!" he yelled at the business agent, "goddamnit, I have a shift to work." That angered the union officer: "You also have a work stoppage," he said as he climbed down.

"What's the problem?" asked the superintendent.

"The winch doesn't work right," said the business agent.

6 In all likelihood, the "actual" number of disagreements over orders is higher than this figure indicates. As the following example suggests, the disputes do not always result in a formal complaint.

The walker jumped in: "There's no problem with them winches; I've called the ship's mate and he says that's the way they operate."

"Get him over here and have him fix them," demanded the business agent.

As the two sides exchanged demands, the winch driver explained to the researcher that just a short time ago he had been fired by this company for injuring either cargo or men with the winches. Now they wanted him to work with equipment that would increase the possibility of injury or accident.

The superintendent came over and suggested, "let's work this shift; we'll fix it tonight and that way we won't lose time."

"No deal," responded the union official.

A little while later one of the ship's crew members came up to check out the problem. He climbed on the equipment with the winch driver and they worked the winches. The crew member said the winches were "fine," and that there was "no problem."

That response infuriated the winch driver; his demeanor changed completely: "He didn't do a mother-fucking thing except watch me operate the machine," he yelled; "and then he's gonna tell me there's nothing wrong with it?! I'm driving it, not him!"

"Get the ship's electrician," the union representative said to the superintendent. While they waited for the electrician, the winch driver explained to the researcher what was at issue: "If the superintendent had come up in the beginning," he explained, "and said something like, 'I know there's a problem; let's try and do our best to get through the shift; be careful, but try,' I would do it." But since they were denying the problem, he "had to protest."[7]

Had the winch driver protested without the business agent's encouragement, he probably would have been fired and cited for "refusal to work as directed." But the dispute in this incident was not about refusing orders. The issue was the winch driver's personhood, and his right to be treated as a citizen on the docks. The winch driver did not refuse to drive the winches until he was told that what he thought was a problem was not a problem. He initially told the business agent that the difficulty was not

---

7 Based on field notes.

"too big a deal." He did not become upset or angry, and refuse to work, until a representative for the ship's management – a mate and therefore an officer – said there was no problem. He remembered being disciplined under similar circumstances when the company would not take responsibility for the equipment's repair. Had management publicly recognized the problem, acknowledging and respecting the winch driver's intelligence, he would have been willing to work despite the difficulty. But that would have required that the supervisors explain their wishes in relation to a larger context, not just impose an order.

Refusing to acknowledge the problem amounted to a denial of the winch driver's humanity. By minimizing the difficulty, the employers essentially ignored and discounted his ability to assess the winch's safety. Because they were disregarding his capacity to think about the work process, the supervisors did not need to explain their thinking. Thus, the superintendent announced an order, and the ship's mate concurred. But the order denied the winch driver's common sense, and therefore produced a protest.

The conflict over personhood and citizenship rights does not always get expressed so obviously. Sometimes it surfaces in very undramatic ways, produced by rather unlikely sources. The requirement that longshoremen wear hard hats, for example, hardly appears likely to spark a conflict between principles. It seems quite reasonable to require that workers exposed to serious danger wear protective head gear. Thus, it is surprising to discover that a number of complaints filed against Local 10 members, in one two-year period, charged them with not wearing a hard hat.

The small number of these formal complaints does not accurately reflect the magnitude of this dispute. Anyone walking along the San Francisco waterfront is struck by the contempt with which hard hats are treated. Some hats spend more time on the docks than on people's heads. And when they are worn, the men typically wear them quite casually: head straps are missing, the helmets are perched on stylish tams, or located precariously near the back of the head. Hard hats are the subject of constant banter on the waterfront. Supervisors threaten and cajole people to wear the equipment; in response, longshoremen either go through the motions, or ignore the injunctions.

Why should such an apparently reasonable requirement cause so much difficulty? Longshoremen advance a number of explanations for their behavior. The hard hat is less comfortable than most head gear. Moreover, given certain cargoes, the helmet itself becomes a problem: "The god-damn hat is a menace sometimes," said one. "When you're handling the hook it's just about impossible to keep the fucking thing on your head." The individualism of longshoremen also explains why they refuse to wear hard hats. People take pride in their physical appearance and they don't like what hard hats do to their hair.

A deeper appreciation of the issue, however, became evident when one longshoreman who had been fired for not wearing the hat showed up at a Grievance Committee meeting. "The hard hat is the one safety rule that the employer's got religion on," a business agent said to committee members.

> You can have the goddamnedest violations of everything else in the safety code and still those motherfuckers will march around telling people to put on their hard hats. The employers insisting we wear hard hats is more harassment than anything else. It's not because they're concerned about our safety – if that were the case then all this other unsafe shit wouldn't go on in a lot of these other operations on the waterfront. (Field notes)

His observation reveals an otherwise hidden source of tension produced by the hard hat requirement. The dispute was not about hard hats. It was over conflicting ways of being told what to do. Longshoremen know that employers routinely violate or "work around" the safety code. It is virtually impossible to work on the waterfront without knowing this. Insisting that one section of the safety code be strictly enforced while others are violated is not just inconsistent. It makes longshoremen act as though they do not know that safety standards are routinely ignored, and that is an attack on their intelligence. Not wearing hard hats, then, is another way to resist a management order that denies the longshoremen's personhood.

When supervisors use the language of command, the conflict over personhood and citizenship becomes explicit. And if the order is not restated, little gets accomplished. This was the lesson learned by a rather youthful looking superintendent early one winter morning as he prepared to unload a passenger ship. Unbeknownst to him, the night before the union had changed eligibility requirements for longshoremen handling passengers' baggage. Until that evening, employers requested "baggagemen" by name from a jointly agreed-upon list. The new policy abolished the list and made all longshoremen on the dock board eligible for a baggage job. Since the superintendent did not know of the new policy, he had ordered two baggagemen under the old system.

The superintendent was drinking coffee aboard ship when a union business agent told him the men he had ordered would have to return to the hiring hall. A new order would have to be placed. That made the superintendent angry: "How come nobody told me about this? I have passengers coming off this ship right now. Can't we work this out later?"

"No," the business agent said firmly.

The superintendent began to argue: "This is unfair. I have people coming off the ship now and they need people to handle their baggage. Why wasn't I told!?" The business agent pointed out that the argument was wasting time. He suggested that if the supervisor wanted men to meet the passengers, he'd be best off sending the original men back and getting two new baggagemen through the hall.

As the two men started to leave the ship's mess hall, the superintendent said to the union representative: "Send me two men quickly."

"Is that an order?" asked the business agent.

The superintendent reformulated the communication: "I need two men right now."

"I'll do it," the business agent said; "but that's not an order." The superintendent got the point; he said nothing else (based on field notes).

Part IV

WAGING THE BATTLE FOR WORKPLACE CONTROL ON CONTRACTUAL TERRAIN

I T could be argued that longshoremen's objections to the language of command, their active defense of personhood and integrity, their willingness to impose codes of conduct and enforce standards for accountability are examples of radicalism driven underground. Like wildcat strikes and other sorts of insubordination, they could be considered versions of phantom unionism, "weapons of the weak" in James Scott's terms (1985, 1990). Although they are potential sources of power, it could be said, they do not amount to actual institutional or organizational power. Thus, these acts of resistance would not undermine the theories of labor's demise. Longshoremen, it might be argued, like other American workers, are unable to challenge management's authority contractually, and in this respect, the issue of shopfloor regime has been essentially settled. Like other American unions, it might be said, the ILWU has signed agreements with employers that formally grant management control over the work process. The battle for workplace control has, therefore, for all intents and purposes, ended; and, in the strict sense of the term, class conflict has been replaced by various forms of class cooperation.

The M&M Agreements could be read to confirm this view. They apparently did to the ILWU in the 1960s what earlier contracts had done to the CIO in the late 1930s. The agreements undermined longshoremen's ability to effectively dispute management's rule on the docks.[1] According to the terms of the M&Ms, the ILWU agreed to eliminate restrictive work rules and permit employers to introduce more efficient work practices. In return, longshoremen were guaranteed lifetime employment and an

1 See, for example, Mills (1978a); Mills and Wellman (1987); Swados (1961); Theriault (1978); Weir (1964).

employer-subsidized fund to compensate for any losses in earnings.[2] Referring to the initial fund created by the agreement, Harvey Swados called it, "a $29,000,000 bribe to buy back certain working conditions that have been in force for a generation" (1961:449). "Gone was the right to take direct action on the job to correct contract violations," wrote Stan Weir, "except in matters involving 'safety'" (1964:25). In historian James Green's view, the agreement brought the ILWU to "heel" (1980:213).

It may have taken thirty years, this interpretation suggests, but like the contracts signed by other CIO unions, the M&Ms relinquished workplace control to management. The ILWU, it could be said, struck a political bargain much like the deal agreed to by CIO unions in the late 1930s and early 1940s. In return for lifetime employment, the ILWU apparently agreed to dismantle union organization on the waterfront. Citizenship issues at the workplace were evidently conceded to the employers.

The controversy created by the M&Ms is as stubborn as it is angry and polemical. The agreements still generate disagreement among longshoremen. The argument over steady men is just one example of the persistent differences. The debate over the modernization agreement revolves around two questions. The first is whether the agreement was a "good deal." This is an argument over which side benefited most economically from the bargain.[3] The second question is whether management's control of the waterfront can be contested by the union in the post-M&M era. With notable exceptions, a consensus has emerged suggesting that it cannot. With the signing of the M&M Agreements, it is argued, the contractual relationship prevents longshoremen from seriously challenging their employers' orders on West Coast ships and docks.[4]

Although the present study is unable to add much to the debate over which side benefited most from the M&M Agreements, it can shed light

2 For a thorough and balanced discussion of the M&M agreement, see Fairley (1979).
3 Those arguing that the union lost more than it gained include: Jacobs (1964); Swados (1961, 1962); Weir (1964). Arguing the other side is Fairley (1962). More recently, however, Fairley (1979) has argued that the union might have gained more, had it not abandoned work restrictions wholesale. See also Ross (1968). For an assessment of the productivity gains resulting from the M&M Agreement, see Fairley (1979) and Hartman (1969).
4 The exceptions are Fairley (1962) and Finlay (1988). Obviously the union disagrees. See Goldblatt (1971). Proponents of this view include Mills (1978); Swados (1961); Weir (1964).

on whether or not the struggle for waterfront control has ended. As the last three chapters indicate, the matter is not a simple one. In San Francisco, when citizenship rights are ignored, or personhood is unrecognized, political fault lines are exposed and fundamental differences between labor and management get expressed openly. The next three chapters provide a close look at Local 10's recent contractual encounters with the PMA. This look reveals that the issue of workplace regime has not been settled by the contract. Indeed, the battle for control of the shopfloor is waged on contractual terrain.

10

WHO DECIDES HOW TO WORK?

I LWU longshoremen have always used two weapons to challenge management's control over the docks. One is their working know-how: the cultural and technical knowledge analyzed in the last three chapters that is necessary to do autonomous work and, when appropriate, is used to resist management's efforts to direct that work. The other is the contract, a document that contains procedures for redressing grievances. Sometimes differences cannot be settled informally on the docks; either an accommodation is impossible, or longshoremen refuse to work around a problem. When this happens, disagreements over how to work move from the waterfront to contract negotiations or the grievance machinery. Over the past fifty years, then, including the post-M&M period, the ILWU has consistently waged a struggle for job control on two fronts: informally, on the docks; and contractually, in the grievance machinery. The question of workplace regime has never been settled. It was not settled when the first contract was signed in 1934, and it was not settled with the M&M Agreements in the 1960s. The current disagreement between the ILWU and PMA, moreover, is remarkably similar to the one that divided the two sides in the 1930s. The issue is still who will control the dockside workplace? And, as in the past, it is frequently disputed on contractual terrain where both sides can use the contract as a weapon. The contest is about whose rules will be obeyed, and as the following three chapters illustrate, the battle is fought on three fronts: (1) Which side's rules for how to work will be followed? (2) Which side's language will govern the workplace? And (3) which side's method for determining merit will prevail?

Every Wednesday morning in San Francisco at approximately 9:00, ILWU officials and PMA representatives meet to hear and exchange complaints.

They have been doing this for over fifty years. Contractually known as the Local Labor Relations Committee, or, as longshoremen call it, "the LRC," these meetings are the opening moves in a complicated grievance process. Complaints are noted and responded to officially. Around the bare text of official complaint and response, a discourse develops in private caucuses and public exchanges. If disagreements are not settled here, they go to an "Area Labor Relations Committee" or, ultimately, the "Coast Labor Relations Committee."

The full range of the conflict between longshoremen and their employers becomes clear when the complaints leveled against each side are spelled out. Since both parties are required to voice the reasons for their complaints, underlying issues and implicit expectations are made explicit. The revealed differences are fundamental and systematic; the complaints are neither random nor petty. The points of contention contain a set of regular features, and they go to the core of class relations.

The range of complaints against longshoremen adds up to the claim that they are impossible. The scope of grievances against owners, on the other hand, holds them to be constitutionally prone to reneging on commitments made in the collective bargain. The basic terms of conflict are reflected in the kinds of complaint each side lodges against the other. Nearly three-quarters of each side's grievances manifest the name of the other group. Seventy-four percent of management's complaints are about longshoremen not working; 72 percent of the grievances against waterfront capitalists are about their not paying.

In one recent two-year period, 828 complaints were exchanged by Local 10 and the PMA. Four hundred forty of the grievances were lodged by the union, and 388 by the employers. Although thirty-one categories of grievances appeared in the union's accusations, a high proportion of the total grievances was concentrated in several key categories: Seventy-two percent of the cases complained about "pay shortage" (153 complaints), "lost work opportunity" (108), and "unjust firing" (105). When the next most frequent category, "time-in-lieu" (43), is added, 82 percent of the grievances are accounted for.

The same pattern of concentration is found in the employer complaints, although not quite to the same extent. Of the 388 complaints lodged in this period, thirty-one categories were used. Three categories, however,

206

count for 60 percent of the employer complaints: "fail to show" (87), "refusal to work as directed" (64), and "walked off the job" (80). When a fourth category of various complaints pointing to different ways of missing work is added (57), 74 percent of the total complaints are covered.[1]

This pattern of complaint reproduces not only the wants of each side, but the very names of the classes as well. What is wanted from the working class is work, and what is wanted from the capitalist class is capital. Thus, the characteristic grievance of longshoremen is that capitalists represented by the PMA often do not pay; whereas the typical complaint of the PMA is that workers in the ILWU often don't work. This coincidence of outer and inner designation indicates a meaningful relationship between class structure and grievance process.

Counting categories of complaint is one window into the conflict between longshoremen and their employers. It reveals the class location of complaint. Taken by themselves, however, the accusations do not tell what is at issue. The pattern of complaint needs to be interpreted in the LRC context. The interpretive task is facilitated by a formal record of accusation and response that has been created before grievances reach the LRC. Prior to each session, both sides are provided with documents containing written complaints and responses. When the meeting is convened, talk focuses on these texts. Contained in the text and talk are clues for deciphering the issues dividing the ILWU and the PMA.

In order to decode these records, however, it is necessary to suspend the inclination to determine what actually caused a grievance to be filed. Instead of trying to figure out what "really" happened, the task is to unravel what is being disputed. By noting what is explicitly being grieved, the regular elements of contention between longshoremen and employers are revealed. Contained in these points of difference are the basic terms of conflict between the two sides.

The issues dividing longshore labor and management become visible when the observer approaches grievances in a twofold manner: (1) by taking seriously the surface accusation; that is, by accepting charges at face

1 This fourth category, however, is analytically constructed, being made up from the actual categories of "failed to return to work" (32), "late to work" (2), "extended relief" (4), "left work early" (3), "missing from the job" (3), "left job without authorization" (4), "failed to replace" (3), "late from lunch" (11), and "failed to wait for replacement" (4).

value instead of immediately discounting them or reading in hidden meanings; (2) by analyzing the talk about the charge that occurs between the two sides on paper, in private caucuses, or publicly. This methodological posture asks two questions of each complaint: What is the accusation; and how is it talked about? The answers to these questions suggest what is being complained about in the grievance machinery. Regular elements of contention between dockworkers and their supervisors surface in the contractually sanctioned arena for settling differences.

A close reading of the complaint and response text of LRCs indicates that longshoremen and their employers continue to disagree seriously over principles for management. Three kinds of disputes are contained in the 828 complaints exchanged during one twenty-two-month period: (1) What work is being done and who should do it? (2) What are the limits of flexibility? And (3) who gives orders? Taken together, these three categories of disputes add up to a struggle over how to work. The grievances suggest that, stated rules to the contrary, longshoremen do *not* always work as directed; and the employer's interests are regularly disregarded. Thus, the question of workplace regime has *not* been settled by the contract. Quite the opposite. The accusations that are leveled, and the talk about them, indicate a profound disagreement over who decides how to work.

WHAT IS BEING DONE AND WHO SHOULD DO IT?

Disagreements over how to work sometimes erupt before the job begins. Longshoremen arrive at a dock and discover that cranes have already been positioned alongside a ship. Or, cargo has been "lashed" by carpenters. Or, "reefers" (refrigerated containers) have been disconnected. Or, vans have been cleaned by independent contractors.

These discoveries provoke arguments over a very basic issue; namely, what is longshore work? The same kind of disagreements also erupt on the job when walking bosses are discovered driving lifts, or hooking on cargo; or, when machinists drive automobiles off ships; or, when a ship's crew is spotted rigging gear; or, nonlongshoremen are doing "pump" jobs.

Technically speaking, these are complaints about jurisdiction. But longshoremen use different language. They accuse employers of "lost work opportunity" or "pay short," and demand "time-in-lieu" (pay in lieu of the work someone else did). Regardless of what it is called, the disagreement is basic. The very definition of longshore work is at stake. So deep are the differences between the ILWU and the PMA that they do not agree on what longshore work is and what it is not.

When they agree on what is longshore work, they routinely disagree about how *many* longshoremen should do it. Does the job need four winch drivers or three; two bulldozer operators or one? Twelve men have been dispatched to a job; is a gang boss necessary? Does it take six or eight linesmen to handle a vessel? Are four swing men needed, or will two do? Predictably, the union insists on the higher number. And it typically accuses employers of a "lost work opportunity" if it finds too few working. Employers, of course, are convinced the minimum number is sufficient. If longshoremen disagree, and "stand by," they are fired for "refusing to work as directed."

Numbers are not the only issue in these disagreements. The dispute is actually a very serious one. It is an argument over whose understanding of the job will govern the workplace. The disagreement is about who has the power to define work, and hence, who is to be included and excluded from the work process. A seemingly simple question, like how many linesmen are required to work a vessel, for example, can be answered only by settling a prior issue, namely, is the ship being "hauled" or "let go"? When a ship is "hauled," it is moved in its berth, or to another pier. "Letting go," on the other hand, means a ship's lines are released, and it is leaving for another port. But the distinction is usually blurred: If a ship is released from one dock and loaded at another in the same port, is that "hauling"? Or is it "letting go"? Since one activity is known by different names, the labeling process is consequential: "Hauling" requires six longshoremen; "letting go" calls for eight. The dispute is therefore not a minor one. Up for grabs is the definition of work.

This disagreement surfaces in other disputes. For example, differences arise over which longshore categories can do what work. Can people dispatched to container freight stations be required to do a sweeper's work? Can utility lift drivers be used to work against a ship? Can 9.43 men do basic longshore work? If an agreement is not reached, the union typically accuses employers of creating a "lost work opportunity." Management, on the other hand, responds to the disagreement by charging longshoremen with "refusal to work as directed."

At first glance, the disagreement looks like a straightforward jurisdictional dispute. Like the argument over numbers, however, this dispute is about competing definitions of work. Whether or not steady men can do basic longshoring depends on the context. Speaking abstractly, both sides agree 9.43 men will not operate fork lifts in a ship's hold. That is basic longshore work, and it is done by people dispatched from the hall. If, however, the job is a "specialty operation," then 9.43 men can drive lifts aboard ship. The question then becomes: Is the job a "specialty operation"? How the sides answer depends on their interpretation of the activity. The dispute, therefore, is not simply jurisdictional; it is also conceptual.

Arguments over occupational turf extend to disputes about equipment. Are the ramps used to discharge automobiles part of the ship's "structure"? Or, are they "stevedoring equipment"? Is the ship's gear called "winches" or "whirly cranes"? From an outsider's vantage point, ship's gear by any other name is still equipment for loading and unloading cargo. From this perspective, the disagreement is superficial and petty, a minor argument over nomenclature. Waterfront workers, however, have a more complicated point of view. They make fine distinctions when they talk about the relationship between ships and gear. Naming equipment, moreover, has serious consequences. If ramps are not part of the ship's structure, then winch drivers must be hired to operate them. If, on the other hand, the two sides agree that the ship's structure includes ramps, sailors as well as longshoremen can operate them. Similarly, when a ship's equipment is certified as "whirly cranes," steady men can operate them. If, on the other hand, the cranes are called "winches," then they have to be driven by longshoremen dispatched from the hall.

Equipment disputes are rooted in a deep disagreement. Nothing about ship's gear inherently makes it "winches" or "cranes." How equipment will be known, then, is decided by the people working it. But their definition of *what* gear is cannot be separated from *who* operates it. Each side's definition of equipment is therefore socially located *and* competing. Thus

210

the issue in the argument over equipment goes to the heart of class relations; the question is: Which side shall decide who does the work? Conflicts over the fine points in contracts, and arguments about terminology, disputes that the American public lampoons and minimizes when it talks about unions, take on added meaning when viewed in this light. These are not pettifogging activities. Rather, they are disputes over the power to define work. Ultimately, they are disagreements about the distribution of rewards and burdens for the work process.[2]

BARGAINS, PREROGATIVES, AND FLEXIBILITY:
ESTABLISHING THE LIMITS OF PERMISSIBILITY

Disagreement does not end when the two sides agree on what is being done, who can do it, in what numbers, and on which equipment. The contest over how to work continues while ships are being loaded and unloaded. Given the economics of maritime shipping, disputes are inescapable. Profit margins in this industry are especially sensitive to "turn-around time," the time when ships are loaded and unloaded in port. Because ships make money only while they are "under way," turn-around time reduces profits. To complicate matters, and increase costs, ships generate expenses while in port. Steamship lines therefore want vessels in and out of port as rapidly as possible. So do stevedoring companies. They bid competitively for contracts to load and unload ships, and labor is their biggest cost.

Turn-around time is reduced when management is not required to strictly comply with contractual technicalities and details. The contract, however, was not written to minimize turn-around time. And when it is enforced strictly, longshoring takes time. On the other hand, if the contract is applied loosely, or ignored completely, time is saved. But longshoremen have no immediate stake in reducing turn-around time. They are hourly or monthly employees. Thus, it is not always to their advantage to make contractual concessions that save time. Every time ships are tied up, then, the scene is set for serious contests over how to work.

2 I am indebted to Jeff Lustig for this insight.

211

How much flexibility will management be allowed?

As might be expected, one basic disagreement erupts when management uses the contract flexibly. This dispute surfaces in two situations: (1) when longshoremen are shifted from one job to another; and (2) in disagreements over operating principles. The first dispute arises when, for example, men dispatched to lash are ordered to handle lines; or lift drivers sent to "short duration" jobs are shifted to another operation; or, during the course of a shift, longshoremen dispatched to one stevedoring company are transferred to another. When longshoremen are shifted, the union interprets the contract strictly and objects. If the practice is reported to the union, employers are charged with "pay shortages" or "creating a lost work opportunity." The employers, on the other hand, define these contested activities permissively. They want maximum use of the people on their payroll.

A classic example of this disagreement began late one September morning. Six holdmen had been dispatched as lashers on the *Falcon*. When they finished, they were told to release the ship's lines, have lunch, and then go to work aboard another ship, the *Aubrac*, to finish the shift. At day's end, the union filed a grievance. It charged the company with a "pay shortage." The union claimed that

> The lashers were illegally ordered to stand by to let the lines go on the FALCON. Instead, they should have been shifted to the AUBRAC until noon; sent to lunch and then returned back to the AUBRAC at 1:00. By ordering the men to stand by and let the lines go on the FALCON, the Employer created stand-by time for the purpose of not hiring linesmen. The Employers artificially created dead-time to avoid hiring linesmen.[3]

The employers did not deny the union's account. They agreed that the gang had worked on the *Falcon*, finished at 11:30, and let go the lines at 11:45. Disagreement occurred, however, over the union's charge that the stand-by order was illegal. In the employer's thinking, dead-time was not artificially created between 11:30 and 11:45.

> Because the crane was moving to the next berth and the ship work was being organized, there was no work for the lashers. They were used to

3 UC 149/RD 76.

let go the lines on the ship they had finished. The ship was off the dock at 11:45. The principle of using unskilled members of the gang to release a vessel is not in dispute.

Both sides agreed there was no work for fifteen minutes. But they disagreed about whether the men should have "stood by" and released the lines. The union thought they should have been shifted to another ship as soon as they were finished. The employers disagreed. Management's response describes the event as a process: "The ship work was being organized." This language builds flexibility into the very account. Given their interpretation, supervisors can use longshoremen to work in various categories.

The employer's account is self-interested. It saves money in two ways: Linesmen do not have to be hired, and the ship can be released immediately after it is loaded.[4] There is no need to rely on estimated times for departure. This is important because estimates can be costly. When they are incorrect, linesmen arrive early but are paid to stand by. If they are late, the ship is delayed. Thus, the employer's flexible version enables them to reduce turn-around time, and therefore costs. The union's dichotomous description and its strict reading of the contract, on the other hand, understandably restrict employer options.

Flexibility is also an issue in conflicts over operating principles. When management's flexibility interferes with established working rules, serious disagreements erupt. One of the waterfront's important working rules is "hatch rights." A gang assigned to a hatch has contractual claim on that work; the gang is entitled to work that job until it is completed. Hatch rights, however, are not inviolable because the maritime industry is unpredictable. Tides, storms, and other factors over which no one has control can ruin even the most well-intentioned plans. Recognizing this, both sides agree that, under certain circumstances, hatch rights may be suspended. Such circumstances, however, are rare. They occur only when a situation is "beyond management's control." Expectably, the two sides rarely agree that a situation is beyond management's control. The unspoken but obvious issue is how much flexibility will management be permitted? If the union thinks a situation is not beyond management's

---

4 Linesmen are longshoremen hired to take and release the lines that secure ships to docks.

213

control, they accuse supervisors of "creating a lost work opportunity" and they demand "time-in-lieu."

The exchanges are heated and angry. Both sides have a version of what is beyond control. For the employers, it is unforeseen circumstances, like weather changes. Thus, they mention weather when gangs are released one day and replaced the next, even after assuring longshoremen that additional gangs would not be needed. Employers also insist they have no control when gangs are unavailable the next day to do unanticipated work. The union's understanding of employer's control, on the other hand, is narrow. "Beyond the employer's control," according to the union, means management has no options. When these two competing definitions of control are debated, basic issues are revealed. In one dispute, "a lost work opportunity" was attributed to negligence by a ship's clerk, something clearly "beyond the employer's control." The employer wrote that: "Had Mr. X' not made his error, Hatch #1 would have been finished within the one hour provided in Section 2.4431 and the night gangs would not have had to rework the hatch; therefore, the claim is denied."[5]

At the LRC, a union representative spoke first:

"I don't give a shit whether a clerk made a mistake or not," he said.

"Why not?" asked the PMA spokesman, "that obviously makes it beyond the employer's control."

"They could have left that container for the next shift or put it in another cell," the unionist replied.

"And lose revenue?!" exclaimed a manager.

"You're not listening to our suggestion," said the union official, "you're gimmicking the contract. In effect, you're saying you won't go along with the agreement. This is not beyond your control because you had options."

"Companies make decisions on the basis of economics not whether or not there are options," responded the PMA representative matter of factly.

"Economics is not, however, a circumstance beyond your control," the Local 10 officer retorted in disgust. "Oh the hell with it," he said, "let's agree to disagree and go to the arbitrator."[6]

Supervision had very few options in this situation. They are paid to get

5 UC 28–78/RD 108.
6 Field notes.

ships in and out of port as quickly as possible. That task is facilitated by interpreting the contract loosely, even when they risk violating hatch rights. The union, on the other hand, is not obliged to reduce turn-around time. Thus, in this instance, a strict contract reading works to the union's advantage. These different obligations produce conflicting agendas for how to work: One requires flexibility; the other depends upon enforcing the agreement to the letter.

What are the limits to managerial prerogative?

Longshoring produces other conflicts between agendas. Because ships carry multiple cargoes, it is common for jobs to change during a shift. What begins as a job off-loading containers turns into a steel discharge job. When the work changes, another kind of argument surfaces: Can supervisors replace one longshore category with another? The union contends that when a longshoreman is dispatched to a specific job, it is his for the duration. The employers disagree. If a job changes, they counter, the original longshoreman can be replaced. One grievance over a pay shortage is typical:

> Brothers B and M drove lift in the hold with #3 crane unit for 8 hours. Men were bumped by two 9.43 drivers Saturday, being denied their rightful callback. The gang worked 10 hours Saturday.

The employers responded,

> the operation changed on Saturday to H/L (Heavy Lift) coils and using 15-ton lifts. Steady men are permitted on this equipment. Claim denied. (UC 230/RD 79)

The issue in this dispute is flexibility. If a job changes, can employers replace longshoremen? The stakes are not insignificant. Steady men are on the payroll whether or not they work. Thus, employers want to use them whenever possible. The union, on the other hand, is committed to providing work for its entire membership. It is therefore not easily persuaded to grant management flexibility in these disputes.

Management's flexibility is contested in other contexts as well. This frequently occurs when employers enforce the contract strictly instead of loosely. For example, when jobs are overstaffed, and the work almost

215

finished, employers will sometimes invoke contractual grounds to lighten the payroll. A gang is sent back to the hall because it is working "short-handed." A winch driver working without a "skill card" is fired. In these instances, applying the contract rigidly saves employers money. But this is a serious departure from management's tendency to interpret the agreement permissively. When employers reverse their field like this, an argument surfaces about their prerogatives, and flexibility becomes a weapon.

In one of these disputes, the employers denied a pay claim. In their estimation, the gang was not entitled to pay because it had not been "turned to." The reason offered was: "One of the winch drivers, a San Pedro man, did not have a winch card and the hall did not have a qualified winch driver."[7] When the dispute reached the LRC, a union official leveled a serious accusation: "You don't check skill cards when a ship is about to leave," he told the employers present. "You wanted to get rid of a gang this time." The issue of prerogatives was nearly explicit when he continued: "If you want people port-certified, then that's all we'll send. But you can't have it both ways. We want this inconsistency resolved. We're going to write a formal letter to the company asking for an official clarification of their policy."[8]

Management's right to hire longshoremen was not questioned by the union. The disagreement was over *the grounds on which* longshoremen would be hired. Depending upon one's perspective, the company's hiring policy was either "flexible" or "inconsistent." And *that* was the issue. By honoring the employer's right to hire skilled longshoremen, the union restricted their flexibility in hiring. Thus, the union effectively married the disputes over skill certification and flexibility. It used the resulting combination to attack management's hiring prerogatives.

Disputes over prerogatives and flexibility do not always emerge spontaneously. Sometimes they are pursued self-consciously to force an issue. The outer limits of permissibility are established by probing the periphery of tolerance. Eventually these excursions appear on an LRC agenda. In some instances the strategy is acknowledged explicitly. Thus, in one ex-

7 UC 231/RD 64.
8 RD 64.

216

change, a longshoreman accused employers of abusing the "short-duration" lift driver category. The formal charge was that:

> He arrived on the job and immediately started relieving five lift drivers (including Gang Lift Drivers). He did nothing else. This is a gimmick of the short-duration.

Responding officially, the employers justified the practice by paraphrasing contractual provisions that permitted it.

> The short duration L/D was supplementing a skill man of the same skill already on the job. Claim is denied.

When the disagreement reached the LRC, the employer's representative made his intentions explicit: "We want to see if this can be done," he told the assembled people.

The union was outraged. Officials threatened a port-wide work stoppage using whatever technicalities could be found. "It just ain't cricket," protested one business agent. "I'll find something to tie you up a whole goddamn day."

Sounding almost apologetic, the PMA spokesman said firmly, "We feel we have to force the issue; it's the only way we can find out if we can do this."9

Living up to informal agreements: How much latitude do longshoremen have at work?

Like a double-edged sword, the dispute over prerogatives and flexibility cuts two ways. Waterfront employers are not the only ones to benefit from reduced turn-around time; flexibly enforced contracts can sometimes be advantageous for longshoremen. The quicker a job finishes, the sooner the men can go home. And since they are paid by the shift, longshoremen can leave early without losing money. When the contract is applied permissively, work proceeds more flexibly, and that is also an advantage for longshoremen. They can spell each other, work out of category, arrive at work a little late, or leave early. Flexibility encourages the deals described earlier. These informal agreements are possible, however, only under two

9 RD 39.

conditions: when longshoremen are permitted to work in "violation" of the contract, and when quid pro quos are honored by both sides. The deals break down if either condition is violated.

Since waterfront work is not standardized, chances are good that conditions will change during a shift. And unofficial agreements made under one set of circumstances are likely to be broken under another. Permission to leave work early may be granted when it looks like the job is nearly completed. It will probably be revoked, however, if the work takes longer than expected. Every time a deal is struck, then, the stage is set for a serious dispute. Another two fundamental points of contention emerge when this occurs: How much flexibility will *longshoremen* be permitted; and, what is the standing of informal agreements?

These disputes surface in three kinds of complaints. Officially speaking, the employers are accused of "pay shortage" and longshoremen with "walking off the job," or different ways of "missing work," including: "late," "failed to return to work," and "missing from the job." Unlike the official charges, narratives introducing and responding to the complaints tell another story. The disagreement is over facts; the two sides have competing accounts of the event. They are not interpreting the same facts differently; they have conflicting facts. Thus, if one relies exclusively on written accounts, it is impossible to know what transpired, or even what the issues are.

A longshoreman is accused of "walking off the job," for example. He files a countercomplaint charging the stevedoring company with a "pay shortage." The employer's response is straightforward: The longshoreman "left the job at 2:00 p.m. without permission from either the walking boss or superintendent and did not return." But this contradicts the longshoreman's account, which states that he "was unjustly removed from the payroll at 2:00 p.m. by persons unknown after he finished his duties and was released by the W/Boss [walking boss]. This job was finished according to the W/Boss."

Were this the only evidence, one would not know what the dispute was about. Fortunately, however, the Grievance Committee added another dimension to the story. The accused longshoreman, according to its report, "stated the W/B gave him instructions that when the box car was finished that would be all of the work. The W/B and lift drivers closed the

218

doors to the pier and left with him."[10] The implication was understood by both sides: A deal had been made, and broken.

Another exchange is typical. A gang is penalized for "walking off the job." The employer reports that the "the men were instructed by W/B to stay to sort some cargo after vessel sailed at 11:00 p.m. They left without getting replacements and were taken off the payroll at 11:00 p.m." One of the accused men had a different version, however. He filed a counter-complaint, accusing the employer of a "pay shortage." He remembers the situation differently: "He was working as a stickman in the yard," reads the countercomplaint.

> After the last load was off the ship he was told by W/B——— to help let go lines on the ship and go home. He did so, but a couple of nights later the W/B told him his time was cut for leaving the job. Man is entitled to balance of night's pay and T.T. [travel time].

The Grievance Committee agreed with the longshoreman's account ruling that the

> W/B told them to finish sticking in the yard and let the ship go and then go home. They followed orders.[11]

Verbal exchanges at LRC meetings sometimes make explicit what the union thinks is the issue in these disputes. During one argument, a union official asked the employers rhetorically: "Why don't you go after the walking bosses in these cases? You know as well as I do what happened. They made a deal and the walker went back on it."[12] A business agent explained why an informal agreement in another dispute was not honored: "The superintendent probably got on this walker's ass about people leaving early," he explained to the employers. "So the walking boss then files a complaint to cover up the deal and put it on the men."[13]

Informal agreements that cut contractual corners are routine on the waterfront. Because they reduce work time and increase productivity, deals are mutually beneficial. They also create flexibility for both sides. Without these agreements, longshoremen would have to work by the

10 EC 109/UC 244/RD 132.
11 EC 115/UC 225A/RD132.
12 RD 63.
13 RD 112.

letter of the contract even if that involved unnecessary work and unproductive time. Thus, one of the issues contained in these disputes is, how much latitude will longshoremen be allowed? Should they determine the work pace and quitting time? Or, are these issues contractually specified?

Sometimes the bargains themselves are an issue. Although their legal standing is shaky, unofficial agreements are not taken lightly. Once made, each party assumes the other will abide by the bargain. Obviously, however, this does not preclude someone from trying to wiggle out of an agreement. When that happens, either the employer accuses longshoremen of "walking off the job," or the union charges the employer with "pay shortage." The two sides then focus their attention on the agreement's standing.

In one emergency, for example, management agreed to pay linesmen an extra two hours to release a ship and tie it up. Tug boats were standing by and the supervisor didn't have time to wait for a new complement of linesmen. When the men received their checks, however, they were not paid for the two hours. They therefore filed a grievance claiming a pay shortage.

"The superintendent only agreed to pay because he had no choice," responded a PMA representative when the complaint reached the LRC.

> The pilot had berthed the vessel in the wrong place and when that was
> discovered the company wanted it moved. The men claimed that was a
> second job for them and refused to handle the lines unless they were
> paid extra. They said he should have more linesmen dispatched. Supervi-
> sion agreed to pay them only in order to get the vessel untied and
> changed.

The union disagreed. "Once an agreement is made," said an official, "it's binding."

"What if we made a deal to pay a guy a dollar an hour less than the contract," countered a PMA representative, "you wouldn't say that's binding would you?"

"If he struck the deal, we'd expect him to stick to it. But he wouldn't have to make the deal if he didn't want to. There is grievance machinery for him to use that would protect him."[14]

14 UC 260/RD 84.

Summing up the union's position, a Local 10 officer stated the issue candidly: "Look," he said, "The problem we have here is, what do you do when people strike a bargain and then it's not held to?"

WHO GIVES ORDERS? CONTESTING MANAGEMENT AUTHORITY

Disagreements over how to work can be basic and explicit on the San Francisco waterfront. For example, a longshoreman is told to sit on his lift truck and wait for cargo. He does not. "He was warned several times to stay with his unit," reads the employer complaint. "He continued to leave his lift to talk to other longshoremen and was eventually fired." The longshoreman does not dispute the employer's account. Reporting to the Grievance Committee, he states that "supervision had been on his back all morning and after coffee break ordered him to sit on his lift and not stand by watching longshoremen palletizing. He was fired at this point."[15] The disagreement over work in this case is simple: The longshoreman was told to do one thing, and he did another.

Other disputes about how to work are equally fundamental. A gang is discovered working shorthanded. "Only three men were working while the other men were sitting down," the employer complains. "They were told three times by the Walking Boss to assist the other three men working in the square with hand trucks. They refused and the gang was let go at 2:30 a.m." The gang does not dispute the essential facts. "The gang started at 7:00 p.m.," they respond.

> All the men worked until 2:10 a.m. At this time the gang took a unit break. The Walking Boss came to the hatch and said he wanted 6 men working. The W/B repeated that he wanted 6 men working. The steward told the W/B that the men were going to continue working in about 10 minutes when their break was over.[16]

A longshoreman is "warned several times to drive his Taylor machine in reverse motion. He was driving his machine in a forward motion, and was

15 EC 89A/RD 130.
16 EC 225/RD 89.

consequently fired." The accused worker responds simply: "He had been doing his job conscientiously and there was no reason to fire him."[17]

The issue in these complaints is quite basic: An order is given and it is disobeyed. There is no argument over what happened, and there are no interpretive differences. The two sides agree on the facts. It is therefore appropriate that when someone is fired in these disputes, the language is straightforward: Longshoremen are charged with "refusal to work as directed."

Sometimes there is an argument over orders. The discussion around these disputes reveals deep differences. For example, two lashers accused of refusing to lock cones (secure the devices that attach containers to one another and the ship) told the Grievance Committee:

> at 7:55 a.m. the Superintendent requested that two men go and lock the cones. It was 5 minutes to quitting time. *The Supt. told the crane driver this.* The men said that *they were not given any order to lock any cones by the Walking Boss.*[18]

The disagreement in this account extends beyond following orders. If, as the men claimed, the orders were passed through the crane driver, the directives have no standing because the contract does not authorize crane drivers to direct work. Thus, the lashers were not contesting the order. They were challenging the authority of the person giving it.

Management's authority is periodically contested explicitly. An employer explains why one longshoreman was fired for refusing to work as directed in the following terms:

> the Walking Boss instructed him to build loads of loose lumber. ———— was merely watching other holdmen working at this time. ————refused saying that the Walking Boss should not give him direct instructions, but rather, have the gang boss give him orders. He was fired.

The Grievance Committee report expressed a different understanding of the incident: "Brother ———— stated that he didn't refuse to work as directed," it reads. *"He wasn't given any orders.* He stated that this is usual harassment by this W/B."[19] Since, technically speaking, only gang bosses

17 UC 133/RD 47.
18 EC 191/RD 82, emphasis added.
19 EC 57/RD 112, emphasis added.

are authorized to direct work, in this longshoreman's estimation, no orders were given. He therefore didn't refuse the order; he refused to hear it.

When longshoremen refuse to hear the orders of supervisors, they are disputing management's very right to give orders. This is sometimes made explicit in the conversations about grievances. For example, one longshoreman filed a grievance for an "unjust firing" after he was fired for refusing to work as directed. His formal complaint reads:

> he was told by Walking Boss——— to go into the hatch at 4:30 p.m.
> from his job on the dock. At that time *he told the Walking Boss that the gang
> boss was the one supposed to give him orders.* At that time the W/B fired him.

The employer's official response stated that he

> was properly instructed by the Walking Boss. When he refused to work
> as directed, he was fired; therefore the claim is denied.[20]

When the matter was discussed at an LRC, the employer's representative spoke first:

"You know the chain of command doesn't exclude supervision from giving orders," he said.

"The walking boss oversees gangs, not individuals," interrupted a Local 10 officer. "Only the gang boss can fire a man," he continued.

Another union representative had a question: "What was so urgent that the walking boss couldn't tell the gang boss to order the men to shift?"

"It wasn't a matter of urgency," explained a longshoreman who had witnessed the event and was present to testify. "What it was, was that the walker said, 'no one refuses a direct order from me.'"

Quite clearly, and openly, this longshoreman was challenging the right of certain supervisors to give orders. He *told* the walking boss that he followed only the gang boss's orders. And if the witness's account is accurate, the walking boss knew what the issue was too: As he allegedly said, "No one refuses a direct order from me."

Despite explicit contractual language stating otherwise, San Francisco longshoremen do not always work "as directed by" or "in the interests of" the employer. Disagreements over work are standard and profound. The most obvious dispute occurs when longshoremen challenge manage-

20 UC 273/RD 96.

ment's authority by refusing orders. Although dramatic and obvious, this is, however, only one manifestation of the disagreement over how to work. The union and management also argue over bargains, prerogatives, flexibility, what is being done, and who should do it. They operate with conflicting definitions of longshore work; they disagree over what long-shoremen can properly do. In other words, they read the same contract differently. These oppositional readings, understandings, and definitions are socially located and systematic. They are not individual, idiosyncratic disputes. The two sides inhabit different locations in the work process and this produces conflicting agendas for how to work. One side wants con-tractual flexibility; the other wants the contract enforced strictly.

The disagreement between the two sides, then, continues to be a funda-mental one. Each side has a different perspective on the work process, a different interpretation of it. The two perspectives, moreover, are mutu-ally exclusive and competitive because only one view can prevail at a given time. Thus, the disputes that surface in the grievance machinery reflect an ongoing struggle over how longshore work will be done. Contained in the complaints about pay and work performance are arguments over princi-ples for management, disagreements over which side's rules will govern the workplace. The issue dividing the two sides is still fundamental. The conflict is over who decides how to work and who will control the water-front workplace.

11

WHICH SIDE'S LANGUAGE SHALL GOVERN?

IMPORTANT as it may be, the struggle over how to work is only one front in a larger battle for control of the waterfront. Formulating and interpreting contractual language is another theater in this war. Despite fifty years of collective bargaining, and almost thirty years after the M&M Agreements were signed, the differences between Local 10 and the PMA are so deep that the two sides operate with different vocabularies; they do not even agree on the very language specifying the terms of their cooperation. When the collective agreement is being formulated, they battle over whose language will be used; when it is signed, the struggle continues, and the issue becomes whose understanding of the contract will prevail? Thus, even though they live by the same contractual language, they battle over the naming of disputed activities. These disagreements surface in two contexts: in contract negotiations, where contractual language is constructed; and in the grievance machinery, where operating definitions of disputed activities are contested.

"TRYING TO COME UP WITH LANGUAGE WE CAN BOTH LIVE WITH": WORDING CONTRACTS

Negotiations are set up to try to get rid of problems. You've got certain problems, we've got certain problems. You've got certain things that stick in your craw, we've got certain things that stick in ours. You've got certain things you can't live with, we've got certain things we can't live with. What we're trying to do in negotiations is to get language on issues that we can both live with. We're not trying to cut your throats, we're not trying to ruin your operation. We're trying to come up with language that we can both live with in this situation. (PMA representative to ILWU negotiator)[1]

The struggle over words in contract negotiations gets waged in two kinds of arguments. One occurs when the two sides use different language for the same activity. The other emerges when the two sides use the *same language* for an activity, but attribute *different meanings* to the words.

"Unions make demands; employers make proposals": Naming the same activity with different words

Disputes over language erupt very early in contract negotiations. One set of negotiations had been in session only for two days when a disagreement surfaced over what to call the activities. After carefully scrutinizing and elaborating the union's demands, an ILWU representative asked, "When will the employers have their demands ready?"

"Unions make demands," replied the PMA spokesperson sternly, acknowledging the power of names and barely able to hide a humorous barb; "employers make proposals" (field notes).

Even though the dispute is minor, the depth of disagreement is not. The issue in disagreements of this sort is, which side's language will prevail? The establishment of the Special Equipment Operator's Board is a case in point. When negotiations began, both sides agreed to the idea in principle. The union liked the new board because it reduced steady work opportunities. The employers were also pleased because the board preserved the steady man category. The two sides did not agree, however, on the language specifying eligibility requirements.

"Trainees must have a valid California Driver's license," read a provision proposed by the PMA.[2] "Trainees must be able to read and communicate in English," stated another requirement.

ILWU representatives objected to this language. "Whether or not people can drive has nothing to do with if they have a driver's license," pointed out one negotiator. "You can find that out by giving them a driving test."

1 Field notes, RD 133.
2 The subsequent two paragraphs are based on field notes.

"And if they don't know how to drive," interjected someone else, "teach 'em."

"We want the valid driver's license provision struck from the eligibility requirements," said the union's official spokesman.

"We also want you to change that language about being able to read and communicate in English," he continued. "A lot of our guys are illiterate, or can't speak English, but that's no reason why they should be disqualified from becoming Special Equipment Operators. These guys have devised all sorts of ways for communicating and they all don't involve English or reading."

The union wanted different language to qualify longshoremen for the training program. So far as the union was concerned, the criteria for waterfront citizenship was not literacy in the formal sense of the term. Rather, it was one's ability to participate in the work process. Thus, a union official suggested that the employers "substitute the phrase, 'be able to communicate in language necessary to perform the job,' for your phrase, 'read and communicate in English.'" The apparent dispute over language ran far deeper than surface manifestations indicated. As the union saw it, the issue was who belongs and who does not.

"We'll take that under advisement," responded the employer's spokesman.

The struggle over language does not end when the contract has been signed. "I've learned that everything in this business is negotiable," quipped a PMA official.[3] Being admitted into the SEO training program was no exception. When PMA representatives passed a proposed admission form across the table, union officials insisted on a number of changes. The first line of the form, next to the date of waterfront registration, asked longshoremen to check one of two boxes. Were they class "A" or "B" longshoremen?[4] The union was opposed to the question: "We want those

---

3 The following three paragraphs are based on field notes, RD 141.
4 In effect, "B-men" are apprentice longshoremen. They are registered waterfront workers – not casual labor – who work out of the hiring hall and the presumption is that they will eventually become "A-men." They are dispatched after A-men have had an opportunity to work. The joint PMA-ILWU Coast Committee decides when there is sufficient work in a port to register B-men as A-men.

227

boxes struck and the form to read, 'date of original registration,'" said the union spokesman. The PMA agreed to the new wording.

"We object to the second line," he continued. "It currently reads, 'I am presently certified in a skilled category: day, night, active, inactive, reserve,' and we want all of that left out so that it simply reads, 'I am presently working on the ——— board.'"

Union officials were also unhappy with a question pertaining to the "skill categories" of applicants; they wanted different wording. "Just say, 'indicate the waterfront equipment with which you've had experience,'" suggested a union official. The two sides continued to argue about language specifying deadlines, methods for choosing teachers, and how to appeal being disqualified.

At first glance, the arguments over qualifying language seem to be trivial, petty, and misguided attempts to assert power over insignificant matters. On the contrary, the stakes are high in this dispute. The issue underwriting these differences is whether contract language will be permissive or restrictive. The union wants language to be permissive. It wants to qualify as many men as possible so that more people have access to the work. Thus, union officials object to detailed specifications for admitting longshoremen into the training program. They want to define the criteria for eligibility as loosely as they can. The employers, on the other hand, want restrictive language. They want language that will reduce the number of dockworkers eligible for training. Thus, the language they propose provides grounds for exclusion. This struggle over words is a critical one. The language the two sides agree to live with determines who will be on the Special Equipment Operator's Board.

Disputes over permissive versus restrictive language occur routinely in contract negotiations. They usually surface in arguments over which side's language will name a contested activity. A disagreement about how to describe gearmen's work is typical. The PMA spokesperson read the union's understanding out loud: "Gearmen shall be employed to build, repair, handle, and haul all stevedoring equipment."[5] He stopped reading and commented, "gearmen are hauling all equipment now. Why do you want to put that in the agreement?"

---

5 The following three paragraphs are based on field notes.

"We want it in writing," answered the union negotiator.

"Hauling isn't a good word," replied the employer representative.

We all know what it means but it means so many different things. And there's another problem: what is 'equipment'? How do you define equipment? I'm concerned with the fact that sometimes superintendents or walking bosses will need a filler for a respirator, go up to their car, pick it up, come back and you guys will consider that 'equipment' and say they are 'hauling' it. If it's not a problem, why create one?

"The issue isn't fillers for respirators," responded a union spokesman. "The issue is superintendents and walking bosses who sometimes get on equipment and move it. This happens especially on the night side when there's no gearmen working. These guys have free reign to do whatever they want."

Uncharacteristically, the union wanted restrictive language in this instance. And they were almost explicit about it:

"We want that language in writing so we can stop them from doing our work."

"But this is already covered in the section that defines what a gearman is," said the PMA official, nearly unable to contain his frustration, "we don't need it here."

"If you'll agree that gear work belongs to gearmen," someone from the union side said quietly, "then you'll have to go along with our language."

The PMA officer shook his head and tried another approach: "There's a fuzzy line; there's a gray area in the middle where it's not clear exactly what is gearmen's work and what isn't."

What was clear, however, was that both sides attached importance to the words and that the struggle over them was a fundamental one. "I guess we need to come up with some different language if we're going to be able to work this out," he concluded.

"GIVE US AN EXAMPLE OF WHAT YOU MEAN BY . . .":
SHARED LANGUAGE/MIXED MEANINGS

Which side's language will name disputed activities is but one front in the war over words. Language disputes also surface when union and management use the same word to describe different activities. These disagreements center around the meaning of words rather than the words themselves. Arguments happen in three circumstances: when implicit rules are made explicit; when dated language is maintained; and when ambiguity is untangled.

Writing unwritten rules

> I've learned that when something ought to be in the contract, you better put it in or else it will come back and bite you.[6]

Discussing sweeper's work, the PMA wanted to eliminate any reference to cleaning dock offices. The union objected, accusing the employers of trying to reduce ILWU jurisdiction.[7] The argument quickly turned on competing definitions of a "dock office."

"We could include language on dock offices," said a PMA representative, adding an important qualification; "but it depends on where the dock offices are."

"Give me an example of what you mean by a dock office," challenged his union counterpart.

"Shacks in the immediate area of the dock are not 'dock offices.' Neither is the supercargo's shack, or the shacks on the pier. These are administrative offices, not dock offices."

"Don't give me no bullshit!" exploded someone from the union's side of the table, "This is jurisdictional. We used to have all them places."

The ILWU spokesman calmly interjected himself into the exchange: "You're trying to take the offices away from us," he asserted. "Is that the intent? Are you trying to take away our jurisdiction?"

"No," responded a stevedoring company representative, who was making the employer's intention explicit. "What we're trying to do is clarify the situation as it truly exists now."

The union did not challenge the employer's assessment. The unionists did, however, object to making explicit an arrangement they had never formally ratified, and one that cost them jobs. "Just because we don't work a particular facility doesn't mean we have waived our jurisdiction to it," explained the ILWU representative. The argument, then, went beyond

6 Union official to PMA representative, field notes.
7 The next two paragraphs are based on field notes.

jurisdiction. It was a dispute about formalizing the informal, making the implicit explicit. Thus, a PMA executive countered, "we're not trying to take anything away; we're trying to identify what you already do in a better way."

In the argument over dock offices, the employers pushed for contractual language to reflect operant realities. This strategy, however, cuts two ways. Thus, when the union made the same argument in another context, the employers objected.

"Would you explain what you mean by this?" asked a PMA negotiator about proposed language requiring that, after holding union office, gearmen be returned to their original job category.[8]

"What we mean is that if a man is a gearman and he runs for office, he's still in the category of gearman after his office expires."

"But that's already an unwritten rule," protested the employers; "that already happens."

"We know that," said the union representative summarizing the dynamics of the disagreement, "but we want to put it in writing."

"Just because we operate in good faith," added someone else from the union side of the table, "doesn't mean we trust you."

Keeping language current

Sometimes words are used even when the circumstances that originally created them have changed. The words survive while their meanings change. This typically occurs in industries experiencing rapid and profound technological change. In these instances, contractual language is frequently not synchronized with shopfloor realities. The language was designed for circumstances that no longer exist. When discrepancies are detected between the contractual vocabulary and waterfront realities, another kind of dispute over language emerges in negotiations.

The contractual definition of coopers is a case in point. On the waterfront, the term "cooper" refers to workers who repair cargo containers. Historically speaking, coopers repaired wooden barrels. In some sectors of working-class culture the term also has an abstract meaning. It is a syn-

---

8 This paragraph is based on field notes.

onym for fixing up or repairing. For example, longshoremen can be over-heard to say, "let's just 'cooper-up' this machine." On the Pacific Coast waterfront, contractually speaking, coopers "repair cargo containers." The meaning of "cargo containers," however, has changed radically since 1958. Cargo containers are no longer pallet boards or wooden boxes that can be "coopered up." They are now huge metal vans and sophisticated machinery is required to repair them. When making this observation in recent negotiations, PMA representatives proposed changes in the language per-taining to longshoremen repairing cargo containers.

The union, however, was not easily persuaded. "We assume that coopers will continue to repair containers," said Local 10's representative. "Any language that you would propose would be restrictive language. We think that the original language is pretty good."[9]

"But there's a clarification that's needed," argued a PMA official. "The present language assigns container repair to coopers, not to gearmen. That has changed."

"There's no advantage for us to change the language," the union spokes-man said simply. "We'll take your proposal under advisement."

Untangling ambiguities, matching meanings

"We want that in there," said a union representative, "because it puts in writing what we've already agreed to. We want to nail down that principle."

"We have no problem with the principle," responded the PMA repre-sentative, "our problem is with the language you propose." (Field notes)

Another dispute over language surfaces during negotiations when the two sides use the same words, but with different meanings. The words they use often contain multiple meanings; and definitions of them are neither obvious nor located in the words themselves. Because the two sides define words self-interestedly, using meanings that work to their advantage, they frequently operate with different meanings of the same word. And, when the meanings don't match, an argument erupts over which side's under-standing of the disputed word will go into the contract.

9 This paragraph is based on field notes.

For example, discussing the issue of pay guarantee, a union negotiator said to his counterpart: "In your last sentence you say, 'subject to disciplinary action.' Give us an example." He had no trouble with the words per se. He was, however, worried about how they might be interpreted. Thus, he asked the PMA official to specify the grounds on which someone might be denied the guarantee.

"A man doesn't show up on a given day," replied the employer representative, adding: "and he doesn't have a bonafide reason."

"What do you mean by a 'bonafide reason'?" asked the unionist; "what about an emergency?"

"If he has an emergency, he can call."

"Call who? The hall?"

"No, the employer."

"That's redundant," said the union spokesperson, "there's already disciplinary language in the Master agreement."

"Are you saying that you have trouble with that?"

"No, I'm saying it's in the agreement already, you already do that."

"I know, but we want to be explicit," said the PMA negotiator.[10]

This dispute is not about which side's words will prevail but rather whose definition of the words' meaning will operate. In this instance, the interpretation of words like "bonafide reason," "emergency," and "call" is the terrain on which a battle over language is waged. Substituting one side's words for the other's will not resolve this difference; the issue is whether the words will be permitted. Thus, in this instance, the argument moves away from the question of disciplinary action to the issue of redundancy.

"What does this mean?" asked a union negotiator in a similar dispute. The employers had proposed language that would "obligate" longshoremen with skill cards to work in their skill category when it was "required."[11] "What do you mean by 'obligated'?" asked the Local 10 officer.

"It means that they have to work when they are required."

"What's your definition of 'when required'?" probed the union official.

The employer's negotiators recalled that a large order of tractor drivers

---

10 Field notes.
11 The next paragraphs are based on field notes.

had recently gone unfilled. The order went unfilled, in their estimation, because longshoremen who were available and skilled chose not to take the jobs. In other words, the problem was not a shortage of credentialed tractor drivers, but that qualified longshoremen chose not to do this work. Since longshoremen didn't take the jobs, the employers had to find people outside the hiring hall; thus they hired "casuals" (people available through unemployment offices). " 'When required,' " he concluded, "means it's up to the men to make themselves available when their presence is necessary to do a job."

"But one of the privileges of having a skill card," explained a union representative, "means that you don't have to take a job when you don't want to. This wording would take away that privilege."

The word "require" became more ambiguous when another question came from the union's direction. "What happens when a man has three skill cards and chooses to use one rather than the other? What does 'require' mean in this situation?"

"I can see the union's point," said an employer's representative candidly, "this would restrict people's choice. But what about the other side?" he asked, observing that the union's word-sword was double-edged. "What would happen if jobs go unfilled because there are not enough men to fill them?"

"I can see your point," said the union spokesman. But even though he could see the point, he would not accept language proposed to resolve it. "Does this mean," he asked, "that a man can be forced to give up an unskilled job if he has a skill card and he's needed in that particular skill? If it does, we can't go along with this language."

A similar dispute arose over which side's understanding of "dead-time" would be written into the contract.[12] "Are we clear on the meaning of dead-time?" asked a union person, as a bargaining session began. The employer's representative was surprised by the question. The answer seemed obvious. So far as he was concerned, "dead-time is that time at the beginning, middle, or end of a shift when there is no work for longshoremen."

"That's not our interpretation," shot back the union spokesman. "So far

12 The following three paragraphs are based on field notes.

234

as we're concerned, dead-time only occurs when the men have completed the work for which they were dispatched, and when there's nothing left for them to do." Dead-time could occur only once in the course of a day. The union's understanding was that it "had to be at the end of a shift."

The interpretation of this concept had serious implications for the assignment of work. If the union's understanding of dead-time, when longshoremen were on the payroll but not working, was written into the contract, it would be called "stand-by" time not "dead-time." The distinction is an important one. Longshoremen cannot be shifted from one task to another when they are "standing by." They can be moved around, however, on "dead-time." Thus, if the union's meaning of "dead-time" were implemented, longshoremen could not be shifted around during a shift. If, on the other hand, the employer's interpretation was given contractual standing, longshoremen could be shifted whenever they were not working since not working would mean there was "dead-time."

The distinction was sufficiently important to engage the two sides in an argument that lasted over an hour. When the arguing ended, the disagreement was still not resolved. The dispute was precipitated by an argument over who could be required to tie up a ship during a shift. The stakes were high. If the employer's permissive reading became the written understanding, longshoremen could be shifted to take lines when there was a lull in the work. This would increase employer prerogatives. It would also save money because fewer linesmen would be needed. Were the union's restrictive understanding maintained, however, employer options would be minimized and their costs increased.

NAMING DISPUTED ACTIVITIES

The struggle over words does not end when the contract is signed. The grievance machinery enables longshoremen to challenge the employer's discretion on matters of pay and work assignment. When Local 10 members feel they have been paid for fewer hours than they actually worked, they file a grievance alleging a "pay shortage." And if supervisors permit nonlongshoremen, like sailors, to do traditional "longshore work," the practice can be challenged by filing a grievance that directs the employers to pay "time-in-lieu" to people who otherwise would have been working.

235

On the surface, these disputes seem rather simple and straightforward: The issue appears to be jobs and money. But the ways in which the two sides argue about these grievances indicate that the disagreement is not just over dollars and cents; the dispute goes much deeper than the formal charges suggest. Closer inspection reveals that each side often uses a different vocabulary to describe the event in question. The conflict between waterfront labor and management is so deep that the two parties cannot even agree on what to name the activities producing disputes over pay and job jurisdiction.

Arguments over claims for "time-in-lieu" are typical.

• A walking boss is accused of "driving" a crane known as a "cherry picker." Since supervisors cannot do longshore work, the union demands "time-in-lieu," a day's pay for a longshoreman. The employers deny the claim. They argue the supervisor was not "driving crane"; he was "checking out" the "equipment."

• Another walking boss is seen "tending hatch." The union wants one winch driver paid for eight hours because supervisors cannot tend hatch. The employers refuse to honor the claim. "The walking boss was down in the hold to supervise longshoremen," they respond. "He was in *communication* with the crane operator but did not perform the duties of a hatch tender."[13]

• A gang claims they saw a ship's crew "rigging" gear. They feel entitled to "time-in-lieu" because the ship's crew was doing their work. The employers disagree. The crew was not "rigging gear"; they were "*securing* the ship for sea. This is properly their work."[14]

• Another gang demands two hours' "time-in-lieu," claiming that a ship's crew was seen "lashing." The employers literally see things differently. In their words, "the crew was, in fact, *stowing* lashing gear."[15]

In each instance the two sides agree that the disputed activity happened. That is not what the disagreement is about. The dispute is over how to *designate* the activity. Was the walking boss "driving" the cherry picker or "checking it out"? Was he "tending hatch" or "communicating" with the crane driver? Was the ship's crew "rigging" gear or "securing" the ship for

13 Emphasis added, RD 78/UC 141.
14 Emphasis added, RD 66/UC 226.
15 Emphasis added, RD 62/UC 189.

sea? Were they "lashing" or "stowing" lashing gear? The disagreement is so deep that the two sides cannot agree on what to call the activity causing the dispute. Thus, they don't have language that enables them even to argue. One union representative reached this conclusion and therefore angrily decided to leave an LRC meeting. "If we can't agree on the difference between 'rigging' gear and 'stowing' it," he said, "then there's no sense talking."

His anger extended beyond the disagreement on nomenclature. More was at stake than naming disputed activities. The employer's position, in his view, insulted longshoremen's intelligence: "It's like saying we don't know the difference between rigging gear and securing it," he continued. "And once we've reached that kind of impasse, we just can't talk to each other any longer."

Similar kinds of disagreements emerge in disputes over the hours longshoremen work and the money they are paid. Since the contract explicitly specifies a shift's duration and the amount of hourly wages, it is hard to imagine how differences could develop over pay. However, because the two sides know and name activities with conflicting assumptions and vocabularies, profound and disruptive disputes over pay regularly crop up in the grievance machinery. The following examples are typical.

• A gang that is discharging autos feels the operation is unsafe.[16] One of the winches is operating erratically, even though the ship's electrician has already repaired it once. The ship's boom is short so that cars are being landed within four feet of the bull rail at the end of the pier. The men estimate that tidal currents are running nearly ten knots per hour. They think the situation is unsafe and thus they ask the superintendent to sling a safety net between the ship and the pier. When he says "nothing doing," the gang stops work. They "hang the hook," alleging that the operation violates the safety code. At this point, the walking boss fires the gang and returns them to the hiring hall. The gang protests, arguing they cannot be fired for raising a safety issue. Supervision disagrees, and takes them "off the payroll."

The disagreement was arbitrated immediately with a conference call between a PMA representative, the local arbitrator, the gang steward, and

16 Examples are based on RD 88/UC 100–70/EC 64.

the superintendent. When the call was concluded, the four had agreed that the gang was "improperly fired" and, after a safety net was rigged, the men would resume work. By the time the net was rigged, however, three longshoremen had gone home, thinking they were fired. After their replacements had been ordered, it was already time for the lunch break. The remaining gang members returned to the job after lunch and waited thirty minutes for the replacements. When it became apparent that additional longshoremen were not coming, the gang was released at 1:30.

Members of the gang received their pay checks two weeks later. Each of them had been paid only for showing up; none of them were credited with the time worked before they were fired. The men filed a grievance for a "pay shortage."

The employers, however, saw the situation differently. They lodged a complaint against the gang. The men who stayed on the job were accused of an "illegal work stoppage." The longshoremen who had left during the safety dispute were charged with "leaving the job without authorization."

• Another gang was discharging steel beams on the night shift when, between 11:00 and midnight, they temporarily ran out of work.[17] The gang "stood by" during the hour and then went to lunch. When the men returned to the ship at 1:00 a.m., they were fired for "failure to work as directed." The discharged longshoremen immediately called a business agent and filed a grievance for a "pay shortage."

When the dispute reached the LRC, the employers explained that earlier in the evening the gang boss had been told the lunch break was at 11:00. They claimed he failed to inform his gang of the change and that was why the gang had no work between 11:00 and midnight. The employers claimed that, when asked why he didn't tell the gang of the new lunch time, the gang boss's "reply was that when he went to tell his gang, someone in the gang told him that it was changed back to 12:00." Unsatisfied with this explanation, the employers justified their complaint by saying, "he should have confirmed it with the walking boss."

The union's account reads quite differently. Gang members insist there was no mention of a changed time for lunch break. They recalled being asked by the walking boss if they would take a half hour for lunch at

17 Example based on EC 197–8; quotes are from field notes.

midnight and the remaining thirty minutes later. They declined the offer and thus stood by between 11:00 and midnight since there was no work. In the union's view, the men were entitled to a full night's pay because they were improperly fired. The accusation of "pay shortage" was therefore legitimate to their way of thinking.

• In another pay dispute, all four gangs working a ship called a business agent to complain about the vessel's gear.[18] They felt that some of the goosenecks and blocks needed to be greased and they wanted someone to inspect the sheaves in other blocks. They were worried because vessels with similar gear had recently been found with scarred and worn sheaves. The business agent arrived at 1:10 that afternoon. He went directly to the superintendent's office, a visit that is required contractually. Finding no one in the office, he went aboard the ship and told the walking boss that he intended to inspect the gear.

It was approximately 1:50 p.m. when the business agent finished inspecting the gear at hatch #1. That was the time the superintendent arrived. He was, in the union official's words, "quite agitated,"[19] and asked the walking boss what was going on. The business agent interjected himself, explaining that ships like this one had been discovered operating with unsafe gear. The union was therefore inspecting the ship's gear, he said, and would also be looking at the vessel's gear certification papers. He said the employers had been notified that this would happen at an LRC a couple of months earlier. The business agent thought the superintendent seemed "satisfied, if not happy" with the explanation.

The union representative left the ship ten minutes later. As he was leaving, a hatch tender told him that the chief clerk said the gangs would all be docked fifteen minutes because of the inspection. The men wanted to know if that was, in fact, the case. The business agent went back to the superintendent and asked. He was assured no one would be docked and left the vessel.

Two weeks later, when checks were distributed, the men discovered they had been docked fifteen minutes' pay. Predictably, the union filed a grievance, charging a "pay shortage." The employers denied the charge,

18 From RD 86/UC 835.
19 Quotes are from the written text accompanying the complaint.

however. In their view, they did not short the men pay. Rather, the union conducted an "illegal work stoppage," which meant the men were "not under the company's supervision" for a fifteen-minute period. They were therefore not employed by the company at that time, and "thereby not entitled to payment."

These kinds of disputes erupt because each side sees the same activity through different lenses. The gang discharging autos thought the operation was unsafe; the superintendent, on the other hand, saw no reason to do things differently. The gang unloading steel beams "stood by," in the walking boss's eyes, because they refused to take lunch early. The gang members, however, insist they stood by because they saw "no work." The stevedoring company would not pay longshoremen fifteen minutes of stand-by time because the business agent, in their view, created a "work stoppage"; he did not conduct a "safety inspection."

In each instance the two sides interpret the same activity differently; they use competing language to describe one activity. What longshoremen call "pay shortage," the employers call "left work without authorization." "Pay shortage" for longshoremen is "refusal to work as directed" so far as management is concerned. And the employers counter the union's allegation of a "pay shortage" with the accusation that the union created an "illegal work stoppage."

Given what they see, and the language used to describe it, the remedies proposed by each side make sense. The difficulty, however, is that the two sides operate with conflicting assumptions. Sometimes the disagreement surfaces humorously. "How come when we take advantage of the contract it's called 'gimmicking,'" asked a high-ranking management person rhetorically during an LRC, "and when you do it, it's called 'rights under the contract'?"[20]

But the differences contained in these disputes are not inconsequential. They are deeply divisive, disruptive, and not easily resolved. None of the above disagreements were settled in the LRC. No informal agreements were arranged. Never did the two sides amicably agree to disagree. In each instance the dispute was either arbitrated by a third party, or left unresolved. The atmosphere was usually highly charged and both sides made

20 Field notes.

very thinly veiled threats to resolve these differences outside of the grievance machinery.

The exchanges produced by these disputes indicate the depths of the disagreement. "Fuck it," said a union official at the LRC meeting who was discussing the disagreement over safety in which gang members received less than a full shift's pay.

> "I've been fucked by these people before and I know what to do. The next time they fire someone on a safety beef, we'll pull the whole goddamn ship and stop the entire operation. Fuck it. That goddamn walking boss is an idiot. Those men should be paid."
>
> "Your ass!" responded the PMA official. "Those guys left the job without asking anyone. It's their own goddamn fault they didn't get paid."[21]

"How do you want to handle this?" asked another union representative, when the two sides could not agree on whether longshoremen had been shorted pay or refused to work as directed.

"Let's find them guilty of 'refusing to work as directed,'" said a PMA representative, "and accept the loss of pay as 'sufficient penalty.'"

"What did they refuse to do?" asked the union.

"Not taking lunch when told to."

"My God!" yelled the union representative. "We can't agree on that. The hell with this goddamn LRC, we'll settle this matter on the docks."[22]

In each of these settings, the two sides either talk about the same activity using very different language, or operate with competing meanings for the same words. The two sides "see" or interpret activities differently because they share neither concepts nor social location. They use alternative words or competing meanings for the same words because they see issues from different vantage points. The disputes over language and its interpretation are therefore conducted like a war over words. This war determines which side's language will prevail. The outcome is fateful to the way work will be done because the side whose language prevails controls the grounds upon which working rules are interpreted. Thus, the struggle for words is a battle for advantage in the formulation of explicit rules.

21 Field notes.
22 Field notes.

12

BY WHOSE PRINCIPLES WILL
MERIT BE REWARDED?

E XCEPT for the people affected directly, disputes over pay and promotion are rarely viewed as deep disagreements between employers and unions. Rather, they are considered expressions of greedy, narrow-minded, self-interested economics, examples of the "mere" in Gompers's "mere economism." But regardless of how much importance is attributed, or not attributed, to monetary differences, most of labor's observers agree that the issue in these disputes is *not* workplace control. In fact, it is often assumed that labor's right to make financial claims is its reward for *relinquishing* control over the workplace.

A different understanding emerges, however, when one observes disputes over pay and promotion in settings of their most routine occurrence: in negotiations defining a fair day's pay, choosing supervision, and determining skill. In this context, the two sides argue about the grounds for promotion and the bases for salary differentiation. These arguments reveal a third front in the battle over workplace control. The two sides disagree over principles for acknowledging merit. The issue is hardly narrow or merely economic. The gap between the union and management is as wide as the differences are deep. The dispute is, whose principles for promotion and pay will prevail?

HOW MUCH MONEY? FAIRNESS VERSUS HIERARCHY AS PRINCIPLES FOR DETERMINING PAY

When the two sides talk about wage scales during contract negotiations, it becomes clear that pay disputes extend beyond money. As local negotiations were concluding, the PMA and ILWU representatives remained deadlocked over a wage rate for gearmen. Financially speaking, the two sides were not far apart: The employers offered $9.72 an hour; the union wanted $9.97. As a union spokesman said, "the difference between us is a lousy two bits an hour."

He was wrong.

The financial discrepancy reflected a much deeper difference between the two sides. They were not just divided over twenty-five cents an hour. Their respective offers were based on two different assumptions about what was a fair day's pay.

The union's position was that a fair day's pay should be fair. They justified an additional twenty-five cents an hour by linking merit and equity. Gearmen, they maintained, were "much more skilled than winch drivers," and yet people in the two categories were paid the same.[1] The employers' proposal, on the other hand, did not acknowledge the difference between gearmen and winch drivers. The union also argued that gearmen were "at the heart of the longshore industry"; without them nothing would move. Despite their importance, however, gearmen were paid less than longshoremen driving trucks on ro-ro ships.

"How is it," asked a union representative, "that a man who drives a trailer onto a ro-ro ship gets a sixty-cent-an-hour pay differential and a man who the industry depends on and who drives huge rigs on the highways doesn't?"

The union also argued that gearmen were loyal employees. In fact, some people considered them "company men." Putting a positive spin on the issue, the union said they had "the best interests of the company at heart." But unlike other loyal workers, gearmen were not rewarded for this quality.

"We're much more important than walking bosses," said one gearman who was sitting in on the negotiations, "and we're also special employees. How come we don't get as much as they do?"

Each claim joined the principles of merit and equity. The union did not argue gearmen should be paid more just because they were skilled, important, or loyal. Rather, they argued longshoremen in comparable categories were paid more. And that was not fair.

Comparability was connected to fairness in a different way during an-

1 Field notes.

other argument over gearmen's pay. While the negotiations were in session, San Francisco gearmen called their friends up and down the West Coast and asked them about wage settlements in other ports. They were disturbed by their discovery. In Portland, Oregon, gearmen were awarded $11.00 an hour; and gear locker foremen were granted an additional 15 percent differential. The report from Los Angeles was equally upsetting: They had already agreed to fifty cents an hour more than what was being offered in San Francisco.

"Gearwork in Portland and San Pedro ain't no different than gearwork up here," said a gearman to PMA representatives.[2] "They shouldn't be getting more than us for doing the same work. It ain't right."

"There may be reasons for pay differences on the Coast," interjected a union official, "but these differences are too great. The least you can do is give us the twenty-five cents we're asking for. That would be fairer."

The union's commitment to equity was so strong that the gearmen rejected an employer proposal that would potentially benefit them but also create a division in the local.

"If you're worried about people driving trucks aboard ship making more than you, why not propose a sixty-five-cent-an-hour pay differential for gearmen driving trucks," suggested a PMA negotiator. "We might even agree to that."

The union called for a caucus. "What about that offer?" a union official asked the assembled gearmen when they met behind closed doors. "Should we go for it?"

> "We discussed that ourselves earlier," said one of the gearmen. "We don't want a differential among gearmen. We want all gearmen to get the same pay."
> "The union is divided enough already," said another. "There isn't any point to dividing us up more. It would be just like the situation between the steady men and hall men." (Field notes)

When the caucus ended, the union negotiator reported back to his counterpart: "No deal. We want twenty-five cents an hour for everyone."

Equity was not a principle the employers invoked. They did not use the language of fairness to justify counter-offers. They barely mentioned skill

2 Field notes.

and never disputed the merits of gearmen. The employers restricted their talk about a fair day's pay to economics, to dollars and cents.

"It's not like we haven't given them anything," said the PMA negotiator, barely disguising his disgust. "We're offering gearmen what amounts to a $1.10 an hour more than they were making on June 30th. Gearmen are making $437 a week," he continued.[3] "That's $1,670 a month straight-time and doesn't include overtime. So far as we're concerned, that's an awful lot of money. Our position is $9.72 an hour for gearmen. And in my estimation, that's one helluva increase."

The employers connected equity and comparability differently than the union did. In their view, equity could not be established by making comparisons across job categories. The employers focused their attention more narrowly. They primarily talked about pay rates within the gear category, and only in San Francisco.

"We see things differently," said a management spokesman responding to the union's argument that it wasn't fair for gearmen and winch drivers to be paid the same. "We don't equate gearmen with winch drivers," he said. "Try to see the matter through our eyes," he suggested. "Don't look at our offer as the same as the winch driver rate. Look at it as fifty cents an hour over base pay. Consider it a fifty-cent-an-hour pay raise."[4]

Each side's understanding of fairness is based on a different vantage point. Looking across categories, fifty cents an hour is not much and therefore "unfair." Removed from that context, and viewed within the category, however, fifty cents an hour is a substantial increase and thus, "fair."

The employers extended their principle of internal comparison to the gearmen in other ports.

"That Portland agreement is the culmination of thirty years of negotiation," said a PMA representative responding to the union's proposal for coastwide parity among gearmen. "There's a difference between the work gearmen do in Portland and the work they do in San Francisco. *What was agreed to in Portland has no relevance to what we agree to in San Francisco.* Our final offer is $9.72 an hour."[5]

3 Field notes.
4 Field notes.
5 Field notes, emphasis added.

The two principles for determining pay and the conflict between them became clear in an exchange that followed.

"All we're really asking for is two bits above what you've offered," said the union negotiator.

"No way," responded the PMA spokesman quietly.

"We want parity with gearman on the coast," continued the union official. "We feel we should have it. These guys work hard and are important."

"We're not questioning their ability," the employer's representative replied. "What we're saying is that we're offering the same differential we've been offering gearmen in San Francisco since 1957. In fact what we've done is upped it from twenty-five cents an hour to fifty. That's quite a bit."[6]

But fair did not figure in the employers's thinking. If anything, that was an unrealistic expectation and therefore beside the point. In the employer's view, inequality was an inevitable feature of economic life. Appeals to equity and merit were therefore irrelevant. When asked to justify pay differences between heavy lift operators and gearmen, one PMA official responded candidly, and without additional comment: "There's always going to be inequities."[7]

The two men crossed swords over the same issue two weeks later. "Paying gearmen the same as winch drivers is ridiculous," said the union person. "There's more skill involved in being a gearman than a winch driver."

"It's all relative," responded the PMA negotiator, stating the employer's principle for determining pay: "Every job has a value and this is the value we've assigned to this job."[8]

Pay equity was not the principle employers used to decide wages. Neither was being fair. This became explicit in the negotiations over a pay scale for gear bosses (foremen). Once again, the two sides argued over twenty-five cents a hour. The union wanted $10.17 and the employers would agree only to $9.92 an hour. The principal issue dividing the two sides, however, was not twenty-five cents an hour. "We're willing to in-

6 Field notes.
7 Field notes.
8 Field notes.

crease gear bosses ten cents an hour over what they get," said an employer representative. "That would bring them up to $9.92 an hour. But we're not willing to increase their pay to $10.17 because that's what walkers (walking bosses) get."[9]

Money wasn't the problem for management. The issue was maintaining a financial distinction between supervisors and hourly employees. Thus, the PMA explicitly refused to accept supervison's pay scale as the grounds for increasing gearmen's wages. "We're proposing a twenty-five-cent differential above winch drivers," said the union side. "That's with $9.97 as a base. They would start out with twenty-five cents more on that base. That comes to $10.17 for a gear boss."

"I don't care how you figure it," shot back the employer spokesman, "just as long as it doesn't add up to what walking bosses get."

The employer's notion of a fair day's pay assumes and reinforces hierarchy in the work process. It is based on distinctions between supervisors and hourly employees, and it is intended to maintain that distinction. The idea of gearmen and walking bosses earning the same amounts, and thereby being financial equals, was symbolically unacceptable. Unlike the union, meritocracy and equity are not the principles employers use for negotiating wage scales. And when the union raises them, they are characteristically ignored or dismissed by the PMA. Thus, the two sides often talk past each other when financial matters are being negotiated. They speak different languages because they operate with conflicting assumptions about what is fair in a fair day's pay. What divides them, then, is not simply dollars and cents. The deeper division is that they use different principles for establishing fairness and rewarding merit.

CHOOSING SUPERVISION AND DETERMINING SKILL:
SENIORITY MERIT VERSUS MANAGERIAL MERIT

It is often assumed that when management and labor argue over promotions to skilled categories and supervision, one of two disputes surfaces. Either the competence of the people being considered is debated or the number of people to be promoted is contested. When promotion is de-

9 Field notes.

bated by the ILWU and the PMA, however, the disagreement is not over competence or numbers. It is about the criteria used for establishing merit. Each side wants to reward different qualities in longshoremen.

The union wants the criteria for merit to be uniform, restricted, and equitable. It wants the grounds for promotion to be explicitly stated and strictly enforced. Skill and seniority are the worker qualities the union wants rewarded. The employers, on the other hand, want merit determined by another set of criteria. The PMA pushes for flexible criteria that permit discretion. They want to reward loyalty.

These differences surface regularly. When one gearman retired, for example, the stevedoring company replaced him with a longshoreman who had previously been a temporary employee. The superintendent called the hiring hall and asked specifically for this person. The morning he started working steady, however, the union returned him to the hall saying he had been selected improperly. Within hours, a special Labor Relations Committee meeting was called by the PMA.

The employers were outraged. In their view, they had hired someone from the "casual gear list," with a "skill card." How could they possibly have selected him "improperly"?[10] But the union had additional standards for selection criteria. It wanted the criteria to be uniform and equitable. "*Everyone* who is on the casual gear list should have a skill card," said a union official, "the fact that he has a skill card isn't a reason for selecting him."

> As things stand, there is no principle by which gearmen are being selected. Since there is no rule, the situation is open to the possibility for discrimination and favoritism. In the past we've gone along with this ambiguity and so maybe we've been implicated in the favoritism that has gone on. But we're not going along with it anymore. We want some principles for selecting these guys and we brought this brother back to the hall to force the issue.

"Under the terms of the contract," the employers representative responded, "this man was properly employed. If the union doesn't like the terms of the contract," he challenged, "you should renegotiate them. But

10 RD 72.

so far as the employers are concerned, we are operating under the terms we agreed upon."

The disagreement was not about who had read the rules correctly. At issue was: Whose criteria for determining merit would operate? Before the PMA representative could continue, a vice-president of a major stevedoring company injected himself into the debate. "The word discrimination is very inflammatory," he said angrily. And then he made the issue explicit: "Selection is not discrimination," he said. "The union is asking us to curtail the precious few prerogatives the employers have left in a very binding contract that we have with the ILWU. For damn sure we ain't going to do that willingly."

The battle lines were drawn. To the union's way of thinking, unless the sides agreed on explicit rules, the selection process could lead to discrimination. Thus, they wanted the criteria for selecting gearmen to be explicit. Management, on the other hand, wanted the right to choose gearmen. And even though they agreed to accept minimal eligibility requirements, they refused to share ultimate choice.

That did not leave much to talk about. "There's no sense screwing around with this issue," said a shipping company executive as he put on his coat and prepared to leave. "We've reached disagreement. Let's go at it."

Disputes over promotion criteria are sometimes part of a larger disagreement about the qualities each side wants to reward in longshoremen. In certain instances both disputes are contained in one disagreement. An example emerged during negotiations over eligibility for the Special Equipment Operator board. Both sides agreed to select people mainly from "active" boards (boards with a lot of work); seniority would determine eligibility among longshoremen on "slow" boards. The agreement, however, was short lived. It ended when the PMA produced a list of people who were *not* eligible. Included on the list were longshoremen in two categories: those accused of drunkenness, assault, or pilferage; and those with training in skilled categories, but who had not worked in those categories for a year or more.

"Why disqualify guys accused of drunkenness, assault, or pilferage?" asked the union negotiator. "What's that got to do with whether they can do the job or not?"

"They're not trustworthy," answered the PMA representative, invoking a new criterion for promotion.

"What's this business about being trained for a skill board and then not working on that board got to do with being eligible for the SEO board?" the union official continued.

"It shows a lack of commitment," replied the employer's spokesman, adding additional qualities to be encouraged among dockworkers.

"We can't go along with that," the union officer said, shaking his head. "Guys should be eligible on the basis of seniority."

After the union carefully examined the list of longshoremen who, by the employer's stated criteria, were not eligible for the SEO board, it became obvious to both sides that the disagreement turned on a different issue: would criteria for promotion be applied flexibly or uniformly.

"Hey!" exclaimed someone from the union side in loud astonishment, "there are guys on this disqualified list who are *already* steady men and are therefore automatically eligible for the SEO board. If you applied your guidelines to them, they wouldn't be allowed to be working steady. These guidelines are ridiculous if they aren't applied to everybody."

The employer's response was not substantive, nor did it challenge the union's accuracy: "The contract says we can do that," said the PMA negotiator invoking a technicality (field notes).

The exchange revealed what the issue was. The employers wanted longshoremen on the SEO board who expressed loyalty. They were looking for people who, in their words, were "trustworthy," who showed "commitment." And, as their list of "disqualified" people indicated, people displaying these desired qualities would be included on the SEO board despite their failure to meet stated criteria. To do this, however, the employers had to flexibly apply the criteria for promotion. The union, on the other hand, wanted to reward longevity. They sought to promote men on the basis of seniority. Thus, ILWU negotiators insisted on strictly enforcing the stated criteria, and uniformly, too.

The union's commitment to equity through seniority is also expressed when longshoremen are promoted to walking bosses. When Local 10 members are invited by a stevedoring company to be a walker, they must first be cleared by the union's Executive Committee. But before clearing anyone, the committee raises two questions: Is racial balance maintained between the people being promoted? And what were the criteria for choosing the new walking boss?

For years, walking bosses have been primarily Euro-Americans. During the last two decades, however, African-Americans and Hispanics have become the largest ethnic groups on the San Francisco waterfront. To insure that the walking boss's local accurately reflects the racial composition of the industry, every second longshoreman cleared by Local 10 is either African-American or Hispanic. Thus, when Euro-American longshoremen ask for clearance, the Executive Committee looks at the ancestry of the last person promoted. If that person was Euro-American, permission is denied until a Black or Hispanic is transferred.

The Local's Executive Committee also tries to establish the criteria by which walking bosses were chosen. The committee is quite suspicious of potential walking bosses with low seniority. They suspect that these people are requested largely because of their loyalty to the company requesting them. Thus, potential walking bosses are asked to describe their relations with company officials and if they appear too friendly, transfers are denied.

When issues like racial balance and union loyalty are raised in connection with walking bosses, the union makes its criteria for promotion explicit. It is also insisting the criteria be applied equitably. Thus, the union wants promotions based on seniority.

The ILWU and the PMA do not agree on the criteria for rewarding and promoting longshoremen. They disagree because each side uses a different method for choosing supervision and determining skills. Their two methods are based on opposing principles: Equity is the principle guiding the union decisions; it tries to divide scarce opportunities as equally as possible. Union representatives therefore object to ambiguous criteria. They insist that the grounds for promotion be applied consistently.

The employer's goal, on the other hand, is to maintain discretion. They want control over who is promoted. In their view, not every waterfront worker is worthy of promotion. They want to promote only those longshoremen who meet management's needs. And they are explicit about this. Thus, when the union insisted that criteria for gearmen be written down and agreed to, a PMA representative responded, "I know the union's feeling, and I know how important the issue of seniority is for you. But the employers must maintain their rights to employ the guy who is best qualified to do the job, as they see it."

The disagreements over promotion are serious ones. Because the two sides do not share the same criteria for promotion and reward, the argument is, in part, over which side's method for choosing supervision and skill will prevail. Another issue also surfaces in this disagreement: namely, which side decides who will inhabit the workplace? Will longshoremen be union- or company-hired workers? Do supervisors get selected from above or below? The union's position stresses the internal politics of control. But union control over the workplace is, from the employers' perspective, unacceptable. Thus these disputes about promotion and reward, like the arguments over wages, are skirmishes in the larger battle for control of the workplace.

Part V

AGREEING TO DISAGREE:
BEING DEFENSIBLY DISOBEDIENT

T HE patterns of disagreement produced by the ILWU–PMA contractual relationship indicate that the divisions between these two
sides run deep. As the last three chapters suggest, the fight for management of the longshore enterprise continues; elements of the struggle over
rival systems for production are still visible in the longshore industry.
Thus, the issue of who governs the waterfront has not been effectively
settled. In this regard, not much has changed since the 1930s.

What *has* changed, however, is that, contractually speaking, the issue *is*
resolved; it was settled years ago. If the question of workplace governance
was not formally laid to rest when longshoremen agreed to the terms of
the 1934 contract, it was certainly established in 1966 when the ILWU
agreed on paper to eliminate restrictive work rules. The collective bargain
states clearly and unequivocally that longshoremen must do as they are
told by employers. They must "work as directed." The employers' right to
direct work was reaffirmed, some would say reestablished, with the M&M
Agreements and subsequently sustained by arbitrators' rulings. Thus, formally and legally speaking, the dispute over workplace regime has been
resolved; and resolved in the employers' favor. On paper, they control the
waterfront.

However, when one analyzes the accusations each side levels at the
other in the grievance machinery, and observes contractual negotiations, it
becomes quite clear that, practically speaking, the question of workplace
regime has not been settled. Despite contractual prohibitions to the contrary, longshoremen continue to dispute managerial directives.

But how can this be? How can longshoremen contest management's
control of the work process when the contract specifically prohibits such
behavior? How can the struggle for governance be waged once it has been

officially settled? Is this the legacy of communist participation in the union's early development, the result of subversive agitators? Or is it produced by less sensational sociological forces?

The answer emerges when one observes how contracts are actually used as weapons in contests for workplace control rather than looking for the rules of class relations in contract books. From this vantage point, one can see that ILWU members have learned to use the document that was intentionally created to minimize conflict – the contract – to contest management's control of the waterfront. They use the contract as a weapon. It enables them to struggle with their employers for shopfloor control by being defensibly disobedient.

Defensible disobedience is a twofold, almost contradictory, process through which each side seeks advantage over the other *and* tries to stay within the language limits of the contract. The contract is used to promote self-advantage, but without undermining the agreement to cooperate. Disputes are waged strategically; complaints are constructed rationally. Each side tries to get a leg up on the other while appearing fair and even-handed. They act deceptively and manipulate appearances. Each side brilliantly orchestrates impression management, acting as if it is upholding the contract when it is actually working around it.

Defensible disobedience is possible under three conditions: (1) Troubles have to be translated into grievable issues; (2) both sides must live by the agreement; and (3) the appearance of cooperation must be maintained. The next three chapters analyze how that happens.

13

TRANSLATING TROUBLES INTO GRIEVABLE ISSUES

"**A**RE you willing to stop work?" yelled a business agent into a phone at Matson Terminals in Oakland. "If we don't try to stop them from doing that, it'll continue," he explained. "Win, lose, or draw, I'd like to try and stop it. Are you willing?" The other person obviously agreed. "Alright then," said the business agent loudly, "I don't want you to work after lunch. If they want a work stoppage, goddammit they'll get one. Is the rest of your gang willing to stop work, too?" he asked. "Good. Then go tell the walking boss and superintendent that you talked to me and you're hanging the hook. If they want, they can call me at this number."[1]

The business agent was talking to a longshoreman working in Richmond, across the bay. The man was unloading chrome ore and felt he was being treated unfairly. He therefore called the union and the official was paged by electronic beeper. Once he heard the complaint and assessed the situation, the union officer had to figure out a course of action. His decision rested on two considerations: Were the longshoremen willing to stop work and act on their complaint? And, could the action be defended contractually? When he determined that the work stoppage could be defended, and used strategically, he told the longshoremen to stop working. The union could protect these men when they refused to obey orders; they were being "defensibly disobedient."

PATROLLING AND AMBUSHING

Sometimes complaints can be translated into contractually defensible disobedience spontaneously, or over the phone, like the previous example.

---

1 Based on field notes.

Usually, however, the process is more strategic. It is typically accomplished through careful work by union officials and the process is time consuming. As part of their job, Local 10 business agents drive along large sections of the waterfront. They stop at docks looking for problems, and they speak with union members. "How's it going?" they ask, "any problems?"

Trouble is frequently spotted in these travels. When driving along a dock, for example, one business agent noticed a lift truck that violated the safety code. The exhaust pipes did not extend above the driver's head. The union representative got out of his car and wrote a note: "Unsafe equipment. Do not drive. Signed, ———— ILWU Business Agent." He carefully placed it on the driver's seat. And before he left the dock, he told a walking boss that the company would have to fix unsafe machines before he would permit Local 10 men to drive them.[2]

Some business agents call this "patrolling." Union officials are not looking for particular problems while patrolling. They are not self-consciously searching for specific contractual violations. Rather, as one business agent put it, "patrolling means going around the docks, looking at the operation without any problem in mind. But you sometimes stumble onto a problem when you're patrolling." Many of these problems can be handled on the spot, like removing lift trucks from operation. But difficulties detected while patrolling can also provide business agents with grounds for further action. In these instances, patrolling sets the stage for "ambushing."

Ambushes are directed toward particular problems. When specific troubles are brought to the union's attention, business agents act on them immediately. But not every complaint can be pursued strategically. For example, to avoid jeopardizing longshoremen's pay, union officials have to find practices that are contestable on contractual grounds. Thus, business agents will explicitly tell Local 10 members when they are looking for particular problems. People are told to look for a "beef we can win." "Ambushing," said one business agent,

> means you're working with a half dozen guys and you're trying to find a particular situation and you've got guys as scouts out there and when you've done the necessary research and found the problem, you jump on it. You sit down and talk with the guys about doing an ambush.

2 Based on field notes.

256

The distinction between "ambushing" and "patrolling" is not always clear cut. While patrolling, business agents sometimes look for contractual violations on specific vessels. And if they are found, an ambush is staged. Some business agents, for example, would single out ships carrying South African cargo for "special treatment." These vessels were inspected with particular care, and the union official looked for reasons to stop work. If a reason was discovered, an ambush would be launched and an unannounced protest against apartheid was accomplished.

Stevedoring companies that have a history of serious, unresolved disputes with the union are also given extra attention by business agents on patrol. If they can find grounds for an ambush, the disagreement will be forced into the grievance machinery, thereby increasing the chances to settle it. Business agents also patrol for specific problems they want to use in future ambushes. In one instance, for example, a union official found dangerous chemicals on a dock while he was patrolling. Since there were no procedures for handling the chemicals safely, he made a mental note of where the deadly cargo was located and prepared for an ambush later on.

Ambushes are also organized while patrolling. Union officials convene informal meetings as they inspect ships. Gathered around a business agent, the men listen while the agent explains what he is looking for and how they can help. Having organized his scouts in this way, he continues to patrol.

Patrolling and ambushing are the first moves the union makes to use the contract self-interestedly but without subverting it. Union officials supervise employers while patrolling; ambushes keep management honest. The threat of work stoppages is incentive for most employers to keep contractual promises, at least minimally. Used together, patrolling and ambushing help the union translate workplace differences into grievable issues. But before dockside disagreements can become grievable issues, the disputes must display certain features. Not every disagreement will do. A "good" beef must be found, or created.

FINDING AND CREATING "GOOD BEEFS"

"Fact of the matter is," said one business agent, "my job is running around, maybe finding problems – discovering them, running into them – and having run into a problem, my job is to translate that problem into a beef. Then, of course, my job is to try and solve the beef in favor of the union." Union stewards are important for translating problems into beefs. Local 10 officials therefore rely on stewards to be their eyes and ears.[3] Business agents regularly attend meetings of the Stewards' Council, which meets monthly. They report their activities to stewards and pass on information they want communicated to the rank and file. Business agents also solicit help from stewards to find dockside disagreements that will clarify contractual disputes. "I want you to be on your toes looking for health and safety violations," said one union representative at a stewards meeting. "When you find one, I want you to call me. Drop a dime on my ass because a B.A. ain't shit without stewards. You stewards are my eyes."[4] Agreeing with the basic proposition, another business agent extended the metaphor:

> It ain't enough to say that the stewards are the eyes of the business agent. The business agent has a real problem of focusing their eyes. My experience then, is that you've got to work closely with the Steward's Council. You want to say, "alright, we're looking for two things this week," or, "we're looking for one thing this week," and go into some depth and really do it. You've got to organize the goddamned effort. It ain't enough to hand the steward a safety book and safety code, and say, "alright, now go out there and take a look."

Problems are not transformed magically into beefs even when stewards become extensions of business agents. Beefs must be organized if they are to be pursued defensibly. One group of stewards, for example, told a business agent that equipment was unsafe at their container yard. When the business agent convened a meeting of the men longshoring in that yard, he said they should challenge the unsafe equipment, and asked if they were willing to stop work. They were. And they also had their own list of troubles they wanted translated into beefs. Strads were operated without windows; underpowered tractors were used to lift overweight containers; the brakes on some machines were so poor that to slow down,

3 Elected by gang members, and in some instances by longshoremen working on docks, stewards serve as the union's on-the-job representative. The constitutional duties of stewards include enforcing the contract and improving working conditions. For a historical account of the evolution of the stewards system in the ILWU, see Mills and Wellman (1987).
4 Field notes.

258

the vehicles had to be banked off the sides of ships; exhaust fumes were discernible in certain ship's holds.

The men also had ideas for creating successful beefs. "Don't come until about 10:30," said one of them; "that way there will be enough time for the fumes to build up and there's no way the arbitrator won't be impressed."

"That's right," said another, "and by then there'll be trucks lined up waiting to drop vans. The company will have to deal with us then."[5] Having worked out a strategy, the union official could turn their problems into grievable beefs, differences that could be disputed on contractual grounds.

Formulating defensible strategies for dockside disputes is complicated; organizing insubordination is not enough. If grievable issues are to be created out of workplace difficulties, each side must must carefully weigh contingencies and think through possible problems. How will the work stoppage actually evolve? How can the price of justice be minimized for one side and maximized for the other? The calculus of defensible disobedience is not easy to figure.

On his way to initiate a work stoppage, for example, one business agent wondered out loud how to orchestrate the beef. He had been called by a gang that was loading chemicals. They thought the operation was unsafe and therefore wanted to stop work. But who would actually stop work? the business agent asked himself. Should it be the lift driver who brought chemicals to the ship? Or, should it be the winch driver who loaded them aboard on pallet boards? Since the dispute was over safety, the choice was critical. The union could stop work only on contractual grounds if it could show that the operation was currently unsafe. Arguing that it might become unsafe would not do. If the winch driver stopped work, the union could invoke safety because the holdmen obviously would be endangered were chemicals to fall off the pallet board. If the lift driver stopped work, however, the union could not make that claim since no one would be at risk were chemicals to fall off the lift truck. Given these considerations, the union official thought the winch driver should initiate the work stoppage.

But there was a complication. The work stoppage would be mediated by an arbitrator. If he ruled against the union, the men who stopped work

5 Field notes.

would not be paid for the time they stood by during the dispute. Were the winch driver to stop work, the entire gang would be docked. If, on the other hand, the lift driver initiated the work stoppage, only he would suffer financially. The union official therefore had to calculate his options strategically. Did the winch driver stop work, claiming the operation endangered holdmen, and risk costing them a couple hours' pay? Or, did the lift driver precipitate the issue, thereby covering the holdmen, but providing the arbitrator with a contractual loophole? (No one was in immediate danger if he spilled the deadly cargo.) "It's hard to play Solomon," said the business agent with mock seriousness as he struggled for a plan that would be defensible before an arbitrator, and in the union hall. He decided on the contractually defensible option: The winch driver stopped work.[6]

Cost, then, is one primary consideration when workplace disputes are translated into grievable issues. Since most disputes can be joined only with a work stoppage, grieving is expensive. Union members risk losing pay while the disagreement is being argued. And because cargo does not move when work stops, the employers lose money either way. Economics are therefore crucial in deciding when to stop work.

The union looks for disputes involving capital-intensive container operations because work stoppages at these locations are especially expensive for employers. Management, on the other hand, is willing to risk work stoppages that tie up entire gangs because this increases the union's liability. Both sides are especially interested in finding disagreements that have precedent-setting potential that will make future work stoppages either unnecessary or illegal. When an issue is joined, each side tries to leverage financial risk in their own favor. Both operate with an eye toward maximizing expenses for the other and minimizing costs for themselves.

"Do we need a work stoppage to settle this?" asked a business agent of a PMA representative. The union official faced a dilemma: He wanted to contest a work practice but worried that his grounds would be unacceptable to the arbitrator. "I don't expect to win this beef at the local arbitration," he said candidly. "Why don't we arbitrate it without a work stoppage so that both of us can cut our losses?"

"I am not willing to arbitrate hypothetical grievances," said the em-

6 Field notes.

ployer's representative, declining the offer. "I will not arbitrate in advance."[7]

The PMA spokesman was making the union pay to challenge a questionable work practice. He was upping the ante. If the union wanted to dispute the issue, a gang would have to stop work and go off the payroll. The employers would incur the cost of a work stoppage if it was also expensive for the union.

Were the union to insist on pressing the issue, the PMA representative intimated, an even higher price might be exacted. Barely disguising the threat, he said that if a work stoppage could not be prevented, he would be "more than happy" to "advise shippers" that the union was increasing the cost of longshoring in the Bay Area. Shippers might therefore want to consider sending cargo through other ports. Both sides understood the threat: Even if the dispute were resolved in the union's favor higher up, the ruling would be counterproductive. Shippers might use other ports, and Local 10 longshoremen would lose work.

DISTINGUISHING BETWEEN "GOOD" AND "BUM" BEEFS

The calculus of defensible disobedience takes into account possible contingencies, potential costs, and contractual/political implications. These three factors determine the chances for transforming workplace disagreements into grievable issues. When union officials have thought through these contingencies, a beef is defined as either "good" or "bum."

A "good" beef

The longshoreman working in Richmond called in a good beef.[8] When the business agent arrived at the Richmond waterfront, he was met by the grievant. "What's the complaint?" asked the union official. The longshoreman explained he had been driving bulldozer aboard ship for the last couple of weeks. Until today, two men were assigned to each machine. That way longshoremen could spell each other. But now only one man worked a machine. He thought the change in practice added up to a

7 Field notes.
8 Field notes.

"manning" violation; the company, in his view, was not ordering enough longshoremen. The business agent explained that the union could not raise "manning" issues, and he changed the terms of discourse. "The problem is 'onerousness,'" he said, substituting new language. Each time the bulldozer operator mentioned "manning," the business agent corrected him, speaking of onerousness.

"Let's take a look at the operation," said the union officer. They went aboard ship and descended into the hold where the longshoreman had been working. After nosing around the chrome ore and machinery, the business agent emerged with a grin on his face. "We got 'em," he announced triumphantly to the gaggle of men surrounding him. He pointed to the bulldozer's exhaust pipe. The pipe traveled up from the engine and extended back alongside the vehicle at the driver's face level. "That's in violation of the safety code," said the union official. "The exhaust pipe is supposed to be a foot over the man's head." As the entourage moved to the remaining three hatches, they detected other safety violations. One bulldozer had no head guard; the exhaust system on two others was illegal. The business agent told the assembled machine operators to "stand by" on a "safety beef."

Having assessed the situation, he left the ship and walked dockside to the superintendent's office. After exchanging a few pleasantries, he announced: "We have a genuine work stoppage here, Paul. That work is onerous; the exhaust pipes on those bulldozers violate the safety code; and I want the air in those hatches tested for pollution. I'm not going to let these men work until we know whether that work is safe."

An argument followed. The superintendent claimed the company had always used one man per machine; there was nothing new about the practice. The bulldozers were rented, and he had not altered their exhaust systems. He was convinced the air was clean. The exchange was civil, even cordial. But the two men did not reach an agreement, and the work therefore could not continue. "It just won't wash, Paul," said the business agent, "we'll have to arbitrate."

From the union's perspective, the beef was a good one: It combined a number of critical features that guaranteed the union could not lose. To begin with, the initial dispute is extremely important for the union. The issue of manning scales is a long-standing source of resentment for Local

10 members; it goes back at least to the 1930s. Moreover, when the M&M Agreements were signed in 1966, the union's contractual right to determine manning scales was weakened significantly. As a result, Local 10 has no contractual remedy when employers reduce the workforce. The Richmond dispute, however, gave the union a unique opportunity to raise the manning issue. With virtually no risk involved, longshoremen could challenge a practice that, on paper, had been settled. Regardless of outcome, then, the union had little to lose. Even if the arbitrator ruled against them, the union would not give up anything because the disputed practice had already been eliminated. Thus, nothing would be lost were the arbitrator to uphold the current manning scale. And if, by chance, the arbitrator agreed that two people should operate bulldozers, the number of men working would be doubled. Thus, the ILWU had everything to gain and nothing to lose.

More important, the union could defend the work stoppage on contractual grounds. As the business agent explained to the grievant, "the problem is 'onerousness.'" Although the union could not challenge manning scales by making numbers the issue, it could claim onerousness. By charging onerousness, the union was protecting men who were actually disputing manning scales. Thus, the union had constructed contractual grounds for challenging a practice that was otherwise settled.

When the business agent discovered safety violations, the dispute became an especially good one for the union. Onerousness is a judgment call; it is rarely obvious and usually creates disagreements. As contractual grounds for protesting manning scales, onerousness was risky. And if the arbitrator ruled against them, the longshoremen would not be paid during the dispute. Safety code violations, on the other hand, are more obvious than onerousness. Moreover, if an arbitrator agrees that a work practice is unsafe, the aggrieved longshoremen are paid for stand-by time. The union therefore had back up if the arbitrator were to rule against them on the question of onerousness. Adding the safety violation guaranteed that the men would be paid for stopping work.

The Richmond dispute was a good one for other reasons. Not only was it inexpensive for the union; it was costly to the employer. Within hours of the initial work stoppage, the entire ship was idle. When the bulldozers shut down, longshoremen transporting ore from the ship to trucks quickly ran out of work. They had to stop working. And the employers faced an expensive problem: The ship was not being worked, yet they continued to pay its operating costs. Longshoremen were standing by and, more than likely, they would have to be paid for doing nothing. Thus, the union had a cost-free opportunity to challenge the employers on a dispute that was already settled contractually.

The most attractive feature of the dispute was that it allowed contractually defensible disobedience. The union could effectively contest the employers' control over the job *and* live by contractual restrictions. To do this, the business agent could not raise the manning issue, and had to convince an arbitrator that the union was concerned only about safety and onerousness. Evidently he succeeded: When the arbitrator ruled, he found some conditions unsafe even though the work was not onerous. The union had correctly assessed the quality of this grievance: It was a good beef because it enabled the men to challenge management's manning decision by being defensibly disobedient.

"Bum" beefs

Every disagreement does not produce a grievable issue. Not all disputes can be used to contest management's rule. Questionable or unwinnable disputes are considered poor grievances; in the language of the industry, they are "bum beefs" because nothing can be done with them. When grievances are determined to have little strategic value, neither side wants to pursue them. Both union and PMA representatives are forthright and candid when they feel a grievance is a bum beef.

"I work for you," said one business agent to a gang that had stopped work. The men felt shortchanged. Their superintendent had offered them extra pay to allow a ship to leave before lashing was completed but they thought his offer was too low.

"You don't work for me," said the union officer, "I'm paid to give you advice. If we put this in the grievance machinery, we might lose. And even if we win, you won't get your money for another six months at least. If you accept the offer, the money's in your pocket. What do you want me to do?"[9]

9 RD 65.

Union representatives sometimes respond humorously when faced with bum beefs. And typically they will accept PMA recommendations for closing the matter. In one complaint, for example, a longshoreman was charged with "sleeping on the job."[10] At the Labor Relations Committee meeting, a union representative responded pseudo-seriously: "Hell, he wasn't sleeping; he was contemplating how to work the cargo." The PMA spokesman ignored the comment and recommended the longshoreman be sent a warning letter reminding him not to sleep on the job.

"Yes," agreed another ILWU official, "that sounds reasonable." And unable to contain a grin, he added, "The workplace is not a place of rest."[11]

More troublesome matters are handled with less frivolity even though the outcome is usually similar. The union, for example, disapproves of longshoremen leaving jobs without replacing themselves with someone from the hall. Thus, when longshoremen are accused of not replacing themselves, and the evidence is persuasive, the union typically agrees to the sanctions recommended by employers. In these instances, the union does not choose to transform the dispute into a grievable issue.

Like union officials, employer representatives are also faced with disputes they cannot win. This occurs when supervisors violate the contract, or return longshoremen to the hiring hall for inappropriate reasons. In these situations, PMA officials, like their union counterparts, speak candidly. They tell employer representatives the PMA is unable to defend against a union grievance, or that a complaint cannot be justified contractually.

"This claim is payable on the face of it," said a regional PMA official to an employer's representative during an LRC caucus.[12] "What happened?"

The stevedoring representative reiterated his company's official response: Because linesmen could not be found, longshoremen lashing containers were asked to release the ship's lines. The order for linesmen

10 RD 68.
11 This was a not very thinly disguised pun. "Point of rest" is the phrase that has traditionally been used in longshore contracts to define the limits of longshore jurisdiction. The 1934 contract read: "Longshore work is all handling of cargo in its transfer from vessel to first place of rest including sorting and piling of cargo on the dock . . ." (Fairley, 1979:123). The "point of rest" was the dividing point between longshore jurisdiction and teamster jurisdiction.
12 RD 78.

had been placed at 9:00 p.m. and when no one showed for work, a business agent gave the superintendent permission to use lashers. The company therefore refused to pay linesmen for a "lost work opportunity."

"There's a number of problems with your position," explained the PMA official. "First of all, the order for linesmen was not placed at the right time." That "bothered" him because, in his estimation, it "weakened the position."

"I'm also unhappy with the language in your response about an agreement between the superintendent and the B.A.," he said. "They can't enter into agreements that are binding." He also thought the company's position was short-sighted. "If you insist on pushing this, even if we win in arbitration, we lose because the union will never let us order men at odd hours." Shaking his head, he looked directly at the employer representative and said: "The union's claim is payable. What will you have me do?" Both sides know when they cannot defend a practice. They also understand that it is sometimes counterproductive to push an issue. "I guess we'll have to pay," said the company representative.

Rank-and-file longshoremen also accept responsibility for mistakes that create bum beefs. "I'd like to shed some light on this problem," a longshoreman said to the Grievance Committee as it considered a complaint against a longshoreman accused of not showing for work and failing to replace himself.[13] "I'm in his gang. He's only been working on the docks six months. His partner picked up the job and never told him about it. His partner is ——— and no one told him that the guy is a drunk. If anyone's at fault, it's me for not telling him. Don't give him time off, give it to me." Committee members pointed out that when longshoremen fail to show for work they jeopardize the entire local. Employers are then able to use their absence as grounds for hiring non-union people. Thus, the committee punished the two men by removing them from the dispatch for seven days.

Bum beefs share a number of characteristics. When grieved, they are expensive. Loss of pay or revenue, however, is not the only penalty; the losing side also pays the arbitrator's expenses. Having one's day in court, then, can be costly. Thus, one feature of bum beefs is they risk financial liability.

13 RD 21.

Bum beefs typically do not arise over differences of principle. Sleeping on the job, or missing work because of alcohol are not union principles; and ordering linesmen late is not an employer prerogative. When neither side is ideological about their differences, they can assess the relative merits of a dispute. And if they find that the expense of grieving exceeds possible benefits, defeat is an acceptable option. Since certain disagreements are not ideological or principled, the two sides do not have to pursue them if the beef is unwinnable or counterproductive. Thus, another characteristic of bum beefs is that they are not principled differences. That is why they can be lost or dropped.

Because principles are not at issue, losing bum beefs does not set precedent, although how and where the loss is settled is crucial. Disciplining longshoremen or fining employers at the local level is a loss. At this stage in the grievance process, however, the loss is relatively painless. The consequences are minimal and limited; precedent is not established. Were either side to pursue the matter further, on the other hand, costs would increase and precedent might be established. The Coast arbitrator, for example, could deregister longshoremen who are repeatedly accused of intoxication. Management's informal dispatching agreement with linesmen could be formally abolished and every Pacific Coast port would feel the consequences. Thus, pursuing a bum beef is like spending money on a losing proposition when the outcome is known to be even more expensive. To understate the matter, bum beefs are not good issues to raise or fight. Pursuing them gains nothing except more risk.

Even if the issues in these disputes are worthwhile, however, it is not possible to pursue them. There is very little either side can do about them. None of the disagreements can be defended on contractual grounds. Thus, perhaps the most distinctive feature of bum beefs is that they do not allow either side to be defensibly disobedient.

14

"WE ESSENTIALLY HAVE NO CONTRACT WITH YOU": KEEPING THE AGREEMENT

"LET'S get this fucking agony over with quickly," announced a business agent to a Special Labor Relations Committee. The two sides were discussing union complaints about a stevedoring company that had hired non-ILWU workers. "They have 9.43 men painting strads," he said, "IAM [International Association of Machinists] people are doing maintenance and repair work; IAM people are hooking and unhooking equipment; sailors are doing lashing and 9.43 crane operators are being contracted out to other companies."

The grievances extended beyond these particulars: "This company burns up too much union time," he continued, "they pay management to find ways for getting around the contract." The relationship between union and management was also an issue: "We essentially have no contract with you," he concluded, looking at the people across the table.[1]

If the charges were true, his assessment was accurate. The union's agreement to cooperate would exist only on paper. There would be no agreement in fact if the company circumvented agreed-upon procedures to resolve disagreements. If each side acts unilaterally, the rules for joint action are difficult to apply; cooperation is problematic. When the contract is not treated as a "living" document, the agreement does not work. The business agent was therefore correct; effectively, there was no "contract." But this presents a problem: If either side is to be defensibly disobedient, the contract must be allowed to "live."

---

1 Field notes.

THE FAILURE OF AGREEMENT

You'd better clean up your act if you want to avoid work stoppages.[2]

Despite an explicit "good faith" agreement to observe it, the contract is routinely violated. Hundreds of complaints and grievances are filed each year indicating that contractual compliance, like good faith, cannot be assumed; it must be enforced and negotiated on the docks. The legal agreement must be made to "work" because, for various reasons, the contract is often ignored, violated, and used for self-interest. Each side explores the limits of contractual possibilities and permissibilities. Because of financial considerations, the union and management have differing and conflicting interpretations of the agreement, and they therefore try and use it to their advantage. Thus, it is understood, and taken for granted on the waterfront, that each side will experiment with the contract and stretch it to cover their needs. Both sides also know that disagreements will erupt in the process. This is expected, and, within certain limits, it is acceptable.

Taking "advantage" of the contract

Under some conditions, it is permissible to push contractual limits even if that triggers a grievance or complaint. For example, walking along a dock early one morning, a business agent heard people working aboard ship. "Sailors are unlashing and removing hatch covers," he said; "that's longshore work and I've caught them red-handed."[3] He asked a clerk where the superintendent was. "On board, in the captain's quarters," was the response. He went aboard ship and walked to the captain's room where he found the superintendent with the ship's chief officer. They were drinking coffee and discussing the discharge operation. When a natural lull occurred in the conversation, the business agent interjected himself, and told the superintendent, "I want 'time in lieu.'"

"For what?" asked the supervisor innocently.

"You know for what; the crew was unlashing cargo."

2 Business agent to a stevedoring company representative, field notes.
3 Field notes.

"Alright," said the superintendent without hesitation, "I'll give you half an hour for one man."

"No you won't. You know better than that. You'll give half an hour for the entire gang."

Acknowledging defeat without surrendering dignity, the company official smiled and said: "Why don't you go bother 'Z' Stevedoring Company and leave me alone?"

"You do the right thing," he was told, "and I will."

The matter was settled easily because there was no dispute. The two men knew the contract had been violated; the only question was how much the agreement would cost. Contractual violations like this one are routine on the waterfront, especially when containers are involved. Capital-intensive technology is expensive, and so is turn-around time. As a result, stevedoring companies cut corners. Since steamship profits are not generated while ships are being loaded, shippers encourage stevedoring companies to violate the contract if that will expedite departure times. It is common knowledge, for example, that steamship companies risk "extended shift violations" to load container ships and have them under way by 6:00. Although not acceptable, violations like this are expected and recognized by both sides. Commenting on the practice, a high-ranking PMA official described the arrangement in these terms:

> They know what they're doing. And when a stevedoring company is ordered to work in possible violation of the contract, they'll tell the steamship company, "you know, we're running the risk of an extended shift violation." The steamship companies tell them, "we're willing to run that risk." If the union finds out, and the claim is deemed payable, the stevedoring company passes on the claim to the steamship line and says, "this is your debt; this is what you owe." They pay the union and add that amount to the steamship company's bill.[4]

These violations are tolerated only if both sides agree that they are contractual transgressions. So long as they are recognized as violations of the contract, the practices are interpreted generously as stretching the agreement. On the West Coast waterfront, this is called "taking advantage" of the contract. As a PMA official said candidly during an LRC meeting: "We

4 Interview with author.

use the contract to our advantage. The contract is there for whatever you can get out of it when it comes to money."[5]

Although taking advantage of the agreement is sometimes unacceptable, it does not jeopardize the contractual relationship. Stretching the contract does not make cooperation impossible. As indicated in an earlier chapter, when employers shift longshoremen without regard for their dispatched category, the union objects and a grievance is filed. But the cooperative relationship is not contested in this dispute. The two sides agree to disagree, and work continues while the disagreement is being settled.

Both sides take advantage of the contract regularly. It happens when management is caught violating the contract and explains that circumstances were beyond their control. Longshoremen making deals to spell one another, working out of category, leaving early, or working around the written agreement are also taking advantage of the contract. The most obvious example arises when a questionable activity is acknowledged and justified as being a way to find out if the practice is contractually acceptable.

In each instance, the contract is stretched. And when it is stretched beyond tolerable limits, a complaint or grievance flags the practice. None of these transgressions, however, undercuts the cooperative relationship between the union and management. The relationship survives because, when the violations are alleged, the practice stops; transgressions are recognized as violations. This public acknowledgment reaffirms shared language and common understandings. No one attempts to wiggle out from under the agreement in these situations. They pay up. Instead of denying the activity, or making excuses, they try to justify it contractually. If that is not convincing, the consequences are suffered and agreed-upon penalties are accepted. Taking advantage of the contract does not mean subverting it. The two sides may experiment with the contract; they can also stretch it. But they do not completely disregard it. The contract can be flexible and used creatively only if it survives and is not totally ignored. Flexibility, then, is one feature of a living agreement. When people on the waterfront talk about taking advantage of the contract, one meaning of the concept is therefore that the agreement lives between them; it has room to breathe.

5 UC 24/RD 98.

"Chiseling," "cheating," and "gimmicking":
Outright violations of the contract

Probing contractual perimeters is not always permitted. Even living agreements have their limits. Thus, there is an implicit distinction between taking advantage of the contract, and outright violations of it. On the Pacific Coast, the latter is called "chiseling," "cheating," or "gimmicking" on the bargain. The difference between violations is not obvious because the definitions depend largely on who does the defining. However, it is possible to recognize the most glaring forms of outright violations.

Clear-cut transgressions would include fighting or threatening supervision with violence; pilferage of expensive products (automobiles or sophisticated stereo equipment) is another example; so is stealing more than one can immediately consume. Although less obvious, most forms of chiseling, cheating, or gimmicking are still detectable.

Some examples:

• Two longshoremen filed a grievance alleging a "pay shortage"; they claimed the time sheets had been altered. Six men were originally listed as working until 5:30, but only two were paid overtime for the additional half-hour. The men contended that the documents had been falsified to justify denying overtime. Thus, when the dispute reached an LRC, the union requested the time sheets. After examining them, one union official said the sheets looked "fishy," as if the numbers had been altered.

"Something else is fishy," added a business agent. "How come there's no gang boss with six men?"

The PMA's response did not address the issue raised; instead, it was legalistic and technical. "If the union is claiming a violation on the grounds that there was no gang boss," said a PMA representative, "then it's an 'untimely claim'; you waited too long to file the complaint."

The atmosphere became tense. All pretenses of cordiality stopped. "Fucking chiseling bastards," muttered someone on the union side of the table.

"You guys insist on openly violating the contract until you get caught," said a union official, "it's becoming a way of doing business for you. You even work in violation of the contract when you know it's a violation. If that's the way you're going to operate, it doesn't make any sense to work through the grievance machinery."

His comments were met with silence.

"We've reached 'disagreement,'" he concluded angrily without dropping his eyes, "let's move on to something else."[6]

• Two other longshoremen were dispatched to a 6:00 job at 6:30. Upon arrival at the job, they asked the walking boss when their pay period started. Even though they had been dispatched late, they thought they should be paid for an eight-hour shift. Thus, they wanted to be put on the official payroll at 6:00. The walking boss disagreed; he told them their time would start by the clock, not the dispatch. Unsatisfied, the longshoremen refused to "turn to"; they returned to the hall and filed a grievance.

The PMA did not dispute the men's claim. In fact, the PMA spokesman conceded that the union was "partially right." The employer's written response concurred:

> The Union may have had an arguable claim had the men turned to at 7:15 p.m.; however, inasmuch as they refused to turn to, the Union has no claim. . . . There is a grievance machinery available to resolve such disputes. The men should have worked and submitted a claim for the time they thought they were due.[7]

"If they had turned to, they would have been paid," reiterated a management representative, "but since they didn't, the claim isn't payable."

"You cheating sons-of-bitches," replied a union person, "you agree these guys were fucked and you still won't pay. Let's reach disagreement and get the hell out of here."

• A gang charged employers with a "pay shortage." The men claimed they had been "turned to," worked for an hour and a half but were paid only for one hour. When a gang is turned to and works, they argued, the gang cannot be released until the midshift meal. The employers saw matters differently. Since the gang was understaffed, it could be released for "cause."[8]

6 Field notes.
7 UC 104/RD 79.
8 UC 182/RD 79.

"They were working shorthanded," said one PMA official, "this company's got a policy of releasing gangs working shorthanded."

"That's an odd way of handling the matter," observed a union representative. Then he raised some pointed questions.

"There was a gang boss present, wasn't there?"

"Yes."

"The gang boss is the employer's representative on the job, right?

"Right."

"Then what he does is company policy, right? If he didn't release them, then it was company policy that they work, right?"

"No," replied the PMA official, "it's not company policy, when a mistake is made."

A verbal explosion erupted from the union side of the table:

"You've got to be kidding!" shouted someone.

"You people are fucking outrageous," chimed in another.

• One longshoreman accused an employer of "bypassing the hiring hall." He claimed that three Local 10 members had been dispatched to work as "button men" (elevator operators) aboard a passenger ship on Saturday. The three were released that evening. When another ship arrived Sunday morning, however, one of them was returned to work. The grievant thought no one could be called back if they had been released the night before. Instead, the new job belonged to the next person in the dispatch. Since he was low man that day, the job was rightfully his. The employer's formal response was technical and narrow: "A registered longshoreman was employed."

The employer representative knew this position was untenable. He was told by PMA officials during a caucus that the claim appeared "payable." He agreed: "We made a mistake and won't do that again." Then he asked, "what's the penalty?"

"The longshoreman under the gun (low man in the dispatch) has to be paid," said a PMA representative, agreeing with the union's conclusion.

"Hey!" exclaimed another stevedoring company manager, "the low-man-out rule should help you guys in this beef. The guy who took the job should not have, since he wasn't low man out. Put it on him. He violated the LMO [low-man-out] rule."

274

A consensus emerged: The ploy might work at least temporarily and the claim would not have to be paid at the local level.

"We admit the employer's action was improper," announced the PMA spokesman when the LRC reconvened. "And we are also cognizant that the man was in violation of the LMO rule."

"Do you want to argue that position in front of the arbitrator?" interrupted a union official belligerently.

"The man had an affirmative obligation to *not* come back," shot back the PMA representative, skirting the arbitrator issue; "the penalties are offsetting."

Another PMA official joined the argument: "Accepting the callback violates the LMO rule. The guy who took the job is as guilty as the company."

"I'm absolutely fed up with this shit!" declared the union spokesman in a loud, very angry tone of voice. "You're making a mockery of the contract! If that's the way you want to do things, then we'll go outside the contract too and clean your fucking clocks. And you can have my book!" he threatened, referring to being deregistered if he actually delivered on the threat. Gathering his papers, he said to an associate, "let's go; I'm done. There's gonna be a work stoppage with these folks at 1:00 this afternoon."

But he wasn't done. Nearly red in the face, he yelled: "There's no excuse for an outright contract violation! If you're gonna make the men responsible for illegal orders, then we're gonna instruct them to refuse *any* order which is in violation of the contract."

An eerie silence came over the room as the two union officers prepared to leave. The quiet was broken, however, when an employer representative said softly in an explanatory, almost apologetic tone of voice, "the guy who filed this complaint didn't lose anything."

"He got fucked out of a job," shouted the union officer before anything more could be said (field notes).

Making outright violations of the contract are different from taking advantage of it. Each of the previous disputes crossed the line from stretching the contract to violating it outright because one of three situations occurred: (1) one side acted unilaterally, ignoring the other's needs, and thereby undercutting the bases for cooperation; (2) all pretenses of

275

working with a contractual agreement were dropped; or (3) the transgressions were so blatant, and the issue so important, that one side could not afford to ignore them.

Outright violations are also recognizable by the formal sanctions they elicit. If it is determined that the agreement has been openly violated, longshoremen can be taken off the dispatch and in some instances deregistered; and PMA members can be fined. But perhaps the most effective sanction for and distinctive feature of outright violations is that when the contract is openly and repeatedly abrogated the cooperative relationship is jeopardized. At that point there is no flexible, living agreement between the two sides. Thus, when the agreement is self-consciously ignored, the employers risk production and the union is unable to protect its members.

"WE'LL SETTLE THIS ON THE DOCKS": TRANSFORMING THE OFFICIAL AGREEMENT INTO A LIVING BARGAIN

Defensible disobedience is impossible without a living contract. Unless both sides keep the bargain, or at least the appearance of keeping it, neither side can be defensibly disobedient. If the agreement is not kept a new one has to be generated or the old one must be reinforced. And when one side acts as if the contract is merely a formal document, which has only legal standing, the other side has to translate the official agreement into a living bargain.[9] To be defensibly disobedient both sides must be more than signatures on the collectively bargained agreement. They also have to be partners. Thus, to be defensibly disobedient, sometimes it is necessary for

---

9 The distinction between living bargains and formal agreements is analogous to the difference between legal realism and legal formalism. The legal realists, according to Derrick Bell (1992:99–101), were a group of legal scholars writing in the 1930s who challenged the classical structure of law, which, at the time, was conceived as a formal group of common-law rules. Like legal realism, the notion of a living contract challenges formalism and conceptualism, and looks instead at the realities of keeping an agreement. Keeping an agreement is making it work, "living" it rather than applying it, and using it flexibly. For contracts to live or be lived, they have to be stretched, to be expanded or restricted depending on the situation, and in this sense, it can be said they need room to "breathe." They require that signatories make them work, or make them "live." Living agreements die when they are not upheld. Formal agreements can remain in effect even after the living agreement has been destroyed.

one side to force the other to abide by the nuances and formalities of their agreement.

Within twenty-four hours after walking out of the LRC meeting described earlier, the union formally protested the employer practices. "It's the opinion of the local union," wrote the four titled officers in a letter addressed to the joint Coast Labor Relations Committee,

> that labor relations at the local level have reached an impasse. The purpose of labor relations meetings is to peacefully settle disputed questions on the basis of the contract. For the meetings to function well requires a spirit of accommodation on the part of both parties and a sincere willingness to see that the memberships of both sides perform in accordance with the agreement as per Section 18.1. We feel that the local employers . . . have adopted a stonewall approach where they automatically say no, regardless of the merits of the claims involved. Matters can not continue as they are. We are requesting that the Coast Committee alert the local employers as to their responsibilities. . . . As things stand now, the local union has no confidence whatsoever in the present working of the grievance procedure.[10]

The union was even more candid with the PMA. "We feel that labor relations in this port have reached an abysmal low," they wrote on the same day.

> At Labor Relations Committee Meetings, it is our feeling that the employers make no attempt to discuss the contractual ramifications of questions raised, but just adopt a stone wall attitude of complete negativeness towards the union's claims. . . . We believe that under such conditions it is a charade to continue holding the regular labor relations committee meetings.
>
> Unless we have some indication that the employers will discuss union complaints on their merit giving full weight to the contract and what it contains, the union feels justified in stating that the local grievance machinery is breaking down and failing to work and therefore . . . we are referring this matter to the Joint Coast Labor Relations Committee.[11]

The letters put in writing what the walkout said about management–labor relations: There was no effective agreement between the two sides. The union felt the contract was not being lived up to, or adhered to

10 Letter in author's possession.
11 Letter in author's possession.

seriously. By walking out, the union was attempting to change the relationship; it was trying to transform an official-legal agreement into an actual bargain, practiced on the docks. Thus, the unscheduled departure was not unexpected. "Things were leading up to this," said one waterfront executive to another when the union was gone, "it had to happen."

It had to happen because when one side violates the contract and the other feels it has no options, the following scenario emerges: Either, (1) the contract will be strictly enforced on the docks, not in the grievance machinery; or, (2) informal deals will be called off and cooperation canceled. The walkout, then, was predictable. It was the union's way of making the employers live by contractual appearances and formalities. The union was trying to make the agreement a living bargain.

When this point is reached, threats are barely veiled. In one exchange, for example, a union official said to the PMA: "We've talked long enough; if this keeps up we're just gonna have to settle this on the docks."[12] In another dispute, the union told management, "If you insist on operating this way, the only option for the union is to deal with our complaints directly and on the job." And when the two sides could not settle a contractual disagreement, one union representative declared: "Let us know the next time this ship is in port. We'll stop work on it and see who's right" (field notes).

The union's message is clear in these exchanges. If the contract is not lived by, the union will not resolve its differences with employers in the grievance machinery. Disputes will be settled on the docks. And that will cost employers time and money. Thus, when the union told the employers it would instruct longshoremen to refuse any orders that violated the contract the message was clear: No one would work around the contract. All deals were off. That, of course, could be expensive to the employers. The walkout and follow-up letters underlined the union's willingness to act on its promises. Union threats were now policy.

The employers got the message. Less than twenty-four hours after the walkout, a Special LRC was convened and it was attended by high-ranking PMA officials. The exchanges were frank; both sides candidly discussed their troubles. The union thought the employers were taking unaccept-

12 UC 79.

able liberties with the contract: "We're tired of being fucked over," said one union official at the outset.[13] Making the implicit explicit, he announced: "The niceties of the contract no longer operate."

Given the state of relations between the two sides, the union was exercising its only option. It would enforce the contract strictly, by the letter, because the spirit of cooperation had been violated. The union hoped this would force the employers to live by the formal agreement. "We've allowed you to work around the contract in the past," explained a union representative. "Maybe that's an error. We're going to have to keep to the specifics of the contract now because when we don't, you fuck over us."

"The only way to make you live up to the contract," said someone else, "is to make it costly if you don't."

"Your problem poses a problem for me," responded a PMA official; "all your beefs are not legitimate. You're partially to blame for this situation."

A stevedoring company superintendent spoke up and argued that the failure to agree was two-sided. The union may not have violated the contract, he said; but it was not cooperating either. And that forced the employers to ignore the agreement. "I didn't want IAM people repairing containers," he insisted,

> but you guys wouldn't write a letter saying it was OK for steady men to do it. And neither would the VP (of the stevedoring company). I wanted customers to use this company. That makes work for all of us. If IAM can't do it, we'll have to truck the containers out and we both lose money. And then you stop me from using hall men on pad eyes. You won't be flexible. But it's being done in Tacoma. And we both lost work because of that one, too. And I'm tired of this fucking painting issue, too. I've been saying "let's arbitrate it" but you won't do that either. I'm willing to lose before the arbitrator. Look, I'm paid to do what I think is right. I have an obligation to do that. But I want things settled. I call the union hall to talk about these things and you guys never return my calls.

"We're not here to give our work away," responded a union spokesman, "and we're not going to let an arbitrator give our work away either. We want some conformance with the contract."

"Look," added another unionist,

---

13 RD 80.

we need some cooperation or else contract negotiations are going to be pretty stormy. We have a membership that's up against the fucking wall. The night side is like a room of gasoline waiting to explode. Business agents can't be hauled out to deal with off-the-wall issues where you openly violate the agreement. You've got us in an untenable situation. You ask us to collaborate to keep the industry going and we do. And then you fuck us. You're not helping.

"We'll pay the button man," said a regional PMA official softly, trying to settle the matter and reestablish an effective relationship between the two sides.

"Why did we have to walk out?" asked a union negotiator.

"We all make mistakes," replied the PMA spokesman in a quiet, conciliatory tone of voice.

MAKING THE SYSTEM WORK

Keeping the agreement sometimes means temporarily not cooperating. When the union walked out, it stopped helping the employers. The rules for cooperation were suspended; the two sides could not even agree to disagree. Although the walkout was successful, it did much more than win a grievance and uphold a union principle. It forced the employers to live by the agreement, to be bound by it. Unless both sides are bound by the formal contract, there is no agreement in the work process. By refusing to use normal channels, the union forced employers to live by the agreement. In this way, the union made the system work. They established an effective contractual relationship where one did not exist. This was an important accomplishment because unless the two sides have an effective relationship – where both are actual parties to the agreement, where the contract is lived by, in spirit, and on the docks – neither can be defensibly disobedient. Making the system work, in this context, therefore means holding both sides to the fullest meaning of the agreement. Like production, insubordination under a collectively bargained agreement is effective only when both sides cooperate.

In this situation, being insubordinate and being able to dispute issues of workplace regime depends upon one side's ability to coerce the other into actually abiding by a living contractual agreement. Thus, making the system work sometimes means making it *not* work by disrupting it. Sometimes it is necessary to threaten the cessation of collaboration to produce cooperation. To defend insubordination contractually, and to struggle for control of the workplace, both sides must live closely by the agreement. When one does not the system breaks down. To make the arrangement work, to be able to be disobedient, the violator must therefore be made to become a party to an agreement that lives. Another feature of defensible disobedience, then, is being able to make the other side act like more than a signature on a legal document.

15

CONSTRUCTING AND MAINTAINING THE APPEARANCE OF COOPERATION

T HE knot connecting the ILWU and PMA is a complicated one. Keeping the living agreement alive involves doing more than following contractual formalities. For the bargain to live and be jointly kept, private agendas are publicly presented as reciprocated efforts. The two sides try to look like they give as well as take, even when they do not. The union and PMA therefore do more than create contractual language to live with. They also cultivate a relationship in which each side can live with the other.

When the appearance of reciprocity is not maintained, one side appears disadvantaged. At this point, living agreements die and defensible disobedience is no longer possible. Making the ILWU–PMA relationship work, therefore, means that the agreement must be kept alive in another sense: The *impression* of cooperation must be maintained even when one side takes advantage of the other. Expressed differently, a fiction must be established for the relationship to live. Constructing this social fiction is a self-conscious process; it is deliberate and two-sided. Each side is involved in making the illusions joint creations. The fiction is produced in a number of observable ways.

CREATING THE ILLUSION OF NEGOTIATION

One example emerged during contract talks. Coastwide negotiations began in May and concluded in the middle of July. However, because the ILWU is a decentralized organization and locals are relatively autonomous, the contract is not signed until working rules are negotiated for each port. Local rules for linesmen became a stumbling block in San Francisco. The union had made three or four demands for new language in the linesmen's

282

agreement and the employers rejected them all. Each time an agreement was reached on another set of differences, the union would return to the disagreements about linesmen. A pattern had emerged by the end of August and both sides were very familiar with the other's position. The same demands were advanced, with the same rationale, and each time the same language of rejection was spoken. Not much progress occurred. The negotiations seemed hopelessly deadlocked.

"What are we going to do?" asked a frustrated union representative in early September. "We're going 'round and 'round." He suggested that maybe the matter should go to an arbitrator.

"We're not turning it over to an arbitrator, or any other outside agency," responded the PMA spokesman firmly, "I don't want arbitrators writing my working rules."

The PMA official then asked a question, and it took the union by surprise. "I'll put it to you frankly," he said. "What are you willing to give up to get a pay differential for leadermen on the lines board?"

"What proposal do *you* have priority on?" asked a union negotiator. "Is it extending the lines dispatch to 9:30?"

The PMA official nodded his head, "yes." And then he offered, "We'd be willing to pay the differential if the union would go along with changing the language on when employers can use nonlinesmen to tie up and let go ships." The employers wanted the option to have gang men release ships. Under certain circumstances, they wanted to avoid calling the hall and having to wait for linesmen.

"We need to caucus," said a union official quickly. He had a strategy that depended on a secret and he wanted his side out of the room before anything more was said.[1]

The secret was that linesmen were already very satisfied with the coast-wide contract. Their work was protected and the new agreement included a substantial pay raise. They were therefore in a good bargaining position; anything negotiated after the coastwide contract was gravy. They could not lose; they could only gain. But only the union knew this.

Nothing could be gained if the secret were revealed. The employers did not have to meet local union demands, and if they discovered linesmen

1 RD 137.

were satisfied, no more concessions would be granted. Thus, even though the union had no surface reason to negotiate, if it were to act strategically, it had a great deal to negotiate. If union negotiators could make it *look like* they were seriously negotiating, the linesmen stood to benefit from local negotiations and gain additional concessions. But if they could not construct that illusion, there was no way to raise the demands.

The caucus was called to create that illusion.

"I think we have them where we want them," said the union official when the caucus room doors were closed. "What is your most important demand and what are you willing to give for it?" he asked the assembled linesmen. The pay differential was pretty important, they said. A couple of men wanted to extend the dispatch time, but only if employers would accept two dispatches, one in the morning and the other at night.

"Look, we got 'em!" said the union official, barely able to contain his excitement. "The dispatch is much more important to them than they're letting on." He read aloud from the transcript of a previous arbitration. PMA officials had told the arbitrator that to use linesmen flexibly, employers needed to extend the dispatch. Flexibility, argued the PMA, was necessary if the employers were to exercise sound business practices.

"We've got 'em!" exclaimed the union officer. "You guys are happy with the contract the way it is. Right?"

The linesmen nodded.

"The employers don't know that," he explained, "they don't know what's important to you or what you're willing to give for the differential. Let's take them up on the offer for a pay differential and throw in a bunch more demands we don't care about. That way they'll think you're unhappy with the coast contract. It will look like we're negotiating and they won't be able to tell what's important to us."

Smiles emerged on people's faces. The mood became upbeat. The linesmen thought the strategy might work and they suggested three demands be negotiated. One would guarantee linesmen four hours' pay at straight time for any job dispatched between 8:00 a.m. and 5:00 p.m., Mondays through Fridays. The second demand was that linesmen be paid four hours' overtime for any work between 5:00 p.m. and 8:00 a.m., Saturday through Sunday and holidays. Finally, they demanded that linesmen traveling outside of Oakland be paid fifteen cents a mile both ways plus travel time and tolls.

"Let's give it a try," someone said, "let's see if it works."

"In the spirit of the employers' proposal," said the union spokesman when the negotiations reconvened, "we'll consider your offer for leadermen's pay if you'll also agree with three union proposals." He elaborated on the demands and concluded by saying, "We think that that's a fair exchange." The employers called for a caucus (field notes).

The strategy enabled the union to look as if it were actually negotiating. ILWU negotiators appeared willing to consider the employers' offer. And if the employers would accept certain union demands, an agreement could be reached. What the employers did not know, however, was that the demands were expendable. The union, on the other hand, knew that the demands most likely would not be approved. But the demands were not made for approval; rather, they were decoys to hide other demands from being detected. The demands were used as weapons to get other proposals accepted. The strategy was to deceive the employers through the impression that the union was seriously interested in proposals that were actually expendable.

Strategically speaking, the union was well positioned. If the employers wanted an item exchanged for pay, the union had something to give up. And what it gave up, of course, was a bargaining chip. Thus it would be giving up a decoy (travel time or extended pay guarantees) for a serious demand (a pay differential for leadermen). Union negotiators therefore conveyed the impression they were engaged in give-and-take when actually they were not.

The strategy evidently worked. When negotiations reconvened, the PMA spokesman said: "We have a counterproposal in connection with your extended hours proposal. We're willing to pay 40 percent of the pay differential to leadermen. We're also willing to extend the four-hour guarantee from 8:00 p.m. Saturday to 5:00 p.m. Sunday and stop it at 6:00 a.m. Monday. That expands the eight-hour guarantee period three hours. Our answer to the overtime proposal is, no. Our answer to travel time is also, no" (field notes).

Given that the linesmen started out satisfied, the local negotiators did exceptionally well. Leadermen received a pay differential, and three hours were added to the eight-hour guarantee. The exchange also enabled the union to appear as if it were seriously negotiating when it actually had nothing to lose and everything to gain.

SAVING FACE FOR THE OTHER SIDE

The appearance of cooperation is established in other ways. After months of negotiation, for example, the ILWU and PMA could not agree on contractual language for gearmen. They disagreed about pay, who provided work clothes, availability, and a starting date for the agreement. By October 10, the two sides had narrowed their differences considerably. The only substantial disagreement was over the starting date for the new agreement. The union wanted July 1, which meant the contract would apply retroactively. The employers wanted September 1. Neither side would budge. Since they could not bridge the gap, talks were adjourned until October 26.

When negotiations resumed the morning of the 26th, very few words were exchanged. The union reiterated its October 10 position and so did the employers. Then the union called for a caucus. The caucus lasted through lunch. It was interrupted in the afternoon only briefly when the employers made a new offer. This proposal narrowed differences on every issue except retroactivity. Late that afternoon the union returned to the negotiating table. It moved the employer's most recent motion, with one revision: The contract would be effective July 1. The employers asked for a five-minute caucus. When they returned, the response was surprisingly straightforward: "Okay, we accept" (field notes).

From all outward appearances, the exchange is unexplainable. After six months of negotiating and caucusing, without any obvious change in circumstances, the employers conceded a seriously contested point and struck a bargain.

Although not acknowledging it publicly, however, both sides knew that between morning and afternoon the situation had been changed. Operating behind the scenes, and hidden from public view, a different set of negotiators was talking. When they reached an agreement, the local stalemate was broken.

Sometimes it is impossible to settle differences across the bargaining table. Then it is necessary to involve people with more power to create an agreement. When this is done unilaterally, without the other side's knowledge, it is known as going over someone's head. Going over an adversary's head is frequently necessary. But it is also rather risky. If the maneuver becomes public, it is not possible to maintain the appearance of equality that underwrites a cooperative relationship. Thus, neither side takes advantage of the other in public, if they want to keep the living agreement alive. Indeed, under certain circumstances, the advantaged side orchestrates scenarios that enable its opposition to save face. That is what happened with the disagreement over gearmen. The union had gone over the head of the local PMA; it came to an agreement with the higher-ups and figured out a way for the local managers to save face.

A couple days before the 26th, one of the union negotiators called international headquarters.[2] The two sides were deadlocked over retroactivity, he reported. He thought local agreements automatically went into effect July 1st to coincide with the coastwide contract. If that was true, retroactivity was not a bargaining issue. "Was this assessment correct?" he asked. The international official thought so and said he would explore the matter further. "Call me," if the issue comes up again, he suggested.

The issue surfaced early on the 26th. The two sides were still divided over the agreement's starting date. When these differences surfaced, the union asked to caucus and called the international offices. An official at the international was asked to call his PMA counterpart and have him "move [the local negotiator] off dead center."

The local official knew he was going over the other side's head. He was aware of the risk and knew the local PMA negotiator would be angry when he found out. He realized the phone call had serious consequences and explained that he had no alternative: "It's the only way I can operate at this point."

Word came from downtown that the appropriate PMA official was not around; someone else would have to be found. The instructions were clear cut: "stall." Thus began a "caucus" that continued through lunch and into

---

2 The following account is based on interviews with union and PMA officials and field notes.

287

the afternoon. But there was nothing to caucus about and so the time was spent swapping stories, sharing gossip, playing cards. The negotiating team received a call from the International within an hour: They still could not find the PMA official they were looking for. Keep stalling. There would be a knock on the door every so often and a PMA person would ask, "are you ready yet?" No, the unionists responded, trying not to laugh. They stalled until lunch and the extra time taken eating helped extend the appearance of caucusing. After lunch, additional time was requested.

Once during the afternoon the caucus was suspended when the employers made a new offer. Everything in the proposal was acceptable except the starting time. Caucusing continued. Late that afternoon, union negotiators received another phone call from headquarters: A high-ranking PMA official had been consulted and he agreed with the union. Local PMA negotiators would be told to modify their position. After waiting to make sure the message was communicated, the union ended its "caucus" and "negotiations" resumed.

When the two sides sat down, it was clear the PMA negotiators had been told to back down. The spokesman was noticeably agitated. Speaking to no one in particular, he said he wasn't "going to allow Coast officials to do Local negotiations." The union advanced a new proposal. They repeated the employers' last offer, with one difference: It went into effect on July 1.

After caucusing for five minutes, the employers agreed.

The Local 10 official explained later that the proposal was a "face-saving gesture." Had he wanted to be vindicated symbolically, he would have publicly announced that the PMA representative was wrong about retroactivity. He would tell him to consult with his superiors who, in turn, would verify the union's position. "I could have made him look silly or ineffective by telling him to speak with his boss. Then it would have been clear that he had no power and had been outdone by the union."

But the union officer saw no advantage in this. "We were maneuvering in a very delicate situation," he said. "We could have rammed it down their throats, but I don't think that would have worked." The PMA had options. They could have reduced their salary offers or dragged out negotiations another couple of months. "By allowing him to save face," the union official pointed out, "nobody felt too bad."

He knew the union could hang tough. Nevertheless, he thought it was smarter to "let them think the motion was theirs. We wanted them to think that we were really negotiating not just going over their head." The gesture was not altruistic. It developed out of the union officer's understanding of the relationship between the two sides. "I couldn't rub his face in the fact that I was going over his head," he said.

> After all, he is a key actor in the Northern California area and he's trying to do his best. I have to live with him after negotiations are over. If it becomes obvious that I've gone over his head, it doesn't look too good for him and he can make *me* suffer later on. He could have redone the offer and negotiated until next year. He could give the union a hard time on every other issue from now on. That's why I wanted to allow him to save face.

Keeping the living relationship alive requires a variety of face work. The faces to be saved vary, and so does the work to save them. During one LRC, for example, PMA representatives were in a difficult situation: On the surface, the union's complaint was legitimate. The accused company, however, did not want to concede; the company wanted to refer the matter to arbitration.

"You've got a weak case," the PMA spokesman told the company representative at a caucus.[3]

"I know," replied the manager. "But we want to go to Area [the second step in a three-stage grievance process that moves from "Local" to "Area" to "Coast" LRC] anyway to find out what the arbitrator will do."

"We'll probably lose," said the PMA officer; "but that's actually good for us. He has a lot of cases in front of him where he's going to have to rule in our favor. If he rules against us on this one, that'll make him look good."

The PMA official had a multilevel strategy. Moving the matter to arbitration gave employers the appearance of taking the grievance machinery seriously. The private agenda, however, was different. By arbitrating, the employers could deny they had made a mistake. That allowed them to maintain face locally. But the most attractive feature of the strategy was that it enabled the arbitrator to rule for the employers on other disputes and still appear unbiased. The maneuver therefore helped the arbitrator maintain the appearance of neutrality.

3 RD 108.

Each side is quite sensitive about public appearances and how they are interpreted. Thus, they both devote considerable energy to strategies for managing the consequences of appearances. Effective face-work is only one strategy. The ILWU and PMA very carefully and skillfully avoid jeopardizing their delicate relationship. They do so in numerous ways.

Victories are rarely named as such. In fact, if negotiations and grievances were assessed solely on the basis of public self-reports, no winners could be found. Victory talk is rarely heard in public; self-effacing talk is more typical. In public, negotiators characteristically dwell on the weaknesses of bargaining positions. Talk of strength is reserved for caucuses. When one side has obviously made a concession, the acceptance is usually cloaked in mock humility:

"Is that the one we win today?" asked a union official when employers agreed to pay a grievance.

"We ain't asking for justice," said another unionist who had just demolished an employer's logic for not settling a grievance, "shit, we'll settle for mercy" (field notes).

Public claims of weakness and humility are understandable. Victory talk is counterproductive: It jeopardizes cooperation because the defeated are publicly identified. It also reflects poor taste. More important, however, victory talk contributes to inactivity. The membership of either group can justify lack of involvement by saying that the organization is doing well without them. But that would be a serious problem because membership participation is necessary for both sides to press their demands effectively. The language of weakness, then, contains a self-interested vocabulary.

The cooperative relationship between union and management is also protected when minor violations of agreements are consciously ignored. Each side operates with implicit priorities and chooses not to challenge every transgression. In colloquial language this is called letting something "slide," or giving someone "slack." One PMA official had another name for it. He called the process a "waltz of the toreadors."

The particular dance he had in mind was a caucus in which the union was stalling.[4] The two sides were deadlocked over whether longshoremen had to cross another union's picket line. Nothing could be done until an

4 The following account is based on interviews and field notes.

arbitrator arrived and made a decision. It was late afternoon and if the issue wasn't settled by 9:00, work would wait until the next day because the hiring hall would be closed. At 3:40 the LRC was adjourned so the sides could caucus.

"I'll give you a half hour," said the PMA official.

At 5:00, the PMA finished caucusing and employer representatives began milling about the corridors. The union was still caucusing at 6:00.

"It's going to be long night," predicted the PMA official.

> We all know what the outcome will be. They're stalling until 9:00. The arbitrator won't get here before suppertime. By the time we break for supper and he rules it will be after 11:00. I have tickets to the ballet for tonight but I've already called the wife and told her to go without me. I won't be home until late. The arbitrator will rule for us, but we won't be able to enforce the decision until tomorrow morning. I know all the moves in this dance; it's a waltz of the toreadors.

Each side made moves that closely followed the choreography predicted by the PMA official. Every so often the PMA would ask the union if they were ready to reconvene. The union would say "no" each time. And even though everyone knew the union was stalling, no one made it an issue. The union's activities were never questioned; neither were its motives. Nobody accused the union of violating time limits on the caucus. The PMA ignored this transgression and allowed the union to make its moves. Thus, the PMA was the union's partner in this waltz. Evidently it was more important for the employers to preserve their delicate relationship with Local 10 than to announce publicly that the union was abusing their patience.

THE APPEARANCE OF JUSTICE

The living agreement is also kept alive by the grievance machinery. Whether intended or not, the agreement is enhanced when serious disagreements appear resolvable and the possibility of justice is maintained. The grievance management process might well have been designed to promote this impression. Whenever longshoremen feel aggrieved, they can file a grievance. And when employers complain about longshoremen their complaints are heard first by an elected union committee. If satisfac-

291

tion is not reached locally, a number of options are available: The matter can be taken to an Area LRC, an arbitrator, the Coast LRC, or the Coast Arbitrator.

The union and management also work very hard to resolve disagreements. Meetings hear grievances weekly and each side puts in many hours. The sessions are public and, when they do not have a job, Local 10 members attend them. Considerable emotional energy is expended during these meetings: Voices are routinely raised by both sides and impassioned pleas are delivered for aggrieved constituents. Ten to fifteen complaints are heard and debated each week. Thus, the formal architecture of the grievance machinery definitely gives the impression that serious differences are engaged and justice is possible.

Even though both sides routinely grumble about the grievance process, they use it rather extensively. In fact, one major complaint is that the machinery is slowed by overuse. Tallying grievances confirms this impression. During one recent twenty-two-month period, over 800 complaints were exchanged. It is reasonable to assume, then, that the two sides believe complaints are actually redressed through the grievance machinery.

But a different understanding emerges when the disposition of complaints is determined empirically. In one recent six-month period, for example, 208 complaints were filed (126 by the union and 92 by the employers). Eighteen LRCs were convened during this period. In the majority of cases (148), a mutually acceptable solution could *not* be found. Put differently, two-thirds of the time, the disputants would either agree to "disagree," "postpone," "close, subject to reopening," "look into," "hold over," or "refer to Area." In only one-third (60) of the 208 complaints filed, did the union and employers agree on a solution. For the most part, then, without even assessing the quality of decisions, the local grievance machinery neither resolves serious disagreements nor achieves justice.

Longshoremen, however, seem to believe something actually happens to their complaints in the grievance machinery. Otherwise, they would not file so many grievances. Apparently they have faith in the process despite its record. Although that process was not necessarily created for this purpose, their belief in it is another fiction that sustains the union's relationship with employers. Faith in the grievance machinery keeps the living agreement alive. It is the political grease controlling the heat produced by the friction of class relations. To paraphrase Erving Goffman, it is a "cooling-out" mechanism.

This faith, however, is not universal. Sometimes the illusion cannot be sustained and the impression of effectiveness breaks down. During one LRC, for example, a longshoreman who did not qualify for the pay guarantee complained that he worked just enough to disqualify himself for unemployment compensation. But the money he made as a longshoreman was insufficient to survive on. A union representative agreed and argued the longshoreman was effectively penalized for working. This policy, he insisted, rewarded people who did not work. "That's not fair," he said; "we need to get some justice on the matter. Something needs to be done."[5]

The PMA's response was candid. It also totally destroyed the impression that the grievance process was about justice. "We realize it's not equitable," said the PMA spokesman, "but given the language of the contract, there's not much we can do."

At another LRC meeting,[6] an injured longshoreman on disability wanted to be pensioned off the waterfront. He found out, however, that he had been deregistered. Because he had been living in and out of his home to protect his wife's welfare check, he was never informed of the deregistration proceedings. Since he had not protested the action when it occurred, little could be done now to help him. He had been legally deregistered.

"Let's take the issue under advisement," suggested a union official, "and study it seriously to see what can be done."

The PMA side did not object. Their spokesman did, however, announce that re-registration was not possible. The man's deregistration had followed contractual procedures. The union official nodded his head in silence. He knew the union could do nothing contractually. He also knew he could not say "tough luck" to a totally disabled man on social security. The union's proposal did not resolve the complaint; nor did it achieve justice. But it did convey concern and it appeared to take the problem seriously. The man was being "cooled-out."

5 RD 33.
6 RD 32.

Sometimes humor communicates that LRCs are often long-winded sessions that settle very little. In one instance, for example, the two sides could not agree on who should be paid after they agreed that a union claim was payable. A good deal of time had been used to argue the issue when an employer representative said with a smile: "If we don't pay, we argue three hours and if we do pay, we argue three hours. I therefore move that the claim be denied so we don't have to decide who gets paid."[7]

In an equally frustrating session, a longshoreman waited hours for his grievance to be heard. Running out of patience, he leaned over to this researcher and said under his breath: "You may find this interesting, but I find it slow."[8] When three hours passed, he could barely restrain himself: "You're a saint to put up with this," he said, "but if that's the way university people get smart, I'd rather be stupid."

The living agreement lives a little less when it is not possible to believe in the effectiveness of the grievance machinery. LRC meetings are sparsely attended; cynicism is expressed openly; neither side attempts to appear serious about the process. When either side loses faith in the grievance machinery, they stop being defensibly disobedient. Instead, people storm out of meetings, verbal explosions take place, and job actions are waged on the docks. In these instances, people know how to be disobedient in defensible ways but they choose not to be because the process has broken down.

LEARNING IMPRESSION MANAGEMENT: HOW TO APPEAR
DEFENSIBLY DISOBEDIENT

Most longshoremen do not know how to create the impression of living by the agreement when only partially following it. They must learn how to be defensibly disobedient. Grievance Committee members typically teach them how to do this. Learning defensible disobedience is like developing photographic negatives. Images emerge slowly; it takes time for the unrecognizable to become identifiable; clarity and resolution evolve out of

7 RD 75.
8 RD 60.

blurs and fuzziness. The principles for being defensibly disobedient come into focus as committee members construct written responses to employer complaints.

"What happened?" the committee chair asked one longshoreman accused of being drunk as well as using "foul and abusive language."[9]

The man explained he had gotten into an argument with the walking boss; words were exchanged, and he was fired.

"Were you drinking?"

"Nope."

"Why does he say you were?"

"I don't know."

"Let's take the story from the beginning," suggested the person writing the committee's report, "you and the walker got into a beef. Right?"

"Yeah, I guess."

"And both of you used typical longshore talk. Right?" prompted the writer.

"Yeah, that's it."

"You have gout, don't you?" suggested the recorder.

"Yup."

"Well, let's add that you'd been taking pills for gout at the time."

The committee rejected the employer's complaint. It stated: "Brother X got into a beef with the walker. They both started yelling at each other using typical longshore talk. Brother X has been taking pills for gout."

Without disputing the facts, the committee's account added information and substituted new language. "Typical longshore talk" is a euphemism for "foul and abusive language." But contractually speaking, people cannot be fired for using longshore language. At first glance, gout appears unrelated to the dispute. Pills for gout, however, produce the symptoms of drunkenness. Thus, although not disputing the complaint, the committee's account established a defense for the man's disobedience. And, in a not-too-subtle way, the accused dockworker was also shown how to construct a defensible account.

The committee is not always successful in teaching longshoremen how to be defensibly disobedient:

9 RD 3.

"Where were you when the walking boss came by?"[10] the Grievance Committee secretary asked of a gang accused of working "four on, four off." Three of them said they were relieving themselves.

"Where were the others?" No one was sure. Extra men had been on the job all day and the walker rotated them in and out of the gang.

"So maybe that's why it seemed you were working 'four on, four off,'" said the notetaker anticipating a defense.

"No, not really," he was told, "the extra men weren't working at that time."

"Besides," said another gang member, "the superintendent was around and he looked in the hatch and only saw four men."

It was becoming clear that a defensible account could not be constructed along these lines. But the Grievance Committee official persisted; he continued to develop a case for why the superintendent did not see what he reported. As the gang boss told of problems with the walker, the union official started writing again. The gang was loading cotton, said the gang boss, and it was unfairly compared with a more productive gang working the same cargo in another hatch. The gang boss thought the two operations were different and it was therefore a mistake to hold the gangs to one standard. Committee members wanted to elaborate on the gang boss's account.

"In other words, it was a speed-up," said a committee member, trying to provide grounds for defending the men.

"Hell," said the gang boss rejecting the cue, "we had ten men; we could have done it."

Given the gang's report, the Grievance Committee could neither construct, nor teach how to construct, a contractually defensible account of the event. When union officials are not given the raw materials for shaping a defensible account very little can be done. In these instances, people sophisticated in the art of defensible disobedience explicitly tell the uninitiated what to say and do to be protected by the union the next time.

Sometimes the lesson is learned the hard way. One longshoreman accused of "walking off the job" explained that he had worked hard for an entire shift. He hardly had a break. At day's end, the walking boss asked

10 RD 6.

him for "a favor." Would he pick up some spilled cargo? The man thought that amounted to being overworked and told the walker to "get me a replacement." Then he walked off the docks.[11]

The Grievance Committee found him guilty of walking off the job and removed him from the dispatch for seven days. The longshoreman was outraged and berated the committee. When he finished, committee members explained how defensible disobedience works. "Look here," said one of them,

> when you guys walk off the job, you make it difficult for the rest of us. You want us to defend you, but you don't give us anything to defend you with. You can't just walk off the job. You've got to replace yourself first. And if you don't do that, then give us some grounds to defend you.

The veteran then told the neophyte how to be defensibly disobedient:

> When you're ordered to do something, never say "I won't do it." Walk over to the container and put your hand on it. Then start yelling about how your back hurts, or your arm. Then we can defend you. If you think you've been treated unfairly, call the B.A. and wait until he gets there. But if you walk off the job, the only person who benefits is the employer.

The advice was not unusual. When a similar complaint appeared months later, committee members used nearly the same language to advise the accused longshoreman. The man had been lashing on a container ship. The work was hard and as the shift ended, his assignment was completed. Thus, when the walking boss told him to work on another part of the ship he felt aggrieved. Besides which, he said, there were other longshoremen available and they had not worked as hard as he had. He thought he was being asked to do their work and so he refused. Even though the committee was sympathetic, it could not defend his behavior. Thus, he was told what to do the next time. "It's like if someone tells you to move a boxcar," pointed out one committee member;

> there's no way a man can move a boxcar. But rather than get fired for refusing to work as directed, he should put his hand on the boxcar and act like he is trying. Next time something like this happens, take your time.

11 RD 6.

Walk very slow. Don't really do the work but act like you are trying to. The walker will get the message. And you won't be asked to do that again. (Field notes)

"Don't just walk off the job," said the committee chair. "Next time wait for the B.A. before you leave. Don't take a hike. We can't defend you if you do that" (field notes).

Contractually speaking, the question of waterfront control has been settled. The employers control the job because the contract says longshoremen must obey their orders. The accusations leveled by each side against the other in the grievance machinery, however, indicate that the issue is hardly resolved. Longshoremen do not routinely obey orders. They clearly know when to be obedient and when not to be. Obedience, then, is a quality over which the two sides wrestle. It cannot be assumed.

The variable nature of obedience has become a weapon in the contest for workplace control. Disobedience is defensible if longshoremen know when to obey orders and when *not* to; or how to follow orders and how *not* to. Knowing how to be successfully disobedient enables longshoremen to exercise control over their work. It empowers them to work in ways they decide and not be fired when they refuse an employer's directive.

This knowledge is power. It enables union officials to make management accept the union's ideas even though, according to the contract, employers need not listen. But for this to happen, longshoremen must be taught some operational facts of life: They need to learn how to use the contract as a weapon for self-defense. When longshoremen know the contractual grounds that protect disobedience and learn how to use them, the struggle for workers' control can be waged even though the collectively bargained agreement prohibits it.

Defensible disobedience means more than defending malingerers. It is not simply about devising clever justifications for bum beefs. Rather, it is learning how to dispute the employers' authority. The ILWU has a long history of teaching its members to be defensibly disobedient. At least as early as 1936, the union established that longshoremen had the contractual right to ask an employer by what right one thing or another had been ordered; and if the employer could not cite a contractual provision, longshoremen had a union obligation to refuse that order.[12] In today's context, defensible disobedience means learning how to present alternative, and sometimes competing versions of the same reality. And just as in the past, learning to be defensibly disobedient today is learning how to assert one's personhood, how to be heard instead of being silent, how to be contentious rather than subservient or dominated. It means learning how to insist on being taken into account, how to insert one's self in the work process even though the contract says otherwise, and how to do that and be protected by the union. In short, learning how to be defensibly disobedient today means what it has always meant in the ILWU: It means learning how to fight with management for control of the waterfront.

Defensible disobedience is not practiced only by the union. As numerous examples in this book suggest, the employers have also devised ways to disobey the rules. A common thread therefore runs through the disagreements dividing the ILWU and the PMA: They are disputes over rules for obedience. This dispute erupts because, even with an agreed-upon set of rules, the two sides have different and sometimes conflicting agendas. The contract, however, prevents them from acting unilaterally on their respective agendas. Thus, each side develops methods for disobeying contractual rules in defensible ways. Put differently, the collectively bargained agreement has forced these two antagonists to be *defensibly* disobedient in their struggle for control of the workplace.[13]

Over the years, the ILWU and the PMA have developed practices that enable them to be defensibly disobedient. Methods have emerged for handling deep differences within contractual parameters. The union has learned how to distinguish good beefs from bum grievances, and how to create good beefs; how to take advantage of the contract without violating it; and how to make the system work by constructing the appearance of cooperation when actually contesting management's right to rule the workplace. Through these practices, it is possible for the two sides to

12 For a more elaborate account of this history, see Mills and Wellman (1987).

13 Modern theoreticians of industrial relations in Germany have recognized a similar relationship between management and labor. They use the concept *Konfliktpartnerschaft*, sometimes translated as "adversarial collaboration," to talk about partnerships based on acceptance of the fact that the two sides have different interests. See MacShane (1993).

uphold the contract, *and* be insubordinate, to pursue serious disagreements, *and* productivity. Ships can be loaded and unloaded while at the same time, in the grievance machinery, workplace control is being contested.

CONCLUSION: TRADE UNION EXCEPTIONALISM OR PREFIGURATIVE POLITICS?

ACCORDING to conventional wisdom, the war between the classes ended decades ago in North America. Capital won, easily and decisively. By most accounts, labor was defeated not only politically, but lost culturally and morally as well. "The myth of the liberating power of the proletariat has dissolved," wrote the formerly socialist Italian novelist Ignazio Silone in the early 1950s, "along with that other myth of progress" (1954:25). Agreeing, the American political sociologist S. M. Lipset observed less than a decade later that intellectuals of the democratic left who once thought the proletariat was necessarily a force for liberty, racial equality, and social progress, faced a "tragic dilemma" (1963:87). They could no longer pin their hopes for a more just and equitable world on the Western working class; alternative visions for the good society would need another agent.

Critical theorists of the Frankfurt school and postmodern scholars concur. As Craig Reinarman notes, they find little hope for opposition in what they see as the debased, commodified culture of the modern world. Most believe that mass consumption culture and the welfare state so dominate social life that critique and resistance is impossible among the manipulated, managed working classes. The "singular achievement" of advanced industrial society, wrote philosopher Herbert Marcuse, is the "containment of social change" (1966:xii). Post-Marxist, poststructuralist theorists share this pessimism. Although some find genuine resistance in "new social movements," the working class is dismissed as an agency for social change. Increasingly, those who view society from the academy see modernist, enlightenment visions of a better world as outdated; the collective dreams of social progress and personal freedom have been eclipsed or co-opted by advanced capitalist culture.

The world looks quite different when one spends more than three years doing fieldwork that carefully explores the everyday working lives of San Francisco longshoremen on the docks and in the union hall. Critical and postmodern theory seem more one-dimensional than insightful after spending another two years analyzing documents produced by union, management, and industry activities. The idea that late industrial capitalism has triumphed over labor seems premature and one-sided. At least in one major American industry, collaboration *and* conflict, cooperation *and* critique, production *and* resistance cohabitate. And in certain crucial respects, radical American industrial unionism has survived.

OLD TRUTHS RECONSIDERED

The persistence of radical unionism in the ILWU raises serious questions about the conventional wisdom contained in social science accounts of American labor. It is therefore time to take another look at the old truths with which this book began, and to reexamine the hypotheses that have been elevated to assumptions about radicalism, class, and the possibilities for social transformation. After looking at the ILWU close up, what can be said of the following assumptions?

• Class conflict is diminished or terminated when labor establishes a binding contractual relationship with capital.

• Left to its own devices, American labor is essentially conservative. Its natural consciousness is merely job consciousness; its natural state of organization is pure and simple unionism. Labor has no critique of capitalism. The radicalism that erupted in the 1930s and 1960s was an aberration introduced from outside; radicalism is not an authentic, indigenous expression of American working-class culture.

• Class is no longer a salient category in American culture; class consciousness is a relic, a leftover from old-left ideologies. It is found in historical archives, not actual working-class lives.

• The struggle over workplace control is driven by artisan or craft skill. The two are correlated. Automation therefore reduces labor's ability to resist capital on the shopfloor. The loss of skill produced by modern technology decreases cognitive activity on the job thereby freeing management from its dependence on labor. Stripped of its essential source of power, labor is unable to contest management's legal authority at work. Thus, the struggle over workplace governance has been subverted by technological innovation and scientific management.

• Unions that continued to be militant after the initial burst of early CIO idealism are deviations from the rule.

The end of history?

When one focuses on the actual activities of working Americans, and not just on what they say, when one looks at their practice, and not only at their ideology, conventional wisdom does not seem very wise. Another world emerges before one's eyes. It is a world in which the war between classes has not been settled; history has not ended. That war may be waged on unfamiliar terrain, and the weapons used may be unexpected or unconventional; but the war is hardly over. On the waterfront, for example, class relations continue to be a spectacle of incompatibility. The two sides have been fighting for a long time, and despite fifty years of contractual cooperation they still essentially resent, dislike, and distrust each other. Although not as polemical and ideological as it was in the old days, the struggle for workplace control has not been eliminated by the contractual bargain. The disagreements that emerge in the grievance machinery indicate that the question of who will govern the shopfloor has not been settled. Indeed, the two sides continue to fight over principles for management as well as principles for establishing fairness and merit. They also continue to fight about whose rules will be obeyed.

The San Francisco longshoremen's unionism is neither pure nor simple, and their differences with employers extend considerably beyond money. The union has not exchanged its pursuit of workplace governance for wages. Rather, it continues to fight with employers for management of the longshore enterprise. The conflict between labor and capital has not been settled by contractual agreement.

Subversive principles and mere trade union consciousness

Another traditional truth therefore needs to be discarded. Contrary to critical and postmodern theories, labor's opposition to capital persists in the midst of a commodified culture. Critique and resistance is practiced by the American working class in the very institutional-legal framework presumed to preclude it. The ILWU, for example, challenges capitalist practices that its members find unfair. Waterfront capitalists are not permitted to use either their capital or their labor unilaterally. They are forced to consult with longshoremen, to recognize their working knowledge, and to honor their codes and ethics. And if this doesn't happen, work either stops or seriously slows down.

The basic terms of conflict on the waterfront still approximate a struggle over rival systems for organizing production. The system promoted and defended by the ILWU challenges traditional ways of organizing work in capitalist society. On the Pacific Coast waterfront, work is organized by a number of principles that can be interpreted (and sometimes are by PMA officials) as being subversive of capitalist values. Principles like equality are affirmed in the dispatch system and the pay scale. The principle of democracy is protected politically in the local's handling of its internal affairs *and* on the docks. This principle is enhanced by the union's anti-hierarchical culture of insubordination and its insistence on participating in promotion decisions. Principles like empowerment and self-actualization are also found on West Coast docks. These principles are embedded in the rotary dispatch, the reciprocation of personhood that occurs between longshoremen and their supervisors, and in the subsequent power longshoremen wield at work. Solidarity is yet another principle that is still found on the San Francisco waterfront. It is practiced in the longshoremen's political culture; their ethical codes give voice to it.

These principles for organizing work suggest that the ILWU has fashioned ways for living at the point of production that challenge management's rule over the workplace. The union promotes principles that empower workers and enable them to exert considerable control over their working lives. These principles also sustain and extend some of the ideals contained in early American industrial unionism. The ideal of racial unity still lives in Local 10. This union continues to care about and tries to eliminate racial hierarchy from the labor force. Internally, it practices a version of multiculturalism. The ideals of equality and solidarity that are routinely practiced by longshoremen at work and in the union hall, and that are codified in their working ethics, also uphold an earlier principle of industrial unionism. This principle continues to challenge the ethos of competitive capitalism that ostensibly permeates the rest of American society. Longshore culture counsels Local 10 members to do the *right* thing, not the expedient thing. "Working union" means thinking in terms of group, not individual, needs. On the waterfront, then, the selfish principles of self-interest and me-first are not the only principles that prevail. Older, more egalitarian principles also operate. Thus, the ILWU continues to articulate an alternative to the ways in which many U.S. industries currently organize production. Although that alternative is not socialism, it is based upon principles that echo the values enunciated by labor in an earlier period. ILWU principles continue to restrict management's opportunities to direct the work; they undercut the authority of property ownership; and they limit the prerogatives of capital. As a result, the ILWU's ideas for managing the longshore enterprise frequently come into conflict with the employer's notions for how to run a private business.

This struggle over management of the longshore enterprise does not mean the ILWU is a revolutionary organization, or that longshoremen have a socialist consciousness. Nor, however, does it mean that a minority of troublemakers have taken over the union and file an inordinate number of ideologically motivated grievances. Union complaints are pretty evenly distributed throughout the membership. The union leadership, moreover, is not exceptionally ideological; and when most union members vote, they vote for the Democratic Party. By surface criteria, then, the union is conventional, even by contemporary standards. The struggle over rival systems for organizing production cannot, therefore, be attributed to some deviant, outmoded ideology smuggled into the union through the backdoor by a clever and manipulative leadership.

Quite the contrary. This conflict is actually produced by what some people trivialize as "mere" trade union consciousness. As the PMA has discovered, however, basic trade unionism is never trivial; it is not, to paraphrase Rick Fantasia, "a simple, narrow, or 'mere' anything" (1988:237). When it stays close to its basic values, trade unionism stands for some very radical principles: solidarity, equality, and democracy. These principles, as V.L. Allen observes, are quite radical because as the essence of collective

305

action they are the antithesis of capitalist values (Fantasia, 1988:237). Thus, individualism, which is the core of capitalist activity, is confronted by trade union collectivism.

The ILWU is radical, then, not because it permitted communists to join in the 1950s, or because its founding leaders were sympathetic to socialist causes, or because it supported unpopular foreign policy issues. Nor is it radical in conventional terms that equate radical with ultra-left politics. It is radical because it promotes trade union values, because it is based on the principles of solidarity, equality, and democracy. It is radical because, in addition to the collectivist impulses contained in the values of solidarity and equality, the union practices and promotes insubordination and individualism. In this respect, the union practices a critique of, and resistance to, the social order of which it is also an important component. To paraphrase Sean Wilentz, the ILWU is radical because it continues to insist that its members be treated as human beings, with their own dignity, autonomy and property, and not merely as commodities, human labor, and the part-time property of other humans (1984:20).

The salience of class as an activity

Local 10 practices radical trade unionism in another sense of that term. On the waterfront, capitalist hegemony is not taken for granted. The power of shipping companies was never translated into authority. ILWU longshoremen never granted their employers the right to dictate who would work and how work would proceed. These are prerogatives employers must fight for and longshoremen do not concede them without struggle. Class antagonism, in other words, is still expressed on the docks. Class persists, in E. P. Thompson's terms, as an activity. It can be observed in action, in opposition to other classes. This meaning of class, as David Montgomery observes, is found in workers' ethical codes where homegrown ideologies like "do the right thing" are cultivated. Class consciousness in this context is not simply an attitude or an ideology measured by answers to survey questionnaires. Rather, it is found in cultural expressions embodied in the traditions, codes, ethics, and institutions of working-class organizations like Local 10. These manifestations of working-class culture are, in Montgomery's words, "the ethical seedbed for reform" (1987:4).

Paraphrasing Sartre, labor historian Herbert Gutman wrote that he was interested not in what "has been done to [working] men and women but what [these] men and women do with what is done to them" (cited in Nasaw, 1988:132). When one considers what working people *do* with what is done to them, how history is made rather than suffered, culture can be seen as a powerful weapon, a source of power in class struggle. Obviously, as David Nasaw points out, this power is not absolute. Often it is no match for the power of capital, especially when that power is reinforced by the state. Nevertheless, as the Local 10 story indicates, political culture continues to be a source of identity, solidarity, and resistance.

The power of that culture is underlined by the ILWU's continuing ability to contest management's prerogatives on the waterfront. Despite contractual language to the contrary, and in the face of a technological revolution, that culture enables the union to challenge management's right to rule. The battle over workplace governance has been extended to terrain most people thought precluded it.

But does this battle over workplace governance add up to a struggle between classes? Or is it merely a fight over job control? Although the mutualistic dimensions of longshore unionism are certainly impressive, there is also an undeniable preoccupation with *"our work"* and *"our* jurisdiction." Does that mean the ILWU political culture represents *job* consciousness rather than *class* consciousness?

How this question is answered ultimately boils down to what one means by class. If class means a class for itself in the classic Marxist sense of the term, if class means explicitly socialist politics and ideology, then class consciousness is not expressed in longshore culture. If, however, one defines class as "a social force, acting in relationship to other social forces" as Kim Moody does (1988:xvi), and if one defines the working class by its "relationship to, dependence on, and opposition to the capitalist class" (Moody, 1988:xvi), San Francisco longshoremen certainly act like a class in this sense of the term. And if one thinks of class consciousness as "the articulated resistance of wage workers . . . to capitalist wage-labor relations" (Wilentz, 1984:6), then one can say longshoremen are "class-conscious" workers. Their consciousness reflects an active sense of class, not just an occupational awareness and commitment.

Their experience of community teaches San Francisco longshoremen to be moral, not just economic, actors. The principled behavior called for by their ethical codes applies to all workers, not just brothers on the docks. The "us" that this community practices, which is reinforced by the daily fights with employers, is sometimes extended beyond the waterfront to workers in other industries and nations. ILWU solidarity is applied internationally. Thus, Local 10 members boycotted cargo bound for Chile's military dictatorship and South Africa's apartheid regime in the late 1970s. These acts of solidarity were organized around lessons learned on the docks. Longshoremen applied waterfront ethical codes when they debated these decisions to boycott. Their experiences with authoritarian supervisors and racial labor principles were the grounds they used to justify their actions. As a result, consciousness produced on the job was used to support people doing different kinds of work in other countries. By most standards, this consciousness was class consciousness.

Local 10's disagreements with management also extend considerably beyond job issues to questions of personhood, citizenship, and authority. The process of defensible disobedience teaches longshoremen how to argue with their employers, how to act when they think they are right and have been wronged. They are taught to not accept an order simply because it is issued by powerful people. They learn to ask of the powerful, by what right is an order issued? And they also learn to refuse an order when that question is ignored. Thus, apparently minor disputes over how to do a job are the surface manifestations of a much deeper disagreement. The disagreement is, which side will govern the workplace? Which class will rule the waterfront? Challenging management's right to rule the workplace is not a jurisdictional dispute based on occupational self-interest. It is an implicit critique of capitalist authority. It is more profound than job consciousness because the issue is not simply one's right to a job. Rather, it is capital's right to rule.[1]

---

1 In this regard, class relations on the waterfront approximate T. H. Marshall's notion of class conflict, which occurs, he writes, "when a common interest unites adjacent social levels in opposition to more distant social levels" (1965:184).

Artisan skill + cognitive labor = job control

Capital's right to rule, however, was supposed to be assured when the waterfront was modernized and automated. Labor was not supposed to be able to contest management's control of the docks. The current state of class relations on San Francisco's waterfront therefore raises questions about the putative correlation between skill and the battle for workplace control. The reigning conception of skill needs to be reconsidered.

Skill is usually equated with artisan or craft work. Skilled workers in the late nineteenth century are the standard bearers for this construction. Their "principal asset or possession," in the words of Frederick Winslow Taylor, the quality that gave them "skill," was their "mass of rule-of-thumb or traditional knowledge," which made their initiative indispensable to the operation of the enterprise. The "manager's brains," to quote Bill Haywood and Frank Bohn, were "under the workman's cap" (Montgomery, 1987:45). Because their initiative was indispensable, because they possessed a carefully guarded, exclusive body of traditional knowledge, these skilled workers could dictate the work pace and therefore control the job.

These, then, are the standards against which future American workers would be judged. Skill would mean traditional knowledge of artisan or craft work, and control would refer to workers' ability to use initiative, autonomy, and craft knowledge to determine work pace. When these two standards are the baseline, history moves in only one direction. "From this starting point," writes Paul Adler, "everything seems to have gone downhill, and examples of 'loss of control,' understood as loss in individual autonomy, are easy to find" (1986a:82). "There is a long-run tendency," writes Zimbalist summarizing Braverman, "through fragmentation, rationalization, and mechanization for workers and their jobs to become deskilled, both in an absolute sense . . . and in a relative one. . . . Even where the individual worker retains certain traditional skills, the degraded job he or she performs does not demand the exercise of these abilities" (1979:xv). The theory is that skill – in the traditional sense of the term – makes job control possible. Thus, if labor's artisan or craft skills could be reduced, management's control of the work could be enhanced and the contest for shopfloor control could be settled in capital's favor. Dead labor would triumph over living labor, Braverman argued, as workers' skills

309

were absorbed by technology. Capital would be substituted for labor and, with fewer opportunities for skill development, the workforce would be increasingly less able to seriously oppose management's rule.

Local 10's experience with modern technology suggests that history does not move in only one direction. Opportunities for skill development, although certainly more limited than before, have not disappeared from San Francisco's docks and neither have the chances for exercising control over the work process. Cognitive labor, moreover, is still an essential part of waterfront work. Workers' skills, then, have not been absorbed by the technology.

This is not unique to West Coast longshoremen. Observing other industries, Paul Adler, for example, concludes that, "As technology develops . . . machine systems grow to encompass broader and broader spans of previously discrete operation. Workers lose their individual autonomy – but not necessarily to the benefit of capitalists. As a general rule, workers lose their individual control to a broader 'collective worker,' encompassing manual workers, technicians, and engineers" (1986a:83). Zuboff confirms these observations. She finds that modern technology does not produce the consequences Braverman predicted. "The new technology," she writes,

> signals the transposition of work activities to the abstract domain of information. Toil no longer implies physical depletion. "Work" becomes the manipulation of symbols, and when this occurs, the nature of skill is redefined. The application of technology that preserves the body may no longer imply the destruction of knowledge; instead, it may imply the reconstruction of knowledge of a different sort. (1988:23)

Two observations follow from these findings. Skill is not limited to traditional craft labor; and the contest for shopfloor control need not end when craft skills are transformed. The relationship between skill and job control is therefore more complicated than conventional wisdom assumes.

New technologies redefine skill; they do not eliminate it. Thus, workers operating advanced technologies can, like their craft counterparts in another era, generate and sustain ethical codes defining acceptable behavior at work. The classic, early industrial skilled worker was able to control the labor process not just because his traditional knowledge and initiative were indispensable, but also because a "mutualistic" work culture and a "demanding ethical code" governed individual behavior on the job (Montgomery, 1987:204). The workers' code celebrated "individual self-assertion" for the "collective good"; "manly bearing" was a moral imperative. "Objectionable orders from bosses" were to be refused, even if it meant quitting the job. "The individual who earned praise from his fellow machinists," writes Montgomery summarizing the code,

> was "conservative" (i.e., not prone to thoughtless actions), highly competent at his trade, scrupulously observant of the craftsmen's ethical code, and fully prepared, if need be, to sacrifice his personal interests to the common good. (1987:205)

Principles like "do the right thing," "watch the game," and "working union," which are currently seen and heard on the San Francisco waterfront, indicate that mutualistic work cultures and demanding ethical codes are not relics from past periods of labor militancy. At least in some places, they are contemporary practices and therefore resources in contests for control of the workplace.

The relationship between skill and job control is complicated in a second way. Because the new technology redefines skill and knowledge rather than destroying them, it does not eliminate cognitive work. Mental labor is clearly still a necessary ingredient in longshoring. If cognitive work persists on the modern waterfront, this means that advanced technologies do not free management from its dependence on workers' knowledge. The modern workplace does not strip labor of this essential source of power. Thus the contest over workplace regime has not been eliminated by technological innovation.

So long as work requires thought, workers cannot be treated like machines. Unlike machine or animal power, human power is generated by cognitive energy. In addition to being paid for their physical labor, workers are paid to think about their work and to act on their best judgments for how to do the job. So long as people are paid in part to think about what they do, it is quite likely that differences will arise in the work process. And because human workers, unlike machines, can verbalize these differences, it is also likely that, given the opportunity, they will "talk back" to their supervisors. Thus, so long as cognitive labor is necessary to the work process, the issue of governance will be raised. The contest over who rules will not end so long as it is possible to disagree over how to work, who decides how to work, and on what basis – despite what Taylorism, Divine Right, Social Darwinism, or de-skilling theory have to say about the matter. And when unions are organized to give expression to these issues, as the ILWU is, conflicts over governance will occur routinely, just as they do on the San Francisco waterfront.

Conventional wisdom becomes problematic when one focuses on the actual practices of working-class Americans in one contemporary union. The accounts of labor's demise seem premature. Despite technological revolution and contractual collaboration, the war between classes continues; some of the values labor articulated in the 1930s have been neither co-opted nor defeated by capital.

Is radical unionism unique or unrecognized?

Conventional wisdom, some will argue, is not rendered problematic by the ILWU experience. One cannot generalize from this case study, it could be said, because the union is much too unique.

Clearly, along certain dimensions, the ILWU is unarguably a unique union. Very few American unions regularly elected international officers who were accused of being communists. Most unions purged communists during the McCarthy era, and they did not allow them to join. Only a handful of American unions have a history of opposing U.S. foreign policy, and not many of them used muscle generated on the job to express their oppositional politics. The ILWU has a long history of expressing its politics on the job, combining pork chops with politics. And rarely have American unions supported third-party presidential candidates, which the ILWU did in 1948 when it endorsed Henry A. Wallace. There is no doubt that in these respects the ILWU is an exceptional American union.

But these features of the union's history have little bearing on the matter of whether the ILWU is too unique to undermine conventional wisdom. It does not matter that the ILWU is unique in these respects because they are not considered "causes" of the class-struggle unionism practiced on the waterfront. Longshoremen do not challenge their employers' right to rule the workplace, and they do not fight with supervisors over control of the job because their union refused to purge communists, opposed American foreign policy, and supported Henry Wallace. Thus, for the purposes of this analysis, it does not matter that the ILWU was unique in these ways because these events are not considered to be directly responsible for the kind of unionism longshoremen practice.

There are, however, other aspects of the ILWU experience that *are* responsible for the class-struggle unionism one finds on West Coast docks: the union's decentralized structure and its participatory democratic culture; its commitment to the principle of racial equality; the working principles and codes of conduct that determine how longshoremen will work; the aggressive use of grievance machinery and the practice of defensible disobedience. These union features may, *or may not,* be unique to the ILWU. But that cannot be assumed in advance. That is an empirical question and it can be settled only by comparative research.

Future researchers might discover that the ILWU is not unique; that the principles, practices, and codes that facilitate militant unionism on the waterfront are practiced in other industries and used by other unions. It might well be that class-struggle unionism is more widely practiced than is assumed but goes undetected for conceptual reasons: Because radicalism has been constructed as ideologically left-wing politics, class consciousness has been thought of as socialist consciousness that is revealed in survey questionnaires, and the operating rules of class relations have been located in contracts rather than activities on the shopfloors. It could quite possibly be that the ILWU is a lot less exceptional when one looks for elements of class struggle in the disagreements that erupt between labor and capital as they routinely negotiate the work process, and when one looks for these contests in actual practices rather than exclusively in written documents.

It could also be that the ILWU *is* unique, that it is the exception that proves the rule. But that can no longer be assumed. One does not know if it is or is not unique because trade unions have not been studied in the manner this book examines the ILWU. Thus, to determine whether the ILWU is unique, one must clarify the meaning of uniqueness from the outset. Will uniqueness refer to the ideological politics articulated and practiced by union members and leaders? Will it be a measure of how closely their consciousness approximates socialist consciousness? Or will it refer to actual practices and principles articulated on the shopfloor and in the grievance machinery?

No matter how these questions are answered, the study of American unions needs to be reopened, reconceptualized, and reframed. Scholars need to take a new hard look at American labor and discover what actually goes on. Only then will it be possible to formulate theories that can explain what happened to the something special that erupted in the 1930s.

YESTERDAY'S ALTERNATIVES OR TOMORROW'S FACTS?

"Social theory," wrote Herbert Marcuse, "is concerned with the historical alternatives which haunt the established society as subversive tendencies and forces. The values attached to the alternatives do become facts when they are translated into reality by historical practice" (1966:xii). By contemporary standards, the unionism Local 10 practices is certainly one of those historical alternatives that has haunted established society. And if historical practice is the benchmark, this union's values have clearly become facts; they have been translated into reality on the waterfront. Although one cannot dispute the reality of this union's historical practice, it is possible to be skeptical about its future. What kind of potential does it have? Does the unionism practiced by the ILWU represent a viable direction for American unionism?

This question is literally a life or death matter for some unions and industries in the United States. If unions are unable to find ways to involve their members organizationally, to pursue the question of citizenship on the job and in their union halls as the ILWU does, they will die. If industries using modern technologies cannot devise strategies that encourage workers' cognitive energies and their active participation in the work process, then these industries will not compete with foreign firms.

Thus, the question raised by an earlier generation of labor historians and sociologists needs to be reformulated. Instead of asking, "what might have been?" the question must become, "what might be done?" How is the modern workplace to be organized? What role will working people play on the technologically advanced shopfloor? What say will workers have in the decisions that affect their everyday lives?

Ironically, the seeds for that program may have been planted more than fifty years ago by the CIO. When union officials, rank and filers, and sociologists of labor talk about "new" ways to organize the modern workplace, they sound remarkably like "old" CIO activists. "Walter Reuther forever talked about the need for workers to have a voice in the decisions that affect them," said Don Ephlin, Director of the UAW's GM Department, recently. And citing concepts like "jointness," "quality circles," and "teams," he continued, "today, to a degree, we have" (Massing, 1988:23). Machinists striking against Boeing Aircraft in 1989 rejected a settlement that substantially increased wages but gave them no say in working overtime. "Why not give us a choice?" asked one striker (Egan, 1989:A9). And, outlining the "radical organizational changes" required for new information technologies to reach their potential, Shoshana Zuboff (1988) writes: "The centerpiece of such a strategy must be a redefinition of the system of authority" (p. 394) currently dominating most contemporary corporations. She calls for "increased equality," and "broad access to information" (1988:394).

Notions like participation, choice, and equality may be new to some unions and industries. They were, however, basic items on the early CIO agenda for workplace and union citizenship. And they never stopped being items on Local 10's agenda. "New" proposals for workplace organization like "quality circles," "teams," and "broad access to information" are therefore old practices in the ILWU. They were established on the San Francisco waterfront in the 1930s by militant direct action and they have been jealously guarded ever since. They survive today in the form of "membership meetings," "gangs," "grievance committees," and "Labor Relations Committees."

But what about the ILWU's adversarial relationship with management, its class-struggle method for handling differences? Has this style become obsolete, as proponents of managerialism like Charles Hecksher (1988) argue?[2] Must unions operating in a post-Taylorist world shift from adversarial to cooperative workplace relations to be effective?

The ILWU experience suggests that adversarial unionism need not un-

---

2 See also Kochan, Katz, and McKersie (1986); Kochan, Katz, and Mower (1984); Piore and Sabel (1984).

dermine productivity and growth. In fact, the watchwords of the "new industrial relations" – "involvement," "commitment," "flexibility" – are quite compatible with ILWU codes for how to work. "Doing the right thing" does not mean being inflexible, uncommitted, or uninvolved in the work process. This suggests that the union's adversarial pursuit of industrial justice is not, as the ideology of cooperation assumes, incompatible with employers' needs for flexibility. On West Coast docks, when both sides make it work, these apparently conflicting goals are brought together: In return for justice, longshoremen work flexibly and conscientiously, and take the employers' interests seriously. Thus, to paraphrase David Brody (1992), it may not be necessary to retreat from adversarialism in order to be responsive to post-Taylorist systems of production.

The ILWU's practice of adversarial unionism also confirms what many unionists have suspected: The mere fact of cooperation, in and of itself, accomplishes very little. Indeed, two researchers have recently discovered that the majority of "Employee Involvement" plans achieve very little, and many actually *reduce* productivity (Kelly and Harrison, cited by Metzgar, 1991). "What is essential," writes Jack Metzgar, "is the *participation* of workers in management decisions from which they have been traditionally excluded" (1991:68). The "'contentiousness' and give-and-take" of relations in unionized settings, conclude Kelly and Harrison, may "actually be an advantage" for achieving production and efficiency (quoted by Metzgar, 1991).[3] Thus, ironic though it may seem, rather than being outmoded, the ILWU's aggressive adversarialist style may well have much to recommend it in the post-industrial world.

What is exceptional about American exceptionalism?

If labor's new program in the twenty-first century turns out to be some version of the old adversarial CIO agenda, the major lesson of the ILWU's experience on West Coast docks might not be that it is an "exceptional" union. When old assumptions are dropped and actual practices are observed, when researchers do not assume class conflict ends if contracts are signed, or that skill is absorbed by modern technology freeing employers

3 Rothstein (1993) provides additional empirical evidence that confirms this conclusion.

from their reliance on workers' knowledge, it may turn out that although the ILWU is not unique, organized labor in North America *is* exceptional, but in ways that are yet to be explored. Instead of being exceptional in the sense that it did not follow the European political path of creating political parties to relocate labor's agenda on the parliamentary floor, American labor's exceptionalism may be that, unlike European labor, it has been free of historical habits of deference and has learned how to fight politically on the shopfloor, and that, compared to European labor, it has been relatively successful in that arena.[4] Thus, the American labor movement may have something to teach its European counterparts. If that turns out to be the case, the ILWU might not be a nostalgic remnant from labor's radical past.

It might be prefigurative.

4 I am indebted to Boy Lüthje for this insight.

317

Longshoreman, Pier 27, San Francisco. Copyright © by Pat Goudvis 1980.

APPENDIX

DOING FIELD RESEARCH: AN ETHNOGRAPHIC ACCOUNT

CONSTITUTING ETHNOGRAPHIC AUTHORITY:
THE WORK PROCESS OF FIELD RESEARCH

I F social scientists were ever granted methodological authority automatically, that is no longer possible. As numerous critics observe (see Clifford, 1988), ethnographic writers cannot ignore the political and epistemological assumptions contained in their research and writing. Ethnographic authority must be established: It can no longer be assumed. It can be established, moreover, with a variety of strategies; there is not one right way to do so.

My method for constituting authority is to describe the work process of my field research, to detail the process through which the account contained in this book was constructed, and to recognize my "indigenous collaborators."[1] Thus, this is not a traditional methodological appendix. Instead of establishing a putative claim for "objectivity" or "reliability," the focus is on the actual makings of an ethnographic research project.

Ethnographic authority, Vincent Crapanzano points out, is often constituted through the claim that the researcher was either invisible or disinterested. The idea is that invisibility insures that what "really" happens is not disturbed or altered by the ethnographer's presence. Ethnographic authority for this book, however, will be constructed along very different lines. If it is successfully constituted, authority will be accomplished first by *acknowledging* both my visibility and self-interest, and then by describing how I managed both, or managed to use both to achieve my ends.

Following this strategy, I hope to avoid the troubles Mary Louise Pratt

---

1 This is the method I used in an earlier work. See Wellman (1993, chap. 3).

correctly associates with the "personal narratives" many ethnographers use to give authority to their experience of fieldwork. These ethnographers' self-portraits, she writes, mystify the experience, "notably the sheer inexplicability of the ethnographer's presence from the standpoint of the other" (1988:42). She also detects "great silences" in these narratives, which she attributes to the power differential between the researcher and the researched, and the ethnographer's "material relationship to the group under study" (1988:42).

I think the mystifications and silences Pratt observes are produced in large part by the framework within which most claims to ethnographic authority are constructed. Authority is established according to grandly theoretical, epistemological, and political standards.[2] As a result, the relationship between field research theorist and field research worker comes perilously close to the theorized relationship between conventional anthropologist and "other." The theorist theorizes about the process of field research without consulting the field-worker's account or understanding of what he or she is doing. Thus, like the other, the field researcher is often evaluated according to criteria that are disassociated from the researcher's own understanding of what he or she is doing.

Field research, however, is not only a version of political practice. It is also work, in the old-fashioned sense of the word. The research site is a work site, with many of the same demands, constraints, negotiated agreements, anxieties, and exhilarating moments. Decisions are routinely based on practical work process considerations, and, if truth be told, the elegant abstractions and political principles that create the silences and produce the mystifications are usually constructed *after* the field work is completed and the field-worker has returned to the university to theorize field research.

I choose to take a different path. Instead of constructing authority through abstract theoretical and political principles, I offer an analysis of the field research work process through which this book was constructed. This account attempts to address the issues that personal narratives have, until recently, either mystified or ignored.

2 Linguistic anthropologists may be an exception. They establish authority by trying to present the details of speech events observed to be recurrent in everyday life. I am grateful to Aaron Cicourel for bringing this to my attention.

Appendix

FROM TOURIST TO HONORARY RESIDENT: CONSTRUCTING
A CRAFT RELATIONSHIP BETWEEN DOCK AND FIELD-
WORKER

Studying an American trade union is not like doing research on colonized peoples in the Third World. Union members have a say over who and how outsiders enter their work world. They must agree to the idea of a stranger in their midst, someone coming to do "research." To complicate matters, university and government bureaucrats insist that the researcher and the researched sign documents purported to "protect human subjects."[3] Thus, a relationship must be negotiated, literally as well as sociologically.

My relationship with San Francisco longshoremen began as a visit and soon became a semipermanent settlement. At first, I was treated as a tourist. Eventually, however, I came to be seen as a "fellow worker," one who practiced another "craft," but a craftworker nonetheless and therefore someone who could be trusted. We had established what I later came to recognize as a "craft relationship," a relationship that enabled me to participate in their world in ways a visitor cannot. My ethnographic authority, if successfully established, is therefore located in that relationship. My method for establishing authority, then, is to detail the process of constructing that craft relationship.

Finding an auspice

The first requirement for making a visit to a field is permission. Because most people treat their work space possessively, a visit that is not enforced by coercion must be done under the auspices of someone who is entitled to bring someone new around. One may "pass" or pretend to be a participant rather than an observer, of course, but such a maneuver risks incurring the wrath later on of people who feel intruded upon or deceived. Thus, before the study actually began, contact was made with Herb Mills, a longtime friend and longshoreman, a former officer of Local 10, and a political science Ph.D. with a background in naturalistic research. Mills became my initial guide through the longshore territory. He arranged

3 For a critique of this policy and an assessment of its negative implications for field research, see Duster, Matza, and Wellman (1979).

interviews, helped make contacts with other guides, and acted as an advisor in a variety of other ways. As the study progressed, other guides quickly became important since too great a reliance on Mills's sponsorship could have been hazardous to the integrity of the study.

During the initial stages of fieldwork, the correspondence between field observation and being a visitor is close. The friendlier longshoremen tried to show me what they thought I wanted to see and made guesses at what was important, taking their cues from the summary presentation of my research aims. Since the summary presentation I developed was itself shaped by, and shaped, the interaction between researcher and field setting, it is worth recounting. Longshoremen were told that I wanted to study the grievance process. When I originally began to formulate the research with David Matza, our interest was more general. We were concerned with the directions taken by the American working class after the Second World War, the allegedly greater conservatism of the working class compared to the prewar period, the possibility of a revival of militancy because of the long stagflation in the 1970s, and a description and location of the form taken by working-class consciousness in modern postindustrial society.[4] The decision to ground these questions in a case study of one union and to focus on the grievance process was shaped by numerous interactions with colleagues and persons who studied and participated in labor unions. They told us that the focus on the grievance process would allow a further exploration of the thoughts, dissatisfactions, and yearnings of workers. We became convinced that the grievance process was an anchor for the more general and amorphous concept of working-class consciousness. The struggle between organized capital and organized labor, it could be said, was located in the grievance process. Another advantage was contained in this summary presentation: A lot of confusion and kidding could be avoided by not mentioning our interest in the larger meaning of working-class consciousness.

The stated reason for studying the union resonated with longshoremen. Many of them were angry about the grievance system; in fact, they were critical of it. My presence was interpreted as giving legitimacy to, if not endorsing, their point of view, and I was actually welcomed aboard.

4 See Matza and Wellman (1980).

Appendix

"I'm very glad you're doing this," a dock steward told me after learning of my reasons for being at the meeting. "The goddamn grievance machinery sure as hell needs looking into. I would do it myself, if I had the time and know-how."

One of my first discoveries, then, was that many longshoremen *wanted* me to be there. I was expecting resistance and reluctance, and was prepared to plead and justify. Instead, I found openness and encouragement.

Being introduced

There was, nevertheless, still good reason to anticipate at least suspicion or mistrust, and perhaps even hostility. In every field research site those being studied want to figure out the researcher. For longshoremen, being told that, "he's from the University of California," was not an altogether comforting or even neutral introduction. In addition to the usual pictures people have of university professors, ILWU members have some long-standing and traditional fears dating back to several unfortunate incidents in which University of California students and professors did not appear to be friends of the longshoremen. During the general strike of 1934, U.C. football players worked as scabs. And General Barrows, who led the National Guard attack that killed two strikers, later chaired the department of political science and had the building that houses the sociology department named after himself. When the union came under attack in the 1940s and 1950s, very few from the university came to the defense of the civil liberties of the union's leaders. And still later, in a years-long law suit that accused the union of unfairly deregistering members, several fairly prominent U.C. faculty members were identified with the plaintiffs. For these reasons, and others, the people in Local 10 might be ambivalent about having a researcher from the University of California in their midst. It could not be taken for granted that someone from U.C. was to be trusted.

Because my sponsors could not assume longshoremen would accept me, they used a number of different methods to assure that this would happen. One method was to phase my entry into a variety of settings. This made it possible for successive and multiple sponsorships and endorsements to be created. I was initially taken to observe three kinds of meetings to study the grievance process. The first was the Stewards' Council. There business agents meet with dock and gang stewards to discuss the kinds of grievances the union wants to pursue on the job. The stewards also report on working conditions at these meetings. In this way the Local can locate issues and grievances that are meaningful within the work situation. Meeting the stewards was important because they are not only the eyes and ears of the business agents, but of their fellow longshoremen as well. As a result of my presence at the meeting, the news that the Local was being studied was disseminated. Within a couple of months, it was suggested that I attend a second sort of meeting: the Local's Grievance Committee, which meets weekly. Officially composed of fifteen members, about half of whom are usually present at a given meeting, the committee hears complaints filed against longshoremen by employers. The longshoreman who is being complained against attends this meeting also. After deciding what stance the union should take on the facts of the matter, the committee recommends a course of action to be taken at a third kind of meeting: the Labor Relations Committee, which involves management as well as union officials. Since management controlled whether the actual workplace could be observed, being accepted by them at these meetings was important for gaining access to the docks. The fourth opportunity for observing the grievance process was to follow business agents as they pursued their various functions, one of which was responding to possible grievances in the work situation. This gave me access to the workplace. Traveling with business agents, and being introduced by them, gave me reason to move about the ships and docks, to observe the work process, and talk with longshoremen on the job.

My various guides' introductions created multiple, but not contradictory, personae for me. Each persona suggested that I had legitimate reason to be there: "He's interested in the grievance machinery," some guides would say; or "he's doing a study of labor relations." Sometimes I was introduced simply, "he's from U.C.," or, "Professor Wellman." One business agent constructed me as "on loan to the staff." The personae created by my guides constituted more than introductions. Spoken by elected officials and unofficial leaders, they were also endorsements.

One persona constructed by my guides included a dress code for university researchers. This was revealed at the end of the first day I accompanied a business agent on the waterfront. Because I knew how easy it would be to ruin clothes on machinery, I wore Levi's blue jeans and a work shirt. Acknowledging my logic, the business agent suggested I wear something else. Longshoremen might not appreciate the reasoning behind my appearance, he commented, and they could interpret it as slumming. "We have an idea of how professors dress when they go to work," he told me, "and it ain't like that."

Introductions were constructed on the assumption that it was normal for me to be there, and logical that I should be accepted. Mills minimized the difficulties of sole sponsorship by introducing me to other union members, and then subsequently introducing me to others as the second person's guest. My presence was always presented as an accomplished fact, not a problematic issue. I was introduced to employers at one of the first LRC meetings I attended with the comment: "This is David Wellman. He's been studying the union and we thought he should come to LRCs. The union has no problem with his presence. Do you?" The same formulation was used to introduce me at union meetings. In each instance, the introducer announced his endorsement of me, effectively putting the onus on others to construct grounds for saying "no." In union-management contexts, the barely implicit challenge was: "We have nothing to hide. Do you?" It wasn't too long before my introductions took the form of "Oh, by the way, this is David Wellman," or simply, "Any objection?"

"Is there anybody here who *doesn't* know David Wellman?" one business agent asked at a negotiation session after I'd been in the field a year and a half.

But I was not always accepted by longshoremen without question. "You trouble me," said an older black longshoreman, as I walked into the hall one morning.

"I don't know why I should trouble you," I responded, extending my hand to him.

"Well, you say you're from the university and you're always hanging out here. I'm worried about what you're doing. What I'm afraid of is that you may use some of this stuff against us."

After I reiterated my purposes, and tried to alleviate his concerns, he concluded by saying: "Well, I've checked you out, and the fellows say you're OK. But I still sometimes worry."

The sequence of introductions reflected my guides' sense of what I needed to see and when I needed to see it: "This is David Wellman. He's been looking at [the Stewards Council, or the LRC], and we think he needs to sit in on [the Grievance Committee, or membership meetings, etc.]." As I drove down Third Street late one night with a business agent, another form of introduction emerged. He pointed out bars and eating places frequented by longshoremen. "We'll stop in at each one in the next couple weeks," he told me. "You need to know something about our lifestyle."

When a guide thought I had seen enough of one territory, I would be introduced to another location, or a new perspective on the old territory. Because I had numerous guides, each one with a different sense of what was important, I was introduced to a vast, complicated, and wonderfully textured territory.

The cynical or suspicious might say I was allowed only to see what my sponsors wanted me to see. Instead of being taken around, they might argue, I was really "taken." That is conceivable. But the theory of contrived appearances is contradicted by certain pieces of evidence. Time and again I saw behavior that contradicted the union's official self-image: People goofed off, told racist jokes, used male chauvinist expressions, and engaged in "un-unionlike," antisocial behavior. If appearances had been contrived, it is unlikely that behavior that incriminated the union's official version of itself or contradicted its ideology would be revealed. Besides which, people can only playact for a while, if at all. The longshoremen had work to do that was more important than acting for me.

Becoming an observer: Constructing an identity and a viewpoint

Finding an auspice and being introduced make a visit to the field possible. They do not, however, create a craft relationship. That can occur only if the visitor is transformed into an observer. For me, becoming an observer meant constructing an identity. The need to do so, and the way that identity was constructed, came as something of a surprise. I had assumed I would identify with the union. Neutrality or objectivity was out of the question. As a graduate student, I was persuaded that sociology was not a science – and probably shouldn't try to be one – and thus I questioned the possibility of sociologists being neutral. Even after reading the classic essays by Max Weber, I seriously doubted that sociologists could transcend, much less avoid, their social location as actors in the world. Thus, I was somewhat taken aback when my guides constructed me as being "objective."

This construction became apparent early in my field work during an LRC. When the management contingent called for a caucus, I got up to leave the room with the union's delegation.

"No, wait a minute, Dave," said a business agent, "you stay."

As I continued to walk, he argued with me, saying that I was "an objective, neutral observer, and should stay." I hesitated for a moment, glancing at the PMA spokesperson.

"I agree, Dave," he said. "Sit down and stay."

Later on, when I began to observe committee meetings at the union's international headquarters, the situation was repeated.

"What are we going to do with our visitor?" asked a coastwide PMA official. "Doesn't he get to sit in on both caucuses?"

I came to realize that my identity as an observer was being constructed by the people I was observing, and that, regardless of my own self-conception, they were constructing me as a "neutral observer." I decided that I had better figure out how to fulfill their expectations. However, being a "neutral observer" at an important intersection in class relations, being "actively situated between powerful systems of meaning" as Clifford (1986) puts it, is more easily written about than accomplished. I discovered just how complicated and difficult the process could be one morning when a PMA official invited me to accompany him on the docks to witness an arbitration.

Because I did not expect to be on the docks, I did not bring my yellow hardhat that day. Yellow is the color of hardhats worn by longshoremen; management wear white hardhats. Since the union had given me a hardhat, mine was yellow. When we arrived at the docks, the employer's representative told me, "when you go with management, you have to wear a hardhat," and handed me a white one. If I wore the white hardhat on the docks after being at an LRC, I might be seen by some longshoremen as being with the PMA. If I didn't, I could not go on the docks.

An opportunity for getting off the hook occurred when the PMA official told me he had to speak with a superintendent and asked if I wanted to go with him. I declined the offer, saying that I needed to get a sandwich and would see him later at the ship where the job was being arbitrated. In the meantime, a union official arrived and I began speaking with him. As the time for arbitrating arrived, I put the hardhat under my arm, and stayed close to the union representative. At a certain point during the arbitration, I put the hardhat on the dock and under a box where it would not be seen. I retrieved the hat as the encounter was ending, handed it to the management official, thanked him for the use of it, and said I would not need a ride back since one of the union people lived near my house and would take me home.

Being a neutral observer meant not being partisan in the conflict between management and labor. Thus, I did not express opinions at the meetings of the LRC considering grievances. At the request of both sides, I also attended caucus meetings of each and sat between the two sides rather than on one side or the other during LRC meetings.

Although I acceded to the longshore industry's construction of me as a neutral observer, I did not, however, adopt multiple or pluralist standpoints. The social location from which the knowledge constructed in this book would be derived was the standpoint of labor. I adopted this strategy in order to produce description that was not only factually accurate but deeply appreciative of a particular subjective reality. To recreate the world of workers and their subjectivity required empathy with their position and the various attitudes contained in it.[5] By accepting the viewpoint of labor, the possibility was created for catching on to the insights and understandings of that particular view of the world.

Being accepted

I knew a threshold had been crossed and a test period passed when I walked into the union hall one evening without guide or sponsor and was

---

5 It is not impossible to apply such an approach to multiple perspectives (e.g., Institute for the Study of Social Change, *The Diversity Project*, 1992), but it would certainly require more resources than were available for this particular study.

immediately recognized. Handshakes, smiles, small talk, and encouragement welcomed me.

"How you doing?"

"Hey, aren't you the guy that's studying us?"

And even: "Brother Wellman!"

The transition from tourist to fellow worker moves closer to completion when the observer's *absences* are recognized:

"You missed some fireworks last week," a Grievance Committee member told me quietly when I sat down at a meeting after a week's vacation.

"Where you been, man?" said a holdman in another context, "I haven't seen you in two weeks."

The transition is completed when one is not simply recognized, but recognized as a *worker*. A number of months passed before my construction as a worker emerged. Initially, I was constructed as a student. Many people assumed that being from the University of California and doing field research meant I was writing a dissertation. When I told them, no, I had completed the Ph.D., they expressed surprise. My construction as a worker became explicit in this context. As I chatted with a hatch-tender aboard ship one afternoon, he asked how my dissertation was coming. I explained I was no longer a student, but rather was "doing research" on a university project. He looked at me quizzically and said: "Oh, so you're on your job now."

The craft nature of fieldwork was recognized after I had been on my research job nearly six months. During a conversation over lunch, the Local's president explicitly acknowledged as much. He listened carefully when I explained why field research took so much time, pointing out that field-workers focus on processes rather than outcomes. He nodded in recognition when I said I had a pretty good feel for the "forest," and even some of the "trees," but that it would take more time to figure out patterns and processes.

"You're a scientist," he concluded. "And so you look at things very carefully. I like that. Now, if you were a newspaperman, you'd probably have written a couple articles already. Right?"

The extended period necessary to do field research was in this instance an advantage, not a liability. It was interpreted as a commitment to careful work, which is an important element of craft labor. I had unwittingly passed a test. Some people who call themselves field researchers are reputed by longshoremen to visit the field irregularly, briefly, and usually when it is convenient. Evidently my practice of showing up regularly, at 6:00 a.m. in the hiring hall, or 7:30 p.m. at membership meetings, and on the docks all day, was crucial to the construction of a craft relationship. Apparently, I had demonstrated that I was "serious," and therefore could be taken seriously as a craftworker.

The construction of field researcher as craftworker produced its humorous moments. A short, stocky, grizzled dockworker in his late fifties sat down next to me during an LRC, mistaking me for a longshoreman. What had I been "cited for," he wanted to know. When I explained my business, he gave me a piece of advice:

"Look, listen, and learn. And don't make the same goddamn mistakes we do! This situation is all fucked up."

As the meeting recessed for a caucus, I excused myself to get a cup of coffee. But before I could fill the cup, the old-timer walked into the room with an agitated, impatient look about him:

"Hey! Hurry up!" he called to me. "The meeting's about to start up and you're gonna miss something!"

Once I was recognized as a worker, longshoremen asked about the status of my work. Whenever I was in the union hall, or on the waterfront, I would be peppered with questions like:

"How's the study going?"

"Have you found out anything yet?"

"Are you getting something?"

They also checked on my progress in acquiring the various longshore perspectives.

"Can you now see what I meant last week," asked a steward, "when I told you about giving brothers the benefit of the doubt? Do you now understand what I was talking about?"

I was "tested" on what I was learning. People asked me to explain what I thought I was seeing, and if my account was too limited, or in their view wrong, they would either fill in the details, or correct it. As I began to "pass" these "tests," my relationship with longshoremen deepened. We approached a relationship of equals. One indication of this was their joking critiques of my research job:

"Still listening to all them old sad stories?" commented one holdman.

"If that's how you get smart," a winch driver said after watching me sit through endless meetings over a three-week period, "I'd rather stay stupid!"

As I passed crucial tests and my worker status was recognized, my introductions changed. I was no longer introduced as an outside observer, but rather as someone with an understanding of the community. They acknowledged the knowledge I was accumulating:

"Just think," said a dock steward, "you've got 75 percent of the picture, and you've only been here a year. Some guys have been on the waterfront twenty years, and they still don't have the picture."

"You probably know more about this union," said a member of the Executive Board, "than guys that have been down here thirteen years."

"I'll bet you're finding that a lot of the stereotypes about us ain't true," a deckman told me. "Now you know that all longshoremen aren't just big, dumb, burly guys."

Eventually, my presence ceased to be worthy of comment. I became a normal feature of the setting:

"You've become invisible, Dave," said a union official over lunch. "You're part of the furniture."

In some situations, being invisible created problems for me. Although certain longshoremen constructed me as invisible, I could not. And I sometimes felt my presence was inappropriate. For example, one morning Grievance Committee members suspended the official meeting and began to militantly admonish a young longshoreman for repeatedly being drunk on the job. I felt completely out of place. Without being asked to, I left the meeting.

Acceptance brought protection, not only sponsorship. This became apparent late one night in a bar around the corner from the union hall.

"Hey! How about loaning me some money, brother," said a fairly drunk longshoreman in a tone of voice that could be interpreted as being somewhat intimidating. Before I could generate an appropriate response, a rather powerfully built longshoreman with a reputation for physical toughness intervened. "Knock that shit off, motherfucker!" he yelled at his drunken brother. "He's not loaning you any goddamn money. It's time for you to take your drunken ass home."

Appendix

The transition from tourist to fellow worker had been completed and was recognized in various ways:

"Here's to our friendship, Dave!" toasted a business agent one evening, as we socialized about non-union topics in a bar.

"I want Wellman in the picture with me," announced a holdman at a union meeting while photos were being taken.

"The union should make you an honorary member, you been around so long," said an old-timer who initially had been skeptical about my work.

Acknowledging my honorary status as union member, a longshoreman running for office – who knew I could not vote – handed me his campaign card and said: "You know how to vote when you get in the booth, brother Wellman."

RECORDING AND CONSTRUCTING CULTURE:
THE FIELD RESEARCH JOB

Having located ethnographic authority in the craft relationship established between longshoremen and the field research worker, it is necessary to reconstruct the craft of field research, to describe the actual work process of doing fieldwork. My job as field researcher was twofold. First, where none existed, I had to construct a record. And second, I had to reconstruct or discover a culture. Constructing the record was a threefold process.

Developing an ethnographic ear and eye

To begin with, I had to learn how to see and hear anew, and to represent what I heard and saw. These skills had to be learned. The field-worker needs to develop ways for actively listening and hearing, of being involved in conversations without dominating them, and to be able, later on, to reconstruct accurately what is seen and heard, along with the context in which it occurred.

As an observer, I trained myself to remember details by repeating key words and names, actively committing them to memory. I would try to etch details in my memory, hoping that thoughts of weather, smells, clothing, etc., would trigger memories of the more important elements in a scene.

Although I never tried to pass as a longshoreman, and always identified myself as a researcher, I did not feel comfortable carrying the researcher's proverbial pencil and clipboard as I moved among dockworkers. Instead, I carried small 3" x 5" index cards in my breast pocket. When my mind felt as if it would not absorb one more detail, I excused myself and retreated to my car or the restroom, where I would furiously write notes to myself, making more room in my mind for another batch of details. Not taking notes during the actual observation process enabled me to concentrate on what I was seeing and hearing. It also made me feel less intrusive.

Creating text

An ethnographic ear and eye make it possible to construct a record. In order to establish an actual record, however, another step is required. The memories and notes have to be recorded. And the sooner that is accomplished, the richer and more accurate the record will be.

I therefore disciplined myself to write field notes, religiously, the moment I got home or to my office. With note cards as prompters and reminders, I would type up every relevant memory created by the most recent field visit. The process usually took a couple hours, and produced between eight and ten pages of single-spaced text. If the field visit ended late in the evening, or I was too tired, or my memory was reduced by alcohol consumed in the process of doing fieldwork, I would write the field notes first thing the next day. My efforts to develop an ethnographic ear, along with my discipline in immediately transforming observations into text, make me feel I accurately reproduced what I heard in the field. Thus, I am persuaded that I am warranted in using quotation marks whenever the talk I observed in the field is reproduced in this book.

Reconstructing the written record

In certain longshore contexts, a written record is produced by the groups in the encounter. The LRCs and arbitrations, for example, operate with a text that contains official complaints and responses. These written accounts are distributed before the meetings convene, and after I had been accepted by both sides, I was provided with copies of the documents. Therefore I did not have to construct an official record of these meetings.

The written records produced by LRCs did not, however, mean that I was relieved of my job to construct a more complete record for these meetings. Around the bare text of official complaint and response developed a discourse that was expressed at the negotiating table and in private caucuses. The commentary and exchanges produced by these official texts contained candid expressions, uncensored expectations, and insights into class relations. One rarely has the opportunity to hear, in interviews at which official positions are reiterated, a full record of what transpired during these sessions. Thus, my job in LRC meetings and arbitrations was to construct the record that emerged *around* the official text.

The official texts distributed before each meeting enhanced the quality of the work I could do. In addition to providing actual texts, and therefore official records, LRC agendas and minutes gave me an excuse to take notes. Because many people took notes during these meetings, I could write in the margins of agendas without feeling conspicuous. I therefore feel especially confident in using quotation marks around the dialogue recorded during LRCs, arbitrations, and negotiations.

Two additional kinds of materials contributed to the record I constructed. The first was "logs" that business agents wrote and shared with me. A version of journals or diaries, the logs contained written accounts of grievances filed, issues discussed, and meetings convened each day. They enabled me to compare my observations of business agents with the union official's self-reports. The logs also gave me access to events I was not able to witness directly.

I also did approximately thirty in-depth interviews with Local 10 members. These recorded conversations with "indigenous collaborators" contained insights into subtexts and scenarios played out beneath the surface of this culture. The transcribed interviews are an important component of the record created by my field research and the materials produced by them are also identified by quotation marks.

Constructing culture: Managing the predicament of ethnography

"The historical predicament of ethnography," writes James Clifford, is that "it is always caught up in the invention, not the representation of cultures"

(1986:2). The culture I write about in this book was *already invented,* and represented, mainly by its practitioners, long before I arrived in San Francisco. Not only are West Coast longshoremen, and particularly those in San Francisco, a notoriously opinionated and self-conscious community, they have also constructed a fairly comprehensive, self-defined culture that *they* have written about extensively.[6] They have also photographed that culture and painted murals depicting it as well.

This book is therefore not my exclusive invention or representation of longshore culture. Instead, it is often a dialogue between my understandings of longshore culture and the longshoremen's conceptions of it as they themselves have "invented" or constructed it. The dialogue, moreover, was sometimes explicit and self-conscious. For example, Herb Mills regularly read my field notes and commented on them. Before initiating this exchange, we agreed to certain rules. I would not share field notes based on private caucuses with employers, nor would he read interviews with managers. We also agreed on how to handle disputes generated by my notes. At Mills's suggestion, we decided that in disagreements over fact, like how to use longshore language or name parts of the technology, he was the expert, and I would defer to his judgment. With differences about "low-level generalizations" (his term), we would discuss and record our disagreements. "Theoretical interpretations" (also his concept), we would not dispute. Statements of this sort "belonged" to me. I then recorded Mills's reactions to the field notes, as well as my responses to his comments, and included them in the analysis.

Out of this dialogue has emerged a new construction of longshore culture: mine. Throughout the text, I have tried to include and be sensitive to the longshoremen's constructions, make our differences explicit, and give reasons for the difficulties I have with their representations. In doing so, I am recognizing that ethnographic knowledge is a collaborative production and that it could not be constructed without "indigenous collaborators." I have tried to acknowledge the dialogical nature of this cultural construction by reproducing field notes in the text, quoting indigenous collaborators, and striving to indicate where they leave off and

6 See, for example, George Benet (1979); Gene Dennis (1979); Eric Hoffer (1969); Herb Mills (1976, 1977, 1978a, 1979b); Reg Theriault (1978), and Stanley Weir (1974). For a collection of writings by and about longshoremen, see Carson (1979).

I begin. Ultimately, however, I must accept responsibility for the authorship of the culture represented in this book.

LEAVING

Knowing when one part of the job is done and another phase needs to begin is a critical element in craft labor. I recognized this gradually and sporadically. Although the self-consciousness of being a visitor eventually wore off, the sense of being in someone else's place never left completely. The anxiety of being an outsider was chronic, right up until the end. No matter how many visits I made, I always went to the waterfront with a stomach full of butterflies. After three years in the field, however, the end came into focus when I realized I was treating the fieldwork as a job. I needed to generate energy for going to "work." On the "job," I had to resist temptations to cut corners, like following fewer leads, writing fewer field notes, and tuning out longshoremen instead of actively listening to them. I found myself resenting some of the positions in which I found myself, such as being a mental health worker for some union members and a political consultant to others. I also discovered that, without intending to, I was declining access to further union resources. I was no longer capitalizing on offers to organize interviews or introductions.

Like most people who regularly work overtime for an extended period with very little time for themselves, I was getting tired. The job was taking its toll on me. I was also getting lonesome for friends in the life I left to settle semipermanently on the waterfront. It was becoming time to go home.

Impatience followed fatigue. I found myself less sympathetic to stories and exchanges repeated endlessly, and my ability to record them faithfully was decreasing. I knew my job in the field was completed when I discovered the source of my impatience. I had heard the stories, witnessed the exchanges, and observed the events so many times that I knew how they would end when they began. I could predict the process as well as the outcome. To paraphrase Anselm Strauss, my research categories were saturated. To convince myself that saturation was not simply an expedient excuse for fatigue, I tried to predict how the actual process would unfold. When I succeeded, I knew the time to leave had come.

Deciding not to just disappear, and promising to stay in touch, I spent a week thanking my sponsors, guides, collaborators, and friends. I left and turned my attention to the next phase of the field research job: analyzing and writing up the record constructed in the field.

REFERENCES

Adler, Paul. 1986a. "Technology and Us," *Socialist Review,* no. 86, pp. 67–96.

Adler, Paul. 1986b. "New Technologies, New Skills," *California Management Review,* vol. XXIX (Fall), pp. 9–27.

Aronowitz, Stanley. 1973. *False Promises: The Shaping of American Working-Class Consciousness,* McGraw-Hill, New York.

Atleson, James B. 1983. *Values and Assumptions in American Labor Law,* University of Massachusetts Press, Amherst.

Barbash, Jack. 1948. *Labor Unions in Action,* Harper & Brothers, New York.

Bell, Derrick. 1992. *Faces At the Bottom of the Well: The Permanence of Racism,* Basic Books, New York.

Benet, George. 1979. "Lew Welch," "Overheard in a Bar," "Longshore Joe," "The End of Ben Catlin," in *The Waterfront Writers: The Literature of Work,* Robert Carson, ed., Harper & Row, San Francisco.

Bernstein, Irving. 1950. *The New Deal Collective Bargaining Policy,* University of California Press, Berkeley.

Bernstein, Irving. 1970. *Turbulent Years,* Houghton Mifflin, New York.

Blauner, Robert. 1964. *Alienation and Freedom: The Factory Worker and His Industry,* University of Chicago Press, Chicago.

Braverman, Harry. 1974. *Labor and Monopoly Capital: The Degradation of Work in the Twentieth Century,* Monthly Review Press, New York.

Brecher, Jeremy. 1974. *Strike!* Fawcett Publications, Greenwich, CT.

Bridges, Harry. 1943. *Women in the War,* ILWU Education Department, San Francisco.

Brinkley, Alan. 1990. "The Best Years of Their Lives," *The New York Review,* pp. 16–21, June 28.

Brody, David. 1964. *The Emergence of Mass Production Unionism,* The Ohio State University Press, Columbus.

Brody, David. 1969. *The New Deal,* Weybright and Talley, New York.

Brody, David. 1972. "Labor and the Great Depression: The Interpretive Prospects," *Labor History,* vol. 13 (Spring), pp. 231–44.

Brody, David. 1975. "Radical Labor History and Rank-and-File Militancy," *Labor History,* vol. 16 (Winter), pp. 117–26.

References

Brody, David. 1980. *Workers in Industrial America: Essays on the 20th-Century Struggle,* Oxford University Press, New York.

Brody, David. 1985. "The CIO After 50 Years: A Historical Reckoning," *Dissent,* pp. 457–72 (Fall).

Brody, David. 1992. "The Breakdown of Labor's Social Contract," *Dissent,* pp. 32–41 (Winter).

Burawoy, Michael. 1979. *Manufacturing Consent: Changes in the Labor Process under Monopoly Capitalism,* University of Chicago Press, Chicago.

Burawoy, Michael. 1985. *The Politics of Production,* Verso, New York.

Carson, Robert, ed. 1979. *The Waterfront Writers: The Literature of Work,* Harper & Row, San Francisco.

Clawson, Dan. 1980. *Bureaucracy and the Labor Process,* Monthly Review Press, New York.

Clawson, Mary Ann. 1989. *Constructing Brotherhood: Class, Gender, and Fraternalism,* Princeton University Press, Princeton.

Clifford, James. 1986. "Introduction: Partial Truths," in *Writing Culture: The Poetics and Politics of Ethnography,* ed. James Clifford and George E. Marcus, pp. 1–26, University of California Press, Berkeley.

Clifford, James. 1988. *The Predicament of Culture: Twentieth-Century Ethnography, Literature, and Art,* Harvard University Press, Cambridge, MA.

Cochran, Bert. 1977. *Labor and Communism: The Conflict that Shaped American Unions,* Princeton University Press, Princeton.

Cohen, Lizabeth. 1990. *Making A New Deal: Industrial Workers in Chicago, 1919–1939,* Cambridge University Press, New York.

Commons, John R., et al. 1918. *History of Labor in the United States,* Macmillan, New York.

Cornfield, Daniel. 1989. *Becoming A Mighty Voice: Conflict and Change in the United Furniture Workers of America,* Russell Sage, New York.

Cornfield, Daniel. 1991. "The U.S. Labor Movement: Its Development and Impact on Social Inequality and Politics," *Annual Review of Sociology,* vol. 17, pp. 27–49.

Crapanzano, Vincent. 1986. "Hermes' Dilemma: The Masking of Subversion in Ethnographic Description," in *Writing Culture: The Poetics and Politics of Ethnography,* ed. James Clifford and George E. Marcus, pp. 51–76, University of California Press, Berkeley.

Davis, Mike. 1986. *Prisoners of the American Dream,* Verso, New York.

Dawley, Alan. 1976. *Class and Community: The Industrial Revolution in Lynn,* Harvard University Press, Cambridge, MA.

Debs, Eugene V. 1921. *Industrial Unionism,* New York Labor News Co., New York.

DeLeon, Daniel. 1921. *Industrial Unionism,* New York Labor News Co., New York.

Dennis, Gene. 1979. "A Bill of Sate," "Footnotes to the Glory Years," "Loading Rice at 14th Street," "Monopology Capital and the Interpenetration of Imperial Markets at Pier 27," in *The Waterfront Writers: The Literature of Work,* Harper & Row, San Francisco.

DiFazio, William. 1985. *Longshoremen: Community and Resistance on the Brooklyn Waterfront,* Bergin & Garvey Publishers, South Hadley, MA.

Doeringer, Peter B. and Michael J. Piore. 1971. *Internal Labor Markets and Manpower Analysis,* Heath, Lexington, MA.

Dubofsky, Melvyn. 1986. "Not So 'Turbulent Years': A New Look at the American 1930s," in *Life and Labor: American Working-Class History,* ed. Robert Asher, pp. 205–23, State University of New York Press, Albany.

Duster, Troy, David Matza, and David Wellman. 1979. "Field Work and the Protection of Human Subjects," *The American Sociologist,* vol. 14 (August), pp. 136–42.

Edwards, Richard. 1979. *Contested Terrain: The Transformation of the Workplace in the Twentieth Century,* Basic Books, New York.

Egan, Timothy. 1989. "For Boeing Strikers, Walkout Is Welcome Respite," *New York Times,* p. A9, October 6.

Emch, Tom. 1978. "The Cargo that Doesn't Arrive," *The San Francisco Examiner,* February 26.

Epstein, Albert and Nathaniel Goldfinger. 1950. "Communist Tactics in American Unions," *Labor and Nation,* vol. 6 (Fall), pp. 36–43.

Fairley, Lincoln. 1962. "The West Coast Longshore Contract," *Dissent,* vol. IX (Spring).

Fairley, Lincoln. 1979. *Facing Mechanization: The West Coast Longshore Plan* (Monograph No. 23), Institute of Industrial Relations, UCLA, Los Angeles.

Fantasia, Rick. 1988. *Cultures of Solidarity: Consciousness, Action, and Contemporary American Workers,* University of California Press, Berkeley.

Fink, Leon and Brian Greenberg. 1989. *Upheaval in the Quiet Zone: A History of Hospital Workers' Union, Local 1199,* University of Illinois Press, Urbana.

Finlay, William. 1988. *Work on the Waterfront: Worker Power and Technological Change in a West Coast Port,* Temple University Press, Philadelphia.

Fraser, Steve. 1983. "Dress Rehearsal for the New Deal: Shop-Floor Insurgents, Political Elites, and Industrial Democracy in the Amalgamated Clothing Workers," in *Working-Class America: Essays on Labor, Community, and American Society,* ed. Michael H. Frisch and Daniel J. Walkowitz, University of Illinois Press, Urbana.

Fraser, Steve. 1989. "The 'Labor Question,'" in *The Rise and Fall of the New Deal Order,* ed. Steve Fraser and Gary Gerstle, Princeton University Press, Princeton.

Fraser, Steven. 1991. *Labor Will Rule: Sidney Hillman and the Rise of American Labor,* Free Press, New York.

Freeman, Joshua B. 1983. "Catholics, Communists, and Republicans: Irish Workers and the Organization of the Transport Workers Union," in *Working-*

References

Class America: Essays on Labor, Community, and American Society, ed. Michael H. Frisch and Daniel J. Walkowitz, University of Illinois Press, Urbana.

Friedlander, Peter. 1975. *The Emergence of a UAW Local: A Study in Class and Culture*, University of Pittsburgh Press, Pittsburgh.

Galenson, Walter. 1974. "Communists and Trade Union Democracy," *Industrial Relations*, vol. 13 (October), pp. 228–36.

Garson, David. 1973. "Beyond Collective Bargaining," in *Workers' Control*, ed. Gerry Hunnius, G. David Garson, and John Case, Random House, New York.

Gerstle, Gary. 1989. *Working-Class Americanism: The Politics of Labor in a Textile City, 1914–1960*, Cambridge University Press, New York.

Gibbons, R. 1972. "Showdown At Lordstown," *Commonweal*, March 3.

Giddens, Anthony. 1979. *Central Problems in Social Theory: Action, Structure and Contradiction in Social Analysis*, University of California Press, Berkeley.

Giddens, Anthony. 1984. *The Constitution of Society: Outline of the Theory of Structuration*, University of California Press, Berkeley.

Glaberman, Martin. 1980. *Wartime Strikes: The Struggle Against the No-Strike Pledge in the UAW During World War II*, Bedwick Editions, Detroit.

Glaberman, Martin. 1984. "Vanguard to Rearguard," *Political Power and Social Theory*, vol. 4, pp. 37–62.

Glaser, Barney G. and Anselm Strauss. 1967. *The Discovery of Grounded Theory: Strategies for Qualitative Research*, Aldine Publishing Co., Chicago.

Glazer, Nathan. 1961. *The Social Basis of American Communism*, Harcourt, Brace & World, New York.

Goldblatt, Louis, ed. 1971. *Men and Machines*, ILWU-PMA, San Francisco.

Goldfield, Michael. 1987. *The Decline of Organized Labor in the United States*, University of Chicago Press, Chicago.

Gooding, Judson. 1970. "Blue-Collar Blues on the Assembly Line," *Fortune*, pp. 69–71.

Gordon, David, Richard Edwards, and Michael Reich. 1982. *Segmented Work, Divided Workers: The Historical Formation of Labor in the United States*, Cambridge University Press, New York.

Gorz, Andre. 1970. "Workers' Control," *Socialist Revolution*, vol. I (November–December).

Gorz, Andre. 1980. *Farewell to the Working Class*, South End Press, Boston.

Green, James. 1975. "Fighting on Two Fronts: Working-Class Militancy in the 1940's," *Radical America*, vol. 9, no. 4–5, pp. 7–48.

Green, James. 1980. *The World of the American Worker: Labor in the Twentieth Century*, Hill and Wang, New York.

Hamilton, James. 1979. "In the Hold," in *The Waterfront Writers: The Literature of Work*, ed. Robert Carson, Harper & Row, San Francisco.

References

Hardman, J. B. S. 1928. *American Labor Dynamics in the Light of Post-war Developments,* Harcourt, Brace and Co, New York.

Hartman, Paul T. 1969. *Collective Bargaining and Productivity: The Longshore Mechanization Agreement,* University of California Press, Berkeley.

Haywood, William. 1905. *Voice of Labor,* p. 8 (May).

Heckscher, Charles C. 1988. *The New Unionism: Employee Involvement in the Changing Corporation,* Basic Books, New York.

Hill, Herbert. 1987. "Race, Ethnicity and Organized Labor: The Opposition to Affirmative Action," *New Politics,* pp. 31–82 (Winter).

Hirschhorn, Larry. 1984. *Beyond Mechanization,* MIT Press, Cambridge, MA.

Hobsbawm, E. J. 1967. *Labouring Men: Studies in the History of Labour,* Anchor Books, Garden City, N.Y.

Hobsbawm, Eric. 1974. "Labor History and Ideology," *Journal of Social History,* vol. 7.

Hoffer, Eric. 1969. *Working and Thinking on the Waterfront, A Journal: June 1958–May 1959,* Harper & Row, New York.

Homans, George C. and Jerome Scott. 1947. "Reflections on the Wildcat Strikes," *American Sociologial Review,* vol. 12, pp. 278–87.

ILWU and PMA. 1978. *Pacific Coast Longshore Contract Document, 1978–1981.*

Institute for the Study of Social Change. 1992. *The Diversity Project,* University of California.

Isserman, Maurice. 1989. "Unions on the Left – I," *The Nation,* pp. 282–4, September 18.

Jacobs, Paul. 1964. "Harry, The Gag Man," *The New Leader,* pp. 12–13, July 6.

Jacobs, Paul. 1969. "The Failure of Collective Bargaining," in *American Labor History in the 20th Century,* ed. Jerold S. Auerbach, Bobbs-Merrill, New York.

Jennings, Ed. 1975. "Wildcat! The Wartime Strike Wave in Auto," *Radical America,* vol. 9, pp. 77–105.

Kampelman, Max M. 1957. *The Communist Party vs. the CIO: A Study in Power Politics,* Praeger, New York.

Kazin, Michael. 1982. *Barons of Labor: The San Francisco Building Trades, 1896–1922,* Department of History, Stanford University.

Kerr, Clark and Abraham J. Siegel. 1964. "The Interindustry Propensity to Strike – An International Comparison," in *Labor and Management in Industrial Society,* ed. Clark Kerr, pp. 105–47, Doubleday, Garden City.

Kessler-Harris, Alice. 1987. "Trade Unions Mirror Society in Conflict Between Collectivism and Individualism," *Monthly Labor Review* (August).

Kimeldorf, Howard. 1988. *Reds or Rackets: The Making of Radical and Conservative Unions on the Waterfront,* University of California Press, Berkeley.

Klare, Karl E. 1978. "Judicial Deradicalization of the Wagner Act: The Origins of Modern Legal Consciousness," *Minnesota Law Review,* vol. 65, pp. 265–339.

Kochan, Thomas A., Harry C. Katz, and Nancy R. Mower. 1984. *Working Participa-*

tion and American Unions: Threat or Opportunity?, W. E. Upjohn Institute for Employment Research, Kalamazoo.

Kochan, Thomas A., Harry C. Katz, and Robert B. McKersie. 1986. *The Transformation of American Industrial Relations,* Basic Books, New York.

Kornhauser, William. 1959. *The Politics of Mass Society,* Free Press, Glencoe.

Krauss, Henry. 1985. *The Many and the Few: A Chronicle of the Dynamic Auto Workers,* University of Illinois Press, Urbana.

Kremen, Bennett. 1972. "No Pride in This Dust," in *The World of the Blue Collar Workers,* ed. Irving Howe, Quadrangle, New York.

Kuhn, James W. 1961. *Bargaining in Grievance Settlement: The Power of Industrial Work Groups,* New York.

Kusterer, Ken. 1978. *Know How on the Job,* Westview Press, Boulder, CO.

Larrowe, Charles P. 1955. *Shape-Up and Hiring Hall: A Comparison of Hiring Methods and Labor Relations on the New York and Seattle Waterfronts,* University of California Press, Berkeley.

Larrowe, Charles P. 1977. *Harry Bridges: The Rise and Fall of Radical Labor in the United States,* 2d ed., Lawrence Hill, Westport CT.

Lens, Sidney. 1959. *The Crisis of American Labor,* Sagamore Press, New York.

Levison, A. 1974. *The Working-Class Majority,* Penguin, New York.

Lichtenstein, Nelson. 1989. "Unions on the Left – II," *The Nation,* pp. 284–7, September 18.

Lichtenstein, Nelson. 1977. "Ambiguous Legacy: The Union Security Problem During World War II," *Labor History,* vol. 18 (Spring).

Lichtenstein, Nelson. 1982. *Labor's War at Home: The CIO in World War II,* Cambridge University Press, New York.

Lichtenstein, Nelson. 1983. "Conflict Over Workers' Control: The Automobile Industry in World War II," in *Working-Class America: Essays on Labor, Community, and American Society,* ed. Michael H. Frisch and Daniel J. Walkowitz, University of Illinois Press, Urbana.

Lichtenstein, Nelson. 1984. "Industrial Sociology for Labor Historians," *Reviews in American History,* pp. 419–24, September.

Lichtenstein, Nelson. 1989. "From Corporatism to Collective Bargaining: Organized Labor and the Eclipse of Social Democracy in the Postwar Era," in *The Rise and Fall of the New Deal Order,* ed. Steve Fraser and Gary Gerstle, Princeton University Press, Princeton.

Lipset, Seymour Martin, Martin A. Trow, and James S. Coleman. 1956. *Union Democracy: The Internal Politics of the International Typographical Union,* Free Press, New York.

Lipset, Seymour Martin. 1963. *Political Man: The Social Bases of Politics,* Anchor Books, Garden City, NY.

Lipset, Seymour Martin. 1985. *Consensus and Conflict: Essays in Political Sociology,* Transaction Books, New Brunswick, NJ.

Lynd, Staughton. 1971. "Personal Histories of the Early CIO," *Radical America,* vol. 5 (May–June).

Lynd, Staughton. 1972. "The Possibility of Radicalism in the Early 1930s: The Case of Steel," *Radical America,* vol. 6, pp. 57–64 (November–December).

Lynd, Staughton. 1976. "Worker Control in a Time of Diminishing Workers' Rights," *Radical America,* vol. 10 (September–October), pp. 3–14.

MacShane, Denis. 1993. "Do Europeans Do It Better: Foreign Lessons for U.S. Labor," *The American Prospect,* no. 14 (Summer), pp. 88–95.

Marcuse, Herbert. 1966. *One Dimensional Man,* Beacon Press, Boston.

Marshall, T. H. 1965. *Class, Citizenship, and Social Development,* Anchor Books, Garden City, NY.

Massing, Michael. 1988. "Detroit's Strange Bedfellow," *New York Times Magazine,* pp. 20–7, February 7.

Matles, James and James Higgins. 1974. *Them and Us: Struggles of a Rank and File Union,* Prentice Hall, Englewood Cliffs, NJ.

Matza, David. 1961a. "The Disreputable Poor," in *Contemporary Social Problems,* ed. Robert Merton and Robert Nesbit, Harcourt Brace, New York.

Matza, David. 1961b. "Subterranean Traditions of Youth," *The Annals,* no. 338, pp. 102–18.

Matza, David and G. Sykes. 1961. "Juvenile Delinquency and Subterranean Values," *American Sociological Review,* vol. 26, pp. 712–19.

Matza, David. 1964. *Delinquency and Drift,* Wiley, New York.

Matza, David. 1969. *Becoming Deviant,* Prentice-Hall, Englewood Cliffs.

Matza, David and David Wellman. 1977. "Managing Grievance in the Urban Workplace: Research Proposal Funded by NIMH," Institute for the Study of Social Change, University of California, Berkeley.

Matza, David and David Wellman. 1980. "The Ordeal of Consciousness," *Theory and Society,* vol. 9, pp. 1–27.

Matza, David and David Wellman. 1981. "Outline Toward An Analysis," Institute for the Study of Social Change, University of California, Berkeley.

McConnell, Grant. 1966. *Private Power and American Democracy,* Vintage Books, New York.

McWilliams, Wilson Carey. 1973. *The Idea of Fraternity in America,* University of California Press, Berkeley.

Metzgar, Jack. 1992. "'Employee Involvement' Plans," *Dissent,* pp. 67–72 (Winter).

Michels, Robert. 1962. *Political Parties: A Sociological Study of the Oligarchical Tendencies of Modern Democracy,* Free Press, New York.

Miller, S. M. and Ira Harrison. 1964. "Types of Drop Outs: The Unemployables," in *Blue Collar World,* ed. A. Shostack and W. Gomberg, Prentice-Hall, Englewood Cliffs, NJ.

Miller, Walter. 1958. "Lower Class Culture as a Generating Milieu of Gang Delinquency," *Journal of Social Issues,* vol. 14, pp. 5–19.

345

References

Millis, H. and E. Brown. 1950. *From the Wagner Act to Taft-Hartley,* University of Chicago Press, Chicago.

Mills, C. Wright. 1948. *The New Men of Power: America's Labor Leaders,* Harcourt, New York.

Mills, Herb. 1976. "The San Francisco Waterfront: The Social Consequences of Industrial Modernization, Part I," *Urban Life,* vol. 5 (July), pp. 221–50.

Mills, Herb. 1977. "The San Francisco Waterfront: The Social Consequences of Industrial Modernization, Part II," *Urban Life,* vol. 6 (April), pp. 3–32.

Mills, Herb. 1978a. "The San Francisco Waterfront: Labor/Management Relations – on the Ships and Docks, Part One: Conventional Longshore Operations," Institute for the Study of Social Change, University of California, Berkeley.

Mills, Herb. 1978b. "A Rat's Eye View of History: Story Telling on the San Francisco Waterfront," Unpublished paper.

Mills, Herb. 1979a. "The San Francisco Waterfront: Labor/Management Relations – on the Ships and Docks, Part Two: Modern Longshore Operations," Institute for the Study of Social Change, University of California, Berkeley.

Mills, Herb. 1979b. "The San Francisco Waterfront: The Social Consequences of Industrial Modernization," in *Case Studies on the Labor Process,* ed. Andrew Zimbalist, Monthly Review Press, New York.

Mills, Herb. 1980. "The Men Along the Shore," *The San Francisco Examiner,* September 7.

Mills, Herb and David Wellman. 1987. "Contractually Sanctioned Job Action and Workers' Control: The Case of San Francisco Longshoremen," *Labor History,* vol. 28 (Spring), pp. 167–95.

Milton, David. 1982. *The Politics of U.S. Labor,* Monthly Review Press, New York.

Montgomery, David. 1979a. *Workers' Control in America,* Cambridge University Press, New York.

Montgomery, David. 1979b. "The Past and the Future of Workers' Control," *Radical America,* vol. XIII (November–December).

Montgomery, David. 1980. "To Study the People: The American Working Class," *Labor History,* pp. 485–512 (Fall).

Montgomery, David. 1987. *The Fall of the House of Labor: The Workplace, the State, and American Labor Activism, 1865–1925,* Cambridge University Press, New York.

Moody, Kim. 1988. *An Injury to All: The Decline of American Unionism,* Verso, New York.

Nasaw, David. 1988. "The Democratic Historian," *The Nation,* pp. 132–4, January 30.

Nelson, Bruce. 1988. *Workers on the Waterfront: Seamen, Longshoremen, and Unionism in the 1930s,* University of Illinois Press, Urbana.

References

Nisbet, Robert. 1953. *The Quest for Community,* Oxford University Press, New York.

Noble, David. 1977. *America By Design: Science, Technology, and the Rise of Corporate Capitalism,* Knopf, New York.

Noble, David. 1984. *Forces of Production: A Social History of Industrial Relations,* Knopf, New York.

Norman, Geoffrey. 1972. "Blue-Collar Saboteurs," *Playboy* (August).

Pacific Maritime Association (PMA). 1980. *Annual Report,* San Francisco.

Pelling, Henry. 1960. *American Labor,* University of Chicago Press, Chicago.

Perlman, Selig. 1928. *The Theory of the Labor Movement,* Macmillan, New York.

Pierpont, R. J. 1967. "New Stage in the Longshore Struggle," *New Politics,* vol. VI (Winter).

Pilcher, William W. 1972. *The Portland Longshoremen: A Dispersed Urban Community,* Holt, Rinehart & Winston, New York.

Piore, Michael and Charles Sabel. 1984. *The Second Industrial Divide.* Basic Books, New York.

Pratt, Mary Louise. 1986. "Fieldwork in Common Places," in *Writing Culture: The Poetics and Politics of Ethnography,* ed. James Clifford and George E. Marcus, pp. 27–50, University of California Press, Berkeley.

Preis, Art. 1964. *Labor's Giant Step: Twenty Years of the CIO,* Pathfinders Press, New York.

Prickett, James C. 1974. "Anti-Communism and Labor History," *Industrial Relations,* vol. 13 (October), pp. 219–27.

Quam-Wickham, Nancy. 1992. "Who Controls the Hiring Hall? The Struggle for Job Control in the ILWU During World War II," in *The CIO's Left-Led Unions,* ed. Steve Rosswurm, Rutgers University Press, New Brunswick, NJ.

Radosh, Ronald. 1966. "The Corporate Ideology of American Labor Leaders from Gompers to Hillman," *Studies on the Left,* vol. 6 (November–December), pp. 66–88.

Rawick, George. 1983. "Working-Class Self-Activity," in *Workers' Struggles Past and Present,* ed. James Green, Temple University Press, Philadelphia.

Ross, Philip. 1968. "Distribution of Power Within the ILWU and ILA," *Monthly Labor Review,* no. 91, pp. 1–7.

Rothstein, Richard. 1993. "New Bargain or No Bargain?" *The American Prospect,* no. 14 (Summer), pp. 32–47.

Rubin, Lillian. 1976. *Worlds of Pain,* Basic Books, New York.

Sabel, Charles F. 1982. *Work and Politics: The Division of Labor in Industry,* Cambridge University Press, New York.

Salzman, Howard. n.d. "The New Merlins in Taylor's Automation?" Boston University Center for Applied Research, Boston.

Schatz, Ronald W. 1983. *The Electrical Workers: A History of Labor at General Electric and Westinghouse, 1923–1960,* University of Illinois Press, Urbana.

Schwendinger, Herman and Julia. 1976. "Delinquency and the Collective Varieties of Youth," *Crime and Social Justice,* vol. 5, pp. 7–25.

Scott, James. 1985. *Weapons of the Weak: Everyday Forms of Peasant Resistance,* Yale University Press, New Haven.

Scott, James. 1990. *Domination and the Arts of Resistance: Hidden Transcripts,* Yale University Press, New Haven.

Selznick, Philip. 1957. *Leadership in Administration: A Sociological Interpretation,* Row, Peterson, and Co., Evanston, IL.

Selznick, Philip. 1960. *The Organizational Weapon: A Study of Bolshevik Strategy and Tactics,* Free Press, Glencoe, IL.

Sewell, William H., Jr. 1990. "How Classes Are Made: Critical Reflections on E. P. Thompson's Theory of Working-Class Formation," in *E. P. Thompson: Critical Perspectives,* ed. Keita McClelland, pp. 50–77.

Silone, Ignazio. 1954. "The Choice of Comrades," *Encounter,* vol. 3 (December).

Spenner, Kenneth. 1983. "Deciphering Prometheus: Temporal Change in the Skill Level of Workers," *American Sociological Review,* vol. 48.

Stepan-Norris, Judith and Maurice Zeitlin. 1989. "Who Gets the Bird? Or, How the Communists Won Power and Trust in America's Unions," *American Sociological Review,* vol. 54, pp. 503–23.

Stepan-Norris, Judith and Maurice Zeitlin. 1991a. "'Red' Unions and 'Bourgeois' Contracts? The Effects of Political Leadership on the 'Political Regime of Production,'" *American Journal of Sociology,* vol. 96, pp. 1151–200.

Stepan-Norris, Judith and Maurice Zeitlin. 1991b. *Insurgency, Radicalism, and Democracy in America's Industrial Unions,* Institute of Industrial Relations, University of California, Los Angeles.

Sternsher, Bernard. 1983. "Great Depression Labor Historiography in the 1970s: Middle-Range Questions, Ethnocultures, and Levels of Generalization," *Reviews in American History,* pp. 300–19 (June).

Swados, Harvey. 1961. "West-Coast Waterfront – The End of an Era," *Dissent,* vol. VIII (Autumn).

Swados, Harvey. 1962. "Reply to Lincoln Fairley," *Dissent,* vol. IX (Spring).

Theriault, Reg. 1978. *Longshoring on the San Francisco Waterfront,* Singlejack Books, San Pedro.

Thurow, Lester. 1975. *Generating Inequality: Mechanisms of Distribution in the U.S. Economy,* Basic Books, New York.

Tocqueville, Alexis de. 1945. *Democracy in America,* Vintage Books, New York.

Tomlins, Christopher. 1985. *The State and the Unions,* Cambridge University Press, New York.

Veblen, Thorstein. 1964. *The Instinct of Workmanship,* Norton, New York.

Verba, Sidney and Kay Lehman Schlozman. 1977. "Unemployment, Class Consciousness, and Radical Politics: What Didn't Happen in the Thirties," *Journal of Politics,* vol. 39 (May).

Weinstein, James. 1968. *The Corporate Ideal in the Liberal State: 1900–1918,* Beacon Press, Boston.

Weir, Stan. 1964. "The ILWU: A Case Study in Bureaucracy," *New Politics,* vol. III (Winter).

Weir, Stan. 1969. "The Retreat of Harry Bridges," *New Politics,* vol. VIII (Winter).

Weir, Stan. 1970. "USA: The Labor Revolt," in *American Society, Inc.,* ed. M. Zeitlin, Markham, Chicago.

Weir, Stan. 1973. "Rebellion in American Labor's Rank-and-File," in *Workers' Control,* ed. Gerry Hunnius, G. David Garson, and John Case, Random House, New York.

Weir, Stan. 1974. "A Study of the Work Culture of San Francisco Longshoremen," M.A. Thesis, Department of Labor and Industrial Relations, University of Illinois, Urbana.

Weir, Stan. 1975. "American Labor on the Defensive: A 1940's Odyssey," *Radical America,* vol. 9, no. 4/5, pp. 163–86.

Weir, Stan. 1983. "The Conflict in American Unions and Resistance to Alternative Ideas from the Rank-and-File," in *Workers' Struggles Past and Present,* ed. James Green, Temple University Press, Philadelphia.

Wellman, David. 1968. "Putting-On the Poverty Program," *Transaction,* pp. 9–18 (April).

Wellman, David T. 1993. *Portraits of White Racism,* 2d ed, Cambridge University Press, New York.

Werthman, Carl and Irving Piliavin. 1967. "Gang Members and the Police," in *The Police,* ed. D. Bordua, John Wiley, New York.

Wilentz, Sean. 1983. "Artisan Republican Festivals and the Rise of Class Conflict in New York City, 1788–1837," in *Working-Class America: Essays on Labor, Community, and American Society,* ed. Michael H. Frisch and Daniel J. Walkowitz, University of Illinois Press, Urbana.

Wilentz, Sean. 1984. "Against Exceptionalism: Class Consciousness and the American Labor Movement, 1790–1920," *International Labor and Working Class History,* vol. 26 (Fall), pp. 1–24.

Willis, Paul. 1978. *Profane Culture,* Routledge Kegan Paul, London.

Willis, Paul. 1990. *Learning to Labour,* Columbia University Press, New York.

Witt, Matt. 1979. "Dangerous Substances and the U.S. Worker: Current Practice and Viewpoints," *International Labor Review,* vol. 118 (March–April), no. 2.

Zieger, Robert. 1985. "Toward the History of the CIO: A Bibliographic Report," *Labor History,* vol. 26 (Fall), pp. 487–516.

Zimbalist, Andrew. 1979. "Introduction," in *Case Studies on the Labor Process,* ed. Andrew Zimbalist, Monthly Review Press, New York.

Zuboff, Shoshana. 1988. *In The Age of the Smart Machine: The Future of Work and Power,* Basic Books, New York.

NAME INDEX

SUBJECT INDEX

Subject index

grievance process, 206–8; class structure and, 207
grieving: cost of, 260–1, 266, 267

habituation, 30–1, 32
hall men, 172; and skill debate, 129, 130, 132
hard hat requirement, 197–8
hatch rights, 213–15
hatch tender, 150–1, 155
hierarchy, 15, 21; in conventional hold work, 147; in pay determination, 242–7; social location of, in containerized longshoring, 171–7; social location of, in dockwork, 152–6
hiring hall, 51, 60–3, 82–3, 129; architecture of, 61–2, 71; bypassing, 154; and equality of opportunity to work, 74; freedom of expression in, 79–80; holdmen and, 147
Hispanics, 101, 102, 103, 251
holdmen, 138, 152, 169, 177; and supervision, 171–2; and winch drivers, 153–4
holdwork: cognitive dimension of, 140–4; in containerized longshoring, 162–5, 171–2; in conventional longshoring, 138–44, 151; social organization of initiative in, 144–9
Hospital Workers' Union – Local 1199, 6
how to work: in contract, 13; cooperative decisions regarding, 146; disputes about, 191–2, 221–4, 308, 312; principles for, 178–9; right to dictate, 306; rules for, 8, 147–8, 205; who decides, 205–24; winch drivers, 153

iconoclasts, 17, 26
ideological politics, 33; of CIO unions, 26–7, 31
illegal work stoppage complaint, 238–9, 240
illusion of negotiation, 282–6
impression management, 254, 294–300
income inequality, 72, 73
Independent Textile Union (ITU), 6, 28, 43–4
individualism, 93, 198, 306
industrial citizenship; see citizenship
industrial democracy, 36–7
industrial labor: work categories, 11–13
industrial relations, 36n2, 316

industrial sociology/psychology, 30–1
industrial unionism, 3–4, 44–5, 304–5; success of, 19; transformed into business unionism, 50
inferential analysis, 29–30, 31, 32
ingenuity, 161; of holdmen, 139, 140, 142, 144, 145, 146
initiative, 11, 133, 137, 138, 161, 178; organization of, 177; social location of, in containerized longshoring, 171–7; social location of, in dockwork, 152–6; social organization of, in holdwork, 144–9
institutional limits (Local 10), 89–95
insubordination, 22–5, 63, 124, 201, 280–1, 300, 306; culture of, 91–3, 123, 304
interest groups, 18, 104
intermodal system, 12
International Association of Machinists (IAM), 268
International Longshoremen's and Warehousemen's Union (ILWU), 6, 27–8, 37, 47, 55, 304, 312; attack on, 51–3; democracy in, 83n1; disruptive potential of, 14n8; expulsion from CIO, 51–2, 54; principles of, 305; relationship with PMA, 253–4, 282, 290–1, 299; uniqueness of, 8–146, 45, 312–14; see also Local 10
iron law of oligarchy, 96n12
issues: cohorts and, 99–100

job action, 3, 8
job categories, 103–4, 215; cognitive work and initiative needed in, 138–56, 159–77; and kind of work, 209–10; modified, 127; politicos and, 120–1; see also boards
job consciousness, 18, 302
job control, 308, 309–12; debate over, 129; see also workplace control issue
job shifting, 212–12, 215, 235
jurisdictional disputes, 208–11
justice, 316; appearance of, 291–4

knowledge: in containerized longshoring, 159–77; in conventional longshoring, 137–56; of craft, 12; in holdwork, 145; management dependence on worker, 127, 128, 148, 311, 317; management's appropriation of, 21, 22; of skilled workers, 309; as weapon, 124; of winch drivers, 150, 153

labor: conventional wisdom about, 302–3; defeat of, 301–2; *see also* potential power of labor; theory of labor's demise
labor costs, 160, 211
labor history, historians, xii, 4–5, 17–19, 46
labor intensity, 187
labor–management relations, 46–7, 49; CIO and, 41–2; contract in, 277–80; fundamental differences in, 203; issues in, 207–8; technology and, 172
labor movement, 4, 18–19, 38, 317
labor process, control of, 127; *see also* workplace control issue
labor radicalism: and conventional wisdom, 3–16
labor relations system, 4
Labor Relations Committee: Local, 87; Area, 108–11; Coast, 206–8
laborers: dockworkers as, 11
language, 8, 47, 123; in battle for control of workplace, 205, 225–41; of command, 198–99, 201; contractual, 9, 225–41; disputes over, 225–9; in disputes over work, 208–9; of fraternity, 64–7; keeping current, 231–2; mixed meanings in use of, 229–35; permissive versus restrictive use of, 228–9; self-aggrandizing, 113; shared, 271; of skill, 130, 131–2; waterfront, 53, 143, 153; of weakness, 290
lashing, 162–3, 164, 172, 176, 179
Latinos, 101
leaders, 6; founding, 28, 306; generational, 100
left (the): legacy of, xii–xiii
legal realism/legal formalism distinction, 276n9
liberty, 57–8, 63, 77–81, 121, 123; threatened by steady employment, 131
lifetime employment, 201–2
lifting: principles of, 140–1, 142, 143–4
linesmen, 282–6
living agreement, 282; and appearance of justice, 291–4; faith in grievance machinery and, 292–3, 294; saving face in, 287, 289; transforming official agreement into, 276–80
local community: and "tumultuous" democracy, 49–55
Local 10, 7–8; being political in, 106–24; bulletins, 89; multisided organization,

97; social strands in political fabric of, 129–33; waterfront generations, 98–100; Appeals Committee, 84–6, 99; Executive Board, 80, 87, 92–3, 94, 99, 102, 120; Executive Committee, 250, 251; Grievance Committee, 85, 87, 218–19, 221, 222–3, 266, 294–7; International Convention Delegations, 99; Labor Relations Committee (LRC), 87, 95, 240, 315; Labor Relations Committee (LRC) meetings, 108–11, 205–8, 216–17, 219–21, 241, 265, 294; Negotiation Committee, 98, 99; Pensioners Club, 98; Publicity Committee, 89, 99; Stewards' Council, 258
lockouts, 13
longshore industry, xiii
longshoremen: latitude of, 217–21; number of (registered), 78, 160
longshoring: isolated character of, 8, 10–11; nature of, 9, 10–11
Lordstown phenomenon, 23–4
lost work opportunity complaints, 206, 208–9, 210, 212, 214, 266
low-man-out (LMO) rule, 74, 274–5
low-rider(s), 24
Low Work Opportunity Port, 111–12
loyalty, 132, 243; to employer, 130, 154–5, 156, 176; to one another, 81; rewarding, with promotion, 248, 250, 251
lunch breaks, 176

M&M; *see* Mechanization and Modernization (M&M) Agreement(s)
McCarthyism, 127
making the record, 108–14, 118, 119
making the system work, 280–1
management: contract violations, 271; control over promotions, 251–2; ILWU adversarial relationship with, 315–16; issues dividing labor from, 207–8; limits on flexibility of, 212–15; recognizing codes of conduct, 193, 195–9; and SEO men, 170, 173–4, 175–6; *see also* challenging management's authority; labor–management relations
management control of work process, 305; contested by longshoremen, 253–4; *see also* workplace control issue
management dependence on labor, 152–3, 161; in containerized longshoring, 161, 172; on SEO men, 173–4

Subject index

values: ILWU, 314; of labor, 312; trade
union, 306
vessels; *see* ships
voluntary associations, 96
voting, 88, 118

wage differentials, 151, 154; *see also* pay;
salary differentiation
wage schedule/scales, 71, 89, 242–3; *see also*
pay
Wagner Act, 43
walked off the job complaints, 207, 218–
19, 220
walking bosses, 73, 102, 145; and codes of
conduct, 193; and containerized longshoring, 171, 172; and pace of work,
165; pay scale, 247; and pilferage, 186;
promotion to, 250–1; and SEO men,
172, 173–5; and winch drivers, 152
"watching the game," 179–82, 183, 184–5,
186, 192–3, 311
Waterfront Employers Association, 52
ways for working: tension between union
and non-union, 187
welfare state, 38, 301
wildcat strikes, 22–5
winch drivers, 138, 177, 243; in conventional longshoring, 149–52; and safety,
180–2; social location of, 152–4
Wisconsin school, 17, 26
women: in CIO, 38; in ILWU, 58n3
Woonsocket, R.I., 7, 41
work: and body, 143; in containerized
longshoring, 159–77; in conventional
longshoring, 137–56; disputes over, 187,
208–11, 223–4; distribution of, 41, 71–
2; flexibility in 107; organization of,
304–5; politicizing everyday life at, 39–
45; power to define, 209, 210, 211, 224;
as social accomplishment, xiii; and
unionism and technological change,
127–33; *see also* how to work
work culture, 310–11
work practices, xi, 187; codes of conduct
and, 179; holdmen, 146, 147; management control over, 201–2; principles in,
192

work process, 35; changes in, 21–2; management control of, 174; negotiating,
313; SEOs and, 175; and shopfloor control, 133
work rules: elimination of restrictive, 253–4
work stoppages, 22n7, 552n8, 191, 255,
304; "good beefs," 262–4; mediation of,
259–61; prohibited in contract, 13
work-to-rule actions, 22
workforce: registered, 60
working class, 3, 18, 69, 301–2; participation in American institutions, 36–7
working-class consciousness, 35, 39
working-class culture, 307
working-class movement, 32–3
working-class struggle: historic forms of, 8,
14, 39
working etiquette: rules of, 182–9
working knowledge, 7, 54, 304; in containerized longshoring, 161; management dependence on, 152–3; as weapon
in battle for control, 205
working partners, 141–2, 176
working principles, 7, 178–99, 313; and
containerized longshoring, 189–92
working rules: in contract negotiations,
282–3
working to rule, 165
working union, 183–4, 186, 305, 311;
defined, 183; and doing the right thing,
187, 189
workplace control issue, xi, 19–20, 28, 30,
31, 33, 34, 39–41, 106, 252, 300; artisan/
craft skill driving, 302–3; community in,
58, 63; contract in, 201–3, 254, 257,
298–300; ILWU relinquished in contract, 13–14, 20; skill in, 309–12; technological change and, 127–33; union
democracy weapon in contest for, 123–
4; weapons in battle for, 124, 179, 205–8
workplace organization, 18, 314–17
workplace regime, 205, 208; dispute over,
settled, 253–4; disputing issues of, 280–
1; *see also* governance
World War II, 22, 38, 50

Yankee Face, 139, 163